ALL FUTURE PLUNGES TO THE PAST

A VOLUME IN THE

NIU Series in Slavic, East European, and Eurasian Studies

Edited by Christine D. Worobec

For a list of books in the series, visit our website at cornellpress.cornell.edu.

ALL FUTURE PLUNGES TO THE PAST

JAMES JOYCE IN RUSSIAN LITERATURE

José Vergara

NORTHERN ILLINOIS UNIVERSITY PRESS
AN IMPRINT OF CORNELL UNIVERSITY PRESS
Ithaca and London

First published 2021 by Cornell University Press

Library of Congress Cataloging-in-Publication Data

Names: Vergara, José, 1988– author.
Title: All future plunges to the past : James Joyce in
    Russian literature / José Vergara.
Description: Ithaca [New York] : Cornell University Press,
    2021. | Series: NIU series in Slavic, East European, and
    Eurasian studies | Includes bibliographical references
    and index.
Identifiers: LCCN 2021002963 (print) | LCCN 2021002964
    (ebook) | ISBN 9781501759901 (hardcover) |
    ISBN 9781501759918 (epub) | ISBN 9781501759925 (pdf)
Subjects: LCSH: Joyce, James, 1882–1941—Influence. |
    Russian fiction—20th century—History and criticism.
Classification: LCC PG3098.4 .V47 2021 (print) |
    LCC PG3098.4 (ebook) | DDC 891.73/409—dc23
LC record available at https://lccn.loc.gov/2021002963
LC ebook record available at https://lccn.loc.gov/2021
    002964

For Jenny

Contents

ACKNOWLEDGMENTS

Where does a book begin and where does it end? This one probably begins in high school when I first attempted *Ulysses* on my own, but stumbled by the time Leopold Bloom's cat starts talking. It was my initial lesson in Joyce's art and in the experience of writing this book: both were more rewarding in the company of others.

And so, my list of interlocutors is long, and to each of them I am deeply grateful.

David Bethea provided guidance and careful readings, particularly in the early stages of this project's development. I found in him an exceptional mentor and advocate. The suggestions offered by Irina Shevelenko, Andrew Reynolds, and Alexander Dolinin also helped improve my analysis in innumerable ways. To Richard Begam I am appreciative for allowing me to write the paper on Olesha and Joyce in his fascinating Joyce and Beckett seminar that would blossom into so much more beyond the class. David Danaher's advice during the writing and revision of this book has proved invaluable.

For their friendship, support, and ongoing conversations, I thank Jesse Stavis, Thomas Tabatowski, Sarah Kapp, and Zach Rewinski. Sarah and her family deserve special gratitude for hosting me and for providing Georgian food during my research trip to Moscow. S.A. Karpukhin has been a wonderful friend, one to whom I turn with seemingly endless questions and from whom I always receive welcome recommendations. Anna Borovskaya-Ellis likewise helped me think through parts of this project in two languages.

Sibelan Forrester has been an exemplary colleague. From reading drafts to supporting my wilder ideas, she has both enriched this book and made teaching at Swarthmore a true pleasure. I was happy to be paired with Tim Harte for the Tri-College Private Peer Review of Works in Progress program; he was most generous with his time and detailed feedback on drafts. Grace Sewell provided instrumental editorial help while I was preparing the final manuscript.

In an independent study on Russian and Irish Modernism, Tim Langen offered a far more productive experience tackling *Ulysses* in what turned out to be the second in a series of transformative encounters with Joyce that led to this book. Much more recently, his comments on the conclusion and his encouragement to challenge the expected helped give it finer shape. Nicole Monnier solidified my love of all things Russian, and I thank her for years of friendship and counsel. I am terribly sorry that Gennady Barabtarlo is not around to see this book's publication; I remain inspired by Gene's loyalty to former students and to Russian letters alike.

I am glad to count Eliot Borenstein and Galya Diment among my book's first readers. They helped me see things that I had written in a new light and sharpened my arguments. Thank you very much to Amy Farranto for championing this project and for making the publication process as smooth as possible. There were a number of interlocutors at conferences whose comments allowed me to take unexpected turns and to clarify exactly what I wanted to say. Among others, I thank Eric Naiman, Meghan Vicks, Ann Komaromi, Rebecca Stanton, Ron Meyer, and Kevin Platt.

The full scope of this book could not have been realized without the participation of the numerous interview subjects featured in its conclusion: Andrei Babikov, Ksenia Buksha, Dmitry Bykov, Anna Glazova, Alexander Ilianen, Alexander Ilichevsky, Ilya Kukulin, Dmitry Ragozin, Lev Rubinstein, Aleksei Salnikov, Alexander Skidan, Grigory Sluzhitel, Ivan Sokolov, Sergei Solovev, Marina Stepnova, Zinovy Zinik, and the Moscow Joyce reading group. I thank them for their willingness to talk Joyce with me. To Mikhail Shishkin, as well as his family, I extend sincere gratitude for his generosity, candor, and hospitality.

To the students spread across three schools and two correctional facilities whom I encountered in the process of writing, thank you for your attention and inspiring conversations. I am particularly indebted to those in my seminar at the University of Missouri, whom I tormented with the five strange, difficult novels I explore here.

I thank the Provost's Office of Swarthmore College for funding my archival research trips to the Department of Special Research Collections at the University of California, Santa Barbara, in May 2018 and to the Russian State Archive of Literature and Art in May–June 2019. The staff at both institutions were tremendously helpful. I am also grateful to the Friends of the Zürich James Joyce Foundation for funding a five-week research fellowship. There, at what became my Swiss Pushkin House, I benefited greatly from the expertise and warm welcome of Fritz Senn, Ursula Zeller, Ruth Frehner, and Frances Ilmberger. I offer special thanks to Fritz for his unparalleled insights and his willingness to share knowledge and anecdote alike.

An earlier version of chapter 1 and portions of chapters 4 and 5 were previously published as "Kavalerov and Dedalus as Rebellious Sons and Artists: Yury Olesha's Dialogue with *Ulysses* in *Envy*," *Slavic and East European Journal*

58, no. 4 (2014): 606–25; "The Embodied Language of Sasha Sokolov's *A School for Fools*," *Slavonic and East European Review* 97, no. 3 (2019): 426–50; and "'Return That Which Does Not Belong to You': Mikhail Shishkin's Borrowings in *Maidenhair*," *Russian Review* 78, no. 2 (2019): 300–321. I thank these journals for allowing me to include revised versions of my materials and their editors (Irene Masing-Delic, Yana Hashamova, Barbara Wyllie, Michael Gorham, and Kurt Schultz) and my anonymous readers for their suggestions along the way.

In this book of fathers, I am so appreciative of my mother's sacrifices and support.

The gratitude I feel for Jenny, my wife, truly exceeds what I might express here. She has been a constant source of encouragement, inspiration, and love, as well as a devoted reader, and this project owes much to her. From Moscow to Dublin and beyond, the answer will always be a Joycean "Yes." Finally, I thank Lucia and Paz for the opportunity to continue this book's exploration of what fatherhood means. Its conclusion remains open because of you.

Note on Transliteration and Translations

A slightly modified Library of Congress (LC) transliteration system is used throughout this book. For the sake of readability, names ending in *ii* (Dostoevskii) or *aia* (Tolstaia) are rendered with *y* (Dostoevsky) and *aya* (Tolstaya) within the main body; in the bibliography and in clear references to the bibliography, such names retain the LC transliteration. The same applies to the use of a single *i* (Lidia) in some female names rather than *iia* (Lidiia). Three other notable exceptions are Olesha's first name, which has been transliterated as Yury in place of Iurii; Fyodor instead of Fedor (as in Nabokov's protagonist from *The Gift* and the poet Fyodor Tiutchev); and the absence of straight apostrophes as soft sign markers (Gogol as opposed to Gogol'). Names with recognizable English equivalents and surnames of well-known figures appear in their familiar English-language variants (Alexander and Tolstoy instead of Aleksandr and Tolstoi). Unless otherwise noted, all translations from Russian are my own.

ALL FUTURE PLUNGES TO THE PAST

Introduction

How Joyce Was Read in Russia

> Old father, old artificer, stand me now and ever in
> good stead.
>
> —James Joyce, *A Portrait of the Artist as a Young Man*

When the Russian playwright Vsevolod Vish-
nevsky (1900–1951) visited James Joyce in Paris in 1936, the two had much
to discuss. The Irish writer quickly mentioned that he had heard that his books
were banned in the Soviet Union. Was this true? he wondered. Vishnevsky was
pleased to report that *Ulysses* had been translated "earlier than in many other
countries," suggesting in a roundabout way that the Soviets openly accepted
Joyce.[1] Vishnevsky did not lie about the translation, which was published in
1925, but, as a champion of Joyce's art, he exaggerated. This early translation of
Ulysses by V. Zhitomirsky in fact consisted only of several fragments from a
handful of chapters.[2] Furthermore, the head of the International Information
Bureau of the Central Committee, Karl Radek (1885–1939), had infamously led
a rabid attack on Joyce, which began in the early 1930s at the First All-Union
Congress of Soviet Writers and subsequently characterized much of Joyce criticism for the next several decades in the Union of Soviet Socialist Republics
(USSR). "A pile of dung teeming with worms, photographed with a cinema ap-
paratus through a microscope," Radek proclaimed, "that's Joyce."[3] By 1934 Joyce
had become for many an emblem of Decadence, Formalism, and Naturalism—
the very antithesis of official Soviet art.

Still, some recognized Joyce's genius at the time. Boris Poplavsky (1903–
1935), a young émigré writer and poet, delivered a lecture on Joyce and Mar-
cel Proust in 1930 that was then published in the Paris-based émigré journal

1

2   INTRODUCTION

Chisla. He proclaimed his profound admiration for Joyce in no uncertain terms: "Everything taken together creates an absolutely stunning document, something so real, so alive, so diverse, and so truthful that it seems to us that if it were necessary to send to Mars or God knows where a single sample of earthly life or, facing the destruction of European civilization, to preserve a single book for posterity, in order to provide through the ages and across space an inkling of our fallen civilization, perhaps it would be best to leave precisely Joyce's *Ulysses*."[4] Statements such as those of Radek and Poplavsky reveal the complexities of the contradictory positions Joyce has occupied in Russian culture since the mid-1920s. Their views stand at maximalist extremes, reflecting the wide range of emotions and strong opinions Joyce's texts elicited from Russian readers of different artistic and ideological camps.[5]

Before he became anathema to the Soviet regime in the 1930s, Joyce was frequently discussed, if not widely read. (Then again, has he ever been truly *widely* read?) Afterward, his art turned into a forbidden fruit to be enjoyed mostly in private until the publication of the Viktor Khinkis–Sergei Khoruzhy translation of *Ulysses* in the late 1980s.[6] The subject of Joyce in Russian literature has been largely ignored especially in the West, one suspects, precisely because in the Soviet Union he was persona non grata for decades; it would seem that if one were prohibited from speaking or writing about Joyce publicly, then opportunities to respond creatively to him would be limited as well.

Nevertheless, Joyce became a symbol for a branch of Western literature that attracted numerous writers in the Soviet Union and Russian émigré communities.[7] What they appreciated in his texts varied widely: a radical approach to literary language, new forms and devices, the ability to transform one's experience as a budding artist into a national epic, the zenith or nadir of Western literature, a dangerous or progressive influence on Russian culture. Overlap can be observed even amid these various points of emphasis, revealing how Russians crafted a personal version of Joyce ("my Joyce") for themselves, while in the process addressing similar concerns, history and paternity foremost among them.

This book explores the evolution of Joyce's special impact on Russian literature from the mid-1920s to the early 2020s through a series of principal case studies: Yury Olesha (1899–1960), Vladimir Nabokov (1899–1977), Andrei Bitov (1937–2018), Sasha Sokolov (1943–), and Mikhail Shishkin (1961–). In addition to including Joycean subtexts in their writings, these authors have each explicitly spoken or written about Joyce in interviews, essays, and other paratexts. They also offer a neat line of influence. Nabokov's discriminating taste gave Olesha and Sokolov high marks, despite their technical status as Soviet writers, and both Bitov and Sokolov have expressed appreciation for their predecessors' art. Shishkin, too, speaks movingly of the Russian Joyceans. All five belong to a tradition that can be traced back to Joyce and that keeps their art open to his aesthetics and ideas. Two writers come from the prewar period, two from the postwar era, and one from the post-Soviet age. Such chronological range helps illuminate the development of Joyce's literary reception in Russia. Nabokov's and Shishkin's positions as émigré writers add a further nuance to this scheme.[8]

It is very important to note that the presence of Joyce in these authors' works, whether explicit or more hypothetical, does not erase what came before him or what was taking place around them. He was part of a broader landscape, both national and international, and his impact is not necessarily more definitive than that of other figures significant to these writers, such as the symbolist Andrei Bely (1880–1934) or the Russian Formalists. Nonetheless, Joyce and his art stood as an important alternative both in literature and in life. The very criticism of his work could make a later Soviet writer curious. Joyce's project to alter his past and his future through writing, as exemplified by his protagonist Stephen Dedalus's aesthetic theories in *Ulysses*, appealed to them for numerous reasons.

Indeed, while Russian literature's conversation with Joyce touches on many subjects, this particular idea serves as a major through line. These writers are fascinated by, even obsessed with, the question of literary heritage. The Russian historical experience irrevocably altered how authors might relate to their predecessors by violently cutting them out from the tradition, by limiting access to a lineage and a place in the development of world literature. Partly for this reason, Stephen's Shakespeare theory serves as a productive lens through which to examine these writers' relations to Joyce, as well as—in some cases—a direct point of contact between Joyce and his Russian counterparts. Laid out in episode 9 of *Ulysses*, Stephen's idea suggests that a writer can rewrite the past by creating lasting art and by selecting a literary forefather to supplant the biological one. Stephen uses the example of Shakespeare to make his case. According to him, Shakespeare became a father to himself by writing *Hamlet* and, therefore, engendering the world's conception of the Bard, at once father and son. Furthermore, in referring to historical accounts of Shakespeare having played the role of King Hamlet in a performance of the play, he emphasizes how this artistic master also plays a role, literally and figuratively. In this way, the Bard rewrites personal history and inscribes himself into world literature, liberating himself of servile filial bonds. All five Russian writers observed this idea in *Ulysses* and responded to it in turn based on their personal circumstances. The following chapters focus on why they were drawn to this theme, along with related ones such as cultural lineages and history, in their readings and artistic reinterpretations of Joyce. The latter's creations served as an impetus for their literary experiments, but this exchange also functions as a mirror by which their anxieties and goals can be observed.

Simultaneously, while each of the analyzed Russian writers responded to Joyce in an individual manner, the sum of their methods reveals common concerns. This subject raises the issue of how throughout the twentieth century cultural values changed in the Soviet Union, Russian emigration, and the post-1991 Russian environment. Their works, in dialogue with Joyce, reveal how writers in these various times conceptualized how they might make space for themselves within such an increasingly crowded field, and how historical changes affected their sense of political positionality. These authors incorporate Joyce's ideas into their books in ways that illustrate Russia's broader place in world literature. What was possible? What was desirable? Where did Russian literature belong? Their responses to Joyce's texts, particularly *Ulysses* (1922) and *Finnegans Wake* (1939), speak to how they tackled such immense questions relative to their own time and place.

Finally, as this introduction lays out and the ensuing chapters argue both implicitly and explicitly, these case studies highlight shifting understandings of influence and, more to the point, intertextuality. The Russian authors' works constitute not only examples of various kinds of intertextuality but also representative steps in and explanations of the evolution of intertextual theory. To that end, this book considers the connections between, say, Nabokov and Joyce to be a dialogue between texts and readers, rather than a monologic exchange of meaning from a single text to another. It is critical to recall that the Joyce whom Nabokov read is much different from Shishkin's Joyce in the 1990s. Naturally, the conversation is ever-expanding, as the conclusion demonstrates by incorporating the voices of more living Russian writers and critics.

Who's Afraid of Influence? Methodology and Theoretical Framework

Heinrich F. Plett, in his essay "Intertextualities," describes two approaches to the titular subject. According to him, the synchronic perspective "claims that all texts possess a simultaneous existence. This entails the leveling of any temporal differences; history is suspended in favour of the co-presence of the past."[9] "Such an attitude," he continues, "suits the creative artist, not the discerning scholar."[10] In essence, he argues that while all texts may be productively and creatively compared with one another to find, for example, transhistorical linkages, intertextuality as practiced by his "discerning scholar" instead takes into consideration the temporality of a text, its place within a history that cannot be ignored. This study's approach will be grounded in the evidence of each writer's contact with Joyce, whether firsthand or secondhand, in accumulated references and parallels between their works, and in responsible comparative readings that illustrate shared concerns among the various authors.

Joyce pervaded the air of the Soviet literary scene. Many authors became familiar with his texts and ideas in roundabout ways. Still, the goal is not simply to read *Ulysses* "next to" *Envy*, as it were, but instead to explicate a not yet fully explored connection, one that tells us something about Olesha's novel that would otherwise remain obscured. For that reason, what Plett calls the diachronic perspective appears most productive. "Being more of a traditionalist than a progressive," Plett writes, the intertextualist historian of literature "does not hunt after sounds in a diffuse echo chamber but rather prefers well-ordered 'archives' . . . of meticulously researched intertextualities."[11] Each Joycean subtext then serves as one layer in a given work that can then be used to explain with greater clarity the fabric of that same text if analyzed properly. The individual parts (intertextual allusions, parallels, echoes, and so on) shed light on the whole (a given novel's many-layered meanings).

However, this second view, at least as described by Plett, ignores valuable sociocultural information. To counter this inclination, each chapter contextualizes a given writer's literary response to Joyce within the circumstances of where and when he wrote it and offers a different kind of synchronic reading. The five authors investigated here faced their own individual anxieties of influence—that infamous sense of needing to overcome one's predecessors described by critic Harold Bloom. Olesha's dialogue with Joyce was naturally influenced by the culture of the New Economic Policy (NEP) period in which the author found himself, and this fact finds its reflection within *Envy*. Likewise, Nabokov's experience as an émigré who had lost his home dictates that his understanding of Joyce's ideas be markedly different, just as Bitov's and Sokolov's must necessarily be given their status as self-described belated writers of the post-Stalin era. Shishkin, too, would eventually read Joyce in light of the tremendous changes Russia underwent during perestroika and glasnost and through the turbulent 1990s. In short, this study deals not with a single Joyce but rather with five different ones.

Julia Kristeva, in a recapitulation of her notion of intertextuality, emphasizes that, as she understands it, the term "has always been about introducing history into structuralism."[12] Citing Stéphane Mallarmé's interest in anarchy and Proust's in the Dreyfus affair, she goes on to suggest that "by showing how much the inside of the text is indebted to its outside, interpretation reveals the inauthenticity of the writing subject: the writer is a subject in process, a carnival, a polyphony without possible reconciliation, a permanent revolt."[13] For her, then, intertextuality is an "intersection of . . . texts."[14] It is not only about identifying sources but also about exploring the shapes that these intersections, collisions, and polyphonic dialogues take within a cultural artifact. Kristeva emphasizes this same view in her original essay on intertextuality, "Word, Dialogue and Novel" (1966), which draws on the work of the Russian critic Mikhail Bakhtin (1895–1975): "By introducing the *status of the word* as a minimal structural unit, Bakhtin situates the text within history and society, which are then seen as texts read by the writer, and into which he inserts himself by rewriting them. . . . The only way a writer can participate in history is by transgressing this abstraction through a process of reading-writing."[15] In other words, Kristevan intertextuality describes the process by which authors insert themselves into other texts within a historical or social context. She aims to "define the specificity of different textural arrangements by placing them within the general text (culture) of which they are a part and which is in turn, part of them."[16] Such an approach to writing about an intertextuality that recognizes both vertical and horizontal lines of contact between Joyce and Russian writers yields great insights. For this same reason, each case study is both an example of and an explanation for the development of our understandings of intertextuality throughout the twentieth century and into the first decades of the twenty-first century. In the ways these five novelists approach their connections to the past vis-à-vis Joyce, we come to know better how literary heritage was conceived across this range of time.

Thus, for Olesha and Nabokov, who in their fiction at least frame their links to the past in terms of paternal struggles, a Bloomian approach feels most apt, as they exhibit a more traditionally modernist understanding of literary hierarchies and relationships. According to Bloom, influence involves a Freudian clash between predecessor and novice where "figures of capable imagination appropriate" what their precursors have already created.[17] If Bloom's brand of intertextuality has fallen somewhat out of favor, it nonetheless offers some insights into the relations between certain authors and how they challenge Joyce's example. These writers are all, to be sure, fascinated by questions of paternity, but perhaps even more importantly, they also pick up and modify parts of Joyce's works, engaging in what Bloom calls "poetic misprision."[18] It is also easy to see in Nabokov's efforts to wrest primacy from his forefathers, for example, something of a Bloomian Oedipal conflict. Perhaps even more pertinent is Bitov's sense of belatedness, which runs throughout *Pushkin House* as he attempts to come to terms with literary history and to find a resolution that does not involve combating the past through literature. Each chapter addresses precisely these kinds of issues, while keeping in mind Bloom's suggestion that "influence-anxiety does not so much concern the forerunner but rather is an anxiety achieved in and by the story, novel, play, poem, or essay."[19] The tensions found in and between texts, then, should be the focal points of an intertextual study.

To enact this kind of analysis, Bloom proposes six "revisionary ratios" by which authors "misread" their forebears.[20] These vary from the "clinamen" (a swerve away from the original text) to the "apophrades" (a text that makes the original feel like a copy). Arcane as these terms may be, they help conceptualize how authors transform Joycean models. For instance, Nabokov's *Gift* "corrects" *Ulysses*'s Shakespeare theory as Nabokov translates Joyce's idea into his own émigré context. He "misreads" *Ulysses* to unite literary and biological fathers rather than split them apart. Bloom stresses that the "revisionary relationship between poems, as manifested in tropes, images, diction, syntax, grammar, metric, [and] poetic stance" plays the greatest role.[21] The same principle applies to prose: the relationship between Joyce's texts and those of these selected Russian figures can be productively examined in terms of the images, motifs, themes, diction, and tropes that descendants borrow and alter to remarkable effect.

One of the mainstays of intertextual criticism has been the concern that noting links between texts implies a qualitative judgment regarding the author who does the quoting. In an otherwise illuminating reconsideration of the word "allusion," for example, Gregory Machacek suggests that "such terms as *source*, *borrowing*, and *echo* imply that the allusive text is of lesser stature. . . . The terminology can give the impression that the earlier text possesses an admirable creative plenitude, while the later text is secondary not just in time but in value—derivative, unoriginal."[22] Not for nothing did Bloom call it the anxiety of influence. Nonetheless, such hedging feels unnecessary—a justification for a practice that has no need of one. Even if authors may experience such a tension, critics need not. To suggest that a text derives something from a precursor is not to imply a lack of originality, and anyone who argues so misses the point. It is simply in the nature of literary works to comment on themselves and others. Writing decades before Machacek, Gérard Genette acts as a transitional figure of sorts in this history when he writes in his monumental *Palimpsests* (1982) about "a text derived from another preexistent text": "This derivation can be of a descriptive or intellectual kind, where a metatext . . . 'speaks' about a second text. . . . It may yet be of another kind such as text B not speaking of text A at all but being unable to exist, as such, without A, from which it originates through a process I shall provisionally call *transformation*, and which it consequently evokes more or less perceptibly without necessarily speaking of it or citing it."[23] Again, the anxiety is palpable, for no text can be so dependent on its antecedents as to be unable to exist otherwise.[24] By the end of his study, Genette does seem to backtrack when he speaks of hypertexts that may be read without reference to their hypotexts and left completely comprehensible. In the chapters that follow, the Russians "speak" about and to Joyce's works through their reformulations of his images, plots, and ideas, but their novels remain intact originals even without the reader's awareness of Joyce's writing.

This relationship is no less pertinent when it comes to Bitov, Sokolov, and Shishkin—three titans of contemporary Russian fiction whose works likewise evince a shift in the historical understanding of intertextuality. Critics such as Patricia Yaeger have advocated for a return to and renewal of intertextual studies. She pushes for "a swerve from vertical theories of intertextuality to intriguingly horizontal ones."[25] This move, playfully couched in Bloomian terminology by Yaeger, "will allow us to explore the way citations, translations, and Web crawling open hyphenated spaces where choruses of overlapping voices and metaphors fold and unfold like butterfly wings, where we encounter intertext as thread, cocoon, nectar, entanglement."[26] In short, they are exactly the kinds of intertext that later writers, including Bitov, Sokolov, and Shishkin, engage in. For different reasons, they turn away from the vertical, hierarchical schemes of Olesha and Nabokov; generational conflicts concern them no less, but they channel their creative energies elsewhere to resolve the question of literary lineage.

For example, Bitov's *Pushkin House*—a densely intertextual novel and a seminal work of late Soviet dissident literature—is on the surface concerned with obeisance to predecessors. In the way it draws from countless sources in ludic fashion, the novel, however, becomes what Yaeger calls a "ménage," where Bitov's fellow authors, including Joyce, "become wardrobe masters or mistresses proffering old styles for the pleasure of messing around in someone else's clothes: wringing import from adornment."[27] Of course, it is Pushkin House—literary institute and symbol—that receives the special adornment. In this space, elements from others' works decorate and supplement Bitov's Pushkin House/*Pushkin House*; they are ultimately not sources of extreme anxiety, but rather what Yaeger calls "a momentary escape from the weight of history and invitation to turn the past into play."[28] By draping his *House* under citations and quotations from Alexander Pushkin, Mikhail Lermontov, and Fyodor Tiutchev, Bitov can play with different narrative masks and views of history. They are its facades and inlays, its trimmings and curtains—simultaneously essential and purely ornamental. Sokolov takes things even further along this horizontal axis by viewing intertext as "fold or entanglement."[29] His debut novel, *A School for Fools*, challenges chronological and narrative time by blending its protagonist's past, present, and future in a freewheeling, multivocal account. In much the same way, Sokolov proposes the relativity of literary phenomena. There is no hierarchy to speak of, as he references and incorporates all manner of source material. They become entangled when there is no inside or outside to history. His referents—his play with Joycean style, in particular—become equal with his own words in the "circling of source and citation."[30] Finally, the intertexts in Shishkin's *Maidenhair* can be viewed as both "hyperactive ghosts" and, potentially, "unread citations."[31] Again, this author does not fear the past or feel burdened by it. Instead, he celebrates the recyclability of past works. Shishkin takes on Joyce's mantle of "scissors and paste man" to great effect.[32] The result is a dramatic shift from intertextuality as a struggle between two writers(-readers) to a game between author and reader. This approach, Yaeger maintains, "calls readers, perhaps against their wills, to claim alien or abject kinship groups."[33] Shishkin's polyphonic, multivalent citations aim at no less immense a task than uniting disparate traditions, in the process asking the reader to see their interconnectedness amid the violence and misunderstandings of the wars Shishkin depicts in his book. But what if a reader misses a citation? Does Shishkin's dense web of intertexts and borrowed materials shrivel up? Or is that simply part of the game, Shishkin's invitation to "transcend mere identity by seeking a deliberate bliss and entanglement" in the interconnectedness of words?[34] Much like Joyce in *Finnegans Wake*, Shishkin strives toward a universal heritage for both text and reader.

In this multitude of ways, the case studies that follow embody not only strands of intertextual relations between authors but also the very development of our understanding of intertextuality throughout the twentieth century. As the earlier writers (Olesha, Nabokov) exhibit an alternately destabilizing or stimulating fixation on their positions within a tradition, the later writers (Bitov, Sokolov, Shishkin) acknowledge and celebrate the inevitability of repetition. The Russian writers saw exactly what they needed to see in Joyce's work at their respective times. This study endeavors to highlight their intertextual connections, as well as what is most "Joycean" about these figures and their views on literary lineage.

Before proceeding, perhaps it would be well worth considering Mary Orr's description of influence, a term that can feel outdated or misguided:

As opposed to the hierarchical, astral, Bloomian paradigm, the pertinent model for influence here is "that which flows into," a tributary that forms a mightier river by its confluences, or the main stream that comprises many contributors. Influence as baton to be passed on thus understands the "situatedness" of texts not as a synchronic system or electronic network, but as a complex process of human (inter)cultural activity in spaces and times including those of subsequent readers. Texts are the productions of multiple agencies and a plethora of intentions, from pleasure to instruction, exemplification to enlightenment. . . . Thus, the reader is the transmitter and interpreter of a work as cultural artefact that has relevance to real worlds but is not a mere video recording of them.[35]

This notion of intertextuality takes into consideration all aspects of a text's creation—the author, the reader, the cultural and historical contexts—and stresses the connections and tensions between them. It moreover paints an accurate picture of how *Ulysses* spreads its so-called influence in various directions, rerouted into singular streams by each writer's divergent interpretation of its messages, as well as by individual contexts. If a book is composed of many such sources, then it seems logical that its functions or purposes would be manifold, from pleasure to enlightenment. Finally, Orr's definition places an accent on the reader's role as cocreator in interpretation. This facet of influence-intertextuality has a twofold quality, as Nabokov's reading of *Ulysses* comes into contact with the subsequent reader-critic's interpretation of *his* response to Joyce. The analyses that follow aim to provide a more substantive understanding of the myriad ways a group of Russian writers read, misread, and transformed Joycean prototypes. The connections highlighted speak to matters fundamental to their respective worldviews, aesthetics, and contexts. Furthermore, these readings simultaneously present fresh insights into these writers' novels and elucidate the many facets of a central narrative in twentieth-century Russian literature: to use Joseph Brodsky's term, the "Gorgon-like stare of history."[36] This fascination with, and frequently fear of, history, whether personal, national, or literary, is by and large the primary point of reference in Joyce's writing that these authors take up in their quest to come to grips with various temporal and paternal structures.

Structure and Chapter Summaries

While the particular nature of each writer's reading of Joyce determines individual points of analysis, all five chapters follow a shared structure. They are split between details regarding an author's access to and statements on the Irish luminary and readings of the writer's major novels with a focus on their intertextual and thematic resonances with Joyce's work.

Chapter 1 is devoted to Olesha's use of *Ulysses* as both a subtext and a counterdiscourse throughout his short novel *Envy* (*Zavist'*, 1927). Supplemented by archival research, it serves in part to demonstrate that Joyce's impact on Russian writers began early, just a few years after the publication of *Ulysses* in 1922. Despite his complex and seemingly contradictory attitude toward Joyce, Olesha inscribed several direct parallels and inversions of various elements from Joyce's novel into *Envy* in order to counter the idea that the gifted, creative artist may rewrite his past by selecting a literary forefather. Stephen's project, Olesha intimates, was simply not possible under the Soviet system. Thus, while Olesha valued Joyce's project, which aligned with his respect for individualism and Western art, *Envy* is as a counterresponse to many of *Ulysses*'s basic modernist premises.

The second chapter focuses on Nabokov's *Gift* (*Dar*, written 1935–37, complete version published 1952).[37] Although scholarship on Nabokov and Joyce has been far more robust than that on the other four subjects of this book, many more points of contact remain to be explicated. One such area concerns how Nabokov's protagonist, Fyodor Godunov-Cherdyntsev, follows the Joycean system of electing a literary forefather not to alter his paternity, but rather to merge the father of the modern Russian literary language, Alexander Pushkin (1799–1837), with his deceased father to recover a lost birthright. In this sense, *The Gift* is as a transposition of *Ulysses* in a Russian émigré key. Nabokov willfully mistranslates *Ulysses*, writing another tale of a budding artist, but refuses to sever links to the past that Stephen denounces. In addition, reading both *The Gift* and Nabokov's second English-language novel, *Bend Sinister* (1947), alongside *Ulysses* brings Nabokov's dialogic stance toward Joyce into better focus. His treatment of Stephen's theory in *Bend Sinister* is not only an artistic critique of Joyce's aesthetics but also a personal and even political statement.

Skipping past the dark times in which Joyce's name was rarely mentioned, chapter 3 shows how the younger Bitov recognized that Soviet policies disrupted literature's natural progression, resulting in a sense of belatedness for his "post-" generation: post-Stalin, post-Thaw, and newly postmodern. The Joycean intertext in Bitov's celebrated novel *Pushkin House* (*Pushkinskii dom*, 1964–71) spotlights the sources of the author's anxiety of influence and the character arc of his protagonist, Leva Odoevtsev. The latter attempts to rewrite his past by proposing alternative father figures but falters due to a distorted historical perspective. At a higher level, Bitov uses his novel, and its extended conversation with *Ulysses*, to demonstrate how a writer can escape the self-imposed limitations that come with comparing himself with predecessors, even while taking joy in quoting from past works, including those of Joyce.

The fourth chapter continues tracing this course of thought by addressing Sokolov's first novel, *A School for Fools* (*Shkola dlia durakov*, 1976). For various reasons, Joyce's initial impact on Russian literature remained largely, though not exclusively, on the levels of theme, plot, characters, and so on until Sokolov. Although *School* contains fewer of the explicit references to Joyce found in his predecessors' works, Sokolov's style suggests a potent Joycean presence. In short, this text *reads* more like Joyce. Points of comparison include style (particularly stream of consciousness), structural play, and "forking characters" with fluid identities. While *A School for Fools* continues to draw on modernist models and Sokolov engages with *Ulysses* and *Dubliners* (1914), plot and character are dissolved almost entirely, much as in the protean *Finnegans Wake*. Additionally, chapter 4 demonstrates how Sokolov's transformation of the Joycean model involves a disappearance into texture. The protagonist's story is less about his coming into his own as an artist through a revision of the past than it is about how language, style, and the novel's very structure supersede the artist as hero, in essence carrying Joyce's project to a new level.

Finally, chapter 5 considers how Russian writers fit into history after the fall of the Soviet Union. For Shishkin, this reckoning—an awareness of how Russian culture had fallen behind the times—presented both a shock and an opportunity. In 2005, he spoke of merging the West's "love of the word" with Russian culture's "love of man."[38] For him, the former is embodied by Joyce, the latter by Nikolai Gogol (1809–1852). Shishkin thus saw a need to reintegrate Russian literature into world culture after the end of the Soviet Union, and, to do so, he has written works that are heavily intertextual, crafting a vision of the world deeply enmeshed across centuries. Shishkin's third novel, *Maidenhair* (*Venerin volos*, 2005), engages with Joyce in multiple related ways. Like the subjects of the first three chapters, Shishkin weaves themes, character traits, and situation rhymes, but more like Sokolov, he also makes use of a Joycean style. He engages in Joyce's radical brand of citation and borrowing seen most prominently in *Finnegans Wake*. Both Joyce and Shishkin have been accused of plagiarism, an oversimplification that ignores how some writers explicitly transform works created by their predecessors. Moreover, Shishkin develops Joyce's stream of consciousness technique into what can be called "stream of collective consciousness," as he entwines voices in a chaotic blend. Again, he aims to show the interconnectedness of seemingly disparate cultures and traditions and to give Russian letters equal footing on the world stage after the catastrophic Soviet era.

The publication of the complete Russian translation of *Ulysses* in the late 1980s reverberated throughout Russia, though never uniformly. This study of Joyce's impact on Russian literature concludes by reflecting on how writers through 2021 have responded to his texts, taken up some of his key themes (fatherhood, history, literary heritage, exile), and viewed him as either a welcome foreign contributor to their national tradition or an influence best worth ignoring. To do so, selections from interviews with a range of writers and critics are put into dialogue with one another. These voices include Dmitry Bykov, Anna Glazova, Marina Stepnova, Zinovy Zinik, Aleksei Salnikov, Ksenia Buksha, Alexander Ilianen, Sergei Solovev, Grigory Sluzhitel, Ivan Sokolov, Andrei Babikov, Dmitry Ragozin, Ilya Kukulin, Lev Rubinstein, Alexander Skidan, and Alexander Ilichevsky, as well as members of the Moscow-based Joyce reading group Territory of Slow Reading. This collective holds weekly meetings on Sundays via Zoom as they gradually make their way through *Ulysses*, over and over; they also organize an annual Bloomsday walk and celebration in central Moscow. Such various perspectives reveal how the Russian Joyce is no less dynamic today. He has become an exile, a peripheral writer (in both senses of the word), a relic of the past, a gargantuan technical innovator, a symbol for the free spirit of prose, a passing fancy in one's youth, a hooligan, and a master of life-creation (*zhiznetvorchestvo*), among many other things.

Often contradictory, the images of Joyce that abound today, along with this book's primary case studies, serve to demonstrate the scope of Joyce's significant and significantly underappreciated place in Russian letters. His work speaks to issues central to many writers' texts. As the brief chapter précis above suggest, these selected authors, like many of their peers, consistently if not obsessively write about fatherhood throughout their fiction. This phenomenon might be explained with reference to Edward W. Said's theory of filial/affilial relationships: "One very strong three-part pattern . . . originates in a large group of late nineteenth- and early twentieth-century writers, in which the failure of the generative impulse—the failure of the capacity to produce or generate children—is portrayed in such a way as to stand for a general condition afflicting society and culture together."[39] Olesha, Nabokov, Bitov, Sokolov, and Shishkin all take up this exact concept in their works. While some are less concerned with their heroes' physical inability to reproduce heirs, they all demonstrate the many complications that arise when one attempts to defy biology or history in order to change the past. It is not simply a matter of style or of personal history, however. The Soviet project as a whole provoked these questions and left post-Soviet writers reeling with them.

The clash of the artist with a history far beyond individual comprehension lies at the heart of this book. As Hayden White suggests, "The historical past . . . is, like our various personal pasts, at best a myth, justifying our gamble on a specific future, and at worst a lie, a retrospective rationalization of what we have in fact become through our choices."[40] History, a term here understood quite broadly, takes center stage in Joyce's *Ulysses*. It should not come as a surprise that *Envy*, *The Gift*, *Pushkin House*, *A School for Fools*, and *Maidenhair* all likewise probe the depths of history, whether it be personal, national, or cultural. The protagonists of these novels explore what it means to be figured within or without history. Following White's formulation, their authors indicate that it is "only by disenthralling human intelligence from the sense of history that men will be able to confront creatively the problems of the present."[41] This pressing need to overcome the barriers of Stephen's looming nightmare of history in order to engage productively and organically with the present moment reverberates throughout *The Gift* and *Pushkin House*. Nabokov's and Bitov's solutions—if there can ever be a solution to such an enduring problem—diverge dramatically and reflect their particular circumstances, but they share a reliance on Joycean prototypes.

The same prototypes belong to a more general mythologizing trend in twentieth-century literature. The mythic method of Joyce's novel is well known, and it perhaps plays a role in Olesha's *Envy*, Sokolov's *A School for Fools*, and Shishkin's *Maidenhair* in particular. Extrapolating from these techniques, we can see how, as Eleazar M. Meletinsky notes, "literary mythification is dominated by the idea of an eternal, cyclical repetition of mythological prototypes under different 'masks,' which means that literary and mythological protagonists can play various roles and be replaced by a variety of characters."[42] While the writers examined in this study create singular protagonists who are quite memorable for their talents and idiosyncrasies, a broader myth of the "artist as a young man" that frequently combines with more classical myths can be discerned in their texts. Such overlap speaks to the desire in all six writers to carve out a space for themselves in literary history.

These themes, then, serve as some of the central threads of the analysis that follows. In the tensions between, on the one hand, the various polyphonic dialogues with Joyce that these writers cultivate and, on the other, the unities among them, a portrait of an impact as fascinating as it is substantial and multifaceted emerges. For to address Joyce's place in Russian literature of the past hundred years is to begin finally telling a major story of literary history.

CHAPTER 1

Yury Olesha

An Envy for World Culture

> So begin the searches for a father, for a motherland,
> for a profession, for a talisman that can prove to be
> glory or power.
>
> —Yury Olesha, "I Look into the Past"

Speaking at the 1936 General Meeting of the Moscow Union of Soviet Writers, Yury Olesha offered up James Joyce as the face of a negative, alien literary model that must be eradicated. According to Olesha, Joyce exemplified the reason for the urgent need to struggle against Formalism and Naturalism in Soviet letters. His speech was reproduced in the March 20 edition of *Literary Gazette* (*Literaturnaia gazeta*) and included the following remarks:

> The artist should say to man: "Yes, yes, yes," but Joyce says: "No, no, no."
> "Everything is bad on Earth," says Joyce. And thus, all his brilliance is of
> no use to me. . . . In order to understand what is Formalism and what is
> Naturalism, and why these phenomena are hostile to us, I give you an
> example from Joyce. This writer said: "Cheese is the corpse of milk."
> Look, comrades, how terrible. The writer of the West saw the death of
> milk. He said that milk can be dead. Is it well said? It is well said. It is
> said correctly, but we don't want such correctness. We want neither Nat-
> uralism nor formalist tricks, but artistic dialectical truth. And from the
> point of view of this truth, milk can never be a corpse; it flows from the
> mother's breast into the child's mouth, and therefore it is immortal.[1]

On the surface of it, there is nothing particularly special about Olesha's comments, which align with the trend in Soviet criticism from the early 1930s on to denounce Joyce's perceived pessimism and nonprogressive vision of history. As any deviation from state-mandated Socialist Realism was by this time considered counterrevolutionary and artistically suspect, it was inevitable that Joyce would eventually face such condemnation. Olesha, who declared in his speech at the First All-Union Congress of Soviet Writers in 1934 that he had renounced his individualist "beggar theme" and committed his art to the youth of Russia and contemporary moral issues, thus proactively chose to contribute to this body of criticism.[2] By reproaching Joyce early and publicly, as Benedikt Sarnov maintains, he could align himself with the so-called correct critical point of view and potentially avoid greater troubles such as arrest or execution in the future.[3] After all, the year 1937 and Stalin's purges, which made aesthetic preferences a matter of life and death, loomed.

Examined more closely, Olesha's speech reveals itself to be highly contrived and not without contradictions. In the process of covering his own modernist tracks by damning Joyce's formalistic technique and purportedly pessimistic worldview, he alludes to *Ulysses*'s famous lyrical conclusion, Molly Bloom's soliloquy, when she recalls her future husband's proposal: "and then I asked him with my eyes to ask again yes and then he asked me would I yes to say yes my mountain flower and first I put my arms around him yes and drew him down to me so he could feel my breasts all perfume yes and his heart going like mad and yes I said yes I will Yes."[4] Olesha's statements quoted above thus begin with an obvious lie: Joyce's finale undoubtedly ends with a positive affirmation, indeed, one of the most well known in European literature. It stands as an instructive contrast to Olesha's own cynical ending to his novel *Envy* (1927), which finds its protagonists resigned to their undesirable fates. Olesha here allegedly proclaims "No!" to Joyce by appropriating Molly's soliloquy for his own purposes, and he argues that Soviet literature now requires something other than negation, namely, "artistic dialectical truth," a convoluted formulation that bespeaks the jargon of the era.[5] He then goes on to mix metaphors by juxtaposing the milk-corpse-cheese with his own image of a mother's milk offered to a child, an apparently optimistic symbol of immortality. Such an unconvincing and odd juxtaposition raises a host of questions: Just how sincere was Olesha in his speech? Why does he lie about Joyce's pessimism? Was he truly abasing himself, or did he expect his audience to see some other meaning through the subterfuge?

Another coded layer exists within Olesha's speech, one that may be read as a call to admire the depth and novelty of vision that Joyce brought to literature. Despite his diatribe, Olesha implicitly champions Joyce's creative artistry by recognizing the milk-corpse metaphor as strong, if perhaps decadent in some sense. His comments thus represent a subtle form of doublespeak, a way to simultaneously acknowledge and criticize Joyce while remaining noncommittal. Maintaining an ambivalent stance arguably provided not only safety but also an indirect means to promote Joyce's art to the extent that it was possible. Despite the speech's many ambiguities, it raises the issues of Olesha's complicated relationship with Joyce and how he responded to *Ulysses* through his own fiction.

In writing *Envy*, Olesha drew on his interpretation of Joyce's text as well as reviews of the much-debated author, who at this point in the 1920s became a frequent subject of conversation among writers even in Soviet Russia. Joyce's impact on *Envy* goes beyond sporadic allusions to *Ulysses*; Olesha, in fact, establishes a sustained literary response by which he investigates ideas central to his worldview and his situation within a cultural climate growing rapidly hostile toward experimentation and freethinking individualism. This first chapter explores the degree to which Olesha was familiar with Joyce based on his own statements and the general availability of Joyce's work in Russia and then enumerates and analyzes the similarities between *Envy* and *Ulysses* at various important levels including character, plot, and theme. Individually some of these connections may appear coincidental. However, taking such details into account collectively, it becomes clear that the works resonate quite strongly with each other. More broadly, in rereading *Envy* through the lens of *Ulysses*, we better understand the former's thematic complexities. The parallels—and reversals—that Olesha features throughout his text can best be understood as the response from one writer, who attempts to conceptualize the issues facing his generation in a radically unstable period, to the work of another writer who faced analogous concerns in different conditions. In particular, these correspondences and differences develop a conversation concerning one of Joyce's primary themes: father-son conflict and Stephen Dedalus's related project of choosing his own artistic lineage to overcome paternal legacies. Olesha, in turn, addresses this same problem and with his references to *Ulysses* suggests the difficulty, even the impossibility, for a Soviet writer like him to pursue Stephen's path during this period of transition toward an ever more regimented way of life. Though Nikolai Kavalerov engages in a similar undertaking as Stephen Dedalus, the cultural-historical circumstances around him, exacerbated by his own considerable ambivalence, prevent his success. Examining *Envy* in light of *Ulysses* thus helps reveal another layer to the tragic dilemmas presented in Olesha's fiction and his own trying position. It likewise establishes many of the main tropes of the Russian Joycean tradition.

Points of Contact

The more general Soviet interest in Joyce, of which Olesha became an early participant, can be traced back to at least 1923. In the second issue of his journal *Contemporary West* (*Sovremennyi Zapad*), Evgeny Zamiatin (1884–1937) wrote a column discussing *Ulysses*'s overall strengths, use of Shakespearean subtexts, and attention to sexuality.[6] Neil Cornwell rightly suggests that this article "initiated an interest in Joyce among the modernist-inclined writers and intelligentsia in Russia."[7] Copies of *Ulysses* found their way to Russia during these key years. Cornwell, for example, cites Noël Riley Fitch's account of Ivy Litvinov's (née Low) visit to Sylvia Beach in Paris sometime in 1926–27 and her excitement at the thought of bringing Joyce to Russia.[8] This cultural exchange is essential to a comparative study of the two authors. Although the conditions in Soviet Russia would soon change irrevocably, such connections remained possible at this time.

Ulysses's early appearance in translation provides evidence of such permeability.[9] The first known Russian publication of Joyce is V. Zhitomirsky's 1925 rendition of several fragments from *Ulysses* in the Moscow almanac *Novelties of the West* (*Novinki Zapada*).[10] These fragments, all with gaps even *within* episodes, are drawn from the morning episode of "Telemachus," "Aeolus," "Cyclops," "Ithaca," and "Penelope." Additionally, a foreword by E. L. Lann provides an overview of the entire novel and a brief critical introduction to Joyce's life, art, and reputation.[11] Having moved from Kharkov to Moscow in 1922, Olesha would have had access to this volume, and while this is not the place to evaluate the quality of Zhitomirsky's translation, it should be noted that he at times alters lines. Nonetheless, he conveys numerous styles found in *Ulysses*, for example, the deceptively dry scientific catechism of "Ithaca" and Molly's more colloquial soliloquy, including its famous conclusion. These partial translations, along with the foreword, provide an impression of a novel constantly in motion and without a grounded point of view. Olesha would have found in *Ulysses* a satisfying model for displaying varied perspectives. This is not to say that *Envy* should be regarded as formally groundbreaking as *Ulysses*, whether considered solely in the Russian context or not; *Envy* may instead be viewed as a microcosm of such bold modernist experimentation filtered through a different cultural-literary context.[12]

This experimentation was central to Soviet debates regarding Joyce. Even before his 1936 speech with its negative comments, Olesha made several more statements regarding his Irish contemporary, often in reply to others' opinions or as part of a wider debate concerning Western literature. One of Joyce's most outspoken proponents in the 1930s, the well-known playwright Vsevolod

Vishnevsky, answered a series of three negative articles by critic Prince Dmitry Svyatopolk Mirsky (1890–1939) with his own "Know the West!" ("Znat' Zapad!") in 1933.[13] Defending Joyce, Vishnevsky emphatically repeats the need to understand Western literature and hails him as one of its greatest representatives. For support he includes statements by major artists and critics, including the following one from Olesha: "I consider the current of Joyce and Dos Passos innovative. True, I haven't read *Ulysses*, but V. Stenich, who is now translating this book, gave me a keen impression of it."[14] The question of what exactly Olesha meant by his "not having read" Joyce remains unclear, as is often the case with him. Although it is generally believed that Olesha was not fluent in English, the Russian Joyce scholar Ekaterina Genieva, on the contrary, attributes a very thorough knowledge of the Irish writer to Olesha, even suggesting he may have translated *Ulysses*. Without offering any evidence whatsoever, she makes the following cryptic statement: "I think that a lot in the stories about Joyce belong to the realm of myth. But proving that is difficult, because far from all archives are open and no one can say with certainty whether or not Yury Olesha translated *Ulysses*."[15] So, did Olesha mean that he had not read Joyce in English, or was he protecting himself against possible accusations of overestimating decadent Western literature? In spite of his evasive answer, he had surely followed the controversy surrounding the book for the previous ten years and read translations, published or not, available to him. While the culture of 1920s Soviet Russia contributed to Olesha's awareness and subsequent adaptation of Joycean motifs, his interest in European literature ran much deeper. His memoirs attest to the fact that he kept up with literary trends and knew the history of European literature rather well. Olesha even believed that "a writer's work is to some degree like a settling of accounts with the impressions that the writer receives in the course of his entire life . . . [b]ut also with the impressions received from literature."[16] In turn, Olesha's incorporation of elements derived from *Ulysses* into *Envy* evinces such a heavily intertextual practice.

By all accounts, *Ulysses* pervaded the air of the time. A memoir of Olesha by Lev Nikulin recounts a conversation with the author, Mirsky, the satirist Mikhail Zoshchenko (1894–1958), and the publisher Valentin Stenich (1897–1938) in which Joyce's and U.S. novelist John Dos Passos's (1896–1970) names appear. Olesha challenges Zoshchenko's claim that Stenich is translating Dos Passos, suggesting that he makes it all up as he goes along, and states: "Dos Passos, Joyce, Dos Passos, Joyce! Everybody says, 'Joyce,' but no one has read him!"[17] At Mirsky's suggestion that Joyce is nevertheless a great writer, Olesha balks with his typical irony: "He wrote a chapter without punctuation marks? I heard! In Odessa, brokers have long been writing telegrams without commas and periods."[18] Such statements on Joyce by Olesha appear relatively frequently in memoirs from this period. Discussing literary technique in 1934, Olesha gives Lev Tolstoy (1828–1910) high praise and even states that in some respects he reminds him of "what they now call Joyceism [*dzhoisizm*]."[19] Two years later, he remarked in an article published in *Literary Critic* (*Literaturnyi kritik*), "They consider Joyce a great writer. I only know excerpts. Yes, all that's remarkable, what Joyce writes."[20] He then goes on to call Joyce "formally interesting" and acknowledges his "sharp eyes" and "subtle psychological analysis."[21] Nevertheless, Olesha claims that he wants "to know that life is beautiful" and raises the same issue as in his Union of Soviet Writers speech: "I don't want to read a writer who talks about cheese, that cheese is the corpse of milk."[22] These statements utilize a familiar tactic: Olesha guardedly compliments Joyce for features he himself possesses as a writer (bold imagery, striking metaphors), only to cut him down for politically incorrect failures (pessimism, formalism). Tellingly, such traits can also be spotted in his own work.

In his private diary, however, Olesha would "bow before the shade of Joyce" and go on to praise *Dubliners*' "Araby" as "one of the best stories of all time."[23] The fact that "Araby" struck Olesha so profoundly should not come as a surprise. Joyce's story shares many features with Olesha's own short fiction: a protagonist faced with the challenges of maturity, an epiphanic moment, sharp details, and a concise, tensely wound plot. Given this clear, prolonged engagement with Joyce's work, as well as the two authors' similar aesthetic principles, Olesha's turn to *Ulysses* for inspiration in spite of the dangers of being interested in the controversial writer should therefore be explored more fully, especially since *Envy*'s characters and thematics bespeak an unmistakable impact by Joyce on his art.

While such dangers became more fatal than rhetorical during Joseph Stalin's reign, the pressures against writers including Olesha were already mounting by the mid-1920s, an experience to which *Envy* clearly gives voice. He began composing what would become *Envy* in 1924, that is, only seven years after the Russian Revolution. These intervening years saw immense changes in the literary scene, as writers' unions brought aid and community to authors, while others chose emigration. With each passing year, debates ramped up. As Evgeny Dobrenko has put it, "By the early 1920s, the term 'Russian literature' already begins to fall out of usage. Instead, other definitions emerge for the literature developing in the country, such as 'proletarian' literature . . . , 'peasant,' 'bourgeois,' and 'petit-bourgeois' literature. The latter was also called 'fellow-traveller' (*poputchik*) literature," a category in which Olesha found himself ensconced and which refers to writers whose work supported the new order up to a certain point.[24] Eventually two broad camps formed: the hard-line Communists who took aggressive stances against the old literary intelligentsia through such venues as the Komsomol journal *Young Guard* (*Molodaia gvardiia*) and the All-Russian Association of Proletarian Writers (VAPP) and those who advocated a moderate approach, including Alexander Voronsky (1884–1937), editor of the journal *Red Virgin Soil* (*Krasnaia nov'*), who saw the value of authors such as Olesha and the equally conflicted Isaac Babel and actually coined the term "Soviet literature." The former aimed to influence the Communist Party into taking more active and aggressive stances on cultural and, specially, literary matters. Voronsky's ousting from the journal he founded and, eventually, the creation of the Union of Soviet Writers spelled their success. But of equal importance is the fact that the audience for works like Olesha's *Envy* was becoming more and more marginalized ever since the end of the Civil War, as populations shifted from the country to the city. The proletarian writers argued, not without reason, that these new readers were interested in less byzantine works than *Ulysses* or, on a smaller scale, even *Envy*. The push toward Socialist Realism, prefigured by works including Maxim Gorky's *Mother* (1906) and Fyodor Gladkov's *Cement* (1925), in turn helped generate the move toward greater verisimilitude in art and straightforward narratives that aligned with party needs, rather than experimentation. In short, a "total infantilization of culture" took hold, something that Olesha draws attention to in *Envy*.[25]

Thus, on the one hand, Olesha was witnessing how literature itself was gradually becoming politicized as a tool for the regime and, on the other, how his art was viewed for the time being at the very least as ultimately too closely linked to the past. This unstable and, in the final analysis, untenable state, of course, would lead to the anxiety found at the core of *Envy*'s narrative. Olesha's confused appreciation for Joyce and everything that he signified to his first readers in the 1920s is wrapped up in these matters, for in *Envy*, Olesha offered a fresh commentary on the role of the creative artist in this new space. Joyce, born to a stultifying and colonized Ireland, could no matter escape the boundaries of his homeland for Europe and the limits of tradition for revelatory innovations in prose. Olesha sought a reader who was disappearing, a continuation of a tradition that was being challenged, and a means of creative actualization that was simply impractical in his time and place. His engagement with *Ulysses* therefore represents a working through of his relationship with the modernist idea(l) of the self-made artist, as well as with the shifting literary-cultural values of the early Soviet era.

Olesha's Three Other Fat Men: Buck, Bloom, and Babichev

While a Joycean imprint on Olesha must not be overstated, the textural fabric of *Envy* and the wealth of echoes in it suggest that Olesha actively engages with Joyce's masterpiece on a deeper level than once suspected.[26] Of course, Olesha has not simply lifted the Irish writer's narrative strategies, themes, and motifs indiscriminately but instead selected elements attractive to him and modified them for his own purposes. By doing so, he creates a web of super-imposed images through which we see many parts of *Ulysses* shimmer. Olesha builds such parallels on numerous levels and then partially severs or upturns them to shape his negative reply to Joyce's text. He thereby underscores the impossibility of pursuing the same path in the USSR, where such individualism was growing ever more problematic. Olesha the writer may have valued innovation and a desire to chart one's own future, but Olesha the pragmatist saw the dangers in publicly saying so.

Olesha's novel is divided into two parts: one narrated in the first person, the second in the third person. It is repeatedly infiltrated by an array of texts and voices that splinter its time frame and narrative, including dreams and fantasies, two letters, recounted stories, and notes. After a drunken brawl, Nikolai Kavalerov, a writer who cannot adapt to the new Soviet way of life, is taken in by Andrei Babichev. Kavalerov's savior turns out to be an older, successful Communist who is constructing a miraculous cafeteria, the Chetvertak, that will do away with kitchen work and who has previously housed Volodya Makarov, an impressive athlete and the future of Russia, the New Soviet Man. After some time, Kavalerov enacts a failed rebellion under the tutelage of Ivan Babichev, Andrei's vagabond brother, when Volodya returns to Moscow and reestablishes his place in Babichev's apartment. Kavalerov, driven by envy, goes to a soccer match with the intention of killing Babichev and claiming Ivan's daughter, Valia, for himself but remains incapable of any real action. Finally, having rejected the Babichev brothers, Kavalerov resignedly crawls back to his landlady, the widow Anechka, only to discover Ivan in bed with her. Already some parallels and inversions should be apparent.

At the level of characterization, Olesha uses blending techniques to engage with *Ulysses* and comment on what Joyce's heroes mean to him. One of the most intriguing amalgamations of characters occurs on *Envy*'s opening pages. This first major correspondence between the two novels sets up the terms of Olesha's interest in *Ulysses* and the primary contrasts with which he repeatedly plays. Here, Olesha re-creates the morning scene from Joyce's novel, which was among the fragments Zhitomirsky translated, by alluding to Buck Mulligan via Andrei Babichev:

> He sings in the mornings in the toilet. You can imagine what a buoyant, healthy man this is. The desire to sing rises in him as a reflex. This song of his, in which there's no melody, no words, but only a "ta-ra-ra," which cries out in various moods, can be interpreted thus:
>
> "How pleasant it is to live . . . ta-ra! ta-ra! . . . My intestines are resilient . . . ra-ta-ta-ta-ra-ri. . . . The juices move properly within me . . . ra-ta-ta-du-ta-ta. . . . Contract, bowels, contract . . . tram-ba-ba-bum!"
>
> When he passes before me from the bedroom in the morning (I pretend I am asleep) through the door, which leads to the innards of the apartment, to the bathroom, my imagination flies off after him. I hear the commotion in the bathroom stall, where it's narrow for his large body. His back rubs against the inside of the door he slams shut, and his elbows poke into the walls, he shifts on his feet. A matte glass oval has been set into the bathroom door. He turns on the switch, the oval is illuminated from within and becomes a beautiful, opal-colored egg. In my mind's eye I see this egg, hanging in the darkness of the hall.[27]

This famous passage opens Joyce's novel:

> Stately, plump Buck Mulligan came from a stairhead, bearing a bowl of lather on which a mirror and a razor lay crossed. A yellow dressing-gown, ungirdled, was sustained gently behind him on the mild morning air. He held the bowl aloft and intoned:
>
> —*Introibo ad altare Dei.*
>
> Halted, he peered down the dark winding stairs and called out coarsely:
>
> —Come up, Kinch! Come up, you fearful jesuit!
>
> Solemnly he came forward and mounted the round gunrest. He faced about and blessed gravely thrice the tower, the surrounding land and the awaking mountains. Then, catching sight of Stephen Dedalus, he bent towards him and made rapid crosses in the air, gurgling in his throat and shaking his head. Stephen Dedalus, displeased and sleepy, leaned his arms on the top of the staircase and looked coldly at the shaking gurgling face that blessed him, equine in its length, and at the untonsured hair, grained and hued like pale oak.[28]

Possessing huge physicality and tremendous joie de vivre, Babichev shares many features with Buck; the latter also enjoys morning routines and pays close attention to bodily needs and sensations. The characters' vigor overflows into Buck's chanting and Andrei's noisy ablutions (ironically called "singing" by Kavalerov). Their antipodes, the writers Stephen and Kavalerov, run counter to them with their sleepiness and sardonic attitudes. Neither Babichev nor Buck, however, feels in the slightest upset by his roommate's gloomy disposition; their complete self-absorption beats all. In addition, the buoyancy inherent to their nature comes through in various restless actions: Buck's ridiculous "rapid crosses" mid-"gurgling," Babichev's "reflex" to sing in tune with his bowel movements and to thrust out his elbows as he knocks against the walls of the toilet while he "shifts on his feet" (*perebiraet nogami*). A crude energy, reflected in the various action verbs featured in both passages, keeps their bodies in motion, pulling other characters into their spheres of influence.

Babichev's famous bathroom scene also clearly owes much to another character from *Ulysses*, Leopold Bloom. This scatological moment can be neatly traced back not to Russian literature but rather to Joyce's hero: "Quietly [Bloom] read, restraining himself, the first column and, yielding but resisting, began the second. Midway, his last resistance yielding, he allowed his bowels to ease themselves quietly as he read, reading still patiently that slight constipation of yesterday quite gone."[29] Put simply, Bloom and Babichev savor the release of their bowels in terms that even naturalistic works previously hesitated to employ. They immerse themselves in the physiological rhythm of this process, finding a supplementary pleasure in the control they exert over their bodies. Such concern for the physical is emblematic of *Envy*, where Kavalerov places so much emphasis on Babichev's fleshy and massive frame, admiring its strength and feeling repelled by it; *Ulysses*'s unflinching portrayal of all aspects of human physicality, from bathroom habits to sexual encounters, offered Olesha and others a model for such candidness.

As can be seen through these examples, part of Olesha's technique involves his conflation of two characters, Buck and Bloom, into one, Andrei Babichev. This fusion serves to emphasize the ubiquity of this human type. Olesha does not directly transplant Bloom or Buck into *Envy*, of course, but rather crafts a figure that strongly recalls these two literary predecessors. All of these shared or modified points of characterization demonstrate both Olesha's ties to Joyce and the more general literary archetypes that he deploys in his fiction. Bloom's role as a source for father figures in *Envy*, for instance, will be further analyzed below.[30]

Another series of images in these opening scenes also links Mulligan and Babichev through shared traits, either material or psychological, and creates a recurring contrast between them and their younger artist counterparts, the aspiring poets Dedalus and Kavalerov. For example, Babichev indulges in ample "ablutions" and wears a "short mustache, right under the nose," recalling Buck's morning wash and shave.[31] These men concern themselves more with the upkeep of their bodies than with the cultivation of the human spirit or imagination, as expressed by Buck's irreverent attacks on faith and tasteless deprecation of Stephen's deceased mother, whom he once called "beastly dead," and by Babichev's NEP-era mind-set, which is epitomized by his famous passion for creating a cheap super-sausage.[32] Perhaps physiology and physicality do not entirely rule these two characters—Babichev feels compassion for overworked women and wants to liberate them from domestic slavery, while Buck participates in Dublin's literary scene and offers to join forces with Stephen to "Helenise" Ireland—but the narratives emphasize external appearances (for instance, Buck's "white glittering teeth"), and point to their existence in empirical-material(istic) reality.[33] Much as we *see* Mulligan's physical movements but never his internal processes, *Envy*'s narration limits us in this opening scene to Babichev's outer world. Such narratological points of view can prove to be pitfalls for first-time, and even experienced, readers. Though *Ulysses*'s opening chapter clearly does not feature the exact same sort of subjective first-person narration as *Envy*'s, it *is* infiltrated by Stephen's internal thoughts and not Buck's. Stephen's imagination "flies off" after Buck and other topics of his musings in a way that recalls the workings of Kavalerov's mind. These perspectives accordingly present a slanted view (influenced by envy in Kavalerov's case, resentment in Stephen's) of Babichev and Buck. While Kavalerov might exaggerate, he also ultimately may well be right about his temporary benefactor.[34]

Buck's mirror, too, finds its reflection, so to speak, in the large glass door inset through which Kavalerov dimly perceives Babichev's abundant girth and hears his "singing." Much like Babichev's sounds and Buck's mock chanting, imagery based on optic effects serves as a symbolic indicator of the characters' mentality, and the way Joyce and Olesha use these images reveals a common purpose. Babichev, for example, fails to notice the latent aesthetic beauty of the glass under certain angles of light; only Kavalerov's observation imbues it with momentary splendor. Babichev simply does not attune his vision to the metamorphoses that reality constantly undergoes beneath the careful eye. He ignores or perhaps does not see intricate details, such as the play of light on a reflective surface, and the sensual pleasures that a new perspective, such as a rooftop view, offers. Kavalerov, by contrast, cleverly perceives the glass oval in the bathroom door becoming an "egg" and the "blue and pink world of the room" whirling in Babichev's "mother-of-pearl button lens"; if Babichev were to register such transformations at all, they would undoubtedly strike him as irrelevant, and he would consider mad those who see and attach importance to such changes.[35] Stephen's vision proves just as sharp as Kavalerov's: "Stephen bent forward and peered at the mirror held out to him, cleft by a crooked crack. Hair on end. As he and others see me. Who chose this face for me. This dogsbody to rid of vermin. It asks me too."[36] He not only sees himself in the object but also confronts deep-seated apprehensions about himself in the reflection it induces; in addition, he views the mirror as a "symbol of Irish art" and turns to focused introspection on larger issues.[37] This moment morphs into a rhetorically loaded exchange with Buck, who reads their situation differently; Kavalerov's numerous encounters with mirrors, such as when he meets Ivan on the street or when he wakes up at Anechka's and recalls his father while looking at himself in one, lead to similar experiences.[38] In this respect, Babichev lacks the playfulness of mind needed for a truly aesthetic response to reality. He ignores the potential for poetic meaning not only in the reflections of light on mirroring surfaces but in most phenomena, whereas the poets Kavalerov and Stephen cannot help but see all reality in constant flux and metamorphosis giving birth to metaphor.

Olesha's fascination with Bloom's notion of cheese as dead milk provides yet another instructive parallel, as the novels introduce milk images early in their plots. Examined retroactively, Olesha's 1936 speech offers an intriguing connection. Following a brief conversation with an old delivery woman, Buck "[drinks a glass of milk] at her bidding," whereupon he praises it as "good food" that could cure Irish "rotten teeth and rotten guts."[39] Babichev as a habit "in the morning drinks two glasses of cold milk."[40] On one level, their consumption of milk connects the two characters through a sign of healthy nourishment, valued both by the medical student Buck and the food-producer Andrei, while adding an infantile quality to their boisterous personalities. After all, according to Kavalerov, Babichev also "washes himself like a boy."[41] In another sense, this seemingly innocuous habit carries more strongly negative implications. In *Ulysses*, Buck, his English friend Haines, who visits Ireland for anthropological reasons, and Stephen each view the woman who brings them milk for their breakfast in different ways. Stephen considers her a symbol of barren mother Ireland deprived of national identity; he observes her "old shrunken paps" and feels perturbed by her inability to recognize the Irish language.[42] Buck treats the withered woman ironically, however, singing a "tender chant" to her as she departs, ridiculing her as old and ugly; he clearly remains unconcerned about her degraded and weakened state that also represents Ireland.[43] He does not care that her breasts may not be able to produce the life-giving milk the country apparently needs to cure—if we extend the metaphor—its "rotten guts." Babichev, too, is a milkmaid of sorts, but a thriving and robust one. As noted by Eliot Borenstein, he has "appropriated the female capacity for creation" by producing his Chetvertak cafeteria, which will feed the population collectively, and by supplanting traditional family structures.[44] While symbolically seizing through industry the so-called female aspect of creativity, that is, birthing and nourishing, the broad-chested Babichev deprives it of its organic aspect. He mechanizes the preparation and consumption of food into a de-individualized and de-ritualized activity. His cafeteria chain disrupts the natural order (at least in Kavalerov's mind) and perhaps serves to hide his sterility and renunciation of family life, which he masks as a sacrifice for the sake of Soviet ideals.

The milk imagery linked to Babichev and Buck then comes to be associated with the idea of corrupted life-giving energies, which can be cultural (ridicule of Irish traditions and aping of English trends) or political-ideological (socialist mass feeding projects and taking in various children but never producing any himself beyond metaphoric ones in the communal cafeteria and cheap but nourishing sausage). Kavalerov, like Olesha, by contrast, repeatedly associates milk with life-affirming energies. Seeing a group of young mothers in white blouses, he says that the "name of this whiteness is milk, motherhood, marriage, pride, and purity."[45] Earlier, he suggests that in place of his standard platitudes Babichev should have mentioned in a speech that the "milk will be thick as mercury" at the Chetvertak, his new revolutionary cafeteria.[46] For the younger man, the milk is symbolic; for the elder character, it remains purely a practical means to revitalize Soviet society.[47] Thus, with some small modifications, much of William M. Schutte's list of the vivid differences between Stephen's and Mulligan's worldviews apply just as well to Kavalerov and Babichev: "At every level the two are in fundamental opposition. . . . Mulligan is generous; Stephen is selfish. Mulligan is popular with all groups in Dublin; Stephen is a social outcast. Mulligan is a materialist without shame; Stephen abhors the material and exalts the spiritual and the aesthetic. Mulligan is a minister to the body (and is respected); Stephen would be a minister to the soul (and is ignored)."[48] Perhaps more than anything, the fact that people ignore him terrifies and annoys Kavalerov, the would-be minister to the old world and the advocate of the antimaterialist point of view. His perspective confuses other characters, leaving him—not unlike Stephen—isolated.

Though Stephen and Kavalerov may seem childish to their contemporaries, the reader recognizes that Stephen probes deeper into the world around him than Buck does, for example, when he makes the barren milkmaid part of a symbolic order, rather than the butt of a joke. He and Kavalerov *create* with the help of their imagination, whereas Babichev and Buck only *consume* and *replicate*, destroying the genuine and the organic. Babichev's and Buck's projects exploit the "female capacity for creation," implying a desire to reduce the world of myth, aesthetics, and tradition to pragmatic convenience. It is the means to an end that is diametrically opposed to the values of independence, individualism, and creativity fervently advocated by Stephen and Kavalerov. Whereas they wish to reinvent themselves and their personal histories primarily by means of art, Babichev and Buck are more interested in promulgating their agendas through such questionable means as the betrayal of cultural legacies, be it to a foreign influence (English as represented by Haines) or an ideology imported from abroad and proclaimed to be native (communism or Buck's goal of Hellenizing Ireland).

The Dispossessed Youth

Opposite the three-part Babichev-Bloom-Buck figure looms—or rather lies—Kavalerov. This would-be writer corresponds to Joyce's stand-in, Stephen. The two are chiefly united by a struggle against their respective father figures, biological and otherwise; these are at least the terms by which they frequently understand their present circumstances. And again, in this parallel Olesha makes his most strident rebuttal against Joyce's position as a Western writer, not one whom he dislikes exactly, but one whose ideas cannot help him in the Soviet Union.

In both *Ulysses* and *Envy* an older man sympathizes with a young artist after an alcohol-induced confrontation leaves him in the gutter. Bloom recognizes in Stephen his own deceased son, Rudy, whose ghost, aged to eleven years in a haunting scene in "Circe," seemingly rises before him as he gazes at the young writer's body on the street. Babichev, too, feels sympathy for Kavalerov primarily out of the paternal feelings he has developed for Makarov, who in a letter writes to him: "I read your [Babichev's] letter, that you remembered me and pitied the drunk [Kavalerov] by the wall, picked him up and took him for my sake, because some misfortune might happen to me somewhere and I could lie there like that too."[49] Babichev, in other words, sees Makarov's shade hovering over Kavalerov's unconscious body, but Makarov rebukes him for a sentimentality he does not accept in this new era. Whatever the implications of their actions, the older men in *Envy* and *Ulysses* take in the young poets: one a rebel against the old order and the other a rebel against the new order. Neither of the two artists' worlds, however, encourages their development as individuals.

From this shared plot point arises one of the primary sources of anxiety for Kavalerov and Stephen: their sense of being dispossessed. They are both turned out from their living quarters, as well as from a bar and brothel, respectively, and these events lead them to experience a sense of displacement that feels equally physical and mental. They believe that they do not belong either with the individuals around them or with society at large—again, a topic that undoubtedly extends beyond the Russian Joycean tradition but that nevertheless unites these two authors and their characters. In "Telemachus," Stephen begrudgingly turns over his key to Buck when they go swimming and calls him "usurper."[50] In other words, as with the cracked mirror, Stephen treats his peers as symbols of a divided Irish culture, for he disagrees with Buck's involvement with Haines and his anthropologic interest in the Celtic Revival. Kavalerov feels much the same way about Makarov's return to Babichev's apartment after his time visiting family: "Kavalerov told Ivan about how an important person had thrown him out of his own home."[51] They feel a sense of entitlement over their living space, never mind the convoluted questions of priority and ownership involved therein.

In each case the implications of being usurped go beyond a simple domestic dispute. More importantly, issues of national and cultural dispossession besiege the two. Stephen, for his part, feels uneasy about Buck's involvement in the Englishman Haines's taking up residence in the Martello tower. As L. H. Platt suggests, Haines's presence becomes symbolic of Stephen's concerns: "From the first pages of *Ulysses* [Stephen] has seen himself as a servant, a dispossessed son. . . . The usurper in *Ulysses* is not Mulligan or Haines, but the Anglicised culture that they partially represent."[52] The difference is negligible, however, as the artists take out their frustration on Mulligan and Makarov. The latter's reclaiming his couch and relationship with Babichev, and the way Kavalerov responds to this event, may be read as a statement on the cultural dispossession of an old order and as a judgment on men like Kavalerov, whose prestige was rapidly deteriorating in the Soviet state. His abrasive personality and pursuit of what others might consider purposeless aesthetic moments also do not permit him to adapt, just as historical circumstances prohibit him from recovering his preferred cultural heritage. Kavalerov and Stephen in this way respond to their physical dispossession intellectually, seeing the loss of their identity in the intrusion of new cultural forces. Their idealism clashes with the harsh realities that their opponents represent. Thus, how they endeavor to confront such issues by reinventing themselves and their lineage is central to understanding the exchange between these two novels and its wider implications for Olesha's art. The way Joyce's novel activates important components of *Envy* brings into greater relief how the Russian writer used his predecessor's ideas to bemoan his present situation.

One More Failed Father

As another problematic father figure, Ivan Babichev, Andrei's wayward brother, exacerbates Kavalerov's problems. Ivan experiences many of the same anxieties that plague his young disciple, and he serves simultaneously as a corrupted version of the kindhearted Bloom and a model for what Kavalerov himself may come to be in the future. If Bloom represents for Stephen more of the same, a path to paternity that is ultimately a dead-end in Dublin, then Ivan exposes Kavalerov to the dangers of his state of mind and the logical conclusion of his unequal war with the new regime. His is an impasse without any redeeming qualities in this era of Russian history. Because Kavalerov wavers between the two Babichevs, Olesha distributes traces of Joyce's older hero among the brothers, further showcasing his creative method by which the Joycean original is dispersed in multiple directions within *Envy*.

As with other characters, the similarities begin with a peculiar, easily identifiable physical detail. Andrei with frustration asks his brother during an argument, "And why do you wear a bowler?"[53] The hat naturally accentuates Ivan's eccentric nature, but its complement can be found atop Bloom's head: "His [Bloom's] hand came down into the bowl of his hat."[54] While Bloom's bowler makes perfect sense in the context of Irish society at the time, Ivan's hat only emphasizes his estrangement from the changing culture around him, marking him as out of step with the times, and it is in this sense that the two are linked by their fashion, for Bloom, too, experiences a sense of his nonbelonging on June 16, 1904, the day on which *Ulysses* takes place. They are father figures set apart from many of the people whose company they share; this quality brings them closer to the constantly roving Kavalerov and Stephen and keeps them on the move.

Across their respective books, the peregrinations that they undertake define Bloom and Ivan. They wander the streets of Dublin and Moscow for related reasons. The former seeks to avoid the domestic site of his wife's betrayal with the loutish Blazes Boylan, thinking at one point, "I hold this house. Amen. He gnashed in fury. Traitors swing."[55] Ivan takes up his itinerant existence with relish, viewing it as emblematic of the dispossession of his natural place in Russia; he even traces this sensation to a childhood rivalry that led to his beating a young girl and proclaiming, "Don't upstage me! Don't take away what might belong to me!"[56] Deprived of their hearth, whether a particular or a general one, the two men transform into figures whose very dispossession prevents them from finding stability. In this way, they are directly linked to their fellow homeless "sons," but it is Ivan who responds with spite, unlike the more reserved Bloom, who only fantasizes about revenge.

The two older characters are further linked by the attention they pay to feminine legs in a couple of memorable scenes. In turn, these moments shed greater light on their personalities and intentions. Ivan takes Kavalerov to spy on his family, and there they witness how his daughter, Valia, exercises: "On her are black trousers rolled up high; her legs are very bare, the whole structure of her legs is on display. . . . She has dirtied, tanned, gleaming legs. These are the legs of a girl who has felt the influence of air, sun, falling on hummocks, on grass, and blows so often that they coarsen, covered with waxy scars from scabs pulled off too early, and their knees are rough, like oranges."[57] Olesha renders this passage through Kavalerov's perspective, but a parallel can be found in *Ulysses* when Bloom masturbates while watching Gerty MacDowell in "Nausicaa": "She leaned back far to look up where the fireworks were and there was no-one to see only him and her when she revealed all her graceful beautifully shaped legs like that, supply soft and delicately round."[58] This thirteenth episode, not unlike Olesha's passage, describes the feminine form in ornate, Romantic language and unmistakably through a domineering male gaze. The scenes further underscore the writers' fascination with the human form seen also in the opening pages. Here, too, Ivan's decision to share, in a sense, his *own* daughter with Kavalerov, to allow him to feast on her body, if only through his piercing vision, marks him as a despoiled version of Bloom. It is, after all, this encounter that pulls Kavalerov and Ivan apart; after the description cited above, Kavalerov runs away and finally confesses to Ivan that he has been planning to murder Andrei. He feels the weight of his passion for Valia and disgust in the company of his benefactor's relatives. These tangled relationships destroy any chance of future communion between Ivan and Kavalerov, while Bloom remains free to have his—problematic—moment with Gerty. Before then, the two had grown close, reflecting a similar relationship to the one Bloom tries to initiate with Stephen near the end of *Ulysses*. These interactions and scenes represent the more surface-level correlation between Bloom and Ivan and their ramifications on the father-son dialectics at play in the two novels. Even more significantly, Bloom and Ivan come to symbolize all that their young, nomadic counterparts fear about themselves and their fathers, and yet the results are much different.

The older men—two biological fathers of daughters—make appeals to wounded surrogate sons but with the added complication that Ivan has ulterior motives. Ivan sees in Kavalerov the perfect representative of envy for his "conspiracy of feelings," a movement that will ostensibly counter the rise of the New Soviet Man.[59] While Bloom, misguided as he may be, earnestly offers financial aid to Stephen, Ivan attempts to mold Kavalerov in his image and to transform him into a disciple in his (largely imagined) war on the Bolshevik cultural zeitgeist.

Ivan expounds on his ideas to Kavalerov at their first meeting, causing the latter to think, "He is reading my thoughts," a sign of their like-mindedness.[60]

Stephen, by contrast, only recognizes the chasm in thought that exists between himself and Bloom. After the excitement of a confrontation with two Englishmen on the street, Bloom and Stephen take a moment to catch their breaths in a cabman's shelter, and here Bloom tells Stephen about his socialist vision for Ireland: "I'm, he resumed with dramatic force, as good an Irishman as that rude person I told you about at the outset and I want to see everyone, concluded he, all creeds and classes *pro rata* having a comfortable tidysized income. . . . I call that patriotism. *Ubi patria*, as we learned a smattering of in our classical days in *Alma Mater*, *vita bene*. Where you can live well, the sense is, if you work."[61] Stephen responds with typical snark and disdain and proclaims that "Ireland must be important because it belongs to me."[62] He seeks no part in a future designed by the fathers, preferring instead to craft his own path in life. He remains uncompromising in his vision as an artist despite all setbacks, including his premature return to Dublin after the death of his mother. In this way, Stephen refuses this potential father figure's imagined world.

This exchange is preceded by another scene in "Circe" in which Bloom imagines himself to be "Leopold the First," a sovereign who can do as he pleases and banish his unfaithful spouse.[63] Much as Bloom envisions this elaborate reality for himself, Ivan takes on the mantle of "king of pillows" in his dramatic and, needless to say, patently false story, "The Tale of Two Brothers," which details how he and his machine-creature Ophelia bring down Andrei and the Chetvertak.[64] In general, Kavalerov is drawn, at least initially, to the boisterous Ivan and his tales of feats of glory. He sees in him a compatriot, someone who truly understands his displacement since the fall of tsarist Russia. Such newfound respect for Ivan is further reflected in the way that the second half of *Envy* shifts to third-person narration from Kavalerov's first-person and Ivan dominates the story. Stephen, on the contrary, quickly rebukes Bloom's vision for the future of Ireland and his own place within it. Kavalerov thus recognizes too late that following a second Babichev brother is not the solution to his problems; furthermore, Ivan becomes an emblem of a future self that is no less a failure than Kavalerov's present identity. Driven by the titular emotion, Kavalerov elects Ivan to be his new messiah and father, but he fails to see the folly and the redundancy in his choice. The peripatetic Ivan, who is not unlike the Wandering Jew type often associated with Bloom, reveals to both reader and character how the sad, young literary men of Kavalerov's ilk will turn out within the new system.

In these myriad ways, Olesha further complicates the schema he has set up throughout *Envy*. Various character traits, behaviors, and ideas stemming

from Buck and Bloom are distributed among such diametrically opposed figures as the two Babichevs. Kavalerov's dual paternal figures fail him for different reasons, even as they accentuate related aspects of their Joycean origins.
How Ivan functions as a corrupted version of Bloom is particularly significant
as it reveals that the reality of the situation is much more complex than a simple
"fathers and sons" opposition. The young *and* the old idealists cannot adapt.
They instead begin to tear themselves and each other apart. While Stephen is
free to turn down Bloom's offers of assistance, which he takes to be yet another trap (a scenario that will be repeated in Bitov's *Pushkin House*), Kavalerov
is shocked to recognize himself in the embittered Ivan Babichev, something
that Stephen avoids doing. Olesha reads *Ulysses*'s plot as an alternative to his
present condition, as conformity became a driving force in the USSR. How
Kavalerov ultimately responds to Ivan epitomizes Olesha's closing statement
in his response to Joyce, *Ulysses*, and all that his novel represents to a writer of
Olesha's generation.

The Generation Gap Shrinks

Much like its beginning, the end of *Envy* supplies a fascinating reformulation
of *Ulysses*. This point has not gone entirely unnoticed. Borenstein in a footnote compares Bloom's homecoming to Molly after her afternoon tryst with
Kavalerov's and Ivan's dual occupation of Anechka's room. Borenstein, however, may slightly misread *Ulysses*. It is not established, as he writes, that Molly
has seen "a long line of men" in her bed.[65] With the exception of Blazes Boylan,
the twenty-five men enumerated in "Ithaca" more likely represents those who
have made Bloom jealous, romantic partners preceding their marriage, or
Bloom's sadomasochistic fantasies. Nor can we say that Stephen remains with
Bloom and Molly that night as Borenstein implies. If anything, the reconciliation between father and son in *Ulysses* is weightier than in *Envy*, where Kavalerov, even if he ends up with Ivan, openly rejects both of his adoptive fathers.
Kavalerov's return to the detested Anechka represents an even more problematic resignation of spirit than Bloom's coming home to his unfaithful wife, in
part because he still loves her. As the two novels conclude with this quite similar bedroom scenario, a comparison begs to be made.

The synchronization begins when Kavalerov returns to Anechka's apartment. Before falling ill, he turns on the water tap and then, after sleeping with
her, dreams of a rushing flow. Likewise, having made his way home with Stephen
in *Ulysses*'s penultimate episode, Bloom turns on a faucet, and the narrative
takes up his fascination with water: "What in water did Bloom, waterlover,

drawer of water, watercarrier, returning to the range, admire?"[66] Bloom and Kavalerov wash themselves and then go to their respective wife/mother figures, creating another instance of Olesha's subverted parallels. Each author employs the image of the water tap as a means of purification, but soon after the reader discovers that the outcomes are substantially different. Kavalerov's cleansing experience with the water devolves into a nightmare. Much as Stephen fears his mother's corpse as an embodiment of the past's hold over him ("Ghoul! Chewer of corpses! No, mother! Let me be and let me live"), Kavalerov considers Anechka a reminder of the history with which he wishes to part.[67] During the scene in which Kavalerov beats the widow, the narrator likens her to a "woman from Pompeii [*pompeianka*]," a particularly vivid simile that emphasizes her status as a largely symbolic figure in the novel; like the ruins of Pompeii, Anechka and the stultifying existence that Kavalerov associates with her will not be stamped out, no matter the intensity of his rage.[68] The sons furthermore envision Anechka and May Dedalus as corpses, incarnations of a death that is both literal and figurative. Bloom, on the contrary, recognizes the unity of man and a life-giving energy in the water. Along with his love for his wife and his recognition of a natural order in the world, this awareness contributes to his apparent acceptance of Molly's infidelity.

The critical difference between the two endings lies in Kavalerov's sharp divergence from Stephen's individualistic path. Olesha closes *Envy* with his hero's complete resignation accompanied by Ivan's ironic "Hurrah!"[69] The latter's grotesque proclamation that it is now Kavalerov's turn to sleep with Anechka frightens him, as these words remind him of his transformation into a paternal figure. He, in a sense, morphs into the Bloomian type, refuting his association with the youthful, artistic Stephen developed so far in the novel and resigning himself to a defeated state of affairs. Ivan Babichev, Kavalerov's second paternal surrogate, is forced by circumstance and by choice into a decadent Blazes Boylan role in this closing scene; he cuckolds Kavalerov by claiming Anechka before his protégé's return, thus ruining the young man's plans to "put the widow in her place," his final botched expression of power.[70] In the widow's bed, Kavalerov's masculinity is challenged and his father's history—or rather the lack thereof—haunts him. He realizes that he will go no further than his predecessor but remains doomed to repeat his insignificant life, a fear not unlike Stephen's regarding Simon Dedalus or the terror Olesha himself experienced when recalling his father in his memoirs.[71] The ironies of this last scene subvert Joyce's text, which allows Bloom to love his wife as she is and Stephen to break radically the patterns of both his elders and contemporaries.

By bookending *Envy* with parallel variants of *Ulysses*'s beginning and conclusion, which, again, Zhitomirsky included in his 1925 translation, Olesha emphasizes the main points of his literary response to Joyce. Kavalerov may begin in a situation comparable to that of Stephen as a dispossessed writer seeking transformation and resolution, but, following a string of challenges he cannot overcome, his project totally collapses by the end of the book. This reconfiguration of the ending results in Kavalerov turning out to be more like an apathetic version of Bloom—without any hope or even love—rather than Stephen, who, unlike Olesha's hero, can boldly proclaim, "In the intense instant of imagination . . . that which I was is that which I am and that which in possibility I may come to be."[72] Olesha does not directly state but cautiously intimates that in Joyce's West there may be cause for sons to rebel against their fathers, but there is also the option for them to go their own way should they have the courage to do so. No such alternative, Stephen's "possibility," exists for men like Kavalerov in the Soviet Union. In this way, Edward W. Said's comments on the problem of filiation and affiliation resonate throughout *Envy*: "Childless couples, orphaned children, aborted childbirths, and unregenerately celibate men and women populate the world of high modernism with remarkable insistence, all of them suggesting the difficulties of filiation. . . . The only other alternatives seemed to be provided by institutions, associations, and communities whose social existence was not in fact guaranteed by biology, but by affiliation."[73] Olesha's and Joyce's heroes turn to these kinds of relationships for salvation in the uncertainty that plagues their young lives.

Bloom's time with Molly at the end of *Ulysses* does not precisely mimic the ménage à trois scenario with which *Envy* concludes, yet it marks one likely source for Olesha's thought.[74] By transposing distinct elements of *Ulysses* into *Envy*, Olesha simultaneously develops a dialogue with a contemporaneous text and actively raises new questions in his own literary context, that of Soviet Russia, where fathers and sons were thrust into vicious ideological battle.[75] Andrei Babichev's lineage can be mapped back to Bloom and Buck, Kavalerov's to Stephen, Ivan's also to Bloom, and Anechka's to Molly, but why would Olesha choose these characters, images, and themes to populate and enrich his own novel through a refracted perspective? In other words, how and why did the connection between *Envy* and *Ulysses* come to be, and what does it ultimately signify?

Fathers, Sons, and the Nightmare of History

Based on its prevalence throughout both his fiction and nonfiction, the topic of a father's relationship with his son clearly struck a deep and personal note with Olesha. In the brief semiautobiographical story "I Look into the Past" (1928), for example, the narrator proclaims, "It seems to me that the development of a man's fate, a man's character, is in no small degree predetermined by whether a boy is attached to his father."[76] Following the torments of childhood insecurity, the "searches for a father, for a motherland, for a profession, for a talisman that can prove to be glory or power" begin.[77] For Olesha's narrator, and likely for the author himself, sons face a great challenge in overcoming the long shadows cast by their fathers or by the lack thereof. Olesha's own relationship with his father, based on the anecdotes in his memoir *No Day without a Line*, was no less complex. He recounts how one day the drunk Karl Olesha, for a joke, placed him, a young boy, on a windowsill and pointed a revolver at him while his mom begged on her knees for him to stop "that."[78] Without reading too far into the biographical elements of this absurd Dostoevskian scene, the combination of strained paternal relations and a more general sense of displacement (felt quite vividly in his literary interests) arguably resulted in Olesha's quest for an alternative point of origin, both in terms of family history and cultural touchstones.

The conflict between Kavalerov and his paternal substitutes, too, lies at the heart of *Envy*. While Russian literature boasts a lengthy tradition involving fathers and children (primarily sons), *Ulysses* offers a fresh look at this eternal theme, as well as those of family structures, sexual relations, and social roles, all topics important to writers of Olesha's generation. Specifically, Joyce's novel raises the question of whether or not one may change one's history and, if so, how artistic creation fits into the equation. The parallels with *Ulysses* analyzed above lead to this primary theme of father-son angst in *Envy*.

In Olesha's book, the notion of the Soviet nonbiological family complicates the father-son relationship. Andrei speaks of Makarov as his son, although he is not related by blood. He attempts to rationalize his feelings with the help of the new Soviet ideology: "I'll drive [Makarov] out if I'm deceiving myself about his being new, not entirely distinct from me. . . . I don't need a son, I'm not a father, and he's not a son."[79] Babichev takes on a son in a system that intends to eradicate irrational human emotions. He claims he will abandon Makarov if he proves to be unworthy of the Soviet state and, most intriguingly if the youth does not want to be like him, Andrei Babichev, in his passionate ideals. Concerns such as these occupy a central place within early Soviet culture and find their reflection in Olesha's *Envy*. Borenstein writes that Olesha uniquely proposes that the bonds of father and son survived the revolution in some form and even became "integral to the new world," as a result intensifying the violent generational conflicts of the era.[80] Katerina Clark makes a similar claim in her seminal *The Soviet Novel: History as Ritual*. She observes in the Soviet novel a recurring trope involving a "spontaneous" young man meeting a "conscious" older man who channels his untrained, directionless energies by leading him to party work.[81] Conversely, Olesha has the son, Makarov, educate the father, Babichev, to reach greater party consciousness. *Envy* therefore reflects the process by which the culture and supermen of the Five-Year Plan (1928–33) overtook the NEP (1921–28) and its representatives, such as Babichev. This plot point is one more example of how Olesha blends models and trends to create something new. Babichev struggles with what are now considered old-fashioned emotions that make him feel compassion for Makarov and Kavalerov. The characters' relationships in this way do not reflect a successful effort to overcome a set of values entirely. They instead expose the fault lines of a system that cannot be fully implemented.

The sons experience a corresponding anxiety. Recalling a childhood memory, Kavalerov admits: "I recognized my father in myself. It was a similarity of form—no, something else: I would say sexual similarity: as if I suddenly felt my father's seed within me, in my *substance*. And as if someone said to me: you're ready. Finished."[82] In this situation he cannot compete with his rival Makarov, who denies that he shares any substance, physical or otherwise, with his biological father. Kavalerov becomes frightened by the idea that he contains his father within himself, that they actually make up identical pieces of an eternal pattern. The bodily / sexual takes on a grave metaphysical meaning in his mind. This is the Joycean theme of father-son consubstantiation replayed in Olesha's terms, which established a pattern seen in one form or another in many future Russian responses to Joyce. Its equivalent can be found in Stephen's ruminations early in Joyce's novel: "Is that then the divine substance wherein Father and Son are consubstantial? Where is poor dear Arius to try conclusions? Warring his life upon contransmagnificandjewbangtantiality."[83] Stephen hears his father's taunts resonate in his mind and fears the similarities between them. The sons cannot bear to find themselves in the image of their fathers and therefore turn elsewhere, seeking a *choice* rather than passive acceptance of eternal recurrence. Kavalerov, as already stated, discovers that he has no choice, no possibility, no real future of his own creation. He will become his father, as Dedalus will eventually become his own man.

In Stephen's interpretation of *Hamlet*, explicated most fully in episode 9, "Scylla and Charybdis," the artist (Shakespeare) becomes a father to himself by producing genuine art (*Hamlet*) and a ghost by playing a role (Shakespeare as the ghost of Hamlet's father in a production of the play). Disillusioned with the past, he may refashion it through creativity: "As we . . . weave and unweave our bodies, Stephen said, from day to day, their molecules shuttled to and fro, so does the artist weave and unweave his image."[84] By adopting a literary father figure who demands no loyalty to legacy and traditions, rewriting personal history, and creating lasting art, gifted writers may inscribe themselves into

world literature and be liberated of all servile filial bonds. This solution is the-
oretically open to Kavalerov as well. He, too, creates masks to alter his identity, leading one of Olesha's best critics, Mariètta Chudakova, to suggest that
his hero "speak[s] about himself as a literary character."[85] Kavalerov repeatedly attempts to assume roles throughout *Envy* as he struggles to come to
terms with his own personhood in contrast to the society around him and the
cultural-literary ideals he cherishes. Like his author, he dreams of having been
born in France and repeatedly looks to the West for inspirational models.[86] In
this manner, Kavalerov strives to renounce the Soviet collectivist spirit and protests against conformity. This behavior in general recalls Stephen, who stands
apart from his father, carries himself as a lonesome Hamlet figure dressed in
mourning, and rewrites personal and literary histories. In *Ulysses* and *Envy*, the
artists portray themselves as the figures they wish to be to varying degrees of
success. The reader's privileged perspective offers access into their thoughts,
revealing gaps in their reasoning. These characters grow to be highly self-
aware, acknowledging their antecedents and manipulating their lives in ways
to better represent their desires. Fluid identity therefore comes to be a major
defining feature of both Kavalerov and Stephen.

It would then seem that the two heroes are brothers dispossessed of culture and positive paternal bonds. The outcomes of their efforts are far from
identical, however. Stephen remains free to accept or reject his adoptive father,
Bloom, and free to turn down all paternal guidance by becoming a father to
himself. He is free to establish himself as a self-fashioned artist, and therefore,
as he says of Shakespeare, "being no more a son," he is free to "[feel] himself
the father of all his race."[87] Kavalerov, on the contrary, feels prohibited from
accomplishing any of these literary and biographical feats, since he can transcend neither his personality nor his paternal legacy and the historical conditions encircling him. Makarov is hailed as the New Soviet Man, linked to soccer
and engineering, while Kavalerov's lyrical outbursts are viewed as the ravings
of a drunk and not as a means to become a new man in his own right. There
can also be no absolute reconciliation between fathers and sons in the world
of *Envy*, even while traces of those bonds remain, since they are now classified as invalid. Though Stephen and Kavalerov head out on their own, the latter's departure is short-lived, and he returns, unable to engage in a project
resembling that of Stephen or to withstand the centripetal force of Anechka's
bed. Even if Dedalus ultimately rejects Bloom's offer, he maintains his own
identity and can write his own course in life and literature. Kavalerov fails to
do the same; his fate is emblematic of the situation facing Olesha during a critical moment in the Russian literary tradition. His hero cannot take the non-

conformist's route and align himself with Western modernist models, just as he cannot find absolution in any father's home.

Torn by the desire to join the masses of the new state or to pursue the enticements of a romantic Western world based on the ideals of the past (as he envisions it), Kavalerov hesitates, as Olesha personally did. *Envy* is neither anti- nor pro-Soviet. Ambiguity prevails, and this contributes to a reading in which Kavalerov is victim and perpetrator all at once. Trapped in the history Stephen famously calls a "nightmare from which [he is] trying to awake," Olesha's protagonist experiences an erasure of his spirit.[88] Curiously, this history is the *recent* past, not the Romantic era of which he dreams. In part because of his inner discord, Kavalerov's personal nightmare is more menacing than the one haunting Stephen. Olesha's text leaves the so-called old-world characters at a particularly muddled standstill: Kavalerov, hopelessly aiming to elect his forebears, and Ivan, abandoned by his progeny, fail to obtain their self-proclaimed inheritance as heirs to the cultural vanguard. To echo Elizabeth Klosty Beaujour, they are pulled between opposing forces, unable to decide for themselves what is best, "doomed to remain stationary" and terribly ambivalent.[89]

"The Golden Shelf" Revisited

Olesha's impulse to draw on and modify works of literature he admired can be observed throughout much of his oeuvre, limited though it may be. A subtle, highly intertextual author, Olesha told the journalist Isaak Glan that he once "thought up such a book" in which he would "simply retell ten classic plots," such as *Faust* or Dante's *Inferno*, in order "to bring them closer to readers."[90] Though Olesha never managed to write this peculiar book, he did recount many plots and ideas throughout his memoirs, which his widow, Olga Suok (1899–1978), famed Formalist critic Viktor Shklovsky (1893–1984), and others eventually compiled as the volume *No Day without a Line*. Olesha uses the chapter "The Golden Shelf" to register his literary interests. In the process of reflecting on the works that influenced his growth as a person and as a writer, Olesha not only describes their contents but transforms them into something of his own creation as well. These stories—*The Divine Comedy, War and Peace, The Idiot*, among many others—take on Oleshian tones as the author highlights particular elements, critiques certain methods, and manages to convey his wonder and amazement on initially reading them. Although Olesha makes no direct mention of Joyce in *No Day without a Line*, Olesha's engagement with *Ulysses* throughout *Envy* represents a similar sort of experimentation with borrowed materials.

By marking his *Envy* with allusions and themes from *Ulysses*, Olesha creates a bold intertextual response, one that evinces his stated interest to retell and reshape stories. Olesha finds in Joyce's gargantuan novel ideas resonant with his eccentric worldview, but he complicates them with his own experience, that of the stalled artist. Babichev echoes Buck and Bloom, while his brother Ivan highlights Bloom's worst tendencies. Stephen devolves into the buffoonish Kavalerov, who by the end of the novel can find no escape from his emotions or social circumstances. Finally, the ephemeral potential for optimism found in Molly's den turns into a murky amalgam of Oedipal myth and misplaced hopes in Anechka's old immense bed.[91] Olesha's narrative amplifies the tensions found in *Ulysses*, just as, in a manner of speaking, it mocks Stephen's ideals and interprets the Joycean model within a dissimilar context.

The unruly feelings driving Kavalerov's final acts in the book recall one other correspondence between *Envy* and *Ulysses*. Early in the latter novel, Stephen witnesses a passing cloud that Bloom simultaneously recognizes in "Calypso": "A cloud began to cover the sun slowly, wholly, shadowing the bay in deeper green" and "A cloud began to cover the sun slowly, wholly. Grey. Far."[92] Kavalerov notices a similar phenomenon: "An enormous cloud with the outline of South America stood over the city. It shone, but the shade from it was formidable [*groznyi*]. The shade approached Babichev's street with astronomical sluggishness."[93] As the cloud darkens the scenes in both books, it summons past and portends future troubles in the characters' thoughts: the bitterness of death, visions of a wasteland, and an imminent confrontation with Babichev. While in *Ulysses* Bloom and Stephen are unwittingly brought together as companions and potentially as adoptive family by Joyce's parallax metaphor, Kavalerov remains simultaneously alone in his quest and grudgingly united with his father figures through envy and despair. This cloud image appears in early drafts of the book, and yet the shared nature of this image demonstrates a resonance between the two works.[94]

In this way, Olesha's engagement with *Ulysses* and deployment of images from Joyce's text signify, above all, two things. First, Olesha pays tribute to a fellow writer who champions individual insight and who shares his epiphanic outlook by which the everyday—a cloud, a conversation, a shout in the street—is transformed into the revelatory. Second, by showing that it was not possible everywhere, Olesha counters the concept in European Modernism that allows the artist to rework history and to develop a self-realized personal literary biography, a task that Vladimir Nabokov will gladly pick up just a few years later in his final Russian novel, *The Gift*. Outside pressures notwithstanding, it is ironic that Olesha would call Joyce a pessimistic writer in his 1936 speech. Olesha's own ending to *Envy* represents a metaphoric and creative impasse, the terminal point of Kavalerov's attempts to redefine himself. The novel culminates with neither a resounding "Yes!" nor a resigned "No." Instead, the narrator abruptly leaves Kavalerov in a limbo-esque state with Ivan, Anechka and her repellent bed, and, most importantly, a toast to the degradation of history and tradition.

CHAPTER 2

Vladimir Nabokov

Translating the Ghosts of the Past

> *What have you learned from Joyce?*
> Nothing.
> *Oh, come.*
> James Joyce has not influenced me in any manner
> whatsoever.
>
> —Vladimir Nabokov, interview with Herbert Gold,
>   in *Strong Opinions*

In November 1933, Vladimir Nabokov wrote to his colleague James Joyce with an offer to translate *Ulysses*.[1] What motivated the young artist to brave such an immense undertaking? What drew him to Joyce's urban epic? Nabokov's *Ulysses*—a staggering feat of translation—is a traditional *Künstlerroman* torn asunder by mirroring devices and a series of nested stories. Its hero, a budding writer of largely untested talent, seeks fulfillment in his paternal relationships. He furthermore attempts to find his place in a land that feels oppressively foreign. In typically iconoclastic manner, Nabokov derived the original title for his translation from a curious source: *Ulysses*'s final line, that famous affirmation at the end of Molly's soliloquy—"Yes." "*Dar.*"

Nabokov would extend this dialogue with his Irish predecessor in his second English-language novel, *Bend Sinister*, where he critiques Joyce's treatment of *his* ancestor, Shakespeare, in *Ulysses*. The two together, *Dar* (*The Gift*, written 1934–37, complete version published 1952) and *Bend Sinister* (1947), function as a highly idiosyncratic commentary on the process of influence and intertext as translation, on haunting legacies. What Nabokov offers in his *Dar* is an answer to the question of how writers might productively deal with the literary ghosts of the past, whether they be biological fathers, Pushkin, Joyce, or even projects abandoned but not forgotten.

For these reasons, and depending on how loosely you play with the dictionary, Nabokov's assertion in his interview with Herbert Gold for the *Paris Re-*

view that he "learned nothing" from Joyce can, on the one hand, be accepted without reservations or should, on the other, be taken with a great deal more than a grain of salt.[2] Always wary of falling under the influence of another writer, especially a heavyweight such as Joyce, Nabokov immediately changes the terms of the discussion from learning to "influence." The latter word, according to Nabokov's line of reasoning, seems to encompass the former, suggesting that it is impossible for him to educate himself on the strategies of a fellow author, and potentially develop them further, without a contaminating influence. Nabokov was, of course, remarkably sensitive about any such accusations. Just after making the aforementioned statements, Nabokov comments that he first read *Ulysses* "around 1920 at Cambridge University, when a friend, Peter Mrozovski, who had brought a copy from Paris, chanced to read to me, as he stomped up and down my digs, one or two spicy passages from Molly's monologue, which, *entre nous soit dit*, is the weakest chapter in the book."[3] Such critical insertions into a more or less straightforward account are also typical of Nabokov's defensive maneuvers against charges of influence.[4] His next encounter with the novel allegedly came "only fifteen years later, when [he] was already well formed as a writer and reluctant to learn or unlearn anything."[5] Here, he unequivocally asserts that an author is immune to another's sway beyond a given point.

However, Nabokov's dates are misleading: he sent his offer to translate Joyce's masterpiece in 1933, that is, shortly before he began work on his final Russian novel, *Dar*—his dazzling rendition of *Ulysses*. The historical facts not only contradict Nabokov's timing but, if one accepts Nabokov's statements regarding the nature of literary influence at face value, demonstrate that he may very well have imbibed more lessons from Joyce than he cared to admit, for he remained engaged with Joyce's work throughout the period when he was still developing as a writer.

Even beyond those years, Nabokov was careful in how he framed his relationship to Joyce. In his lectures on *Ulysses*, for instance, he makes much of the man in the brown macintosh who appears repeatedly in Joyce's novel but is never given a name. With obvious glee, Nabokov writes, "Do we know who he is? I think we do. . . . The Man in the Brown Macintosh . . . is no other than the author himself. Bloom glimpses his maker!"[6] For evidence Nabokov refers to Stephen's suggestion in the National Library about Shakespeare's insertion of his own likeness into his texts. The fact that Joyce scholarship has not readily accepted Nabokov's hypothesis should not divert us from recognizing that he frequently applied this device to his own work.[7] Nabokov's use of the technique became more pronounced after 1930, that is, after he had reread *Ulysses*. Even if Joyce did not intend the Man in the Brown Macintosh to be his "representative," Nabokov interpreted the figure in this way, reading into the novel the sort of multilayered structure he would come to perfect in his own works. In suggesting Joyce was one of the finest purveyors of such a technique and in applying it to his novels, especially *The Gift*, Nabokov affirms the ancestry, so to speak, of these figures. He may be unwilling to admit he "learned" anything from another writer, but he was perfectly capable of placing himself among Joyce's ranks.[8]

Points of Contact

At least in comparison with the other four primary subjects of this study, Nabokov is a special case in terms of his relationship to Joyce. The only one to meet his counterpart in person, Nabokov could support his reading of *Ulysses* with anecdotal knowledge.[9] Nabokov also possessed an impressive, if idiosyncratic, understanding of both technical and aesthetic matters of Joyce's art, as evidenced by his extensive written commentary developed during his tenure as a college instructor. Additionally, the vast number of intertextual references to the Irish writer's texts throughout a lengthy career in two languages simply provides greater material for analysis than Olesha's smaller output.

Before exploring the discrete connections between *The Gift* and *Ulysses* and what cultural-historical factors may have led Nabokov to read Joyce as he did, it will be worth considering their more general, external resemblance. This vantage point provides a base on which the individual items and comparisons come into sharper focus. *The Gift* tells the story of Fyodor Godunov-Cherdyntsev, a young Russian émigré living in Berlin who, at the beginning of the novel, has just recently published a book of poems. Interweaving first-, second-, and third-person narration, Nabokov provides insights into Fyodor's past, his dreams, and his daily existence in a foreign land. Along with a trip to a shoe store, the reader also sees Fyodor at a literary gathering hosted by his family friends, the Chernyshevskys. From there, the novel takes a circuitous path. Chapter 2 focuses on Fyodor's attempts to write a biography of his father, a famed explorer and naturalist who went missing in Asia not long after the Russian Revolution. In Chapter 3, we meet, though not without some authorial winking and tricks, Fyodor's future beloved, his muse Zina Mertz. Chapters 4 and 5 consist of the young writer's controversial biography of the nineteenth-century author and critic Nikolai Chernyshevsky (1828–1889) and, then, the fallout of its publication. In sum, *The Gift* captures over the span of several years some key moments in Fyodor's life along with his artistic development.

Margaret McBride, in her study of *Ulysses*, summarizes the gargantuan novel in the following terms: "It can be viewed, first and foremost, as an amazingly Daedalian *Künstlerroman*. The work nests stories inside stories and includes crucial poetic theories which subtly but substantially influence the narrative line. More specifically, with regard to the character of Stephen, the mirroring devices elegantly resolve his plotline as a sense of autofictive *mise-en-abyme* loops the tale into eternity. Significantly, such a trajectory has been, all along, the goal of the time-obsessed Stephen."[10] One cannot help but notice just how closely this synopsis reads like a description of Nabokov's final Russian novel. In fact, many of the same critical approaches that McBride mentions have long been applied to *The Gift*. Alexander Dolinin has probed the novel from numerous points of entry: father and son relations and aesthetics, to name but two. He does so, to borrow McBride's terminology, in order to "contemplat[e]" its "Daedalian design," which nonetheless maintains an "overall thematic unity."[11] Pekka Tammi, among others, has considered its roots in and departures from the *Künstlerroman* tradition.[12] Sergei Davydov's seminal *"Teksty-matreški" Vladimira Nabokova* describes the novel's nesting-doll design that encapsulates stories inside stories.[13] Fyodor's "poetic theories" and their ties to the overall narrative have also been addressed in many studies.[14] Justin Weir explores Nabokov's use of the *mise en abyme* technique in order to appreciate the novel's overall narrative design.[15] Finally, time is absolutely crucial to Fyodor's thinking throughout *The Gift*'s five chapters, making its presence felt in everything from the manner in which the young writer's three major works reflect his mastery of time to his conception of a true reader being what he calls the future "author reflected in time."[16] The similarity between *Ulysses* and *The Gift*, as exemplified by McBride's précis, exhibits the external cohesion that remains to be tapped at a deeper level and, more significantly, from the vantage point of Nabokov's biography. The combination of various shared narrative strategies, numerous intertextual allusions, and a general thematic overlap more clearly demonstrate Joyce's presence in Nabokov's work. A comparative reading of *The Gift* and *Ulysses* reveals just how much Nabokov may have been indebted to, if not "influenced" by, Joyce and his predecessor's ideas concerning the artist's creative reworking of father-son relations. In other words, by analyzing the theme of father-son consubstantiation presented in *The Gift* in light of what Joyce says about the issue in *Ulysses*, we can better understand Nabokov's situation.

Both Stephen and Fyodor aim to redefine their past vis-à-vis their biological and adopted fathers. While their projects are quite similar, they ultimately produce contrasting ends: Stephen elects a literary forefather to detach himself from his real and would-be fathers; Fyodor chooses a literary father to unite himself with his lost biological one. Nabokov's reworking of Joyce's project serves to correct it according to his beliefs and complex position as an émigré writer. The system of intertextual elements establishes the general thematic cohesion-cum-Bloomian swerve against *Ulysses* built into *The Gift*. Again, cultural circumstances dictate that Nabokov use these tools differently than, say, Olesha. In addition, Nabokov's *Bend Sinister*, in particular its seventh chapter, offers further commentary on one of the primary themes in *Ulysses* against which Nabokov polemicized, that of the son disrupting filial bonds for the sake of literary ones.[17] This project extends from the Russian to the English years of Nabokov's career, even as it blends his engagement with the two different national traditions. Thus, while Monika Greenleaf writes that *"The Gift*'s determined russocentrism suggests the genealogical omission not only of rival contemporary poets but also of European modernists like Proust and Joyce," by probing the nuances of Nabokov's literary exchange with Joyce, we can better comprehend Fyodor's metaphysical exploits in *The Gift*.[18]

Reading Nabokov's work in the context of the 1920s and 1930s Russian émigré community, we find other reasons for his particular approach to Joyce. Writers endeavored during this time of immense uncertainty to make sense of their situation abroad vis-à-vis their cultural heritage. Had Russian literature come to an end with their departure into exile, or would it continue to thrive abroad? Was what was being created in the Soviet Union a perversion of their predecessors' work or something to be admired? Could the new émigré art (or what should it be called?) ultimately exist without direct links to the Russian soil, to the Russian language? Were there now, in fact, *two* Russian literatures? Or was Alexander Voronsky's "Soviet literature," mentioned in chapter 1, the real fate of literature in what was once Russia? It was a time of crisis that shook every generation, leaving no clear demarcations based on age.

One general division, however, arose between those who took an apocalyptic view, seeing an end to things past and demanding a new purified, ascetic art that would better reflect their tormented exilic state, and those, like Nabokov, who held fast to tradition, to the neoclassical ideals of their forefathers. The former were represented by the poet and critic Georgy Adamovich (1892–1972), himself an established figure in prerevolutionary Russian letters, who galvanized younger writers into composing poetry that expressed the sense of despair rampant at the time, moved away from a focus on form and toward expressive "human documents," and broadly aligned itself with trends in Western Modernism, particularly those originating from France. Adamovich, and those other writers who belonged to the so-called Parisian Note school (for example, Anatoly Shteiger, Lydia Chervinskaya, Dovid Knut, and, to a lesser extent, Boris Poplavsky), struck back against Pushkin and all that he represented, seeing in his legacy a failure to provide comfort in a time of despair and an ultimately meaningless attention to craft, rather than emotion. Poplavsky, in the same essay that he writes about Joyce, would actually declare that "Pushkin is the last of the outstanding primary, dirty people of imagination. But isn't even the biggest of worms still just a big worm?"[19] It is, of course, ironic that Poplavsky would use the same imagery as Karl Radek, as already cited in the introduction. One man's worm is another's genius.

On the other end of the spectrum, the poet and essayist Vladislav Khodasevich (1886–1939), who stayed abreast of all developments in émigré literature but avoided joining any one group, continued to champion the Pushkinian tradition. A friend and mentor to Nabokov, Khodasevich believed that Russian literature must continue in this vein by cultivating poetic craft, rather than the self-indulgent, wholly introspective tendencies of the Parisian Note. It was folly, Khodasevich suggested, to mistake Pushkin's alleged simplicity for vapidity, his attention to form for disinterestedness. Responding to Adamovich's critiques of Pushkin, Khodasevich retorted: "Here, finally, our literary (and not only literary) patriotism is offended, for Pushkin is our homeland, 'our all.' . . . Pushkin's is in fact the path of greatest resistance . . . for in the depiction of greatest complexity he takes the way of greatest simplicity."[20] Khodasevich's statement is striking in his merging of Pushkin, a literary-historical figure, who is, of course, much more than simply that, with the very fabric of Russia itself; to deny Pushkin, for him, is to deny the Russian nation. In short, if Russian literature was to survive, then it must retain its links to the past.

Given these polemics, which were waged across the pages of leading Parisian and Berlin émigré periodicals, it then comes as no surprise that Nabokov would have found the idea of denying one's father problematic, to put it lightly. In *The Gift*, Fyodor combines the biological father (Konstantin Kirillovich), the literary father (Pushkin), and the national tradition (prerevolutionary Russian literature), viewing them as inseparable, and, in doing so, he—with Nabokov conducting the same project at a level removed—establishes himself within this very tradition and creates a legacy of his own conception.[21] If for Stephen the fathers may be estranged, then for Fyodor/Nabokov to do so would mean to unravel everything. Nabokov saw the value in Stephen's Shakespeare project, but his own novel, a kind of translation of *Ulysses* in the key of Russian émigré life, in the end opts for an alternative course. Joyce, in turn, acts as yet another prism though which he can engage in these debates.

Finding the Father and Defining the Son in *The Gift*

When Fyodor is introduced to the reader, he is in a period of enormous transition as he moves into a Berlin boardinghouse during his eighth year of emigration.[22] Devoid of a permanent home, in perpetual need of money, and aware of his burgeoning literary talent, Fyodor struggles against the world that surrounds him. The constants in his life are literature, family, and love (for art, for his father, and, eventually, for Zina). As these elements constitute Fyodor's greatest passions, it would only be natural that in his endeavor to recover the past, he would take different turns than Stephen, similar though their respective efforts may be in theory. Moreover, Nabokov's personal history turns the nature of his character's pursuits away from the Joycean path of affiliation (rather than filiation); an émigré whose father was killed in a botched assassination, Nabokov felt a duty to maintain a bond with what he had lost and all that it represented. Unlike Nabokov, Joyce chose self-imposed exile and maintained a positive relationship with his father, John Stanislaus Joyce, until his death in 1932. While the majority of John Joyce's "children grew to dislike him intensely," Richard Ellmann writes, "his eldest son [James], of whom he was most fond, reciprocated his affection and remembered his jokes." At the end of his life, John, "largely neglected by the other children who could still remember the mistreatment they had suffered from him, loved James more and more with the years."[23] Nabokov, however, was forced to *react* to the circumstances of emigration and his father's death. Thus, in Nabokov's fiction as well as in his autobiography, *Speak, Memory*, he often presents an idealized portrait of the family. His dysfunctional family units in various novels—*Lolita*, *Ada*, *The Gift*—serve as perversions of the romanticized ideal. Joyce, by contrast, mythologizes his families far more. That is not to say that his texts' numerous family members lack individual features, but rather that behind their circumstances and actions lies a more generalized backdrop: Stephen as rebellious son, Bloom as kindly father, Molly as earthly mother. At various stages and to varying degrees, Joyce alternately rebelled against or saw the value of familial ties, both personally and creatively. Things reach an extreme when in *Finnegans Wake* much of the plot, such as it is, revolves around the shifting identities of the Earwicker clan: father (Humphrey Chimpden Earwicker, HCE), mother (Anna Livia Plurabelle, ALP), sons (Shem and Shaun), and daughter (Issy). In this book, Joyce asks his reader to trade unique figures for iterations of historical figures and, more importantly, past generations. As ALP puts it in her speech, "What will be is. Is is. But let them. Slops hospodch and the slusky slut too. He's for thee what she's for me."[24] Here, she acknowledges that her children represent versions of herself and her husband, the rascally

HCE. Unlike Joyce, Nabokov regularly presents much more individualized views of families.

A central principle of *The Gift* involves Fyodor's merging of his father, the biological figure whom Stephen Dedalus calls "a necessary evil," with Pushkin, a literary forefather, in the novel's second chapter.[25] Fyodor finds that Pushkin comes to permeate both his own life and the life of his father as he begins work on a biography of Konstantin Kirillovich Godunov-Cherdyntsev: "Pushkin entered his blood. With Pushkin's voice merged the voice of his father. He kissed Pushkin's hot little hand, taking it for another, large hand smelling of the breakfast *kalach* (a blond roll). . . . From Pushkin's prose he had passed to his life, so that in the beginning the rhythm of Pushkin's era commingled with the rhythm of his father's life."[26] What Fyodor attempts to accomplish through writing his father's biography goes far beyond his initial expectations and ultimately extends the very limits of his artistry. This project bears some similarity, if in a refracted form, to the ideas proposed by Dedalus in the "Scylla and Charybdis" episode of *Ulysses*.[27] Sergei Davydov, for instance, writes that Fyodor completes his father's journey, and, due to this "at-onement" with his father, he is able to develop both "spiritually" and "artistically" as he simultaneously completes his quest to find Pushkin.[28]

This process is achieved through similar methods and forms as Dedalus's but is directed toward different ends. It is for these two writers a project equal parts allusive, narratological, and metaphysical. Like Olesha's Kavalerov, Stephen, on the one hand, seeks to put himself at a clear remove from his biological father by means of electing a literary precursor and by fathering himself through his art; this distancing goes further, however, as Stephen rebels against other adoptive fathers along with the original, Simon Dedalus. The father figures in Joyce's and Olesha's books lack a legacy. Fyodor, on the other hand, wishes to unite the biological with the literary, the filial with the artistic. He actually learns from his father—his mentor in various fields including lepidoptery—unlike the heroes in other modernist novels including *Ulysses*. For this reason, he feels an intellectual affinity that transcends boundaries. Konstantin Kirillovich endorses his son as a pupil, and this move distinguishes Fyodor from his literary counterparts. For him, reclaiming a literary tradition by uniting it with his own personal and family histories means overturning recent events and recovering his father, who comes to stand for the culture that is seemingly inaccessible to him as a Russian émigré. He only regrets that Konstantin Kirillovich remains a mystery and that he possesses incomplete knowledge of his father's exploits. This relationship clearly contrasts with those of Kavalerov and Stephen with their respective fathers, as they feel that they completely understand their paternal figures and consequently view them in a negative light. The unknowability of Konstantin

Kirillovich enthralls Fyodor, ultimately in part because it suggests a means to overcome his senseless loss. If Konstantin Kirillovich cannot be summed up, then the idea of him, his mysterious nature, continues on.

Nabokov's Bloomian swerve ("clinamen"—"an act of creative correction") away from Joyce's text emphasizes precisely these crucial differences.[29] Rereading The Gift in these terms, we see that Nabokov revises Joyce's project according to his own views and experiences, something that his lectures on Ulysses confirm. He does not accept the tenets of his precursor, as they will only serve to separate him from the culture he wishes to retain. Thus, Nabokov manipulates the same ideas—selecting one's ancestors, merging fathers—but swerves away from the divisionary component inherent to Joyce's endeavor. Pushkin is here necessary for Fyodor's gift; they are not in conflict. Briefly put, Fyodor seeks to recoup his father and all he represents by selecting a literary predecessor who embodies the ideals, aesthetics, and worldview shared by the two fathers and solitary son. The Gift, and not just in this second chapter, is imbued with Pushkinian references that drive the project's momentum. As Savely Senderovich describes it, Pushkin acts as "a textual source, a historical figure, a literary personage, a cause for mystification, a poetic motif, and a psychological symbol—in a word, an entire continuous [skvoznoi] semantic layer" in The Gift.[30]

A parallel to this strategy of applying associative allusions to unite biological father, literary father, and son can be found in Dedalus's case. The vast number of references to Shakespeare's work throughout Ulysses serve to give the text a Shakespearean tint in characterization, dialogue, and situation rhymes. Of particular relevance are those associations with Shakespeare that are bestowed on Leopold Bloom, Dedalus's would-be adoptive father. Hugh Kenner makes the intriguing observation that in his speech at the National Library Stephen's idiosyncratic portrait of Shakespeare is remarkably akin to Bloom: "a restless man with a lively daughter and a dead son, uneasily yoked to a wife who 'overbore' him once and cuckolds him now, rearranging all this difficult experience in a steady flow of words."[31] As Konstantin Kirillovich is granted Pushkin's traits, so too is Stephen's potential father-substitute, Bloom, serendipitously equated with the young writer's ideal artist, the version of Shakespeare he depicts in his speech. Unlike Fyodor, however, Stephen will meet this hybrid figure but will not realize it and will turn down his well-intentioned offers of assistance in "Ithaca." Fyodor, on the contrary, goes to great lengths to associate Konstantin Kirillovich with Pushkin even if he can no longer access either father in any physical sense; they only exist in his dreams and writings.

One of the subtle allusions to Pushkin in The Gift that, to my knowledge, has remained unexplored can be found in Fyodor's consideration of which fate his father may have faced on his final expedition: "Oh, how did he die? From illness? From exposure? From thirst? By the hand of man? And if by somebody's hand, can that hand be still living, taking bread, raising a glass, chasing flies, stirring, pointing, beckoning, lying motionless, shaking other hands? Did he return their fire for a long time? Did he save a last bullet for himself? Was he taken alive? Did they bring him to the parlor car at the railway headquarters of some punitive detachment . . . having suspected him of being a White spy . . . ?"[32] Compare the preceding passage with Pushkin's poem "Traveling Complaints" ("Dorozhnye zhaloby," 1829–30):

Do I have much time to wander upon this world
Sometimes in a carriage, sometimes on horseback,
Sometimes in a covered wagon, sometimes in a coach,
Sometimes in a cart, sometimes by foot?

Not in my familial den,
Not among paternal graves,
On the highway, it seems,
The Lord judged I will die,

Upon stones beneath a hoof,
On a mountain beneath a wheel,
Or in a water-worn ditch
Under a dismantled bridge.

Or a plague will take me,
Or a cold will freeze me,
Or a sluggish invalid
Will slam my head with a lifting gate.

Or in the forest under a villain's knife
I will be caught unawares,
Or I'll croak from boredom
Somewhere in quarantine.

Do I have much time in hungry melancholy
To observe an involuntary fast
And through cold veal
To recollect the Iar's truffles?

How much better it is to be in one's place,
To go about Miasnitskaya,
To think at leisure
About one's village, about one's bride!

How much better is a glass of rum,
Sleep at night, tea in the morning;
How much better it is, brothers, at home . . . !
Well, let's go, drive on . . . ![33]

If the precise misfortunes do not match exactly, the implications of these constructions are quite similar. In both cases, the protagonist muses on possible deaths, some stemming from external causes, others from internal ones. Details related to civil war–era Russia naturally replace the dangers of Pushkin's time, but the fear of death while traveling is maintained. Additionally, both poem and prose passage depict the clash between the artist and a perilous world, between the mundane and the deceptively quotidian, between an ill-starred death and an enchanted life.

Fyodor concludes his grim musings, much like Pushkin, on a more positive, or at least a more speculative, note: "Once the rumor of my father's death is a fiction, must it not then be conceded that his very journey out of Asia is merely attached in the shape of a tail to this fiction (like that kite which in Pushkin's story [*The Captain's Daughter*] young Grinyov fashioned out of a map), and that perhaps, if my father even did set out on this return journey . . . he chose a completely different road?"[34] This process introduces serious doubt into the imagined scenarios. That is, the questions, as in Pushkin's poem, render null any sense of certainty, leaving the possibility of survival intact. There is an added direct parallel, as both texts end with the persona pressing forth on an unnamed "road." Fyodor includes the following line in his re-creation of the dying Alexander Chernyshevsky's thoughts: "The unfortunate image of a 'road' to which the human mind has become accustomed (life as a kind of journey) is a stupid illusion."[35] He, in a sense, literalizes the metaphor in his description of his father's imagined survival. The inversion, despite Fyodor's (and perhaps Nabokov's) noted distaste for the "life is a road" metaphor-cliché, suggests that both Pushkin's poet-persona and Konstantin Kirillovich ride out of their respective texts into a life that remains incomprehensible and somehow still positive. Although Senderovich writes that Konstantin Kirillovich becomes "associated with the idea of death," the text ultimately grants him, along with Pushkin, a kind of second life.[36] Again, the mystery of his unknown existence speaks to Nabokov's poetics; he, unlike Joyce, sought to retain that wonder, rather than to pin it down. Fyodor's father's life is imbued with a Pushkinian trace. Contrary to Dedalus with his Shakespeare-esque Leopold Bloom, Fyodor is aware of what he accomplishes by making these explicit and implicit connections, which suggest that even if the young writer does not meet either father in reality, he comes closer to reuniting with Konstantin Kirillovich through his contact with Push-kin's texts and thus promotes the possibility of his father's survival. Pushkin's stylistics are Fyodor's means to reach out to his father as he composes Konstan-tin Kirillovich's story. The very narrative fabric, permeated with all its allusions, makes this process feasible for Fyodor.

The entire procedure is bolstered by a reliance on historical sources in both *The Gift* and *Ulysses*. Stephen (via Joyce) cites directly and indirectly the Shake-speare scholars and biographers George Brandes, Frank Harris, and Sidney Lee in his performance-speech.[37] Stephen, who is comfortable raiding the au-thor's life to explain his art, uses these texts to better access, or construct, his version of Shakespeare's world. His focus, though, remains on the literary father figure on whom he has chosen to model himself. Fyodor, adopting Stephen's methods, introduces documentary sources to construct a life of his biological father, all the while aligning them with Pushkinian texts. He samples and transforms travelogues written by famed naturalists such as Grigory Grum-Grzhimaylo and Nikolai M. Przhevalsky in a kind of tapestry or collage.[38] Countless such elements litter chapter 2 of *The Gift* as Fyodor creates a vivid picture of his father's life and travels. The two artists seek out materials from life and from literature in order to strengthen their paternal constructions by means of borrowings from historical records. Both situations concern the artist's desire to equate himself with an idealized model—or two in Fyodor's case.

All this is to say that Fyodor, like Stephen, plays loose with "facts," whether in life, literature, or documentary texts, in order to construct a desired artistic re-sult. This deliberately crafted image includes numerous connections that bridge the gap between Konstantin Kirillovich and Pushkin, between a lost culture and a literary tradition besieged in the Russian émigré community. William M. Schutte writes that Stephen's treatment of sources, "lacks the scholar's fairness and impartiality," as Joyce's hero seeks out "those facts which will bolster his preconceived notions" about his subject. The same may be said about Fyodor's work on either his father's biography in chapter 2 or his book on Chernyshevsky in chapter 4.[39] The imperative of his project—the desire to link his father directly with Pushkin—motivates his deployment of the allusions he chooses. Zina rec-ognizes this tendency in his work and demands a "deeper truth . . . for which [Fyodor] alone [is] responsible and which he alone could find."[40] This truth, a word similar enough to "reality" or "life" that Nabokov may well have suggested it, too, always fall between parentheses, is the artistic creation of the son in an effort to find (or construct) his father.[41] Even if the means are quite similar, Joyce is creating a father, while Nabokov is recovering one.

The Metaphysics of Fatherhood: Time, History, and Tradition

Beyond the allusive and narratological strategies devised by Fyodor to achieve his goal lies a metaphysical foundation. This part of the project may once again be traced back to Dedalus's thoughts in *Ulysses*. Stephen argues that the artist may actually father himself—that is, the world's future conception of him—by creating lasting art, consequently breaking bonds that are in any event based only on a "legal fiction."[42] In other words, the writer's past will be determined by future acts and words that will cast what comes before them. Fyodor follows in Stephen's wake but not without challenging some of the particularities of his theory. The loving composition of his father's biography and his art will restore connections that were once severed and will position him as next in the lineage he chooses for himself in the metaphysical coup over history. As David M. Bethea writes, "The dumbing-down of history that was the Soviet regime and the tragedy that was the death of Fyodor's father (and [Nabokov's] father) is undone by the life's work that lives on. . . . The future is secretly embedded in one's work."[43] Again, Stephen's choice of Shakespeare, whom he considers the greatest symbol of this process, helps explain his theories. Fyodor's approach is much the same—electing a father figure who embodies the concept of a future that transforms the past—but with opposing ends.

Fyodor's and Stephen's statements on time, history, and tradition act readily as keys to understanding Nabokov's response to Joyce. For example, his protagonist proclaims, "Existence is thus an eternal transformation of the future into the past—an essentially phantom process—a mere reflection of the material metamorphoses taking place within us."[44] In analogous phrasing, Stephen reminds himself during his library performance that he must "hold to the now, the here, through which all future plunges to the past."[45] Artistic acuity, at least as these two young writers conceive of it, provides dominion over the past. For them, the only way to make sense of the present moment is to transform events in art and, thus, to redefine them as they become the immortalized "past." As *Bend Sinister*'s hero, Adam Krug, puts it, "Anyone can create the future but only a wise man can create the past."[46] Moreover, the patterns in the fabric of life—coincidences that resemble an aesthetic creation—*can* be perceived but only with the artist's finely tuned attention.

In this way, the two writers' attitudes to history might well illuminate how their views converge and diverge with regard to the topic of time. Stephen, of course, infamously calls history "a nightmare from which [he is] trying to awake," placing history in an adversarial role.[47] His (future) art will then be a remedy to the nightmare, a way for him to triumph over all his perceived tragedies. Nabokov recognized this aspect of Stephen's character in his lectures on *Ulysses*: "Both see their enemy in history—injustice for Bloom, a metaphysical prison for Stephen."[48] Stephen's only recourse, as Robert Spoo argues, is not a true escape from history, which may after all be impossible, but "the ceaseless effort to awake from history's oppressive texts through the weaving and reweaving of alternative ones."[49] Like Fyodor, Stephen combs his personal and cultural pasts for the material that can be used in art. He constantly pushes back against the wave of history that tyrannizes him in its various guises: his mother and her death, English cultural dominance, exclusion from Dublin's literati, his father, and so forth. The young artist plans to create texts that, not unlike *Ulysses*, will amend his experiences by giving them a shape more in tune with his goals and preferences.

Fyodor for his part adopts a less confrontational attitude. The combination of his powerful memory, inspired vision, and confident artistic touch allows him to recraft all that he has lost. In this manner Fyodor may reformulate the past and launch a timeless cultural memory built into and out of literature. Fyodor is thus far more concerned with a shared history than Stephen. He accepts the tragedies that have befallen him and Russia because he is able to tap into a narrative that affirms his role as a young, increasingly distinguished writer. In doing so, he also sustains that same tradition. What matters most to him is not the tragedy itself, all the nightmares of history, but the artist's response to them, the manner in which he makes sense of everything that takes place around him.

Nabokov paid particular attention to this integration of art and time. In the essay "The Art of Literature and Commonsense," he describes the moment of artistic mastery, which involves "the perfect fusion of the past and the present," as follows: "The inspiration of genius adds a third ingredient: it is the past and the present *and* the future (your book) that come together in a sudden flash . . . time ceases to exist."[50] The literary act for Nabokov thus involves a mystical temporal element, something akin to what his character Fyodor experiences when he writes. He suggests that the artist conquers the past by rewriting it, overcomes the present by recognizing that it can be understood in aesthetic terms, and redefines the future by virtue of these artistic changes to previous experiences. Fyodor attempts this feat—to escape time—in his work. The critical difference between him and Stephen is that the former, at least after a period of maturation, does not feel oppressed by history's burden for he can situate himself in relation to past achievements in a manner that allows him to disregard all "the darkest and most dazzling hours of physical danger, pain, dust, death."[51]

As a fellow dispossessed son, not to mention émigré, Fyodor should by all rights feel the need to awake from the nightmare of history, as did his illustrious company. Spoo notes that this nightmare metaphor "can now be recognized as a characteristic trope of modernist historiography, a figure for the desire to break through received textualizations of the past to an unwonted authenticity."[52] He traces its usage through the works of Joyce, Virginia Woolf, and Ezra Pound, among others. In his characteristically iconoclastic manner, Nabokov circumvents precisely this trope when engaging with Joyce: Fyodor, cast adrift into exile by forces beyond his control, seemingly separated by new "textualizations" from the tradition to which he feels closest, simply isolates himself from all these crises, delving deep into the art of memory to overcome his losses. This, then, is part of Nabokov's response to Joyce's efforts; his character will not disrupt bonds even amid the chaos of the modernist period. He wishes to retain the historical record that produced Pushkin, his father, Konstantin Kirillovich, and the cultural legacy that he treasures so dearly—in opposition to the Parisian Note writers.

Calling to mind Stephen's proclamation about history being a "nightmare," Nabokov writes in *Speak, Memory*: "Initially, I was unaware that time, so boundless at first blush, was a prison."[53] He would later renounce this comment: "My exploration of time's prison . . . was only a stylistic device meant to introduce my subject."[54] Whatever his ultimate feelings may have been, Nabokov's regular use of the prison image in his *Ulysses* lectures and his autobiography suggests that the subject and Joyce's treatment of the theme were significant to him. If we take Nabokov's statements at face value, then we see that whereas Nabokov may have once felt the pressures of time in a way similar to Joyce or Stephen, he found the strategies that allowed him to view history differently, not as an adversary. Fyodor achieves transcendence partly by virtue of his ability to overcome a tendency toward egocentricity. His growth in the novel involves the recognition of others' sufferings, journeys, and connections, which are all inevitably marked by time. He appreciates the fact that he can define history himself but that others—his father, fellow émigrés and Berliners, even Pushkin—help make up the cultural past. Not *everything* can be a reflection of the artist, an insight later lost on Bitov's hero in *Pushkin House*.

In his response to Joyce, Nabokov repeatedly maintains the need to remain faithful to the fathers. Part of Fyodor's poem from chapter 3—"To fiction be as to your country true"—comes to mind.[55] For Fyodor, as for his author, the concepts "fiction" and "country" represent more than paper, geography, and politics. They both imply a cultural heritage embodied by fathers from various fields including poetry and lepidoptery. Again, Nabokov's status as an émigré and Joyce's as an expatriate might explain their differing perspectives.

Only by maintaining this pedigree will Fyodor incorporate what came before him and defeat time—represented by historical forces and mortality. In this regard, the difference between Fyodor's and Stephen's approaches to composing the history of their respective fathers plays a key role. There have been various explanations offered as to why Fyodor does not finish the biography of Konstantin Kirillovich, from Weir's "failed attempt" to bring together Fyodor's two selves to Blackwell's lack of his "ideal reader," his father.[56] Furthermore, as the biography's "he" turns into "I," Fyodor realizes he has not observed the appropriate critical distance between his father and his own persona. Again, Stephen feels no qualms about importing wholesale his problems, for example, the idea of usurpation, into the life of Shakespeare. In recounting his version of his "father's" story, Stephen in fact tells his own saga, that of the dispossessed artist who goes on to transform life through art. Fyodor, by contrast, recoils at the thought that he has forced himself onto his father's memory: "I myself am a mere seeker of verbal adventures, and forgive me if I refuse to hunt down my fancies on my father's own collecting ground."[57] The one finds—or rather situates—his reflection in the past, in his conquest over history, and in the literary forefathers he adopts. The other identifies parallels between father figures and himself, stretching materials when necessary, but nonetheless refuses to integrate himself into their beings. Fyodor only wishes to establish a direct lineage. Pushkin, to reiterate, is said to have "entered his blood," not the other way around.[58]

The Artist's Body of Work

This corporeal metaphor is quite appropriate, as many of the Joycean links in *Ulysses* travel in this class of imagery. One particularly arresting image, for example, can be seen in the fifth chapter of *The Gift* when Fyodor finds a dog's corpse in Berlin's Grunewald forest: "Here is a dark thicket of small firs where I once discovered a pit which had been carefully dug out before its death by the creature that lay therein, a young, slender-muzzled dog of wolf ancestry, folded into a wonderfully graceful *curve* [*sognuvshis'*], paws to paws."[59] This specific detail has its Joycean source, one to which Nabokov drew his students' attention in his lectures on *Ulysses*.[60] Early in Joyce's novel, Stephen examines the "bloated carcass of a dog" on the shore of Sandymount.[61] After witnessing another canine sniff the body, he thinks, "Ah, poor dogsbody! Here lies poor dogsbody's body."[62] Finally, the dog's owner calls his pet back: "The cry brought him skulking back to his *master* and a blunt bootless kick sent him unscathed across a spit of sand, crouched in flight. He slunk back in a *curve*."[63] In both scenarios the writers wander alone, immersed in their thoughts, when they either run across or recall a dog's body. How they each respond to their respective encounter and interpret it speaks to the differences in their personalities at these points in the narratives and to Nabokov's broader interaction with Joyce's work.

Two primary concerns overwhelm Stephen here at the end of the third episode of *Ulysses*: the relentless pressure of time and the possibility that he, too, is a pretender. The hydrophobic Stephen associates the dead dog with himself, as Buck previously called him "poor dogsbody."[64] He feels that he may be unable to transcend his current weaknesses and become the artist he wishes. The sight of the other dog's "master" moreover reinforces Stephen's anxieties about the usurpers Buck and Haines and thwarted cultural legacies, which of course served as a point of contact between him and Olesha's Nikolai Kavalerov. Alone on the beach, Stephen sees himself in the dog, as well as in the drowned man whose sad fate was related earlier in the novel and whom Stephen previously linked to the deceased dog.[65] The pull of time, symbolized by the ocean's currents and the shifting sands, drives Stephen to despair.

In his *Gift*, Nabokov creates a clear association to this scene through the image of the dog and related diction, specifically the word "curve." An element of Fyodor can be seen in the dog's body that he finds, just as Stephen associates the corpse and the subservient mutt with himself. Fyodor's dog, first of all, recalls the very nature of his own texts—from his book of poetry opening with "The Lost Ball" and closing with "The Found Ball," which he flips through at the beginning of the novel, to the Chernyshevsky biography and to *The Gift*'s circular construction. Whereas Stephen's dog "curves" as a response to his master's violent kick, Fyodor's dog lies in a "graceful curve," suggesting a more peaceful state. Likewise, Fyodor notes that the dog was of "wolf ancestry." In doing so, he again raises the issue of lineage that motivates much of this thinking throughout the novel. This creature, found by chance, symbolizes Fyodor's belief in an elect ancestral line. Its death and associated decay do not bring misery to his mind. Rather, he sees refinement in the corpse, an emblem of a long-lasting tradition. While Julian W. Connolly does not specifically mention the dog's body, he observes that Fyodor's (Joycean?) epiphany allows Fyodor to recognize the links to the past that are preserved by his art: "The twenty-page description of the Grunewald outing offers a delicate yet brilliant verbal fugue in which reminders of death are interwoven with counterbalancing images of life and vitality."[66] Fyodor no longer fears death in the way he did at the start of the novel, as he writes his father's biography, but instead recognizes that there are artistic means to overcome it. This epiphany recalls a line from *Bend Sinister*: "But the very last lap of [Krug's] life had been happy and it had been proven to him that death was but a question of style."[67] Fyodor comes to the same realization, though his artistic abilities allow him to liberate himself from death.

Stephen, on the contrary, sees only decay in the image of the dead dog. (There is, admittedly, much less grace in the sight of a bloated carcass.) He wishes to reinvent himself in order to avoid becoming another victim of history, another son drowned by Ireland's pull. The living dog sees itself in the dead "dogsbody," just as Stephen glimpses his own death. Nabokov, then, places Fyodor with his acceptance of the dog's "graceful curve" as a counterresponse to this all-consuming dread present in "Proteus." Fyodor realizes that even in death he may become part of a larger chain. His found dog digs its own grave, positioning itself with its "wolf ancestry," within a place of its choosing.

Nabokov also tacitly points to Joyce as an intertextual source through Fyodor's feet. Directly prior to his first imagined conversation with his rival, the acclaimed young poet Koncheev, Fyodor visits a shoe store. There, a salesgirl uncovers his "poorly darned foot" before selling him shoes that are just slightly too small.[68] The shoes, along with a view of his skeletal foot in an X-ray machine, prompt Fyodor to begin mentally composing a poem and to consider his state as an émigré writer. Later, at home, Fyodor dresses and "admir[es]" his new shoes "apprehensively" (*opaslivo*).[69] Something about the shoes disconcerts Fyodor. Linked with the footstep motif that runs throughout the novel, they constrict his physical movement and symbolize the artistic and metaphysical restrictions against which he clashes.

While Nabokov did not introduce the foot/step motif to Russian literature, we can once again turn to *Ulysses* for a comparable treatment.[70] Broadly speaking, Joyce plays up his own motif for all its worth in his city novel. For instance, Blazes Boylan's footsteps, consistently marked by his "new tan shoes," create a portentous footfall, particularly in Bloom's thoughts about his wife's lover.[71] Most shoes in *The Gift* and *Ulysses*, in fact, influence the protagonists' mindsets. Destitute and desperate (much like Fyodor), Stephen borrows his roommate's "broadtoed boots, a buck's castoffs," feeling "the creases of rucked leather wherein another's foot had nested warm."[72] He imagines that his own "two feet in his [Buck's] boots are at the ends of his legs, *nebeneinander*" since he has likewise taken a pair of trousers.[73] Later, in "Scylla and Charybdis," during his crisis, Stephen's thoughts return to these matters: "His boots are spoiling the shape of my feet. Buy a pair. Holes in my socks."[74] Fyodor's "poorly darned foot" has its Irish precedent. Stephen's borrowed shoes, like Fyodor's new ones, impose a metaphoric system of oppression on him that he resists. They are a concrete symbol of Buck's grip over Stephen, his financial stranglehold. Stephen desires nothing more than independence. Likewise, although Fyodor's shoes are not on loan, they produce no less bitter an emotion. In these respective scenes, they realize that they must break free of systems opposed to their worldviews before casting out into the world.

Continuing the technique of physical connections between Fyodor and Stephen, Nabokov suggests an association through their teeth. At the end of the "Telemachiad," Stephen thinks, "My teeth are very bad. Why, I wonder. Feel. That one is going too. Shells. Ought I go to a dentist, I wonder, with that money? That one. This. Toothless Kinch, the superman."[75] In his mental reevaluation of his recently published volume, Fyodor offers the following account of one of his poems: "Here is the description of a drive to this dentist, who had warned the day before that 'this one will have to come out.'"[76] Intriguingly, the original Russian version reads: *"Vot opisanie poezdki k etomu dantistu, predupredivshemu nakanune, chto that one will have to come out."*[77] Both passages feature teeth that are "going," in need of removal for their own respective reasons. Moreover, a Monsieur Drumont is mentioned in the same paragraph in *Ulysses*, and a Monsieur Danzas mentioned in the paragraph featuring Fyodor's reflections. The former is a reference to Nabokov's ancestor Konstantin Karlovich Danzas (1801–1870), Pushkin's close friend and second in the duel with Georges-Charles de Heeckeren d'Anthès (1812–1895) in 1837. Édouard Adolphe Drumont (1844–1917) was a French editor and journalist at *La libre parole*. These odd parallels imply that Nabokov might have had *Ulysses* in mind when composing his scene with its dentistry theme. The patent change from "that" to "this" suggests a playful bilingual exercise. Just as Stephen manipulates his demonstrative pronouns ("That one. This.") and their meanings, Nabokov adjusted his English line, which was conspicuous enough to begin with in the Russian original, to direct the reader to his Joycean source.

Equally important is the fact that at these points in the novels both artists are considering memory and time. As he composes a mental review of his verse collection, Fyodor realizes how his flagging memory can "condemn to extinction" once dear "objects."[78] In a sense, then, he observes the same procedure in action as Stephen, who finds that the world goes on existing even if he is not around to perceive it: "Ineluctable modality of the visible: at least that if no more, thought through my eyes."[79] Both Fyodor and Stephen fuse the mnemonic with the perceptual, associating the artist's ability to give name to things (or come close with demonstratives) with his control over reality.[80]

Something Sinister in Berlin

Allusive strategies and the development of the role of the artist greatly augmented Nabokov's engagement with Joyce and how he translated certain ideas from his predecessor's work into his own. Turning now to *Bend Sinister*, another text with many ties to Joyce that have been mentioned in the past but never specifically in light of *The Gift*'s poetics, highlights a tendency to avoid seeing certain kinds of unities between Nabokov's Russian and English novels. *Bend Sinister*, however, also treats the question of fathers and sons through its own skewed perspective, like *Ulysses* and *The Gift*. The novel takes place in the fictional land of Padukgrad. Nabokov's protagonist, Adam Krug, is a famous philosopher recuperating after the death of his wife. When Krug refuses to submit to the Ekwilist regime, now headed by his former classmate and the object of his bullying, Paduk, the abrasive philosopher faces a terrible fate. Nabokov's second English-language book offers additional commentary on *Ulysses*, in particular its "Scylla and Charybdis" episode, as well as on Joyce's aesthetics more generally. *Bend Sinister* also amplifies many of the techniques and themes developed in *The Gift* and *Ulysses*. Most importantly, Nabokov inverts the son's search for his father, as the Hamletian father of *Bend Sinister*, Krug, loses his son in a horrific turn of events near the conclusion.

A great deal of work has been conducted on the relevant allusions to Shakespeare that appear throughout the novel. In addition to Samuel Schuman's comprehensive *Nabokov's Shakespeare*, Herbert Grabes suggests that this is proof of Nabokov's "outdoing his predecessors," namely, Joyce and Goethe, in their parodic treatments of *Hamlet* and Shakespearean scholarship.[81] The novel is a tribute to Shakespeare, the greatest representative of classic English literature, *and* his modernist heir, Joyce. In choosing these two authors for models, the newly Americanized Nabokov ensured himself a place in an illustrious lineage, much as he did with Pushkin throughout his Russian works. Nabokov in effect once more enacts the same project as Stephen in *Ulysses*. Even so, he cannot help but offer criticism through his parodic treatment of Joyce, now his "brother" as a fellow self-appointed descendent of Shakespeare. The Bard stands metonymically for Pushkin even in the American Nabokov's work, and, thus, that tradition must be exalted.

The conversation between Krug and Ember on *Hamlet* that takes place in chapter 7 of the novel illustrates this form of exaggerated parody well. As others have remarked, this chapter draws on *Ulysses*'s ninth episode for much of its impact. Remarkably, Nabokov offered little explicit commentary on "Scylla and Charybdis" outside of *Bend Sinister*. In fact, in his lectures on *Ulysses* the episode is given only a brief paragraph that summarizes the fundamentals of Stephen's theory and states in categorical terms Joyce's failure: "The discussion in this chapter is one of those things that is more amusing for a writer to write than for a reader to read, and so its details need not be examined."[82] This is a curious statement given that Nabokov himself, who elsewhere ceaselessly champions details, finds much of interest as both reader and writer in this very chapter, as evidenced by the parodic treatment he delivers in *Bend Sinister*. While other analyses of this section of the novel have laudably explicated its intricacies, none has endeavored to bridge the gap between it and what Nabokov does in *The Gift*.[83] Joyce permeates *Bend Sinister* in various guises, directing Nabokov's hand as he shapes the novel's imagery, characterization, structure, and thematics. By this point, Nabokov had read both *Ulysses* and *Finnegans Wake* and could use them to wed himself to the English modernist tradition by setting up his many parodies and parallels.[84] *Bend Sinister*'s own Shakespeare chapter may be considered a continuation, albeit a more ferocious if still playful one, of Nabokov's rejoinder to Joyce begun in *The Gift*. Bringing together all three novels will help reveal further nuances of Nabokov's *Gift*.

The aforementioned conversation between Krug and Ember speaks directly to Stephen's performance in the National Library. Consequently, the dialogue also has ramifications on our understanding of Fyodor's project in *The Gift*.[85] In scenes such as this one Joyce permeates the narrative of *Bend Sinister* in many subtle ways. The connection is set up early in the chapter when, after describing a series of three engravings on Ember's wall, the narrator, referring to Shakespeare, says that "his name is protean," a reference to *Ulysses*'s third episode and Stephen's cogitations on time, change, and identity therein.[86] Brian Boyd, in his commentary to *Bend Sinister*, explains these engravings as a reference to "three inset illustrations from the title page of Gustavus Selenus's study of cryptographic systems, *Cryptomenytices et Cryptographiae* (1624), reproduced in Sir Edwin Durning-Lawrence's *Bacon is Shakespeare* (1910)."[87] Durning-Lawrence was the leading proponent of the Baconian theory in Shakespeare studies, which suggests that Francis Bacon actually wrote the plays. Nabokov thus begins to establish his parody of scholarly perversions by which the author's life is mishandled and art poisoned by extraliterary considerations. For his part, he prefers the details of Shakespeare's texts: "However, the fact that the Warwickshire fellow wrote the plays is most satisfactorily proved on the strength of an applejohn and a pale primrose."[88] The presence of "pale primrose" found in Warwickshire, whence Shakespeare originated, makes a more convincing argument for Nabokov than any inferences to his marriage dug up in a given play. According to Nabokov, all these transformations of Shakespeare ("Shaxpere," "Shagspere," "William X"), like Stephen's manipulations of the Bard's life, only distort and distract from the art created by a man of genius. Fyodor has therefore been previously offered as a response to this process when he refuses to do the same with his father's history.

The two performance scenes are notably similar in structure as well. Without resorting to the type of reading of *Bend Sinister* that Eric Naiman believes has caused "simplification arising out of the scholarly desire to find in it an uplifting message," Ember's room, the home of the scholar, *does* still represent a sanctuary from the trials of the outside world, just as the National Library for Stephen stands as the last refuge for a poet in a pragmatic world that now champions science over art.[89] As Stephen comes to the emotional climax of his speech, Mulligan, cynical double and usurper, interrupts with his ironic commentary: "*Eureka!*"[90] Buck's intrusion manifests the poet's displacement by the medical student both in their individual lives and on a broader symbolic level. He takes the limelight from Stephen when he is invited to the literary evening being hosted by George Moore, while the young writer is left aside. In *Bend Sinister*, the same process is repeated: amid the scandalous discussion on *Hamlet*, the state's crude representatives intrude on Ember and Krug's world, a realm that remains opaque to the state powers who torment Krug's friends in an effort to get the philosopher to comply. This space, which once seemed safe and immune to such interferences, is revealed to be no less permeable. It is, in fact, only a mirage, and one suspects that Nabokov would have it be so because Krug and Stephen encroach on the realm of the greats.

Krug's quasi-literary activities and their consequences can be better analyzed with reference to Fyodor and *The Gift*. Unlike Krug, Fyodor does not sink to the level of the philistine in his deformation of Chernyshevsky in the biography that makes up *The Gift*'s fourth chapter, nor does he ever even consider mocking Pushkin. He certainly drags his Chernyshevsky through the mud, but Fyodor does not do so with the same intentions as Krug, let alone Stephen. Perhaps more importantly, both Fyodor and his maker do not rank Chernyshevsky on the same level as Pushkin, making this performance more acceptable to them. Krug and Ember derive great pleasure from their baroque, bizarre interpretations of *Hamlet*. This relaxed attitude toward the Bard, according to Naiman, is an aesthetic crime in Nabokov's estimation: "Although Nabokov himself was certainly not averse to parody, when characters in this novel parody great authors, their fates are similar to those of the benighted protagonists of Greek myths, punished for poaching on the realm of the gods."[91] Chernyshevsky is at best a demigod in Fyodor's view. What Krug and Stephen do to Shakespeare, however, goes against Nabokov's aesthetics of the father. Reading retroactively, we see how Nabokov viewed Stephen's treatment of *Hamlet* and Shakespeare's life as too crude an oversimplification of a genius's creative process and bring to sharper relief both Krug's and Fyodor's fates.

Krug and Ember raise their spirits after the death of the former's wife, Olga, with these ribald and dubious readings of *Hamlet*, which are in a sense akin to Stephen's. Some are original creations, others taken from coded sources. Much like the quoted historical documents transformed by *The Gift*'s texture,

Shakespearean scholarship is manipulated in *Bend Sinister*. For example, re-counting the hawk-man's plan for a film adaptation of *Hamlet*, Krug reports, "He added he had thought she was eighteen at least, judging by her bust, but, in fact, she was hardly fifteen, the little bitch. And then there was Ophelia's death. To the sounds of Liszt's *Les Funérailles* she would be shown wrestling—or, as another rivermaid's father would have said, 'wrustling'—with the willow. A lass, a salix."[92] This entire scene is a masterful concentration of intertexts. These lines seamlessly mix music, Joyce, and Shakespeare. There is the "rivermaid's father"—a reference to *Finnegans Wake*'s Anna Livia Plurabelle candidly ex-plained by Nabokov in his foreword to *Bend Sinister*—and the Joycean wordplay with "wrestling"/"wrustling" and "a lass, a salix." Ember is then described as "enter[ing] into the spirit of the *game*."[93] References to Joyce ("*cp.* Winnipeg Lake, ripple 585, Vico Press edition"—*Finnegans Wake*) and Pushkin ("*Russalka letheana*"—the uncompleted *Rusalka*) appear directly afterward, once more linking the two in this "game" of crass quasi-literary one-upmanship. This pas-sage makes Krug, Stephen, and, by extension, Joyce culpable. While Nabokov appreciates games and puzzles, those characters who break or even bend his rules and mock the dignity of great artists often face terrible plights. When one challenges the sanctity of his forefathers, the author's wrath emerges. So while Krug is certainly not a criminal like *Despair*'s Hermann or *Lolita*'s Humbert, his grief blinds him, and he takes a misstep. Fyodor, who, again, admits that he is a "mere seeker of verbal adventures" but "refuse[s] to hunt down [his] fancies on [his] father's own collecting ground," opts out of just such a game.[94] He ac-knowledges the limits of his abilities, which *may*, but *should* not, intrude on the life and art of a cherished father figure. As a result, what goes on between Krug and Ember in *Bend Sinister* can be seen as an even further travestied version of what Stephen accomplishes in *Ulysses* and, as a result, what Fyodor *nearly* does in *The Gift* by distorting his father's life (as well as Pushkin's) with his own poet-ics and interests.

Stephen commits two chief aesthetic crimes according to Nabokov's liter-ary penal code. First, he willingly inserts himself and his concerns into the life of Shakespeare. He chooses to "shuffle, twist, mix, rechew and rebelch every-thing," to borrow Fyodor's words about his creative process and its relation-ship to his life experiences, in order to construct an image of Shakespeare according to his pressing needs.[95] Though they do not involve a ridiculous fas-cist interpretation of *Hamlet*, such as the one present in *Bend Sinister*, Nabo-kov finds this practice questionable, to say the least. Fyodor does something similar when he equates elements of Pushkin's poetry and status as a teacher figure with the life of his biological father. There are critical distinctions, though. Fyodor's scheme brings together, rather than divides, the fathers. His undertaking elevates his own position as chosen son by proxy, but he still reveres the fathers. Fyodor transposes elements of Pushkin's art onto his father's life, not the other way around, thus preserving the poet's distinction in this line of development.

Second, in his crime spree, Stephen also mixes life and art in a very literal fashion by developing an interpretation of *Hamlet* that uses sources external to the literature rather than respecting the inviolability of Shakespeare's plays. Nabokov had the following to say on these issues in a 1971 letter to the editor of the *New York Times Book Review* about Edmund Wilson's memoir *Upstate*: "The method [Wilson] favors is gleaning from my fiction what he supposes to be actual, 'real-life' impressions and then popping them back into my novels and considering my characters in that inept light—rather like the Shakespearian scholar who deduced Shakespeare's mother from the plays and then discovered allusions to her in the very passages he had twisted to manufacture the lady."[96] Of course, Nabokov's choice of "the Shakespearean scholar" here brings to mind Krug, Stephen, and their games. He goes on to suggest that "the publication of those 'old diaries' . . . , in which living persons are but the performing poodles of the diarist's act, should be subject to a rule or law that would require some kind of formal consent from the victims of conjecture, ignorance, and invention."[97] The image of "performing poodles" recalls Nabokov's proclamation that his "characters are galley slaves."[98] The difference, of course, is that Wilson has treated Nabokov in a manner that reduces him to a character and his life to material for his writings, essentially enacting Stephen's claim that his past acquaintances will "troop to [his] call."[99] What becomes clear from such statements is Nabokov's aversion to exploiting real life in explaining a writer's art, his distaste for abusing others' (the geniuses of the world) work, and his unwillingness to subject living beings to the manipulations of art, *especially* if he is not the one behind the pen. Fyodor may transform Chernyshevsky into a literary character—Zina becomes "used to considering him as belonging to Fyodor"—but certainly not with the intention of using the life to explain the art.[100] This is a crucial idea Nabokov repeatedly addresses from *The Gift* to *Bend Sinister* and from his autobiography to his critique of Wilson's book.

Another pertinent text is "Pushkin, or the Real and the Plausible" from 1937. This lecture, originally delivered in French and with none other than Joyce in the audience, ostensibly deals with the demanding process of translating Pushkin, but in large part concerns itself with the titular concepts in biographical writings.[101] Nabokov speaks out against "fictionized [*sic*] biographies": "One begins by sifting through the great man's correspondence, cutting and pasting so as to fashion a nice paper suit for him, then one leafs through his works proper in search of character traits. . . . Indeed, what could be simpler than to have the great man circulate among the people, the ideas, the objects that he himself described and that one plucks from his books in order to make stuffing for one's own?"[102] Much of this speech recalls Nabokov's rejoinder against Wilson, not to mention his literary treatments of these issues. Nabokov was clearly opposed to the practice of creating "paper suit[s]" throughout his entire career, as he vehemently established a clear demarcation between his art and his personal life. While what is typically called "life" could be found in his novels, Nabokov felt that knowledge of this kind contributed nothing to a *real* understanding of his work. Whether or not he was entirely successful in this endeavor or consistent in his practice is, of course, an entirely different matter. There are moments when Nabokov playfully mixes the two sides of the equation, even when it comes to his own life. For example, he writes in the foreword to the English translation of *Glory*: "If Martin to some extent can be considered a distant cousin of mine . . . with whom I share certain childhood memories, certain later likes and dislikes, his pallid parents, *per contra*, do not resemble mine in any rational sense."[103]

Concerning Pushkin, though, Nabokov confidently asserts in the lecture, "Those of us who *really* know him revere him with unparalleled fervor and *purity*, and experience a radiant feeling when the richness of his life overflows into the *present* to flood our spirit."[104] Nabokov in this way continues to position himself as a descendent of the true Pushkinian literary lineage, following in the footsteps of many: Valery Briusov's *My Pushkin* (*Moi Pushkin*, 1929), Marina Tsvetaeva's *My Pushkin* (1937), and Vladislav Khodasevich's *Pushkin's Poetic Economy* (*Poeticheskoe khoziastvo Pushkina*, 1924) and *About Pushkin* (*O Pushkine*, 1937). Nabokov, however, "knows the poet" better and "experience[s]" a merging of his past with the present moment unfelt by those not capable of attaining such great artistic heights. The historical past transforms the present as Nabokov (and Fyodor) are able to channel the poetic energies of earlier periods. Those with whom he implicitly contrasts himself render both Pushkin's life and art inert. Long before Nabokov wrote of Wilson's "performing poodles," he had described the "macabre doll" that a man becomes when someone probes too deeply and carelessly into his private life in search of answers to his art.[105] The biographer's perception of the subject turns out to be "plausible, but not true," a deformation of the ephemeral truth that actually lies in the artist's work, not real "life." There is, though, an irony in the fact that Nabokov's statements on Pushkin are no less a contamination of the poet, his life, and his art than those against which he writes. Nabokov simply adds a spiritual element.

The lecture, in other words, presents Nabokov's theory, while *The Gift*'s second chapter illustrates it in artistic form. Nabokov was engaged with the theme of "biography" and its limits at this point in time (1937) when the two texts were composed, a year after "Mademoiselle O," his first major venture into autobiographical writing. Fyodor stops composing his father's history when he realizes he has tainted Konstantin Kirillovich's experiences with a "secondary poetization."[106] He has departed from the realm of the real (his father's art of lepidoptery) and unwittingly plunged into the plausible (elaborate, romanticized descriptions of his father's travels and death). Stephen, however, does not hold back when describing *his* Shakespeare, and neither does Krug in his grief-inspired abandon. The latter, for his part, fails to recognize the aesthetic chain of command, so to speak, that is so central to Nabokov's art. He joins Ember in raiding Shakespeare's art and life for amusement: even worse, he does not do so to make any more sense of his own existence as Stephen does. (Bitov's Leva takes up Pushkin's life in like manner.) On the contrary, Krug only aims to distract himself from his wife's recent death.

Even if the novels under question are each very different, the greatest irony is that Krug seems to understand the power of the past well. On a personal level his mind is constantly taken by memories of his deceased wife: "Long summer days. Olga playing the piano. Music, order."[107] These recollections trouble his consciousness, defining his present moment. The pull of the past, its appeals and idyllic glow, dictate much of Krug's desire to ignore the recent political (and personal) changes he has witnessed. Speaking with an Ekwilist soldier about a mutual acquaintance early in the novel, as mentioned previously, he remarks, "Anyone can create the future but only a wise man can create the past."[108] His comment implies that the teleological drive of *Bend Sinister*'s authoritarian state, as well as its real-world counterparts, focuses on the future at the expense of the past. On another level, though, it makes the by now familiar assertion that the genius artist can restructure the past to refashion the present; the philistine instead looks forward to projects that may ultimately not be realizable or, worse, that destroy the past's greatest achievements. Stephen's statements regarding the past come to mind here, too. Like Krug, he plays with the story of Shakespeare's life and art. The reasons why differ, but their actions betray a simultaneously callous and permissive attitude, at least according to Nabokov's scheme. Even if Krug ultimately disagrees with the "hawk-face" man whose cinematic interpretation of Shakespeare he and Ember critique, the joy he experiences from his interlocutor's conversation as well as those of his own invention reveals at least a partial kinship between the two. Fyodor, by contrast, accepts Pushkin's grace in his own art. He is the wise man who "can create the past"—but only with the cherished help of his forefathers. This is Nabokov's challenge: Hamlet has to avenge his father but be certain that the ghost is legitimate before doing so;

Fyodor avenges his father through his *art*, which denies the finality of history and of his father's death.

"Alas, Poor Ghost!": Crimes and Misdemeanors à la Nabokov

It is particularly telling that Krug's punishment involves a twisted recapitulation of Bloom's past, as well as an inversion of Hamlet's and Fyodor's. Following a blunder by the state's goons, Krug's son, David, is horrifically murdered at an orphanage for violent children. John Burt Foster Jr. has described the similarities between Bloom's vision of an eleven-year-old Rudy at the end of "Circe" and David's prepared body when it is shown to Krug in *Bend Sinister*: colors (mauve), accompaniments (dog and lambkin), and gaudy clothing.[109] The return of the lost sons becomes ghastly. These two events should, of course, be read with reference to the plot of *Hamlet* and, in the case of Nabokov, his struggle to outdo his predecessor, Joyce, who includes a number of ghosts in *Ulysses*.

Despite the Ekwilist state's efforts to render David a literally exquisite corpse, his appearance is far more haunting than Rudy's due to the seemingly innocuous details, such as the "smooth" blanket, that contrast with the disturbing gravity of the situation.[110] More importantly, the destabilizing contrast between life and death in this scene produces much of its effect. On the one hand, David's lifeless face is "skilfully painted and powdered" in an effort to make him seem more animate. On the other hand, what Krug perceives to be "a fluffy piebald toy dog . . . prettily placed at the foot of the bed" turns out to be a vicious "creature" that reaches for the inconsolable father with its "jaws" as he knocks it over in his flight out of the room.[111] The dead elements come alive, while what should live remains dead, threatening Krug's grip on reality and unsettling the reader's sensibilities. Like Joyce, Nabokov makes the son the ghost in his inverted rendering of *Hamlet*. In doing so, the two writers simultaneously link themselves to the greatest representative of English literature and advance their own art with this revision. However, Bloom's vision is of a different order than Krug's: just as Krug has previously manipulated Shakespeare's text, his own life now plays out like a disturbing version of the Bard's plot. Bloom's Rudy serves as a reminder of the possible communion the father may share with the son or with an adopted son (Stephen), while the sight of David's corpse triggers Krug's madness.

Ghosts—a term that should be understood very broadly—are ubiquitous in Nabokov's art.[112] Their treatment in *The Gift* also involves a reworking of the plot of *Hamlet* in various guises. Polina Barskova has cleverly demonstrated how Nabokov "highlights different aspects of *Hamlet* for different families in his novel."[113] She develops a masterful close reading of the three primary clans in *The Gift*—the Godunov-Cherdyntsevs, the Shchyogolevs, and the Chernyshevskys—and the manner in which their fates retell the plot of *Hamlet*. In the case of Alexander Chernyshevsky, he goes mad, as Hamlet pretends to do so. Barskova argues that Fyodor's dream-encounter with the ghost of Konstantin Kirillovich represents a positive alternative to the Chernyshevskys' fate, that of a "life-affirming philosophy" emblazoned in the novel's very title, *Dar*.[114]

Fyodor experiences this dream, in which he is called to his old apartment to meet an unexpected guest, near the end of *The Gift*. This scene establishes a parallel with Stephen's vision of his mother's corpse in "Circe." Of course, Stephen sees May Dedalus in a far grimmer light: "The ghoul! Hyena! . . . The corpsechewer! Raw head and blood bones."[115] Whereas *Ulysses* is much more obviously fantastical in this moment, unusual details reveal to the careful reader the imaginary nature of Fyodor's encounter with his father's ghost in *The Gift*. Once there, Fyodor is bewildered to find himself face-to-face with Konstantin Kirillovich. As much as Fyodor craves his father's miraculous return, he also dreads the possibility. The dream sequence where the two are reunited reveals a great deal about Fyodor's psychology, including his deep-seated anxiety: "His heart was bursting like that of a man before execution, but at the same time this execution was such a joy that life faded before it."[116] The meeting is an "execution," as it is the conclusion of all that has come before it: the young Fyodor's maturation as an artist and an aching hope for his father's return. It is likewise a final judgment. Here, Fyodor's vision of his father will decide his fate, rendering him mute or allowing him to flourish as a writer.

However, until that impending moment, the idea of death permeates the entire scene, associating itself with both the absent father and the expectant son. Fyodor knows that his father must have perished at some point on his return journey, yet the *plausibility* of his return, which he has entertained for so long, not its shameful *truth*, which lies entirely outside the realm of believability, haunts him. Konstantin Kirillovich's corporeal form has passed on, leaving behind only Fyodor's memories of his father and the connections from which he draws. The fear possessing Fyodor passes only when his father speaks to him, an act which reveals "that everything was all right and simple, that this was the true resurrection, that it could not be otherwise" and "that he was pleased—pleased with his captures, his return, his son's book about him."[117] Notably, Konstantin Kirillovich's words are not reproduced in the narrative. They seemingly emanate from the otherworld to Fyodor's sleeping consciousness and thus exist beyond representation. Nonetheless, the (imagined) exchange allows for the two to be reconciled at last. Again, phrases fairly reminiscent of others previously associated with Pushkin and Konstantin Kirillovich, including "woolen jacket" and "big hands" (compare "hareskin coat" and "hot little hand" in the novel's second chapter), unite the two father figures.[118] Curiously, Nabokov's "Pushkin, or the Real and the Plausible" makes the case against trying to resurrect life. If Fyodor witnesses the apparent resurrection of Konstantin Kirillovich, it is only so because he imagines the father's image through his own creative spirit. It represents another tremulous step toward Fyodor's greatest accomplishment: the completion of *The Gift*, the story of Fyodor's principal constants—literature, family, and love.

Fyodor's encounter with the ghost of his father stands in stark contrast to Krug's with David or Bloom's with Rudy and simultaneously produces vastly different results than Hamlet's meeting with the ghost of the king. Some shared details between the various scenes deserve special note. Nabokov's "anthropomorphic deity" at the end of *Bend Sinister* wields an "inclined beam of pale light" to deliver "instantaneous madness" to the protagonist, while in *The Gift* the narrator comments how "a light broke through" (*prorvalsia svet*) during Fyodor's reunion with his father, making him feel at ease.[119] This light, then, is associated with clarity of mind: Krug may go mad, but he understands that he is only a creation of a greater consciousness beyond his world; Fyodor at long last feels reconciled with his father's avatar, which he had crafted since his disappearance, and with his father's indissoluble true memory. Hamlet and Krug are set on a destructive path, emblematic of their own tendencies, due to their respective ghostly encounters. Following his dream, Fyodor, on the contrary, discovers a unity in the world he had had trouble discerning previously: "Pondering now fate's methods . . . he finally found a certain thread, a hidden spirit, a chess idea for his as yet hardly planned 'novel.'"[120] Stephen, like Bloom, is constantly bombarded with reminders of the past that shake him: his mother's corpse, English dominion in the form of Haines's patronage, and the very weight of literary history. In particular, May Dedalus's sepulchral appearance in "Circe" serves as a vivid inversion of Fyodor's experience with his father's ghost. The specters of the past in Joyce's novel disconcert their witnesses. They emphasize a disconnect between past and present that only Fyodor manages to overcome. Krug, too, is haunted by memories of his wife and a past now lost. Nabokov's young hero, though, ultimately meets the past—in the guise of his dead father—unswervingly. In doing so, he takes on the mantle of the artist-son-creator in a manner that tacitly combats Stephen's practice in *Ulysses* with its acceptance of the father.

Émigré Lessons

Nabokov's exchange with Joyce lasted many years and covered vast ground in his letters. It began before Nabokov's turn to English and his impulse to insert himself into that literary tradition. Much more so than the other four subjects of the present study, Nabokov competed with Joyce. This rivalry arose early in his career when he began to define himself against other writers of various eras. By inscribing Joyce (and in particular *Ulysses*) into the pantheon of literary history and simultaneously revising his predecessor's techniques to fit his own particular worldview, Nabokov came to define his art in similarly triumphant terms.

His exchanges with Joyce also served as a means to shape Nabokov's own dialogic position on various subjects: literary interpretation, the development of the artist-god trope, and father-son relations, a theme of utmost importance to Nabokov in no small part because of his personal biography. He very much wished to counter ideas that became common currency in the modernist age, a time when sons were severing ties to their fathers and, as Eliot Borenstein writes, "when biology, like all nature, was a frontier to be conquered, an elemental force to be reined in."[121] This topic was no less contentious in the thirties, when Nabokov composed *The Gift*. To Nabokov, who as a young man had lost not only his father but also his homeland and direct ties to his culture, such a pursuit rang false. To abandon his father's memory would have been tantamount to the betrayal of a cultural heritage that had nurtured his artistic development. In much the same way, Fyodor is free to choose a new literary, affilial father to replace the filial one, as Stephen is, but he refuses to do so. He possesses the talent to transmogrify Pushkin's or Shakespeare's legacies, again as Stephen and Krug do, but he respects the inviolability of those figures whom he considers his forefathers, whether biological or not. Finally, in his encounter with the ghost of the past, he overcomes his limitations, while Krug unravels and Stephen remains in a struggle with himself and with history.

Even if Nabokov's proposed translation of *Ulysses* came to naught, his *Gift* might be considered a transposition of Joyce's book. Some aspects of *Ulysses* find their mirror image: Stephen wishes to go back into exile in Europe, for instance, while Fyodor laments the loss of his homeland. Other aspects of *Ulysses*—the hero's aesthetic theories, representative motifs, the fascination with paternity, legal and otherwise—come through in less altered forms. Still, any translation involves the inevitable shedding of at least some of the source text's domestic features. Nabokov's *Ulysses* delights in the process of revising a predecessor's texts for its own context—that of Russian emigration in Berlin. Like Joyce's text, it similarly chronicles the growth of a young artist who finally begins to understand his path, but the Russian *Ulysses* speaks to the demands—cultural, historical, personal—placed on its author. It cannot be a translation more typically faithful to the original. Instead, Nabokov delivers to readers the spirit of *Ulysses*, a protean work that refuses to be neatly defined and interpreted.

In all these ways, Nabokov actively, enthusiastically, and regularly engaged Joyce's ideas. Despite what Nabokov would have his readers believe and to his credit, much of what he *learned* from his Irish contemporary came in the form of what *not to do*. The Joycean lessons in *The Gift* and *Bend Sinister* demonstrate Nabokov's ability to transform others' creations into something worthy of the appellation Nabokovian. His hero Fyodor may be viewed in this light as a confident reply to Stephen, the anti-paternal artist. Like Olesha, Nabokov could only respond to Joyce in a manner representative of his circumstances. Unlike his Soviet coeval, Nabokov was able to elect (or disavow) a heritage freely in emigration. He did, in fact, gradually associate himself with the Anglophone literary tradition more and more as the years passed. However, the burdens of the past weighed heavy, as they would soon do on Andrei Bitov and Sasha Sokolov. The responsibility to preserve an endangered culture drove many of Nabokov's actions, including his portrayal of Fyodor Godunov-Cherdyntsev as the living embodiment of artistic ideas opposed to those championed by Dedalus.

CHAPTER 3

Andrei Bitov

In Search of Lost Fathers

> What does he need it for?? A souvenir? Found himself
> a Joyce! That puffed-up, unreadable Irishman
> particularly irritated Urbino. Yes, indeed! Joyce himself
> stole the razor!
>
> —Andrei Bitov, *The Symmetry Teacher*

Back in the Soviet Union of the late 1930s and
1940s, Joyce had become anathema to the state and, thus, a topic broached
only in negative terms. Neil Cornwell, in his history of critical responses to
Joyce, notes that a series of articles produced in 1937 by Rashel Miller-
Budnitskaya and Abel Startsev marked the steep decline of Joyce criticism
until Stalin's death nearly twenty years later.[1] A notable exception, though one
that aligns with general critical trends, is Andrei Platonov's (1899–1951) review
of Karel Čapek's *The War with the Newts* (1936). In this short piece, Platonov
argues that Joyce and Proust contributed to the "liquidation of humanity" by
treating life and their characters as if they were atoms in an experiment.[2] In
other words, Joyce allegedly denied the positivist worldview propagated by the
Soviet machine and partook in formalist experimentation at odds with Socialist Realism. These two claims, of course, were not particularly original by this
point. Other publications that referred to Joyce were likewise hostile or extremely cautious. Startsev's obituary of Joyce in 1941, for instance, acknowledged his position in world literature but maligned *Finnegans Wake* as a
complete artistic failure.[3]

And then the critics fell silent. Following the many attacks on Joyce in the
early to mid-1930s, the rise of high Stalinism, and increasingly stringent proclamations regarding the role of literature in Soviet society, Joyce largely disappeared from the public sphere in Russia until roughly 1955.[4] Still, some

continued to access Joyce in the intervening years. The poet Anna Akhmatova (1889–1966), who herself faced extreme repression and personal loss during this time, recalls having read *Ulysses* jointly with fellow Acmeist Osip Mandelstam (1891–1938) in 1937, she in the original and he in German translation.[5] Lidia Chukovskaya's (1907–1996) memoirs about Akhmatova, her close friend and confidant, contain several more conversations regarding Joyce: "I read *Ulysses* last winter," Akhmatova reported to Chukovskaya in February 1939. "I read it four times before I defeated it. A remarkable book."[6] A year and a half later, the poet had apparently read it twice more, and only afterward did everything become clear to her. In 1941, Chukovskaya shared *Dubliners* with Akhmatova. The poet initially found the collection weak, though she was fascinated with how Joyce reused characters and themes in *Ulysses*. This, Akhmatova felt, constituted exactly the same technique she was developing in her highly complex chronicle of her era, *Poem without a Hero* (1940–62). It also stands to note that she quotes *Ulysses* in a redacted epigraph to her poetic cycle *Requiem* (1935–61): "You cannot leave your mother an orphan."[7] In short, Akhmatova's statements show that Joyce continued to seep into the Russian cultural consciousness and into works written for the drawer in these Soviet twilight years. A taboo, an artifact from a quickly fading era, and, most dangerously, an enemy to state-endorsed culture, Joyce also quickly became a symbol of an alternative path for writers who sought means of expression beyond the tenets of Socialist Realism.

These developments bring us to the postwar, post-Stalin period. With the relaxed strictures of Nikita Khrushchev's Thaw, it once more became permissible to mention Joyce's name and even to study his work. During this period (1956–68) when repressions and censorship were relaxed, even though the same kinds of de rigueur attacks persisted, the importance of recognizing Joyce as a forerunner of European Modernism and, thus, of providing a somewhat balanced perspective became more common.[8]

Points of Contact

At this stage, Andrei Bitov comes into the picture. Born in 1937, Bitov began writing in the mid-1950s while studying in the Leningrad Mining Institute's Geology Prospecting Department. He found himself part of the generation of writers that most directly benefited from the Thaw, as certain forbidden Russian classics and Western modernists became more readily, if not widely, available. Joyce, Ernest Hemingway, and the others who arrived late to Russia received a welcome reception and quickly found their places among writers of Bitov's generation whose works became suffused with a complex of influences. While it would take many more years for new translations of Joyce to be published again in the USSR and for the Irish writer to be integrated fully, Bitov, who knew English, eagerly took in all these new possibilities whether through direct or indirect means.[9]

The author Viktor Erofeev (1947–), whose *Russian Beauty* (1982), incidentally, has been compared to *Ulysses*, writes in a review of *Pushkin House* that "it is impossible to enter the same novel twice. A novel flows though time and the reader's perception."[10] He describes the experience of a single imagined reader; however, his point pertains to the broader changes in values and realities that generations undergo in any country. This framework helps explain each writer's individual choices, for example, the types of allusions made and his reading and selection of particular themes from Joyce. Olesha, finding himself amid the turbulent changes of the early Soviet era, felt drawn to Joyce's project in *Ulysses*, yet considered this goal unreachable. He could not overcome the historical circumstances that prevented him from taking on another literary father figure and rearranging his identity. History, by contrast, freed Nabokov; inspired by the tragedies of his exile, his father's death, and his departure from Russian culture, he used a modified Joycean model to reconstruct his identity, the past, and literature itself, recouping all he had lost through the magic of metaphor.

Thus, what was authentic and spoke to older Russian writers, as well as Joyce, for that matter, is significantly different for Bitov and later authors like him. This fact can of course be explained in terms of changing historical and cultural realities. Late to the modernist experiment, he understood that Soviet policies disrupted literature's natural progression. "It wasn't important if these books were written and published twenty, thirty years ago—they were perceived now," he remarks in the extensive commentary that he includes at the end of *Pushkin House*, referring to the influx of texts that appeared after Stalin's death in 1953: "Remarque's *Three Comrades* was a phenomenon of 1956, not 1930. The 'Lost Generation,' which had burst forth with its novels in 1929, was us."[11] Moreover, the weight of literary history places a burden on Bitov as a mid-twentieth-century writer. His texts repeatedly illustrate the psychological struggle inherent in such an experience. In this way, the goals that Joyce and Nabokov could set for themselves—electing a literary forefather, restructuring a literary heritage in one's image, and competing with the past to overcome it—are no longer really applicable to Bitov's situation. He instead takes on Joyce, his texts, and his ideas in *Pushkin House* (1964–71) as part of his efforts to discover a means out of his perceived historical belatedness—a dilemma central to his generation.

Whereas critics have repeatedly noted the connections between Nabokov's and Joyce's fiction, relatively scant attention has been placed on the role of Joyce in Bitov's work. Ann Komaromi remarked as late as 2005: "The importance of the respective cityscapes . . . serves as an obvious point of comparison between [*Pushkin House*] and *Ulysses*, a work Modest Platonovich dangles in front of Lyova, although I have not encountered extended consideration of the parallels."[12] This fact is puzzling given the various explicit references to Joyce throughout Bitov's writings, not to mention the implicit ones.[13]

In a novel infused so systematically with various traces of Russian literature, it would be easy to downplay the presence of Western sources. If *Pushkin House* is the museum-novel its narrator claims, it is certainly not without its foreign borrowings, such as the explicitly referenced Hemingway and Alexandre Dumas.[14] While the allusions to Russian literature, whether classical or contemporary, inform much of Bitov's thematics, Western writers, including Joyce among the foremost, contribute a great deal, too. Within *Pushkin House* at least, intertextuality frequently serves as a way for the author to work through his own position in Russian literature and, concurrently, Russian literature's position on the world stage.

Bitov explicitly addresses the issue of influence throughout his commentary to *Pushkin House*. Written after the novel proper and initially intended to extend the conversation between character and author begun at the end of *Pushkin House*, Bitov's commentary provides page-by-page notes on the realia of the life of its hero, Leva, as well as extraliterary and metaliterary topics. At one point Bitov announces, seemingly with tongue firmly in cheek, that Pierre Benoit was the only writer who had a "direct influence" on him, that he remains "exceptionally sensitive and bluntly honest" on this subject, and that he concedes to everything that must be admitted.[15] Soon after, though, before discussing Proust, Dostoevsky, and Nabokov, he proclaims, "It would be foolish to deny influences," thus taking a different approach than Nabokov himself.[16] What bothers him are accusations of "direct imitation."[17] This distinction is crucial when discussing Joyce's place in *Pushkin House*. Bitov certainly does not follow Joyce in terms of style or language, unlike Sasha Sokolov and Mikhail Shishkin. Instead, Bitov introduces and manipulates themes, characterization, devices, images, and ideas adapted from Joyce for other purposes.

Bitov, in his commentary, develops a fascinating and complex understanding of belatedness (and paternity) that connects directly to his reading of the Irish writer. He says that he "realizes perfectly that secondariness [*vtorichnost'*] is not simple repetition, that it's possible to be secondary and not know that you're repeating, that an influence can be caught even from the air, not only from a book you have read."[18] Bitov expressed a similar view in an interview with Vitaly Amursky in which he described how young Leningrad writers underwent a "self-education," when they would catch "out of the air" or "by chance" a "bit of culture, a means, a method."[19] For these reasons, and because literature is "neither a sport nor a science," writes Bitov in *Pushkin House*'s commentary, two different authors can strive toward very similar goals without realizing it.[20] Bitov also writes that "geniuses as a rule have not invented new things but *synthesized* what was accumulated until their time."[21] If it seems that Bitov protests too much, his statements certainly do reflect an anxiety stemming from literary history's amassed weight. Bitov cannot be the first to describe the tragedy of father-son conflict or the search for an alternative father. Nonetheless, what he contributes to this theme builds on what has come before—Ivan Turgenev (1818–1883), Nabokov, Joyce—and ultimately establishes a new line of thought. If he is influenced by Joyce or if an idea from the "air" entered his fiction, he simultaneously transforms these elements into something new by recombining them and contributing his own post-Stalin, post-Thaw, and post-historical experience to the tradition.

As chapter 1 illustrated, Joyce enjoyed ubiquity in literary circles of the 1920s during Olesha's time, and it would seem the same situation pertained in the 1960s and 1970s even if his books were not yet freely available. In his interview with Amursky, Bitov relates that his generation's familiarity with literature from the 1920s arrived in a roundabout manner: "For example, I know now that I perceived Joyce's existence through translations of S[herwood] Anderson, that is, indirectly."[22] This not uncommon experience resulted in Bitov becoming aware of authors, at least initially, because of both the excitement that surrounded their names and their impact on others. Discussions of texts and piecemeal access to them encouraged his generation to discover new possibilities in writing.

This process of delayed familiarization aligns with Bitov's understanding of influences as something synthesized, transitory, and occasionally indirect. Suddenly exposed to an aerial influence, the traces of an author on everyone's lips, Bitov would eventually adopt similar ideas, refashioning them through the creative act. His novel *Pushkin House*, therefore, represents a disorientating amalgamation of sources. The theoretician I. P. Smirnov, in an interview with Stanislav Savitsky, defines *Pushkin House* as not only "an intertextual novel, but a novel about intertextuality."[23] Indeed, *Pushkin House* can easily be read as a book about how texts are composed. A complex of foreign—in both senses of the word—elements makes up *Pushkin House*'s very architecture. Joyce contributes to this novel a group of themes and images that Bitov ably manipulates in his exchange with his Irish predecessor. For instance, Bitov explained to Savitsky that the idea of a "hypernovel" came to him in the 1960s when he heard, even if only "by hearsay," about the Western modernist experience: "For example, about *Ulysses*. I understood that it's possible to describe a single day, . . . that a new psychologism exists, a new antihero."[24] These newly imported narrative techniques and devices drawn from writers including Joyce would allow Bitov to shake the foundations of Russian literature.

On the subject of the parallels between Joyce's work and his own, Bitov remains somewhat coy. In the 1994 essay "Three Plus One: On the 150th Anniversary of *The Three Musketeers*," he describes his experience as a graduate student at the Gorky Institute of World Literature. Having chosen to write a paper titled "On Dumas's Intellectualism," Bitov foolishly considered his work pioneering: "That's what I thought, already having completed my first postmodern, according to contemporary scholars, novel and finding myself not reading Joyce . . . [but] reading the novel *The Forty-Five [Guardsmen]*."[25] He goes on to say that he cleverly observed modernist tendencies in Dumas. He suggests that, contrary to what would be expected, he had moved *beyond* Joyce by burrowing further into the past, into Dumas's era, and finding some of Modernism's roots there.[26]

For this to be the case, of course, Bitov must have been familiar with Joyce to some degree, and his literary education seems to have played a role in this process. Established figures such as the well-known critic Lidia Ginzburg (1902–1990), one of his mentors, and Mikhail Slonimsky (1897–1972), a writer and former member of the literary group the Serapion Brothers, invited Bitov and other young writers to their homes and exposed them to new ideas and authors.[27] Ginzburg, who wrote on Joyce on several occasions, would likely have discussed such a major twentieth-century figure with her disciple. The commentary to *Pushkin House* provides tangential evidence of such a possibility: "L. Ya. Ginzburg in a conversation led the author [Bitov] to these considerations regarding a comparison of L. Tolstoy and Proust."[28] It seems unlikely that Ginzburg's views on Joyce would not have appeared in their conversations, particularly as Joyce's name was frequently mentioned alongside Proust's.[29]

Bitov also writes that, among his contemporaries, Sergei Volf "could effortlessly understand how Joyce wrote" and led him to "guess who Proust and Joyce were by one of his intonations."[30] Bitov continues: "I will write a story, and [my friend] Iasha Vinkovetsky will read it and say, 'That was in Olesha.' Or 'That's Sherwood Anderson.' I read Sherwood Anderson; I like him, although I don't have a clue that I receive Joyce through him. Thus some information came through all the time."[31] Even if by paradoxical means, hearsay, or filtered channels, Joyce became a significant presence in Bitov's literary universe.

Bitov provides some further insight into his knowledge of Joyce directly in *Pushkin House*. At the beginning of his mini-essay on influences, he states,

"The author doesn't know French, and he hasn't read or seen *Finnegans Wake* (he's not alone)."[32] Of course, the elephant that remains firmly entrenched in the room is *Ulysses*. With all the other obvious, even explicit, references to *Ulysses* in *Pushkin House*, it seems evident that the author *had* seen and likely *had* read Joyce's most famous novel. Bitov knew it at least well enough to provide versions and variants of many of Joyce's themes and images throughout his own book. Through the responsible comparative readings that follow in this chapter, it becomes clearer how the combination of Bitov's circle and the accumulated effect of these various overt and covert allusions suggests a major response to Joyce.

Bitov Reading Joyce

Pushkin House tells the story of a young Soviet academic, Leva Odoevtsev, from multiple points of view. That is, the focus remains on Leva and his experiences, but after devoting the first third of the book to his early years and his relationship with his family, including a visit to his recently rehabilitated grandfather, Bitov turns the narrative back on itself, revisiting moments in Leva's life but now focusing on his peers and girlfriends. Finally, in the third main part, Bitov addresses Leva's time working at the Institute of Russian Literature, a research center based in St. Petersburg known familiarly as Pushkin House. The effect is dizzying—a kind of Cubist kaleidoscope that allows readers to see Bitov's protagonist from different angles and yet asks them to piece together some kind of cohesive picture of the hero. The ending is no less surprising, as Leva dies in a duel with his frenemy Mitishatev over the honor of Russia's greatest poet, the eponymous Alexander Pushkin. Pages later, though, he is apparently resurrected in an acknowledgment of the flexibility of fiction's artifice. Bitov further enhances this effect by incorporating numerous chapters that provide alternative versions of the events just depicted ("Version and Variant"), appendixes that detail the writings of Leva and his grandfather, and a "commentary" to the novel written by Bitov himself.

The narrative thrust of the novel's first part ("Fathers and Children"), and much of the third ("The Poor Horseman"), deals with Leva's struggle to come to terms with his personal lineage and with Russia's past. This feature of *Pushkin House* naturally recalls Stephen's own experience in *Ulysses*. As Leva entertains elaborate concepts regarding his parentage, he also develops similar ones in his critical writings on Russian poets, much as Stephen does with Shakespeare. For all these reasons, the intertextual links between *Pushkin House* and *Ulysses* merit a more thorough critical investigation.

Ellen Chances defines one of Bitov's primary goals as follows: "Bitov . . . plots the process whereby he, as a writer, is breaking away from the authorities of previous literature that, through Bitov's own consciousness of their superiority, must have a deleterious effect upon his own individual creative, original gifts. He must solve Zeno's paradox by refusing to be in the race. *Pushkin House* is the story of his revolution, his rebellion against his 'fathers,' and his ultimate stepping away from that rebellion."[33] The connections to Joyce function as part of this learning process for both author and character. By deploying many different allusions to Joyce, Bitov develops a literary exchange that directly interacts with Joyce's ideas and illuminates his own responses more clearly through contrasts. The Joycean intertext in *Pushkin House* makes up a single layer of a very complex work, but it remains a critical one that spotlights the sources of Bitov's anxiety of influence and Leva's character arc. The reader witnesses Leva, at one level, attempt to restructure his past and falter under the pressures of historical reality. At a higher level, the author-narrator—A.B., Bitov's stand-in—escapes from the version of Zeno's paradox that plagues him in part because of Joyce's existence. Leva struggles with the phantoms of his culture's past and his ties to his family, while, in what might be termed a Russian response to Harold Bloom, the author-narrator realizes he need not raze the monuments of the past to achieve his own greatness. Nor does he need to equate himself with them, a task Leva pursues single-mindedly.[34] Bitov's sense of belatedness and the aesthetic hierarchies championed by his predecessors drive much of this anxiety throughout *Pushkin House*; it informs Leva's project and the author-narrator's deconstruction of the plot.

Leva's attempts to understand his personal identity run parallel with the author's (and text's) efforts to find his (and its) place in history. Mark Lipovetsky, one of the leading critics on contemporary Russian literature, writes that Bitov's generation of writers grew out of "two contradictory tendencies": "On the one hand, there was the need to return to modernism, to use the aesthetic arsenal of the classics. . . . On the other hand, there was the gradual recognition of the impossibility of 'restoring' modernism after decades of totalitarian aesthetics."[35] Bitov's project—an escape from the nightmare of literary history—embodies the desire to recoup the modernist past while coming to terms with the fact that this goal is impossible given the reign of Soviet power. In his (and Leva's) attempts to once again access nineteenth-century Russian culture and the modernist era (Formalism, Alexander Blok, and so on), he runs up against a dead-end for a number of reasons. Given the immense gap between the development of Western letters and Russian writers' deprivation of full access to the related innovations, there is no way Bitov can read Joyce the way even a contemporary in Ireland or Switzerland would read him in the mid-1960s. His sense of cultural-historical development has been too warped for him to do so.

The causes for such distortions are manifold. For one, Bitov began writing his novel in 1964, that is, well into the Thaw (roughly 1956–68). This period, which was named after Ilya Ehrenburg's eponymous novel of 1954 that drew attention to the Great Purge and other atrocities, witnessed immense changes in Soviet society, culture, and politics. After Stalin's death in 1953 and Khrushchev's "secret speech" at the Twentieth Congress of the Communist Party, where the new Soviet leader denounced Stalin's cult of personality, authorities began to institute a number of liberal reforms, including cultural exchanges that permitted Russian writers to access previously forbidden texts, both native and foreign. It was not a complete overturning of policy—and communist propaganda ramped up at the same time—but it led to a serious reassessment of the past, not unlike what was seen in the West. "These were also years when both Soviets and Western Europeans sought to place their time in a long-term historical perspective," write Denis Kozlov and Eleonory Gilburd. "After the attack on Stalin had threatened to de-legitimate most if not all of Soviet history, many people increasingly looked for new historical foundations that could give meaning to their own and the country's existence."[36] In practice, this meant that both conservative thinkers and the new liberal-leaning intelligentsia, each for their own purposes, sought out predecessors who had been removed from collective memory. Many of these names were drawn from the 1920s, though some also reached further back. In other words, even as people (and not only writers) subsisted in expectation of immense coming changes—the spring that follows the thaw—they paradoxically turned their gaze backward for inspiration.

The problem, as Stephen V. Bittner writes, was that "the pre-Stalinist past was not always retrievable. . . . Stalinism was too transformative for it to be otherwise. . . . [N]ot everyone was able to recover what they found."[37] Bitov's novel gives voice to this dilemma and draws out its implications. He saw that such a reliance on the past, whether it take the form of Joyce's Modernism or NEP policies, would only limit his generation's development. Having lived through the rupture of the 1930s, the *shestidesiatniki*—those born between 1925 and 1945 who came of age in the 1960s—could not access even recent history in an authentic way. Bitov would read Joyce's *Ulysses* as a literary cornerstone that will forever remain out of reach due to the temporal rift between Soviet Russia and the West. *Pushkin House* epitomizes this struggle to make sense of a lost heritage.[38] Instead of being adopted wholesale without any critical distance, pieces of past culture enter the narrative in various forms—chapter headings, copious allusions, and so forth—but are transformed within this context. The result is a new type of fiction and a novel style, one that remains *aware* of the past even as it treats the present moment on its own terms without a constant glance backward. John Barth, in the essay "The Literature of Replenishment," puts this same conflict in related terms: "My ideal postmodernist author neither merely repudiates nor merely imitates either his twentieth-century modernist parents or his nineteenth-century premodernist grandparents. He has the first half of our century under his belt, but not on his back."[39]

It is easy for a U.S. writer to express such an idea (and to follow through with it in his art). It is quite another matter for a Soviet author. Nevertheless, the Joycean subtext in *Pushkin House* emphasizes this very process of coming to terms with the past's achievements and the possibility of progress. *Pushkin House* repeatedly modifies elements from *Ulysses*, a high modernist text; all the while Bitov's distrust of stable cultural hierarchies challenges the Joycean model, as he generates a new one for emulation. Through *Pushkin House*'s various allusions to *Ulysses*, Leva's Dedalus-like endeavor to locate a literary and filial father breaks down as gaps in the historical narrative distort his perspective.

Choosing a Location

While a comparative reading of *Pushkin House* and *Ulysses* will illuminate how they overlap in theme, characterization, and images, the spaces where the two novels take place likewise speak to Bitov's intertextual project. The cityscapes serve as fruitful points of comparison. While Bitov certainly draws on the Petersburg Text tradition—the idea that works set in St. Petersburg/Leningrad share a significant number of tropes, images, themes, and so on, and remain in dialogue with each other over the centuries—some noteworthy Joycean tendencies can be observed as well.[40] The novels' respective cities and, by extension, their nations embody Leva's and Stephen's desires, fears, and anxieties related to their lineages.

In the "Eumaeus" episode, Stephen and Bloom sit in a cabman's shelter, drinking coffee and discussing various topics, among them the latter's socialist vision for Ireland. After Bloom explains that Stephen could work as a poet in his utopian state, since both "the brain and the brawn" will "belong to Ireland," the young writer takes offense:

—You suspect, Stephen retorted with a sort of a half laugh, that I may
    be important because I belong to the *faubourg Saint Patrice* called
    Ireland for short.
—I would go a step farther, Mr Bloom insinuated.
—But I suspect, Stephen interrupted, that Ireland must be important
    because it belongs to me.[41]

Stephen implies with his comments that his writing will transform Ireland, not the other way around. He proposes that whatever he eventually writes about Dublin will come to be considered more real than the actual city. Both country and former acquaintances will then be at his beck and call.[42] (Dublin, of course, came to be permanently associated with Joyce's name.)

This concern with the city as a point of inspiration also fascinates Bitov. Speaking in an interview about himself and his family's long history in St. Petersburg, he said, "[The city] is the main influence there is in me."[43] Perhaps partly for this perceived power of Petersburg over the writer, Leva's relationship to his city is the opposite of Stephen's in *Ulysses*. Although Bitov would eventually receive permission to go on work trips abroad (that is, within the Soviet Union), he lacked the freedom to wander that became second nature to Joyce. It is worth keeping in mind that Bitov would read *Ulysses* in this light, as a reminder that the world was much larger, and made bigger by the Thaw, but as yet inaccessible in its totality to him. The cityscape and, by extension, the imposing presence of a country that cannot "belong" to Leva constantly remind him of his secondary nature. As the author-narrator describes it in a footnote, "*Russian literature and Petersburg (Leningrad) and Russia are all, one way or another, PUSHKIN HOUSE without its curly-haired resident* [Pushkin]."[44] This symbol ties everything together: literature, city, and state. Leva feels that he can only be a copy or, at best, a descendent, never an innovator in his own right, whether as a reader or a writer. He therefore believes that Russia, which is equivalent to Leningrad and Russian literature, can never belong to him.

This inability first becomes evident when Leva realizes that he does not understand the city in its totality (unlike Stephen): "With surprise he caught himself thinking that very likely he hadn't left the old city once in his entire life; he *lived* in that museum, not one of his daily routes lay beyond the limits of the museum avenue-corridors and hall-squares."[45] To extend the metaphor, Leva finds himself to be nothing more than an exhibit on display in the city-museum; he lacks the sense of control, confidence, and knowledge that allow Stephen to proclaim dominion over Dublin, Ireland, and Irish literature. Instead, his scope remains partial, while Stephen roams across his city and observes its expanses. The roots of Leva's problems here lie in the turmoil within his family (that is, generational inheritances) as it relates to his surroundings. Stephen's experience features all of these factors as well; however, Joyce's protagonist wills himself to power, while Leva permits himself to be blinded.

Indeed, Bitov's and Joyce's books feature a connection between an urban environment and familial troubles. Peter I. Barta writes that protagonists in the modernist city novel experience "personal displacement" due to an "inability to turn the city into a protective place, the metaphorical 'home,' without which human well-being is inconceivable."[46] At the same time, the city space couples itself with the fear of family histories that plagues the young heroes. Allowing for some differences, this describes both Stephen's and Leva's situations. Difficulties at home produce an uncertainty in the two heroes that forces them to confront the surrounding environs. Stephen returns to Dublin from Paris only after receiving an urgent telegram: "Nother dying come home father."[47] Joyce puns "mother" with "another" and "nother." The mistake suggests a negation of Stephen's mother as well as feelings of estrangement, resentment, and guilt related to her death, as he refused to pray at her bedside. Here, as elsewhere, for Stephen the general idea of "home"—Dublin, Ireland, his fatherland—becomes entwined with that of death in many senses: literal, figurative, spiritual. Connected as it is to this stark reminder of his deceased mother, the home he has quit forces Stephen to face his own mortality. This confrontation, in part, leads Stephen to avoid his father's house: "I will not sleep here [the Martello tower] tonight. Home also I cannot go."[48] Joyce develops the family-home-death association in other oblique ways. For example, both Bloom and Molly compare Stephen to a stray dog: "The crux was it was a bit risky to bring him home as eventualities might possibly ensue . . . and spoil the hash altogether as on the night [Bloom] misguidedly brought home a dog (breed unknown) with a lame paw" and "like the night he walked home with a dog if you please that might have been mad especially Simon Dedalus son his father such a criticiser."[49] To recall what chapter 2 emphasized, Stephen associates dogs with death, drowning, and servitude. Molly, then, makes explicit the connection between Stephen; his father, Simon Dedalus; dogs; and an unhappy home. After inspecting Stephen's unconscious body with Bloom in "Circe," Corny Kelleher says, "Well, I'll shove along. . . . I've a rendezvous in the morning. Burying the *dead*. Safe *home!*"[50] Stephen will thereafter depart to Bloom's home—a symbolic death for the rebellious son and artist should he choose to remain there. However, Stephen is just as unwilling to accept Bloom's invitation to remain because of both the presence of a substitute father figure and the desire to find his way out from the home that is Ireland. Returning to *any* home means accepting his father's supremacy, a thought that Stephen cannot tolerate and that torments Leva, too.

Instead, in his speech at the National Library, Stephen lists the "note of . . . banishment from home" as one of the Bard's primary themes and takes on his elected predecessor's banishment for himself.[51] Self-exile, he believes, will lead to triumph over the space that only drowns his creative promise.[52] Again, Stephen, like Leva after him, understands the concept of home quite broadly: it represents a culture, a history, and, most pressingly, a family. In terms of plot, Stephen's struggle against his family binds him to stagnation and death and forces him to confront the city throughout the novel, particularly in its open-ended conclusion.

In *Pushkin House*, the idea of a corrupted home troubles Leva just as much, if not more. Instead of death, however, an unexpected resurrection produces Leva's feelings of resentment and entrapment. On learning that his grandfather is still alive after spending years in Soviet labor camps, he responds with shock and, then, with anger toward his parents: "He responded childishly: he flared up, shouted, became impertinent. . . . How dare they hide it!"[53] As in *Ulysses*, the domestic space becomes infected with the concept of death, though here in an inverted form. In this way, Leva begins to recognize the control his parents, particularly his father, wield over him. Their responses, that they wished to make it "easier for him in school, so that he wouldn't talk freely," well intentioned or not, strike Leva, at least initially, as false.[54] The reality once hidden behind his grandfather's absence manifests itself just as suddenly as Joyce's name reappeared to Bitov's generation. Chances contrasts these lies—an elision of the truth—with the muteness of Modest Platonovich himself: "This is a life that is lived in muteness, in silence, when that is required by one's inner being, rather than a life that speaks out, distorting the meaning of words."[55] Whether Leva's father omits the truth or lies outright, his actions generate the same result: a corrupted view of the world (limited as it is). Thus, the son's understanding of the city and its true expanses remains obstructed, as does his knowledge of Russian culture and of his family's history. Leva, unlike Stephen, remains oblivious to this fact until his death.

For all these reasons, Leva's relationship with Leningrad remains largely submissive. His experiences mirror many of Dedalus's and reveal the latter's greater flexibility. Only after his resurrection in part 3 does Leva admit, in no uncertain terms, that he belongs to the city-cum-embodied past, not the other way around: "What a city . . . ! What a cold, brilliant joke! Unbearable! But I belong to it . . . entirely. It no longer belongs to anyone. But did it ever? How many people—and what people they were!—tried to attach it to themselves, themselves to it, and only expanded the abyss between the city and [Pushkin's hero in *The Bronze Horseman*,] Evgeny, drawing no closer to it, only receding from themselves, separating from their very selves."[56] For Leva, the weight of the past is too much to bear. If even the great poets who preceded him could not claim Petersburg for themselves, then what use is it trying himself? If the city of Leningrad (and particularly Pushkin House) represents Russian culture and history, then Leva places himself in a subservient position. As explained in the preceding chapters, Stephen argues that he can subsume the past by rewriting it through art and in his image; history may be a nightmare, but the artist can rouse himself by overcoming his forerunners and creating a new reality, therefore taking command of all that Dublin embodies. Bitov shows through Leva's story that this conception of hierarchies is no longer applicable in his time. Time had been disrupted by the Soviet cultural and political takeover. In place of rebellion, what remains for Leva instead is servitude, as links to the past have been shattered, and he suspects that he can never catch up, let alone truly understand the past.

In true Bitovian manner, we already find ourselves near the end of the novel. We must turn back to the beginning and proceed in order. Leva's various attempts at rewriting the past, as well as what Bitov accomplishes in his own right, remain to be explicated, especially as both of these efforts repeatedly draw on and refer to Joyce. Bitov's engagement with the Irish writer demonstrates how the creative individual may synthesize past sources and new energies if one only comes to terms with the experience of arriving late. Komaromi, for instance, has written eloquently about Bitov's contact with the West. She argues that in his novel, the "residents of Pushkin House look toward the West and perceive their own location."[57] According to her, the recognition of Western precedents helps define one's own place. In other words, a parallax is necessary: a combination of the native Russian perspective (first-person, as it were) and a foreign, Western (third-person) point of view on the same subject that produces another original outlook. Bitov treats his chosen modernist forefathers in like fashion.

Although Leva lacks the necessary self-awareness to free himself from the burdens of history, he is not a totally passive protagonist. If Leva's relationship with his city also speaks to much broader issues regarding belatedness and heritage, then how he approaches such topics as paternity, alternative families, and literary traditions will even more clearly illustrate how Bitov responded to *Ulysses*.

The Second Father Hypothesis: Alternative Fathers and Sons

Pushkin House is a book that wears its anxieties on its sleeve. From the beginning, questions of time and primacy beset Leva. The author-narrator gleefully describes his hero's childhood experience of reading Turgenev's classic mid-nineteenth-century novel of generational conflict, *Fathers and Children* (1862). Proud of the fact that he chose this work rather than a simpler children's story to read on his own, Leva questions some of Turgenev's choices: "Leva considered his time better than Turgenev's . . . during Turgenev's time one had to be so great, gray, beautiful, and bearded in order just to write what in our time such a little (though very gifted . . .) boy, such as Leva, masters so well, and furthermore, his own time was better in that he had been born precisely now, not then, precisely in this time Leva, so gifted at understanding everything so early, was born."[58] Leva does later develop some talent when it comes to literature, but the author-narrator's irony is palpable. Leva's confidence recalls Stephen's bold proclamations throughout *Ulysses* (as well as *A Portrait of the Artist*). Both cases, though, reveal an anxiety regarding the protagonists' place in history. Leva stresses the preeminence of his time because of his very presence, recalling the Soviet state's teleological foundations on which, it was assumed, only a glorious future could be built. This approach leads him to question the primacy of the past and, therefore, his fathers. As evidenced here, not only is Bitov referencing Joyce in his exploration of paternity, but the Joycean strand offers intriguing parallels and insights through comparative analysis.

How Leva manipulates his various paternal figures represents his most spirited attempts to rewrite time and overcome his secondary nature. Similar to Stephen with his Shakespeare theory, Leva develops a "second father hypothesis." Leva, however, goes a step further than Stephen by supposing that Nikolai Modestovich is not really his biological father. By comparison, Joyce's hero critiques the idea of paternity as a "legal fiction" and attempts to substitute his own biological father with a literary forefather (Shakespeare);[59] in doing so, he implies that the creative individual may create himself—that is, his legacy, his legend—ex nihilo. Nabokov's Fyodor Godunov-Cherdyntsev, too, elects a predecessor in Pushkin, but strictly as a means to merge the biological with the literary and to come closer to both through his art. Leva, by contrast, systematically explores the possibility that his origin has been a lie. He considers replacement father figures—Modest Platonovich, his neighbor Uncle Dickens, a colleague at the Pushkin House named Blank—as a means to challenge his personal history. (Literary predecessors play an equally important role in Leva's conception of paternity, as evidenced by his "Three Prophets" essay analyzed below).

Leva feels estranged from his father from a very early age: "It seemed to Levushka that he didn't love his father. . . . Father would appear for a minute, sit down at the table, an extra without a line, and his face as if always in shadow."[60] This schism between generations and parents parallels that of Stephen's with Simon Dedalus. As Morris Beja notes, throughout *Ulysses*, Stephen's mother acts as a "vital *presence* in his life," while his father, Simon, is "most notable as an absence."[61] This condition need not be considered a paradox as Beja suggests. Instead, the father's absence drives the two protagonists' search for a replacement. They wish their fathers to resemble idealized versions of themselves instead of the real people with real faults who unnerve them.

In *Ulysses*, Stephen mentions that "the man with [his] voice and [his] eyes" conceived him.[62] Their corporeal likeness reminds Stephen of the similarities between himself and his father that lie beyond the surface level; for example, the physical markers such as his voice and eyes are signs of an inner nature that Stephen hopes to avoid but often expresses. Olesha's Kavalerov faced the same worries, of course: "I recognized my father in myself. It was a similarity of form—no, something else: I would say sexual similarity: as if I suddenly felt my father's seed within me, in my substance."[63] Leva, by contrast, has the benefit of being *dissimilar* from Nikolai Modestovich when it comes to appearances: "Features, eyes, hair, ears—here they really had little in common."[64] Instead, symbolic indicators, such as intonations in his father's voice and gestures, what he considers the "authentic, elusive, true family resemblance," bother Leva.[65] It is not enough to look unlike his father; instead, he must also *act* differently to challenge paternity. He in fact seeks out other kinds of similarities to fuel his rebellion precisely because there does not seem to be any real likeness.

Perhaps hypocritically, Leva toys with a conception of paternity that takes physical likeness into consideration when it suits him. His father's perceived absence, as well as the revulsion that springs from it, leads Leva to imagine that Uncle Dickens, an old family friend recently returned, is actually his father. He examines a faded photograph of Uncle Dickens before a mirror and, making faces, envisions a certain resemblance.[66] This twin image—a mirror reflection and a photograph—reveals the lengths to which Leva will go to deceive himself in the search for his substitute father. When it comes to disowning resemblances between himself and Nikolai Modestovich, Leva rejects the physical. However, he uses precisely this same evidence to allegedly prove paternity in Uncle Dickens's favor. The mirror itself hints at Leva's incapability to see himself from an outsider's perspective; he cannot truly achieve this vantage point and must employ mental acrobatics to produce the desired result. In *Ulysses*, Stephen and Bloom also look into a mirror in "Circe" and experience a shared vision: *"The face of William Shakespeare, beardless, appears there, rigid in facial paralysis, crowned by the reflection of the reindeer antlered hatrack in the hall."*[67] The narratological peculiarities of this particular moment notwithstanding, Joyce, too, uses the mirror image to signal a merging of spiritual father and son (as does Olesha).[68] Do both Bloom and Stephen witness the same vision? Whose perspective is this? Is it Stephen's because he *needs* it more? Bitov significantly departs from his model, however, in deploying similar imagery but making Leva betray himself by changing the terms of his argument when convenient.

Bitov uses a similar method with reference to a by now familiar podiatric trope. Recalling both Joyce and Nabokov, along with Sokolov, as will be demonstrated in chapter 4, the author-narrator focuses on his protagonist's feet in a passage that takes place directly before his momentous meeting with his grandfather:

> A feeling of aching pity, having been conceived within Leva, did not sur-face; rather much more strongly he felt at that moment some unclear triumph over his father and here, at the threshold of the very study at whose doors since childhood he had switched to a whisper with his father, said unexpectedly loudly: "Very well, Father." His voice cut through all that uncomfortable silence and darkness and seemed to Leva himself unpleasant. Turning sharply, he stepped over the threshold; his father somehow trembled awkwardly and ran forward as if to shut the door behind Leva; his father's shadow was flung under Leva's feet, and it seemed to Leva that he stepped over his father.[69]

On the one hand, Bitov conveys Leva's ascendancy through this symbol of a life-altering footstep over the shadow of the father(-past-history). He extends this theme a few pages later when the narrator uses the same wording to re-fer to Leva's relationship with Uncle Dickens, his first potential replacement father: "And it seemed to Leva that he stepped over Uncle Dickens as well."[70] These scenes mark a dramatic change of relations. Leva tries to render for-mer relations null, and now he ostensibly steps into a new state of being.

On the other hand, Bitov carefully, if emphatically, underscores Leva's ques-tionable understanding of both situations. First, the narrative adopts Leva's perspective during these vital scenes: "it *seemed* to Leva that he stepped over his father" and "it *seemed* to Leva that he stepped over Uncle Dickens as well."[71] In a novel that deals with all types of lies and misconceptions, these narrato-logical details place great restrictions on Leva's delusions of grandeur.

Bitov introduces a similar sense of doubt through other, more symbolic means that recall Joyce's work. He challenges Leva's point of view with the image of his hero's strained feet when Leva heads to Modest Platonovich's apartment: "All his sensation became concentrated in his feet: he wore new shoes for the occasion; they pinched. His feet froze and ached, and Leva stood as if not on his own feet but on prostheses."[72] Like Stephen's borrowed shoes in *Ulysses* ("His boots are spoiling the shape of my feet. Buy a pair"), Leva's footwear both physically and mentally constricts his movement.[73] Stephen con-siders the shoes he has taken on loan a mark of his self-betrayal and his de-pendency on Buck Mulligan. Similarly, Leva's feeling that he stands upon "prostheses" emphasizes his disoriented state. He has taken on a role—that of the son who denounces his biological father—but cannot find his footing, so to speak. Even while his shoes and steps symbolize Leva's desire to challenge and move beyond his predecessors, they reveal a peculiar artificiality inherent to his project.

As long as Leva struggles to change the past by finding a new father, playing into the anxiety of historical belatedness, he will fall short of his goals. In fact, the shoe / step motif only further unites Leva and his father. One of Leva's most vivid childhood memories features his father coming home and "step[ping] into a puddle with his white shoe."[74] Leva recalls how he "stared hard at his father's shoe" and the way he cleaned it afterward.[75] Stephen and, figuratively, Leva then sport borrowed shoes. Stephen acknowledges the connection between his pinched feet, Mulligan, and the past, allowing him to begin transcending them. Leva fails to recognize the situation for what it truly is: an allusion to an earlier scene from his life that only the reader can bring together. The solution to his problem, Bitov implies, will not be found in denying one's father and, thus, participating in the system of Soviet repressions that disrupted Russian culture. Doing so only props Leva up on "prostheses."

Leva's fixation on the idea that Nikolai Modestovich might not actually be his biological father clouds his vision to other possibilities. Just before Leva abandons his "second father hypothesis," he turns to Uncle Dickens for advice and comfort. Unlike at previous visits, however, Leva finally perceives Uncle Dickens's personal suffering. His perspective expands, though only temporarily, to allow him to become aware of others' thoughts and needs: "Have I really burdened him with so much? . . . Uncle Dickens, father, grandfather— Uncle Dickens alone fulfilled them all."[76] He continues in a particularly Joycean vein: "And, really, what kind of father could he be to me . . . how could he possibly be father, son, and holy ghost?"[77] Leva comprehends that he has mixed up all his categories. Uncle Dickens has become father to Leva in relationship, grandfather in age, and ghost in miraculous return.

Stephen uses the same formulation to a different end when in "Scylla and Charybdis" he explains to his listeners how Shakespeare became father, son, and ghost all at once: "When Rutlandbaconsouthamptonshakespeare or another poet of the same name in the comedy of errors wrote *Hamlet* he was not the father of his own son merely but, being no more a son, he was and felt himself the father of all his race, the father of his own grandfather, the father of his unborn grandson who, by the same token, never was born."[78] Shakespeare, according to Stephen, played the role of the ghost in *Hamlet*, while placing a great deal of himself into the character of the son, Hamlet, and fathering his art and legacy. With these remarks Stephen refers to the Sabellian heresy, which suggests that the three figures of the Trinity make up a cohesive essence, and applies this formulation to his version of the god-artist.

Bitov in effect parodies this idea through Leva's thoughts and actions. When Leva attempts to rewrite his lineage by casting his family friend in the roles of "Uncle Dickens, father, grandfather" and "father, son, and holy ghost," he misreads the situation. This was, in fact, part of the Soviet intelligentsia's dilemma throughout the middle of the twentieth century. Suddenly faced with entire segments of culture that had been forcibly excised from official records and, often, from family accounts, Leva and his generation felt the burdens of coming too late, historically speaking. The young scholar attempts to bind the present to the past, though not in any organic way. The shock of the Thaw leads Leva to believe that both Russian culture and his family history, which are closely intertwined in the novel, were broken irrevocably. He responds by denouncing his father and attempting to find a replacement in Uncle Dickens. But while this project may be feasible for Stephen (Joyce), Leva's situation is much different. He does not appreciate that by struggling against his condition in this way, he only exacerbates the problem and casts someone else in roles that Stephen adopts for himself. What is more, he betrays his actual father in the process. Modest Platonovich, the voice of (drunken) reason in the novel, catches on to his duplicity immediately: "There's already treachery in the seed [*v semeni*]! In the seed!"[79] However, before Leva can realize that he should focus on his own development rather than the past, he develops his theories of alternative paternity.

Bitov therefore demonstrates a fundamental difference between his protagonist and Joyce's: Leva's hunt for a second father only further deprives him of any sense of resolution. He misses the opportunity to rethink his generation's situation and the sins of their fathers. Instead, Leva discovers too late that "his father was his father, that he, Leva, *also* needed a father, as it turned out one day that his father needed *his* father, Leva's grandfather, his father's father."[80] In a Bitovian move, the idea of fatherhood consumes the narrator's prose as it trips over genitive possessive constructions, emphasizing the omnipresence of fathers in Leva's life. His father cannot be replaced, but Leva *can* choose a course other than denial and emerge from the dialectical struggle to overcome the pressures of the past.

The Grandfather Hypothesis

If the connections to Joyce in the opening chapters of *Pushkin House* are largely implicit, then many of those that appear in the scenes featuring Modest Platonovich are simply overt. After a botched effort to make Uncle Dickens his father, Leva moves a step beyond Joyce's project: "Father had been born to the son. Grandfather is being born to the grandson."[81] Again, his actions imply an exclusionary gesture; Leva digs deeper into the past to cut out his father from his heritage, symbolically placing his grandfather in the image he devises for him. Leva's "grandfather hypothesis" therefore builds on Stephen's theory and suggests that by reaching back to his *father's father* he can enact a cleaner break. By raising the stakes, Leva will simultaneously circumvent Nikolai Modestovich and bring himself closer to his grandfather's generation.[82]

Coming to terms with the reality of Modest Platonovich's resurrection, Leva begins to clarify his "grandfather hypothesis." He raids the scholarly work of the former linguist to implement another model of paternity based on intellectual pursuits: "Grandfather, for Leva there remained no doubts, was undeniably a Great Man, and, in that rank, the formulation 'Grandfather and Grandson' turned out very nicely."[83] In his Shakespeare speech, Stephen hoists his experiences as an exile and the victim of usurpation on Shakespeare in a selective reading of the Bard's texts. Leva wants to accomplish the same thing in his newfound relationship with Modest Platonovich: "He and Grandfather will be together—as man and man! Grandfather will help open [the shutters within him] even wider and will explain what's there, and a completely new life will begin for Leva."[84] Joining himself to a valuable representative of the past will strengthen his self-image and will make him feel less burdened by his position as a latecomer, much as Stephen's Shakespeare project provides him with confidence. The latter, though, uses the playwright as a springboard to define himself and his (future) art, whereas the former gets caught up in the tangles of history and uses his elder's works while not creating new objects himself.

Leva almost always ensnares himself. One of Modest Platonovich's most famous claims is that Russian culture did not perish with the 1917 revolution; instead, it was forever preserved as a Sphinx-like monument. Though Modest Platonovich focuses on the Russian classics—the poets Pushkin, Blok, Lermontov, Tiutchev, Gavriil Derzhavin, Afanasy Fet, Marina Tsvetaeva—Western exemplars, including Joyce, were also dislodged in time. Throughout Leva and Modest Platonovich's conversation, several Joycean strains and a few direct allusions to *Ulysses* appear. Bitov utilizes these references throughout this frenzied section to throw into greater relief his ideas regarding connections to the originals of the past.

The most notable among these allusions occurs when Modest Platonovich explicitly refers to *Ulysses* as a novel Leva's generation "will read in 1980."[85] He selects Joyce's book as a representative example of Western modernist literature from which Leva and his generation have been cut off. This fact alone would be enough to suggest Bitov's close engagement with his Irish predecessor, but a close reading of this particular passage within the context of the entire chapter—"Father's Father. (Continued)"—introduces fascinating points of comparison related to issues such as primacy and time.

Directly before mentioning *Ulysses*, Modest Platonovich rails against Leva's generation. He suggests that Leva and those like him have created nothing themselves and, in turn, take the small protests that they are allowed, "as if by ration cards," to be a mark of their freedom.[86] They do not carve out their own real existence, instead letting the Soviet powers dictate even their illusions for them. This cycle feeds on itself. As long as "they" demarcate the limits of permissible culture, Leva's generation will forever be in their grasp. Simultaneously, Leva only contributes to the corrupted system with his limited thought and repeats existing models. In this way, Leva pursues Stephen's model of filial substitution but fails.

Ulysses stands for precisely this sort of repression in *Pushkin House*. Modest Platonovich, and Bitov behind him, mentions Joyce's novel by name, both because of its reputation and because it deals directly with Leva's aforementioned anxieties. The newly rehabilitated ex-scholar mocks his grandson: "In 1980 you'll read *Ulysses* and argue and think that you have won back this right. . . . At this point the end of the world will arrive. Imagine, the end of the world and you haven't had time to get to Joyce. Your modernity will be more permissible to Joyce than to you. The thought of your dependence is beyond reach for you. You're enviers, losers, you haven't accomplished anything, neither in the past, nor the present, nor the future."[87] *Ulysses*, then, is emblematic of this generation's inability to catch up. Leva may believe that he rebels against his father and the past, and yet without a complete understanding of modernity, as embodied by Joyce's book and the tradition it represents to the rest of the world, Leva mistakes his dependence on the system and the past for freedom and originality. Modest Platonovich prophesizes that the times will change, that Leva will be able to read *Ulysses* in a couple of decades.[88] This event, to a man of Leva's making, will signify a right earned for committed rebellion. In reality, it will only prove Leva's inherently delayed nature. As a result of the breaks in Russia's cultural history, Leva cannot exist in the past, because he can never make full sense of it; nor in the present, because he constantly directs his gaze backward; nor in the future, because he will always feel a step behind.

Modest Platonovich suggests that a radical shift in perspective is necessary for Leva. He will never catch up with Joyce, just as in Zeno's paradox Achilles will never catch the tortoise. By envying the past, Leva remains bound to the system designed by those in power to suppress him.[89] As Modest Platonovich says, Leva's "modernity will be more permissible to Joyce," meaning that the writer's persona and ideas concerning him have existed for over thirty years as a cultural force; Leva cannot come to them fresh, as if discovering *Ulysses* for the first time. "*Ulysses* [is] one of those books which is always 'always-already-read,' always seen and interpreted by other people before you begin," writes Fredric Jameson. "[It is] hard to see it afresh and impossible to read it as though those interpretations had never existed."[90] Joyce's *Ulysses*, which had amassed a great deal of meaning and interpretations by this point in post-Stalinist Russia, will define Leva's epoch as belated if he treats it as something truly novel.

Another key Joycean allusion in this section concerns the idea of sources. When Bloom turns on the faucet in "Ithaca," the narrator attempts to explain the origin of the water in an absurdly long list.[91] Within *Ulysses*, the answer, as well as the information that follows regarding what Bloom sees in water, firmly establishes Bloom's hydrophilic tendencies in contrast to Stephen's aversion to water. Simultaneously, Joyce mocks the idea of complete verisimilitude and absolute knowledge in a third-person narrator, as the passage pushes the idea of the "original" to the brink.

Modest Platonovich offers a direct rejoinder to this passage, not unlike what takes place near the end of *Envy*. In the middle of his conversation with Leva, he brings up water on two occasions. He first suggests that phenomena like gas and electricity are beyond comprehension but wonders about where water comes from: "I want it and I don't understand it and don't want to understand—that's happiness. All right. It can be explained to me, taking water as a given, that there's a spring, a pump, a tower, a pipe—plumbing. I'll understand that a man wants to explain something to me, this I'll understand. But why does it flow to *me*?"[92] Bitov, once again, builds on what Joyce has laid before him. Even if the source of water can be explained, as Joyce's catechism endeavors to do, the *reason* behind this flow of water cannot. Analogously, even if Leva reaches back into the past to find a forefather—his real father, Uncle Dickens, Modest Platonovich, Blank, even his unnamed superior at the literary institute who speaks to him in a "fatherly way [*po-ottsovski*]"—to define himself in the present, *something* remains missing.[93] Modest Platonovich argues that all efforts to find a true root source (as in the passage from Joyce) result in nothing more than nonsense, a mess of words that masks the true nature of the concept at hand. *Ulysses*'s presence in *Pushkin House* highlights the discord experienced when Leva seeks a close relationship with a paternal figure who will justify his existence.

The author-narrator notes that the break in the relations between son and grandson, Modest Platonovich's death, and ten years finally bring together father and son.[94] However, he questions what remains of Leva following these experiences at the conclusion of the first "Version and Variant" chapter:

FATHER—FATHER = LEVA (father minus father equals Leva)

GRANDFATHER—GRANDFATHER = LEVA

We transpose according to the algebraic rule to obtain a plus:

LEVA + FATHER = FATHER

LEVA + GRANDFATHER = GRANDFATHER,

but, after all:

FATHER = FATHER (father is equal to himself)

GRANDFATHER = GRANDFATHER

To what is Leva equal?

And we stand at the board in Einsteinian reverie . . .[95]

These formulations suggest that, in his quest, Leva has defined others but not *himself*. This process becomes tangible as Modest Platonovich's rambling, pages-long speech effectively pushes Leva out of the narrative. The result, once again, is that by constantly pursuing his antecedents, Leva negates his person, whereas Stephen places his own image onto that of Shakespeare. However, Leva's epoch, if not his personality, is far different than Stephen's. As the narrator states, "Time itself was Father. Father, Papa, Cult—what other synonyms are there?"[96] The idea of an omnipotent father figure embedded itself into Soviet historical and cultural fabric early on. Stalin, who goes unnamed in Bitov's novel, is of course the obvious culprit here. However, the problem is more deeply ingrained: the very concept of fatherhood became corrupted over time through shifting expectations and treachery within families and generations. This partly helps to explain why Bitov would place the various references to Joyce and *Ulysses* throughout *Pushkin House*. He adopts a Western modernist model only to subvert it, in the process showing an alternative means to self-actualization. *Why* he does so, of course, is radically different from Nabokov's motivations. The historical-cultural circumstances demand something else.

The Heroes Speak

In the section that recounts Leva's article "The Three Prophets," the author-narrator takes stock of his protagonist's relationship with Pushkin, Lermontov, and Tiutchev—the subjects of his essay and three of Russia's most prominent nineteenth-century poets. A comparative reading of Leva's "Three Prophets" and Stephen's Hamlet theory demonstrates yet another aspect of Bitov's engagement with Joyce. Both authors pause their respective novels roughly at their midway points in order to highlight these similar ideas. On the one hand, Stephen's thoughts filter into the ninth episode's narration.

Of course, they reveal his various apprehensions, but the hero manages to explain his theory in his own voice. On the other hand, Bitov's narrator relates how Leva's article has essentially been lost to the ages. A.B. tries to describe what he remembers of it. The characters' agency in these scenes differs a great deal. Stephen can defend himself against his interlocutors' responses, while Leva's perspective depends entirely on the words and whims of his creator. These differences reflect the most pertinent questions at hand: Leva's loss of control when it comes to his identity and history.

After having Buck Mulligan mock it as algebraic proof that "Hamlet's grandson is Shakespeare's grandfather and that he himself is the ghost of his own father," Joyce lets Stephen deliver his full Shakespeare theory performance in "Scylla and Charybdis."[97] The speech is not without contradictions and inconsistencies, personal bias and loose interpretation, but it reveals a great deal about its speaker's personality and state of mind. It also helps explain some of Stephen's choices throughout the novel. As Karen Lawrence remarks, "Stephen's stress on both the fictionality and power of fatherhood derives, at least in part, from his own personal situation, in particular his ambivalence toward his father."[98] The story he tells, that of Shakespeare's betrayal, is really the tale of his own isolation. Additionally, Stephen proposes that Shakespeare, "being no more a son" after his father's death, felt able to write *Hamlet* and be reborn as a father (of art) himself.[99] He implies that if he gives up his ties to his father (and Dublin), he can consequently become father to his creative legacy.

Leva's article shares many significant parallels with Stephen's speech and project. Most importantly, "The Three Prophets" is, as the narrator suggests, "not about Pushkin, not about Lermontov, and, moreover, not about Tiutchev, but about him, about Leva," much as Stephen's version of Shakespeare's life corresponds with his own experiences and sense of betrayal.[100] All major events and relationships in Leva's life show up in some form in the article's convoluted and highly personal argumentation. The coincidence that all three poets composed the poems under consideration when they were twenty-seven, the age at which Leva writes his article, for example, spurs on the young critic. Lermontov (1814–1841) was in fact twenty-six when he wrote "The Prophet" right before his death. However, Leva asserts that twenty-seven, "give or take a year," is close enough.[101]

One meaningful difference is that Stephen consciously associates himself with Shakespeare, while Leva becomes a modern-day Tiutchev. Metafictionally, Joyce also announces his status as a new Shakespeare or Homer. In *Pushkin House*, Leva idolizes Pushkin (the equivalent of Stephen-Joyce's Shakespeare), but through his article he links himself more closely with Tiutchev, the envier and unrecognized rival. Leva writes "with knowledge and passion" and without direct reference to Tiutchev about the emotions that the poet must have felt in his poetic duel with Pushkin.[102] Leva's "attempt at rapprochement with his grandfather" and his "'devaluation' of the very object of attraction" mirrors Tiutchev's relationship with Pushkin.[103] Slobodanka M. Vladiv-Glover argues that, according to Leva's article, Tiutchev craved "recognition by the Master (Pushkin) that was never granted," and, furthermore, "as he was for Tiutchev, Pushkin is also Lyova's desire."[104] It might be even more accurate to say that Tiutchev, in Leva's reading, sought not Pushkin's recognition but the *primacy* Pushkin represented that he could never possess. Following René Girard's system of triangular desire, Leva reenacts the same conflict in his article: "The mediator's prestige is imparted to the object of desire and confers upon it an illusory value."[105] Leva can comprehend Tiutchev's envy precisely because he experiences it himself. The object (primacy, recognition, prestige) eludes him, so he feels discontent in his relationship with the mediator (Tiutchev).

The author-narrator maintains that "in Tiutchev [Leva] openly hated someone (we don't know whom)."[106] The context, though, strongly suggests that because he has so closely, if unwittingly, linked himself to Tiutchev, the mystery source of Leva's hate must be *himself*. Alternatively, Leva's former classmate and perpetual rival Mitishatev would seem to be the Tiutchev to Leva's Pushkin, the plebeian to his aristocrat: "They were of the same class, but Pushkin was more aristocratic: he *had* it without thinking about where it came from; Tiutchev was already more the *raznochinets*, he *wanted* to have it, but he did not have it."[107] In spite of these relations, Leva's constant need for recognition propels him to sink to Mitishatev's level, in turn leading him to experience self-loathing. In Tiutchev, and in writing about Tiutchev, he gradually recognizes his own fate made up of betrayals and disastrous liaisons. Leva cannot admit this to himself, but through his writing he opens up his mind for closer scrutiny. Indeed, the evidence is damning: "[Tiutchev] is to blame only for . . . Leva's recognition of himself, his impartial confrontation with his own experience. . . . [H]e is to blame that, like Leva, he was born and emerged too late (each in his own time), and Leva the latecomer, having turned with his heart to another epoch, won't forgive Tiutchev his 'contemporary' existence in it."[108] In Tiutchev, Leva eventually espies his own desire to catch up with the greats of the past. He sympathizes with Tiutchev's sense of displacement; he even considers writing another article on the subject with the expressive title "The Latecomer Geniuses." His distorted sense of the historical moment compels him to place himself on the same level as Pushkin in order to justify his somehow posterior existence.

The past for Leva, unlike for Stephen, represents a barrier that cannot be surmounted. Stephen believes that he may outmaneuver time with his art and, thus, overcome any perceived deficiencies: "In the intense instant of imagination, when the mind, Shelley says, is a fading coal, that which I was is that which I am and that which in possibility I may come to be. So in the future, the sister of the past, I may see myself as I sit here now but by reflection from that which then I shall be."[109] While it may seem that the past exists outside of the artist's control, he can change it. Bitov himself has written as much: "The past is utterly defenseless against our attempts to reorganize it."[110] Joyce fully agreed as far as artists were concerned. With Stephen as his mouthpiece, he suggests that by playing ghost, father, and son all at once, and by weaving past, present, and future into a single literary object, the artist creates his eternal art, thus breaking free of any ties that bind him to history.[111] The failure to be acknowledged in his own time, whether by contemporaries or father figures, will not prevent his ultimate success. Leva, however, simply deifies the past, forcing himself into a subservient position relative to the fathers. When Leva challenges predecessors for his right to preeminence, he only ensures his sacrifice in the elevation of their names.

The Tormentor and the Would-Be Savior

In the third and final part of *Pushkin House* proper, "The Poor Horseman," Bitov features some particularly rich Joycean character and situation rhymes. This tactic recalls the one deployed by Olesha in *Envy*. There, Olesha imbues his characters Andrei Babichev, Ivan Babichev, and Nikolai Kavalerov with elements of Buck, Bloom, and Stephen to develop his argument regarding the inability of the artist to overcome the historical situation in the early Soviet Union. Likewise, this intertext in *Pushkin House* provides a background against which to read Bitov's characters.

Although the true extent of Mitishatev's role as sinister double and tempter only becomes clear late in the novel, his presence within its second part, "A Hero of Our Time," helps define a great deal of Leva's character. Introduced as no less than Leva's "friend-enemy," Mitishatev torments Leva by reminding him of his belated nature, his failed rebellions, and his exposure to treachery.[112] These patterns of behavior share a great deal with the tense relationship between Stephen and Buck in *Ulysses*.

In these two novels with so many unusual names, both rivals use their counterparts' surnames to target the respective heritages to which they may be linked. Buck says to Stephen, "The mockery of it! . . . Your absurd name, an ancient Greek!"[113] Stephen's last name indicates his connections to the Greek tradition, developed by Joyce throughout both *Portrait* and *Ulysses*. Mitishatev, too, takes up the "absurdity" of Leva's surname, Odoevtsev, as a subject for ridicule; he frequently refers to him as "Prince Odoevtsev."[114] Leva's surname is a clear reference to the Odoevskys, a family that included the writer Vladimir Fyodorovich (1803–1869) and the poet and Decembrist Alexander Ivanovich (1802–1839).[115] Leva's name suggests his status as a man out-of-time. His so-called nobility is no longer valid in the Soviet Union, even if, as Mitishatev jokes, "you're certain to find yourself next to an ancient scion" at all parties.[116] Leva's name, then, is a reminder that he belongs to a tradition over which he has no control. Moreover, it links him to a past that cannot be recouped. Stephen, by contrast, gradually uses this inheritance as a way to define himself in opposition to his perceived enemies. Leva does not achieve the perspective required to defeat this belatedness, going so far as to smirk and agree that he, too, prefers the title, playing into Mitishatev's double-edged flattery.

Where there is a Buck, though, there must be a Bloom. Bitov likewise constructs his own version of Bloom through the character of Blank. Beyond the phonetic similarity of their names, the two express a remarkably positive outlook despite being constantly derided by others. In his dramatic debate with the Citizen in "Cyclops" regarding, among other things, the Jewish people, Bloom champions "Love," that is, "the opposite of hatred," as the true essence of real life.[117] Similarly, the author-narrator claims that Blank "could not speak ill of people" and that "he spoke of life as a divine gift."[118] This optimistic perspective defines them as potential models for emulation for their adopted sons; they do not perpetuate the system of hate that they experience on a daily basis and maintain their personal dignity.

Both characters know such animosity firsthand due to their Jewish heritage. In fact, the most significant parallels between them are this shared background and their status as potential father figures for Leva and Stephen. While Joyce can devote a great many more pages to Bloom, Bitov carefully paints a clear portrait of his Jewish hero in just a few passages. This link begins with how they relate to the younger writer figures. As in *Envy*, both novels feature a kind, older man who attempts to provide moral and practical guidance to a young writer. For his part, Leva initially welcomes Blank's advances: "Leva eagerly became the person Blank wished to see in him—a person of 'breeding,' of that culture and decency which are in the blood and you cannot substitute, cannot dislodge it. . . . Leva played along, of course, but it afforded him that pleasure, as if Leva remembered something about himself, and there was some truth not yet manifested in his life. He felt natural in this role."[119] In contrast, Stephen resists the desire to "become the man," or, perhaps more accurately, the child (an alternative Rudy), Bloom wishes to see in him. Leva takes up his "role" with glee, as it affords him the opportunities to regress into his past and to be charmed by the attention of a doting elder. One would be hard-pressed to argue that either Bloom or Blank functions as a particularly negative influence; they both advocate generosity, kindness, and understanding, each in his own way. The problem, however, is that by accepting a father figure so readily, Leva renounces his right to self-fulfillment. Stephen understands this point well, which explains why he departs into the night at the end of "Ithaca" and rejects the security offered to him by Bloom, the Jewish substitute for Simon Dedalus.

Bitov introduces another crucial inversion of the Joycean model by having Leva at first accept Blank's temptation and then turn against him. The Jewish theme thus extends throughout the entire novel. One of its early formulations appears in the chapter "The Myth of Mitishatev," in which the anti-Semitic Mitishatev questions Leva about who in their grade school class was and was not Jewish. Leva finds the inquisition tedious, particularly when Mitishatev even accuses him of being Jewish, but as usual he gives into Mitishatev's foolishness. Nevertheless, Leva triumphs over his rival by bringing the Russian classics into the equation:

> "Well, and Fet? You won't deny Fet, will you?"
> "Fet was slandered."
> "Well, and Pushkin?" Leva brightened up. "What about Pushkin?"
> "What does Pushkin have to do with it?" Mitishatev shrugged. "He's a moor."
> "But do you know what a moor is? An E-thi-o-pi-an! And the Ethiopians are Semites. Pushkin's a black Semite!"[120]

This outlandish conversation has its clear counterpart in "Cyclops," where Bloom must combat the tyrannical Citizen's screed against Jews. Bloom's final blow to his enemy sounds a great deal like Leva's: "Mendelssohn was a jew and Karl Marx and Mercadante and Spinoza. And the Saviour was a jew and his father was a jew. Your God."[121] They both refer to great men of history as being exemplary models *despite*—in the eyes of their opponents—their Jewish heritage. Bloom, of course, takes this logic to the very limits by extending it to the Citizen's ("Your") God for rhetorical effect. In *Pushkin House*, the father of Russian letters replaces the Christian God in the polemic but delivers the same blow upon Mitishatev. The symbolic father prevents any possible retort as the apex and summation of primacy in these scenes where the two authors tackle questions of nationalism and anti-Semitism in their respective countries.[122]

The confrontation between Blank and Mitishatev finds its resolution in Leva's betrayal. At some point in their conversation—the chronology loses shape in the chaotic, drunken narration—Mitishatev offends Blank, who turns to Leva for support but finds none. Mitishatev continues: "You hinted that in that case I myself might turn out to be a Jew, too. . . . Right! I might. I don't know my own father after all. . . . In that case, you might turn out to be my father. . . . An original variant of *Fathers and Sons*."[123] The narrator explains that Leva seems to forget what follows, but the next time his consciousness picks up, Blank has disappeared. Only Mitishatev remains. There are two important points to be drawn from such a dramatic, yet understated exchange. First, the matter of fatherhood continues to resound in connection to the Jewish theme. Mitishatev's statements crudely expose the artificiality of Leva's relationship with Blank when Leva fails to stand up for his friend. All of Leva's relations with his many fathers are thus marked by various strains of treachery. Second, Leva's silence and tacit approval of Mitishatev's words reveal his inability to overcome his contemporary's negative influence. Leva denies his substitute father, but in a way far crueler than what Stephen does at the end of *Ulysses*, simply perpetuating a system of repression. Having come out the other side of Stalin's Terror and the process of rehabilitation that followed, Bitov's generation would naturally be more attuned to the consequences of Stephen's theory and to Joyce's book as a whole. A betrayal would sting more in Soviet Russia, and, ultimately, it would resonate with what the Soviets attempted to do in reformulating history, paternity, culture.

Modern-Day Odysseys

Although during this confrontation with Mitishatev Leva stays tightlipped, at many other times the book's characters refuse to remain silent, and the narrative similarly seems unable to conclude itself. Several chapters titled "Version and Variant" offer accounts of the same event, such as Modest Platonovich's return to Leningrad, and challenge the legitimacy of any one report with their multiplicity. This anti-mimetic technique can also be observed on a metaliterary level, as Bitov's reworking of *Ulysses* (and other texts) provides "versions and variants" of familiar events from other traditions and literatures.

Following the author-narrator's analysis of "The Three Prophets," a second version of *Ulysses*'s library scene in *Pushkin House* takes place at the titular literary institute itself. Here, the discussion of Pushkin's life held by the revelers eventually leads Leva to his final confrontation with Mitishatev. If Nabokov presents a duet between Krug and Ember in *Bend Sinister*, then Bitov develops a full chorus. This dynamic series of exchanges between the characters mimics the one between Stephen, Buck, John Eglinton, A.E., Lyster, and Best in Dublin's National Library. Moreover, it emphasizes Leva's desire to link himself with Pushkin, much as Stephen does with Shakespeare. Throughout the novel, Leva's efforts to define himself by moving between father figures culminate with his death defending Pushkin's honor.

For instance, Leva's comments about Pushkin and his wife parody Stephen's regarding Shakespeare and Anne Hathaway. The latter denounces Anne as a traitor and temptress: "If others have their will Ann hath a way. By cock, she was to blame. She put the comether on him, sweet and twentysix."[124] Leva's interlocutors make similar accusations against Natalia Pushkin, implicating her in Pushkin's death. Leva comes to her defense, arguing that no one (except perhaps him) could have understood Pushkin's genius and that Natalia was "innocent and not guilty."[125] Leva's position regarding the poet's marriage yet again shows his desire to be on equal terms with Pushkin. One of the discussants argues that all the "poetesses" of the twentieth century who idolize Pushkin "can't forgive [Natalia] only because they were born too late to correct his mistaken choice. They would have appreciated his genius!"[126] Leva feels compelled to defend Natalia, as he both envies and sympathizes with her; he wishes *he* could have been there to admire Pushkin, to protect his art, to be remembered side by side with the father of Russian poetry. Stephen, in contrast, uses Anne Hathaway as an argument for the artist's need for self-creation and independence. Bitov in this way offers a complex, inverted situation rhyme with *Ulysses* to make his point about Leva's concern with belatedness. If Leva can justify Natalia's relationship with Pushkin, then he can view his own in an even brighter light, but it is to no avail.

By constantly wishing for mutual recognition from Pushkin, obviously an impossible task, Leva places himself in a trap from which he cannot escape. Again, using a Joycean model, Bitov literalizes this process. The theme of keys plays a central role in *Ulysses* and *The Gift*.[127] Bloom finds that he has misplaced his key at the end of *Ulysses*, and Stephen turns over the one to the Martello tower in the novel's first chapter. Both events symbolize the characters' status as wanderers deprived of what they consider to be rightfully theirs. In *The Gift*, Fyodor feels confident that he "took away the keys to [Russia]" when he went into exile.[128] He believes that he will remain happy and free as long as he possesses these links to Russian literature that his talent provides him. Keys play no less a symbolic role in *Pushkin House*'s conclusion. Following Leva and Mitishatev's flight from a policeman, the former struggles to seal the door to the Pushkin House "like [an] inexperienced thie[f]."[129] His clumsy actions imply that he has locked himself into the system that binds him. Nabokov's Fyodor has been banished from Russia, but he continues to open up its vistas with the cultural touchstones-cum-keys he bore with himself into exile. Stephen supports the creative individual choosing an artistic father figure and projects his own image onto the past through art. He turns over his keys, begrudgingly to be sure, but with the knowledge that he steps into the world on his own terms. Bitov himself accomplishes a similar project by means of his novel's engagement with the West, his reading of Pushkin's literary house through other works. He, in other words, takes up the mantle of prerevolutionary Russian literature without feeling beholden to it. Leva, on the contrary, remains trapped inside the house that Pushkin built and that had been appropriated by other forces for their own purposes long before his time. He behaves like a "thief," as if he attempts to steal this repository of culture, the Pushkin House, that in fact "owns" him.[130]

Leva responds to Mitishatev's accusations of cowardice, duplicity, and dependence on his father by impulsively destroying various items from the Pushkin House museum, a violent plundering of the past. He draws the line, though, when Mitishatev breaks Pushkin's death mask. Leva's emotional response demonstrates how he cannot untangle his ties to the past, unlike Stephen, who manipulates what he finds—or even invents—in Shakespeare's life in order to shape his own destiny. Stephen does the opposite: he considers Shakespeare his forerunner, paradoxically a past model of his future glory on whom he places his image. So while Leva may take up Pushkin's visage or words, in doing so he only becomes a simulation of the past. Perhaps for these reasons, Mitishatev's bullet strikes Leva down. Modest Platonovich writes in a fragment from his essay "God Is" that the "People's Artist d'Anthès cast Pushkin from his bullet."[131] Leva faces the same fate—death by dueling pistol—in part because of his desire to emulate his father figures without transforming the experience into something new of his own creation. Leva's life throughout the novel has consisted of repetitions of previous stories and models, so why would his death be any different?

In the three epilogues that follow their duel, Bitov provides an alternative not only for Leva but for himself as a contemporary author as well. While he concedes the importance of links in history and literature in his commentary, here he speaks about the need to strike out on one's own: *"For whether our hero perished or has risen from the dead in the last line—nothing but personal taste guides the rest of the narrative—the logic of development has been exhausted, it's all gone. In fact, our whole useless attempt at a continuation is an attempt to prove to oneself that continuation is impossible; it's an attempt at literary criticism rather than literature."*[132] Read on a metaliterary level—as *Pushkin House* demands from its reader—Bitov's admission regarding the epilogues announces his intention to cut a new path in Russian literature.[133] If Leva could not avoid making serious missteps because of a desire to find and then be acknowledged by a chosen father figure, then Bitov can.

And yet, the author takes pity on his hero when he brings him back to life, hungover but among the living. Leva's resurrection is a Pyrrhic victory, though. While he cleans up the institute, Leva "perceives the full sorrow of crushed rebellion" as he repairs the damage he wrought in the institute in order to avoid punishment.[134] The events still provide Leva with valuable insight. Later, when he takes a visiting U.S. writer on a sightseeing tour, they have trouble finding the site of Pushkin's duel. A parenthetical aside in this section unites Pushkin and Modest Platonovich, two of Leva's treasured father figures: "(for Leva, the circle closed—that frosty visit to Grandfather)."[135] This sense of closure suggests that Leva finally understands the futility of chasing after the past. Seemingly tucked away, functionally absent, Russian culture's greatest monuments remain there, providing the "secret freedom" of inspiration—a phrase from a poem by Blok that Modest Platonovich dwells on—to those who identify them and in turn construct something *new*. Leva takes his inability to find the location of Pushkin's duel as a positive sign; it proves to him that the spot remains "visible only to the devoted, only to the worthy," recalling Nabokov's views on the "real" and the "plausible" Pushkin.[136] In this epilogue that only takes place after his alleged death, Leva escapes his fear of the absent father. The historical circumstances that cut him off from the past cannot be altered, nor can Leva really change his lineage. The best he can do is step away, following his grandfather's advice to let the past lie. Pushkin will forever be the absent father to Soviet-Russian writers.

Leva's Wake

Bitov makes contact with Joyce, among other Western modernists, but does not copy them outright. Instead, he develops his response to Joyce to give a more original and ultimately Russian shape to his own novel. *Ulysses*, and in particular Stephen's experience, exemplifies the project against which Bitov argues throughout *Pushkin House*. The hierarchical demarcations in culture and history that Stephen can uphold and use to his advantage no longer function within Bitov's epoch. Sven Spieker offers a useful dichotomy: the modernist (Joycean) subject is "marked by its preponderance over historical time," while the later (Bitovian) subject "searches for (its own) history without being able to find it" and "loses the modernist hegemony over the realm of history."[137] Bitov's (and Leva's) belatedness requires that he find new means of coming to terms with the past, as direct rivalry and denigration of father figures only implicates him within the system against which he rebels. His ingenious solution is the museum-novel that quotes but misreads, adopts but transforms. To wit, in an ironic footnote, Bitov writes that he considered naming *Pushkin House* "Hooligans Wake."[138] The fabric of *Pushkin House* makes a great case for calling Bitov himself a literary hooligan. In the myriad ways that Bitov experiments with Joycean motifs, recalling and inverting, echoing and subverting, he produces a fertile intertextual layer of *Pushkin House* that has heretofore remained largely understudied. This Joycean presence also makes its way into later texts such as "Pushkin's Photograph" and *The Symmetry Teacher*. In the latter, for example, the writer Urbino Vanoski accuses Joyce, a "puffed-up, unreadable Irishman," of stealing everything from him except his last novel.[139] Ironic intertextuality is Bitov's modus operandi.

Bitov turned to Joyce, among other writers, because of their shared fascination with literary lineages and the oppression caused by domineering regimes. Joyce offered his Russian counterpart—and other writers like him—an alternative option, that of the creative individual who fashions a new history, both personal and cultural. At the same time, Bitov's place in a generation that had begun to awake from its particularly cruel nightmare of Soviet history ensured that his way be different than that of Joyce. In *Pushkin House*, the author comes to terms with his place in a tradition that extends far beyond him and his understanding of shifting historicized accounts.

As Garry Leonard writes, "Joyce favors apparently ephemeral 'moments' of ever-present 'now' because any 'awakening' from history will necessarily be experienced as a 'schizophrenic,' identity-fracturing moment. Far from being ahistorical, such moments expose the phenomenon of 'history' to be a fictional construct."[140] Precisely this energy drives Leva to his death. More to the point, Leva experiences the schizophrenic energy of the late Soviet age, and he unravels after failing to define himself. Only in the miraculous epilogue, when Leva is resurrected by the author-narrator, does the young scholar begin to truly change. He experiences realization after realization that alert him to the gaps in his understanding. Stephen, troubled as he may be, can still be confident in his construction of a *personal* narrative, however exaggerated or premature, when he says that Ireland belongs to him. Leva, on the contrary, remains ensnared by his own complicity. Bitov's plot demonstrates the challenges that face Leva when he attempts a very similar project; at the same time, his novel's very composition reveals the dangers of replicating this idea in 1960s or 1970s Russia.

In his commentary, Bitov expresses a desire to describe the everyday things that escape the contemporary writer.[141] These elements symbolize that which has not been co-opted by grand metanarratives such as Socialist Realism. Bitov sees the possibility of overcoming both oneself and one's cultural heritage in doing so. While both he and Joyce believe in the transcendent nature of the commonplace, the possibility of the insignificant to become consequential, Bitov suggests that this step is sufficient, letting go of Stephen's model of warring with the past. Stephen's project is no longer feasible for writers such as Bitov who would only be betraying themselves to a system that calls for duplicity and the abandonment of paternal ties. Joyce's place in *Pushkin House* underscores how the presence of Western sources are only negative if one feels paralyzed by the awareness of one's secondary nature. Bitov's generation will remain forever displaced from the modernist era epitomized by *Ulysses*, and Leva cannot fully borrow Stephen's methods for his own purposes. For Bitov, the present must define itself independently. The past, the tortoise, and the Irishman will continue on their way.

CHAPTER 4

Sasha Sokolov

"Here Comes Everybody" Meets "Those Who Came"

> And he answered them, the envious and fearful:
> where there is more delicacy—there is more virtuosity.
>
> —Sasha Sokolov, "Gazebo"

On encountering the initial critical response to *A School for Fools* (*Shkola dlia durakov*, 1976) following its publication abroad in *tamizdat*, Sasha Sokolov was surprised to learn that Vladimir Nabokov had influenced him. Although he claims to have read only a few bits of his fellow émigré's work before leaving Russia, Sokolov himself nonetheless acknowledged some possible similarities in style and technique. This recognition in turn led Sokolov to seek a new path for his second novel. As D. Barton Johnson, one of Sokolov's earliest and most astute critics, describes the situation, "Sokolov's language-obsessed novel arose in part as a conscious reaction against Nabokov's style—not in the sense of a rejection (for Sokolov greatly admires Nabokov) but in a successful attempt to sound a voice utterly distinct from that of the older writer."[1]

The result was *Between Dog and Wolf* (*Mezhdu sobakoi i volkom*, 1980), a novel of wild imagination, trying verbal density, and an incredible concentration of cultural referents.[2] Until recently considered untranslatable, *Dog* tells the story of a murder.[3] One night, the drunken knife grinder Ilya Zynzyrela kills a dog that he mistakes for a wolf. In retaliation, the animal's owner, the game warden Yakov Palamakhterov, steals the one-legged Ilya's crutches, leading Ilya to kill two more dogs. This Gogolian cycle of violence concludes with Yakov and his friends drowning Ilya. However simplified—and therefore misleading—this brief summary may be, the real impression the novel delivers is much different.

As has been pointed out many times, the novel's title refers to twilight, when a farmer may have difficulty telling the difference between his dog and a wolf. Thus, confusion reigns in the book, as the titular metaphor and many others are realized. Characters blend into one another and even submit letters of complaint from the land of the dead; the reader also witnesses several versions of these characters' lives play out. Language itself takes center stage as puns turn into reality, and Sokolov delivers a linguistic tour de force in prose and poetry, *skaz* (narration that mimics oral speech through dialect and slang), and stylized parodies of the classics. Perhaps not surprisingly, numerous scholars have suggested that the novel "has claim to being the *Finnegans Wake* of Russian literature" and provided a broad, though vague, range of parallels in style, structure, and allusions.[4]

Here, at the intersection of *Finnegans Wake*'s Joyce and the Nabokov of his Russian period, we find a curious blend of influences. Though Nabokov expressed great admiration for *Ulysses*, he called *Finnegans Wake* Joyce's "tragic failure" of a novel: "I detest *Finnegans Wake* in which a cancerous growth of fancy word-tissue hardly redeems the dreadful joviality of the folklore and the easy, too easy, allegory."[5] As Sokolov sought a new language in *Dog* to escape Nabokov's pull, he tapped into a vein of twentieth-century literature that his Russian forebear explicitly denounced. While it would be inaccurate to suggest that Sokolov did so deliberately after reading Nabokov's comments, his development as a writer does reflect an intriguing fusion of traditions. Sokolov, in essence, moved from one extreme to another that had not been seen before.

And yet, Sokolov's use of the Joycean model extends further back. If in *Between Dog and Wolf* his engagement with Joyce's later devices, techniques, and style achieved a fuller realization, then this literary adaptation can be felt even in *A School for Fools*. More so than previous authors, Sokolov also took up Joyce as a *stylistic* alternative.

Points of Contact

As described in chapter 3, discussions regarding Joyce gradually began to take place in the Soviet Union once more, thanks to the Thaw in the 1950s. D. G. Zhantieva, for example, published a short monograph in 1967, and Ekaterina Genieva submitted her dissertation—the first on Joyce in the Soviet Union—in 1972.[6] It was in this shifting atmosphere that Sokolov came into his own as a writer. On February 12, 1965, he joined a public reading organized by a group of avant-garde writers calling themselves SMOG (Smelost', Mysl', Obraz, Glubina [Courage, Thought, Image, Depth] or Samoe molodoe obshchestvo geniev [the Youngest Society of Geniuses]).[7] Among this crowd, Sokolov developed his interests in Western and counterculture literature. In a 2011 interview with Irina Vrubel-Golubkina, Sokolov recounts that at this time he read Joyce alongside figures such as Sherwood Anderson (as Andrei Bitov did), Gertrude Stein, Walt Whitman, and Guillaume Apollinaire. He adds that the "formal innovations" he sought as a new writer were not to be found in works by writers such as J. D. Salinger, William Faulkner, or even Andrei Platonov.[8] Instead, he turned to Joyce and Edgar Allan Poe, "names that cannot be ignored" according to Sokolov.[9] Aiming to establish his status as a European cosmopolitan, Sokolov elevates Western writers over Russian ones: "Joyce and company are more important to me than Platonov."[10]

Curiously, Sokolov's stance on Joyce's role in his literary development has shifted over the past few decades, recalling, in a way, what Nabokov said about the Irish classic. Speaking with John Glad in 1986, in a public access TV interview later published in the volume *Conversations in Exile*, Sokolov maintained that he had actually *not* read Joyce, Nabokov, or Jorge Luis Borges in his youth.[11] This statement, which contradicts what he later told Vrubel-Golubkina, may be read in two ways. Either Sokolov was dissembling in 1986 when he was still a young writer at the height of his fame and, perhaps, the peak of his anxiety of influence (however one defines these terms), or he is dissembling *now* (that is, in 2011), using Joyce as a means to associate himself with an elite strain of world literature. However, given both the texture of *A School for Fools* and the cultural milieu from which Sokolov sprang, it seems that he originally distanced himself from Joyce to ensure that his work did not seem derivative.

Sokolov has elsewhere used Joyce as an example to defend the complexity of his work. When asked by well-known writer and critic Viktor Erofeev in 1989 if he believes that *Between Dog and Wolf* could ever be translated into other languages, Sokolov responded, "They even translated Joyce. A translation is without a doubt possible, but one has to spend several years of one's life [working on it]."[12] He almost certainly has in mind here the formal complexities he shares with Joyce. In his essays, he makes such a connection explicit. For example, in the programmatic "The Key Word of Belles-Lettres" (1985), Sokolov, perhaps oversimplifying matters, suggests that "the conversation concerning *what* and *how* is an echo of an eternal discussion between materialists and idealists. What came first, argue these philosophers: matter or spirit? Substituting matter with the concept *what* and spirit with the concept *how*, we attain the formula for our problem. The obvious advocates of the latter in art are Kandinsky, Flaubert, Rimbaud, Joyce, Shostakovich, and other idealists. Supporters of *what* are Socialist Realists and Capitalist Primitivists."[13] Sokolov firmly aligns himself with the camp of artists who champion, in different ways, "art for art's sake" and technical proficiency over writing with a message and an emphasis on content. In another essay with an apposite title, "A Portrait of an Artist in America: Waiting for the Nobel" (1985), he says that his generation "idolize[s] Nabokov, Beckett, Joyce, and Borges," precisely those writers whose impact he downplayed in his conversation with Glad from around the same time.[14]

Sokolov's *A School for Fools*, to be sure, contains fewer of the explicit references to Joyce than can be found in Nabokov's and Bitov's novels. For instance, none of his characters, in this book at least, refers to *Ulysses* by name, as Modest Platonovich does in *Pushkin House*. His style, along with key details, however, suggests a powerful underlying Joycean presence. In short, this novel reads more like Joyce. While Sokolov's style has occasionally been identified as Joycean, surprisingly, no extended study of this connection exists.[15] Sokolov drew such stylistic elements as stream of consciousness, structural play, and so-called forking characters from Joyce, but why he did so and how he made them his own—or not—enriches this story. There are, of course, other potential sources for these techniques, but the evidence at hand (statements, clear allusions, parallels, and so on) demonstrates how Joyce's works were a central source of inspiration.

Furthermore, as with the previously examined texts, strong thematic connections—the creation of an artistic identity, generational relationships, language, and writing—also unite Sokolov's and Joyce's experimental novels. An even more advanced dissolution of Joyce's paternal project takes place in Sokolov's book. While *A School for Fools* continues to draw on modernist models and Sokolov engages with Joyce's novel on various levels, plot and character are dissolved almost entirely, much as in *Finnegans Wake*. Sokolov imbibed the lessons of the *Wake*, ones that were not yet written by Olesha's time, rejected by Nabokov, and apparently still unavailable to Bitov, who wrote in the commentary to *Pushkin House*: "The author doesn't know French, and he hasn't read or seen *Finnegans Wake* (he's not alone)."[16] Furthermore, writing his novel in the early 1970s, Sokolov could not help but respond to Joyce in ways different from those who preceded him. The protagonist, Nymphaea or Student So-and-So, struggles with his own identity as well as his relationship to his father, but Stephen's project takes a remarkably different form here.[17]

This transformation of Joyce's Shakespeare theory involves two distinct operations. First, the search for the father becomes a disappearance into style or texture. In general, both the Student and Stephen face a generational gap that cannot be bridged; the younger artists have an idealized view of the world that contrasts with the fathers' practicality and materialism. However, whereas Stephen adopts a literary father to escape his present conditions, forging his identity in the tradition of a particular forebear, Student So-and-So escapes into language itself. His story is less about his identity as an artist or about his coming into his own through revisions of the past than it is about language's playful potential to transcend mundane reality. Language in the Student's narrative becomes a means of substitution. The search for the father—both filial and affilial—dissolves away as Sokolov points out the relativity of all cultural values, including literary lineage, and the power of the literary imagination. Sokolov borrows and modifies Joyce's stylistic devices in order to overcome the sense of belatedness that plagues a writer of his generation. Here, language supersedes the artist as hero of the book.

This not insignificant revelation leads to the second component of Sokolov's revision of the Joycean model. *A School for Fools* recapitulates *Ulysses*'s penultimate episode, "Ithaca," which features Stephen vanishing into the early morning to find his own way. Sokolov, however, now has the Student meet his (authorial) maker at *School*'s end. At this point when author, narrator, and hero merge, Sokolov makes a paralogical move. By inserting himself (or his avatar) into the textual fabric of his novel, he averts the need to complete Stephen's project on his precursor's terms. Though his use of a Joycean subtext motivates his own endeavor and manifestly demonstrates the importance of the Irish writer for Sokolov, he chooses no explicit literary father figure by the end of the novel; Sokolov instead shatters the boundaries between character and author, between real time and novelistic time, asserting in the process a new angle on the question of primacy that plagued Olesha, Nabokov, and Bitov. For Sokolov, in his literary universe, time is entirely relative, so whether he comes late is really beside the point. He takes his place among his forebears through this flattening of historical and literary perspective.

How Sokolov Translated Joyce's Language

All three of Sokolov's books are notoriously difficult to summarize, each in its own way. *A School for Fools* established this pattern by breaking with many norms of fiction. Perhaps reflecting the hero's condition as a (young?) man with mental issues, the writer's debut novel lacks a clear chronological plot, and numerous characters are also imbued with different personas. The action mostly takes place either at the Student's dacha community or at his school, where his teacher, Savl/Pavel Norvegov, works. His parents, who go unnamed, act as foils, particularly his father, who makes Student So-and-So copy propagandistic articles from Soviet newspapers as a cruel reeducation. The hero also spends his time pining for Veta Akatova, a teacher and the daughter of a scientist who lives nearby.

But all is not so simple, for the protagonist suffers from a disease that makes him (or, read more positively, permits him) to travel in time. Instead of experiencing the passage of time as a linear progression, he imagines a simultaneity, in which he can drop his consciousness into any moment of his life. The practical effect of this condition—allegedly inherited from his grandmother— is that contradictory situations can coincide within the novel. For instance, after several exchanges shared by the Student and Norvegov, it is finally revealed that his mentor had died at some earlier point. Elsewhere, Student So-and-So's conversations with Veta's father morph into encounters with Leonardo da Vinci. Chapter 2 of the novel likewise breaks readers' expectations as the narrative shifts away from Student So-and-So and is dispersed among twelve short vignettes. These stories take place in the same general setting as the rest of *A School for Fools*, as evidenced by overlapping characters and locations, but the change can be quite disorienting. It is within this atypical novel that Sokolov engages in his revolution of the word.

The most pressing and in some ways obvious correspondence between Joyce and Sokolov is their radical use of language. Of course, "Joyce's language" can refer to a multitude of styles: the deceptive realism of *Dubliners*, the episodes in *Ulysses* inflected with free indirect discourse, the phantasmagoric drama of "Circe" that presages *Finnegans Wake*'s dense, pun-heavy prose. This caveat applies just as well to what we call "Sokolov's language," a remarkably diverse phenomenon even in only three novels.

One key stratagem Sokolov and Joyce share is what is usually termed the stream-of-consciousness technique. Though at first glance it does away with logic in favor of immediacy and emotion, stream of consciousness belies great technical skill and attention to form in the two writers. In the first case of this prototypically modernist technique from *A School for Fools*, Student So-and-So's narrative morphs into an even looser form of its already frenzied state. Here, his words serve as an incantation that brings the character Veta into existence:

but the branch is sleeping, having closed its flower petals, and the trains, stumbling on joints, will not wake it ever and will not shake off a single drop of dew from it—sleep sleep branch smelling of creosote in the morning wake and bloom then wither scatter petals in the eyes of semaphore signals and dancing to the beat of your wooden heart laugh at the stations sell yourself to those who pass and those who depart weep and yell baring yourself in the mirrors to the train compartment whats your name I am called Vetka [Branch] I am Vetka of the acacia I am Vetka

of the railroad I am Veta pregnant by the tender bird named Nightin-
gale I am pregnant with the coming summer and the crash of the freight
train here take me take me I am wilting anyway its not at all expensive
I cost no more than a ruble at the station I am sold by tickets but if you
want go without paying there wont be a conductor hes sick wait I will
unbutton myself see I am all snowy white well shower me all over
shower me with kisses no one will notice the petals arent visible on white
and I am bored of it all sometimes I seem to myself simply an old lady
who has spent her whole life walking along glowing engine slag on the
mound she is all old ugly I dont want to be an old woman.[18]

In Sokolov's hands, stream of consciousness functions as a means to explore
the connections the mind creates and the rhythm of thoughts themselves, at
least within the imagination of his narrator. On another level, Sokolov adapts
this technique from Joyce as a means of escape from the fossilized artistic and
linguistic forms that define his era. Amid the Soviet state's calls for art that
concerns itself with social questions and places an emphasis on content rather
than form, Sokolov turned to modernist prototypes. Incidentally, in an interview with Olga Matich, Sokolov proposes—not without a hint of self-defense—
that he learned a great deal from the "modernist" Tolstoy, who "used stream
of consciousness as a device long before Joyce."[19] True as this may be, Sokolov's stream of consciousness looks like Joyce's much more than Tolstoy's. On
a purely visual level, the two writers manifest stream of consciousness through
the use of nonstandard punctuation and syntax; this holds true even in comparison to The Sound and the Fury (1929), in which Faulkner restricts the technique to thoughts and logic much more than to the text's structure or syntax.
Sokolov may have learned from both the proto-modernist Tolstoy and the high
modernist Joyce, but the product of these literary mentorships resembles the
latter. Molly's soliloquy is precisely the sort of "formal innovation" that Sokolov describes in his interview with Vrubel-Golubkina and represents a release from formal strictures.[20]

Here, language itself, rather than plot or character, dictates the progression
of the novel. In the passage quoted above, the railway branch (severnaia vetka)
transforms into a branch of an acacia tree (vetka akatsii) and, finally, into the
multifaceted character Veta/Vetka, teacher, railway prostitute, and beloved all
at once. While Joyce's heroine, Molly, does not perform exactly the same sort
of linguistic sorcery, her soliloquy features similar jumps in thought that carry
one idea onto the next: "then you have to look out of the window all the nicer
then coming back suppose I never came back what would they say eloped with
him that gets you on on the stage the last concert I sang at where its over a

year ago when was it St Teresas hall."[21] But in *Finnegans Wake*, this principle can be found on nearly every page: "Dogging you round cove and haven and teaching me the perts of speech. If you spun your warns to him on the swish-barque waves I was spelling my yearns to her over cottage cake. We'll not disturb their sleeping duties. Let besoms be bosuns. It's Phoenix, dear. And the flame is, hear!"[22] Puns, homonyms, suggestive roots, and all sorts of sound play build up the impression of a text that has become both overwhelmed by the power of language itself and self-consciously captivated by its own possibilities, much as in Sokolov's *A School for Fools*. The major difference, again, is that Sokolov is nowhere nearly as interested in multilingual play as Joyce.

It is by now a commonplace of Joyce scholarship that Molly's language in "Penelope" is not particularly aberrant beyond its lack of punctuation. In fact, as an introduction to his scathing critique of stream of consciousness as device in "Penelope," Nabokov himself suggests that "readers who want to break down the flow of this chapter need to take a sharp pencil and separate the sentences."[23] Periods, commas, and other marks can indeed easily be inserted to produce entirely lucid, if colloquial, prose. Derek Attridge suggests that Joyce "exploits readerly habits to fuse speech and writing, or more accurately to demonstrate the inseparability and interdependence of speech and writing in a literate culture."[24] Molly's speech thus represents not simply the rapid thought processes of a woman in a restless state but rather a *transcription* of those thoughts in the semi-educated style that would have marked a woman's writing of the time. In other words, it approximates a strange mixture of speech, thought, and writing rendered over some thirty-seven pages, reflecting the reality of a literate culture in Dublin of 1904.

Sokolov's novel may be read in much the same way, although it has not. While logical connections may frequently blur in the so-called stream-of-consciousness passages, simply adding periods and commas, along with tracking the frenzied and lyrical connections between words and sections, can produce clear, though poetic, prose. If the Student's narration seems to be a freewheeling expression of his mind, it has less to do with the thoughts themselves than the way they are presented on the page. Regardless of whether Sokolov's protagonist knows where the punctuation should lie, we take the frantic nature of the printed word in these stream-of-consciousness passages to be representative of the Student's thoughts or speech, in essence interpreting a visual sign (the words and omitted punctuation on the page) as an aural or mental one. Not surprisingly, this connection has been reinforced by the Student's condition as a pupil in a special school, as we expect the protagonist to have thoughts that are devoid of logical coherence and that persistently shift in focus, particularly when he becomes excited by his feelings for Veta.

The Student's narrative, which also includes occasional intrusions by an authorial figure, has been called many things, from "a brilliant literary performance showing the possibilities and capacities of artistic imagination at work" to the problematic "crazy talk" of the narrator.[25] Some, like Vladimir Bondarenko, have proposed that Sokolov relays his hero's "speech" and "broken glimmers of consciousness," while others emphasize his use of "stream of consciousness" in what Fred Moody calls "exchanges and arguments between the two voices."[26] The author of a fascinating anonymous review, produced in the USSR and published by the *Russian Language Journal* in 1977, defines it as follows: "A dialogue between the author and the hero, 'Student So-and-So,' and, ultimately, a central dialogue between 'Student So-and-So' and the very same 'Student So-and-So' that is held in the bifurcated consciousness of the main hero."[27] These assorted descriptions highlight how critics and reviewers have typically rendered *A School for Fools* in either of two limited ways for more than forty years after its initial appearance: as an oral conversation or as the Student's thoughts themselves—in other words, exactly how Molly's episode is frequently read.

The tendency to view Nymphaea's narrative as an unstructured, unnatural speech or thought act, as with Molly's "flow," however, tends to exaggerate its deviancy. Indeed, while logical connections may frequently blur, to say the least, inserting punctuation marks, along with tracking the surrealistic connections, can easily clarify a great deal within passages such as the one above. Like Joyce's "Penelope," Student So-and-So's narrative, particularly these highly stylized sections, paradoxically emphasizes the constructed nature of the novel's *text*ure by upsetting typical writing practices. The Student's stream of consciousness records not his thoughts directly so much as a physical, frenzied *transcription* of those very ideas that flitter through his mind. In this way, just as Joyce's heroine is embodied by her text, so too is Student So-and-So. His peculiar language becomes the only apparently concrete thing the reader can identify with a character who remains so nebulous in many respects—age, mental capacity, occupation, identity—throughout the novel. It is in this enigmatic state (fluid language, textualized character identity) that Joyce and Sokolov overlap most in terms of style.[28]

While Sokolov appropriates the Joycean stream-of-consciousness technique, *why* he does so may be more complicated. The extended list of examples from both Russian and Western sources cited above demonstrates that the inclination to use this metaphor has been typical of Sokolov criticism since the novel was first published, even if it is not one of Sokolov's preferred descriptors when discussing his writing. *A School for Fools* has also often drawn comparisons to major modernist works, such as *Ulysses* and *The Sound and the Fury*. Along these lines, Vári Erzsébet has argued that "Sokolov's *povest'* [short novel] represents the first authentic narrative form in post-Soviet [*sic*] belles-lettres to convey 'stream of consciousness.'"[29] Sokolov's approach to stream of consciousness, however, may be less directly modernist than it appears. The stylistic parodies of *Between Dog and Wolf* have been documented widely.[30] Likewise, Alexander Zholkovsky has determined how Sokolov must have read the works of Laurence Sterne (1713–1768) and how his third novel, *Palisandriia* (1985), belongs to the Sternean genre of parodic narratives.[31] *School*, by contrast, has generally been read as a relatively less parodic work. Its complexities can mystify the reader, but its message and the Student's discourse are usually taken straightforwardly because of the apparent lack of ironic narrative masks familiar to readers of Sokolov's later work. However, given how the author complicates stream of consciousness throughout *School*, there is more to it than meets the eye. It is, after all, not "simply" the Student's mental ramblings but rather an intricate amalgamation of speech, thought, and, ultimately, writing that makes up his narrative. In fact, reading Student So-and-So's stream of consciousness through the lens of parody helps clarify its peculiarities. Like Sterne's *Tristram Shandy* (1759), *School*, too, is a largely plotless, highly verbal adventure.

Formalist critic Viktor Shklovsky famously explains in his article on *Shandy*, originally published in the early 1920s, that it is in the nature of the novel as a genre to parody conventions of narration, making Sterne's book "the most typical novel in world literature."[32] In *School*, Sokolov picks up a similar goal, while setting his sights on a different target than the nineteenth-century classics (Pushkin, Turgenev) that *Dog* takes on. Here, it is the modernist stream-of-consciousness novel that is warped by Sokolov's pen. A belated entry into this genre, *School* uses the device even as it subtly unsettles our expectations of what it may do and, consequently, of our understanding of the interdependence of writing and thought in a literary work. These examples illustrate how language itself becomes an intertextual referent to *Ulysses* in Sokolov's fiction. In using the stylistic register of a forebear, he transcends it through various strategies: imitations, extensions, and inversions. Molly's kisses and Joyce's style intermingle with those of Veta and Sokolov. Simultaneously, his tactic permits Sokolov to overcome the commands of any official, state-backed language of Soviet literature.

Constructing a Joycean Novel

Language being the fundamental building block of both Sokolov's and Joyce's art, how they employ it to give shape to their novels deserves closer inspection as well. Three particular Joycean elements in Sokolov's *School for Fools* should be examined further: the use of lists as a simultaneously organizing and destructive principle, a catechistic exchange that complicates the text's epistemological foundations, and a chapter that challenges expectations through a series of short vignettes featuring different perspectives on familiar characters and scenes.

In a detailed formal analysis of *A School for Fools*, Johnson argues that Sokolov's catalogs, which number over sixty and enumerate items from the single digits to more than a hundred, "display an enormous variety in terms of subject matter, internal conceptual organization, and grammatical format."[33] The use of lists as a literary device extends from Homer to Joyce and beyond; Richard C. Borden also links the Sokolovian list to Valentin Kataev's (1897–1986) literary experiments.[34] While Sokolov's lists do not necessarily allude to Joyce alone, they exhibit the same modernist interest in the enumeration of the everyday and the mundane present in *Ulysses*. For example, the Student describes the items dacha commuters carry in their bags: "tea, sugar, butter, salami; a fresh fish with whipping tail; macaroni, buckwheat, onions, prepared foods; more rarely— salt."[35] A not dissimilar example details the contents of Student So-and-So's mother's purse: "a little case for glasses, keys to the apartment, a pincushion, a spool of thread, matches, a compact and the key *to grandmother*."[36]

In *Ulysses* lists can be found in numerous episodes, providing one consistent structural device across a range of styles and points of view. The most comparable to the catalog of the commuters' belongings examines Bloom's drawers in "Ithaca," where items such as a "handwriting copybook," "an old sandglass," and "1 prospectus of The Wonderworker, the world's greatest remedy for rectal complaints" intermingle.[37] Others, such as those in "Cyclops" and "Oxen of the Sun," both emphasize the phonetic play built into the lists and foreground the device as such. For example, the narrator in "Cyclops" provides the following roster of imaginary wedding guests:

Lady Sylvester Elmshade, Mrs Barbara Lovebirch, Mrs Poll Ash, Mrs Holly Hazeleyes, Miss Daphne Bays, Miss Dorothy Canebrake, Mrs Clyde Twelvetrees, Mrs Rowan Greene, Mrs Helen Vinegadding, Miss Virginia Creeper, Miss Gladys Beech, Miss Olive Garth, Miss Blanche Maple, Mrs Maud Mahogany, Miss Myra Myrtle, Miss Priscilla Elderflower, Miss Bee Honeysuckle, Miss Grace Poplar, Miss O Mimosa San, Miss Rachel Cedarfrond, the Misses Lilian and Viola Lilac, Miss Timidity Aspenall, Mrs Kitty Dewey-Mosse, Miss May Hawthorne, Mrs Gloriana Palme, Mrs Liana Forrest, Mrs Arabella Blackwood and Mrs Norma Holyoake of Oakholme Regis.[38]

Here, alliteration ("Mrs *Maud Mahogany*, Miss *Myra Myrtle*"), assonance ("Miss Blanche *Maple*, Mrs *Maud Mahogany*"), rhymes ("Mrs Glori*ana* Palme, Mrs *Liana* Forrest"), and all kinds of other stylistic markers augur Sokolov's engagement with catalogs. Such play, of course, is nonetheless largely rooted in the two authors' belief in the power of the word to create a reality. Sounds and words in their texts, particularly *A School for Fools, Ulysses*'s wildly nonmimetic sections, and *Finnegans Wake*, conjure up images that come to life as if on their own. In an interview with David Remnick, Sokolov stresses this transcendent power of language: "Language is more important than life. So if you deal with language, you are creating not only texts, but also something more important than life. It's been said many times, of course, but it is true that first there was the Word, and God created the Word, the Word is God, and God is more important than life."[39] His novels, in turn, reflect these beliefs, as Sokolov prioritizes the intricacies of his language over plot, character, and setting.[40] Evidence suggests that Sokolov's generation of Soviet nonconformist writers adhered to and developed the myth of language as a substitute reality. Joseph Brodsky, for instance, proclaimed in his Nobel lecture that the poet is "an instrument of language for the continuation of its existence."[41] These writers endowed their stylistic and narrative experiments with metaphysical value. The USSR was, of course, a space made up of competing discourses—inner versus outer, kitchen table versus public realm—and, therefore, realities; by playing with the tension between speech and writing, by pitting different characters' approaches to language against each other, and by engaging in all kinds of experiments with words and sounds, *School* foregrounds the power of the word to shape life itself. Both Sokolov and Joyce take pleasure in the freedom that language provides and in the irony that, by constructing these textual worlds, the sound play only emphasizes their constructed nature.

Their inventories achieve this goal in other ways, too. In nearly all cases, whether brief or extended, lists derail the narrative, forcing the reader to work through a dense net of references that switches the focus from what precedes it. Frequently ornamental to the point of being emptied of any real meaning, such lists also contribute to the fabric of the novels on a level beyond plot. This tendency is precisely the sort of stylistic lesson that would have drawn Sokolov to Joyce. Under the guise of coherence and verisimilitude, their lists do more to disrupt the reader's progression through the novels than to organize the textual worlds for easy consumption.

Sokolov's and Joyce's lists frequently stem from another device that functions as a structuring principle: the catechism. The most famous example of the modernist catechism is, of course, Joyce's "Ithaca" episode. Here, as Karen

Lawrence suggests, the cold, yet somehow comic language the narrator(s) use(s) obscures much of the emotional content:

> Alone, what did Bloom feel?
>
> The cold of interstellar space, thousands of degrees below freezing point or the absolute zero of Fahrenheit, Centigrade or Réaumur: the incipient intimations of proximate dawn.
>
> Of what did bellchime and handtouch and footstep and lonechill remind him?
>
> Of companions now in various manners in different places defunct: Percy Apjohn (killed in action, Modder River), Philip Gilligan (phthisis, Jervis Street hospital), Matthew F. Kane (accidental drowning, Dublin Bay), Philip Moisel (pyemia, Heytesbury street), Michael Hart (phthisis, Mater Misericordiae hospital), Patrick Dignam (apoplexy, Sandymount).[42]

Sokolov's catechistic device, though, runs throughout the entirety of *A School for Fools*, starting from the very first line: "So, where to begin, with which words? It's all the same, begin with the words: there, at the station pond."[43] In Sokolov's book, the very act of cross-examining an interlocutor drives forward in its quest for meaning what is traditionally called the narrative. That the novel begins with a question is telling. From this early point the reader is alerted to the fact that Sokolov is *not* interested in concrete matters, tidy solutions, or incontrovertible facts.

On one level, the Student's interactions with his teacher, Norvegov, and the scientist Akatov represent a typical catechism, as the disciple is tested even as he gains knowledge from his experienced tutor: "'What did you understand?' asks Akatov, 'share it.'"[44] The Student seeks to understand better his surroundings and the people that populate it. As in Joyce, however, there is little that is typical about the novel and its devices. For example, his (self-)catechism raises important epistemological questions. Speaking of the dacha commuters, his two voices question their actions: "But why didn't they go to the river? They were afraid of the whirlpools and main channels, the wind and the waves, the deep spots and bottom reeds. And maybe there just wasn't any river? Maybe. But what was it called? The river was called [*nazyvalas'*]."[45] The act of naming the river essentially wills it into being in the Student's strange narrative, much as Veta morphs into a character by means of his linguistic play. Both Sokolov and Joyce, then, use the catechism as a means to explore the power of the imagination and its ties to reality. Each exchange builds on the previous one to construct a richer world in which rivers have names and thus exist and in which a long explanation of the piping system elucidates the source of water, as seen in chapter 3.

There are, however, important differences. In *Ulysses*, "Ithaca"'s structure probes and interrogates the very limits of absolute knowledge as it simulates the most complete and scientific answers possible. The mass of words that spill out, supplemented by overly complex syntax, often obfuscates the reality behind them. Joyce thus demonstrates language's inherent ability to deceive or, at the very least, to remain lacking through quasi-scientific detail. Sokolov certainly addresses this possibility through the Student's exchanges with himself, but the epistemological (and ontological) tension is weaker. Whether or not the river truly exists matters less than the fact that Nymphaea *believes* in this river and that the language of the novel brings it into being. Sokolov therefore adopts Joyce's model but also an attitude that more readily dispels any anxiety regarding the reality of the situation, which has significant ramifications. The two sides of the Student may debate the veracity of the other's claims, but ultimately no resolution can be found: They are both right in their contradictory exchange, which again brings us by circuitous route to the *Wake*.

Such fiercely anti-mimetic techniques, used early in chapter 1 ("Nymphaea"), make the appearance of chapter 2 ("Now: Stories Written on the Veranda") all the more perplexing. After having established the novel's (at least) dual-voiced quality, Sokolov suddenly shifts to a series of vignettes told from a number of perspectives. In twelve short scenes he explores the same dacha community environs and portrays the same characters as in the rest of the novel; the key difference is that Nymphaea recedes from the novel's narrative foreground, becoming more of a traditional character in the process.

Johnson, drawing from conversations with Sokolov, has offered two explanations for this strange chapter. First, the "author" may be the subject of "The Last Day," a young man discharged from the military who now writes the short stories and, later, the extended tale of Student So-and-So that makes up the rest of the novel. Alternatively, Sokolov suggests that a "'third force' behind the screen" composed some parts.[46] Here, Sokolov's second theory, as reported by Johnson, recalls the concept of the Arranger first proposed by David Hayman in 1970 to explain *Ulysses*'s narrative distortions and intrusions. Hayman calls the Arranger "a figure or a presence that can be identified neither with the author nor with its narrators, but that exercises an increasing degree of overt control over increasingly challenging materials."[47] The Arranger inserts bits of the narrative that neither characters nor narrators would be able to supply or be likely to do so. In the case of chapter 2, following Sokolov's suggestion, the "third force" is a Sokolovian version of the Arranger, one who is closer to the Joycean Arranger from the second half of *Ulysses*: more explicit than implicit, taken by linguistic/narrative play, and strikingly self-reflexive.[48]

More specifically, this device has its precursor in *Ulysses*'s tenth episode, the equally disorientating "Wandering Rocks." After nine episodes that trace Stephen's and Bloom's physical and mental peregrinations, "Wandering Rocks" disrupts the reader's expectations by turning to a number of short descriptions featuring Dublin personages and their actions during a single hour on June 16, 1904. The reader's task, or at least a possible one, is to trace the correspondences between scenes in order to define the entire picture, as it were. What Joyce does on a grand scale throughout *Ulysses*, he completes in a smaller form in "Wandering Rocks." Joseph Frank, in his landmark essay "Spatial Form in Modern Literature," argues that Joyce "composed his novel of a vast number of references and cross references that relate to each other independently of the time sequence of the narrative. These references must be connected by the reader and viewed as a whole before the book fits together into any meaningful pattern."[49] Thus, in the episode's second section, Corny Kelleher converses with an acquaintance as "a generous white arm from a window in Eccles street fl[ings] forth a coin," and, in the third, a one-legged sailor receives a coin from a "plump bare generous arm."[50] A similar principle applies to Sokolov's veranda stories. For example, the young girl in "The Tutor" later becomes the telegraph operator in "Amid the Wastelands," and a young man departs from the army in "The Last Day" and returns in "Now" at age twenty. Elsewhere, in "As Always on Sunday," Sokolov provides another perspective on the Student's family, particularly his father's relationships with his wife and in-laws, thus extending the frame of the chapter further—another Sokolovian self-reflexive narrative move. This technique of splitting perspective demonstrates how Sokolov and Joyce emphasize the subjective nature of reality.

The Joycean connections run even deeper in chapter 2's tales, bringing together the novel's structure and thematics, and even further, reaching back to *Dubliners*.[51] Describing the second chapter, Alexandra Heidi Karriker mentions its "laconism and bare sketchiness" and suggests that the narrator is "a withdrawn, detached observer of phenomena without emotional ties to characters or incidents," which "gives an existential quality to the excerpts."[52] While it is true that a writerly narrator can be detected in several of the stories, particularly those that implicitly or explicitly give the impression of a sketch in the process of its composition, Karriker's descriptions of the chapter misconstrue its true nature. There is not a single narrator but several, from the woman of "The Tutor" to the Oleshian speaker in "Amid the Wastelands" and to the particularly cold and distant voice who describes the death of the eponymous "Guard." The glazier in "As Always on Sunday," too, speaks in a particular brand of *skaz* as he complains about the Student's parents.

Amid this multitude of voices, Sokolov builds a series of tales interconnected through theme and mood. The atmosphere that pervades these stories "written on the veranda" is one of degradation. If Sokolov here adopts Joyce's method of using "a style of scrupulous meanness" to "write a chapter of the moral history of" his country, he does so to demonstrate more clearly the stagnation of these Soviet dacha-dwellers' lives.[53] Thus, the courtship between the repairman's daughter and the young boy in "The Locale" is seemingly recounted without apparent interest, only the air of indifference or inevitability, much as Joyce's narrator describes the boy's failed romance in "Araby" or Farrington's rage in "Counterparts." In fact, however, the sheer laconism of these scenes masks the authors' taut narrative construction.

This technique can be felt quite plainly in the framing stories "The Last Day" and "Now" from *A School for Fools'* second chapter and "The Sisters" and "The Dead" in *Dubliners*, respectively. With the latter tales, Joyce contrasts the deaths of Father Flynn and Michael Furey. The young narrator of "The Sisters" attempts to come to terms with the death of his idol, Father Flynn. He recalls how he would "[gaze] up at the window" as he "said softly to [him]self the word *paralysis*."[54] Joyce plays with this connection between the window and death when, at the very end of "The Dead," he has Gabriel Conroy "turn to the window" as he considers his wife's former love, of whom he was not aware.[55] The omissions regarding Father Flynn's death (from what did he suffer? what caused his paralysis and suffering? why do the adults speak in half-finished thoughts around the boy?) are inverted here in "The Dead," where the blank space, the omission, of Gretta's past romance comes into relief for her husband and provides amazing new insights to him: "Generous tears filled Gabriel's eyes. He had never felt like that himself towards any woman, but he knew that such a feeling must be love. . . . His own identity was fading out into a grey impalpable world: the solid world itself, which these dead had one time reared and lived in, was dissolving and dwindling."[56] In other words, Gabriel's newfound appreciation of true love leads to his understanding of other people beyond himself; he can now potentially break away from the moral, spiritual, and physical squalor that haunts the rest of *Dubliners*.

Sokolov picks up these same techniques in "The Last Day" and "Now." The former begins with a young man, about to enter military service, visiting a girl. Despite the fact that she does not reciprocate his feelings, he recalls how "in the evenings he had paced under her windows until very late, and when the windows went dark, for some reason he would keep standing there and standing there, glancing at the blackened glass."[57] Like Joyce, Sokolov uses the window as an image to symbolize the penetration (or non-penetration) of an admirer into the heart of the admired. It is at once a barrier that keeps the young boy and Sokolov's narrator from really coming into contact with Father Flynn and the girl, respectively, but it also allows careful observation. In "Now," though, Sokolov inverts the Joycean model. Having returned home from his service early due to a radiation accident, the young man takes up work as an attendant in a morgue. One day he realizes that a car crash victim is the same girl he used to watch: "But later he recognized her, although for some reason he couldn't remember her last name and kept looking at her and thinking about how three or four years ago, still before the army, he loved this girl and wanted, very much wanted, to be with her constantly, but she did not love him, she was too pretty to love him. And now, thought the attendant, it was all over, it was all over, and it was unclear what would come next."[58] The attendant's graphic encounter with the past in the form of his beloved's charred body produces mixed results. He resembles a combination of Gretta, who witnessed her love's sickness and death in the past, and Gabriel, who comes to terms with this romance and death in the present but looks forward to the future and his "journey westward."[59] Sokolov's hero loses the window, the protective barrier that separates him from death. He can come to a better understanding neither of the past ("he couldn't remember her last name") nor of the future ("it was impossible to know what the future would bring"). All he possesses, then, is the titular present, a not particularly solid foundation. The eponymous dead of Joyce's story bring about great revelations for Gabriel, while in "Now" they only undermine the character's stability. They render the simultaneous gulf between and interconnectedness of romanticized thought (the girl behind the window) and concrete reality (the body in front of the attendant). Just as the reader may approach *A School for Fools* as the romantic, unrestricted thoughts of Student So-and-So, the man previously viewed his beloved in idealistic, intangible terms. The reader must pay attention to the book's emphasis on language as a means of simulating (that is, crafting) a physical reality. In this way, *A School for Fools*' second chapter offers a microcosm of the novel as a whole, particularly as it engages with and subverts Joycean themes, style, and structures.

Forking Characters

If Sokolov disrupts plot, language, and structure in such myriad ways, his approach to character only solidifies his status as an iconoclast. As evidenced by the essay "Palissandre—c'est moi?," Sokolov himself takes pride in these methods: "I want to take the loaf of *belles-lettres*, extract from it all the raisins of plot and cast them all as alms to the surrounding voracious masses. And the daily bread of the primordial, autonomous word I want to give to the humble in spirit, to the persecuted, and to the other chosen ones."[60] Breaking away from mimetic representation, he asserts that he moves beyond the limits set up before him by literary history. Indeed, one of the most distinctive facets of Sokolov's art is his use of "forking characters." Writing about *Between Dog and Wolf*, Leona Toker observes how "characters of the novel form groups whose members merge into one another, so that each character seems to branch, or to fork into that of his neighbors."[61] Thus, all women are a version of the main female character, Orina (under various guises and names), and Ilya and Yakov take on different forms who are also the same all at once. While critical similarities between character variants do exist, this reading helps explain how Veta in *A School for Fools* can be both train-station prostitute and teacher and Student So-and-So both man and flower. Such self-aware play with character obviously occupies a greater role in *Between Dog and Wolf* and *Finnegans Wake*. However, its roots can be observed in Sokolov's and Joyce's earlier novels, too.

Turning to the central artist figures in these novels, in the contrast between the two halves of the Student's mind—the artistic, free-spirited individual and the other, more demanding identity that tries valiantly to remain in control and to tame his more spirited side—echoes of the relationship between Shem the Penman and Shaun the Postman in *Finnegans Wake*, as well as parallels with Stephen's own trials in *Ulysses*, emerge. Shem has traditionally been associated with Joyce and Shem with his brother Stanislaus, the more pragmatic of the two.[62] Descriptions of the Shem/Shaun dialectic by Joyce scholars could very well apply to the Student's divided self: "Shaun . . . accuses Shem of refusing to be a proper member of society. Shem is accused of being a sham and a forger, . . . constantly imitating others in his writing. His immense pride goes together with an absolute refusal to join in the patriotic struggle which would offer him the chance of achieving true manhood. Instead he prefers to occupy himself with the affairs of women," and "Shaun is, first, the public that receives the poet's message, ridicules and belittles it when it cannot ignore it."[63] Indeed, the more obedient half of the Student's mind constantly questions the other's flights of imagination and tries to temper any creative suggestions with references to reality and authority. The "patriotic struggle" in this case concerns the standards of Soviet society, something the Student fails to uphold in nearly every regard. Less successful than Shem in romance, the Student still devotes a great deal of his narrative to women, particularly Veta, and expresses an urgent wish to understand sex.

Both authors, though, complicate matters by constantly merging and splitting apart the two figures. In the *Wake*, Joyce's brothers undergo crisis after crisis, fight after fight, and yet they can become one: "With this laudable purpose in loud ability let us be singulfied."[64] The Student, too, experiences moments of complete internal discord ("Oh, I was mistaken, sir, that one, the *other* one, dreams of becoming an engineer") as well as of agreement ("But why did you pluck it . . . Of course, I shouldn't have, I didn't want to, believe me, at the beginning I didn't want to, never wanted to").[65] In *Ulysses*'s "Scylla and Charybdis," Stephen proposes that a person's character shifts and constantly reflects back on itself, as it takes on new versions, often self-created iterations: "Every life is many days, day after day. We walk through ourselves, meeting robbers, ghosts, giants, old men, young men, wives, widows, brothers-in-love, but always meeting ourselves."[66] This insight, of course, plays a great role in his Shakespeare theory, which is itself tied closely to his conception of art as a vessel for the creation of one's identity. Student So-and-So explicates a similar idea near the end of the novel: "The song of years, the melody of life. All the rest is not you, all the others are alien. Who are you yourself? You don't know. You'll only find out later, stringing the beads of memory. Consisting of them. You yourself will be memory."[67] Reduced to this state of being, one need only piece together recollections, artistically reconceived and joined together, to fashion a personality, whether it draws on the efforts of one's predecessors or not.

Elsewhere, though, Stephen and the Student consider the world external to their memory and mind and come to different conclusions. Walking along the beach in "Proteus," Stephen closes his eyes to pay attention to the noises around him. He notes various sounds, worries about falling, and ultimately turns his gaze to his surroundings once again: "Open your eyes now. . . . Has all vanished since? If I open and am for ever in the black adiaphane. *Basta!* I will see if I can see. See now. There all the time without you: and ever shall be, world without end."[68] Stephen learns two things here. First, he comes to appreciate the world of the audible more deeply with his vision removed from the equation. Second, and more importantly, once he opens his eyes and recognizes the beach around him, the fact that the world exists independently of his recognition of it strikes him with full force ("*Basta!*").

Sokolov includes a similar episode in the first chapter of *A School for Fools*. Here, the Student has just undergone his transformation into Nymphaea, the river flower: "Having taken several steps along the beach I looked back: nothing resembling my tracks remained on the sand. And nevertheless I still did not want to believe. You never know, as it happens, first, it could turn out that it's all a dream, second, it's possible that the sand here is extraordinarily firm and I, weighing a total of only so many kilograms, did not leave tracks in it because of my lightness, and, third, it is quite probable that I didn't disembark from the boat onto the shore yet, but to this point still sit in it and, naturally, I could not leave tracks where I had not yet been."[69] While his realization that external reality does not depend on his perception frustrates Stephen's ego,

Nymphaea examines the sand for proof of his existence and finds none, yet his response is not despair but bemusement. Setting aside the fact that this scene, along with all those in *A School for Fools*, is entirely imagined by the Student, Sokolov emphasizes the transient nature of reality, art, and character in a parallel with Joyce's novel. If Stephen's certainty in structures and the artist's vision is (at least temporarily) disturbed by the incident on the beach, then Nymphaea's dissolution comes into sharper focus here. Sokolov's protagonist leaves no marks in the sand—only on the page with his narrative—dissolving, as it were, into the truly protean stylistic texture of language and non-plot.

The Student's third identity, Those Who Came (TWC), subverts Joyce's texts further. Limited to five references in *A School for Fools*, this nickname brings to mind Joyce's Here Comes Everybody (HCE) from *Finnegans Wake*. The most famous of Earwicker's monikers, Here Comes Everybody represents his universal character: "An imposing everybody he always indeed looked, constantly the same as and equal to himself and magnificently well worthy of any and all such universalisation."[70] He becomes all sorts of heroes throughout the novel, and, at the same time, he exhibits traits seen in Bloom, Stephen, other characters from Joyce's works, and various historical figures. Here Comes Everybody therefore is the complete embodiment of Joyce's extreme approach to character development. He does not maintain a stable identity as he shifts according to the story's needs.

Sokolov references HCE openly with Those Who Came. The first appearance of TWC takes place during one of the Student's strange digressions regarding his efforts to learn the origins of a pair of pajamas, which in turn becomes a short tale about workers reading Japanese literature.[71] Elsewhere, near the end of the novel, Nymphaea speaks of the name with great elation: "And wherever we came, they said about us: look, there they are—Those Who Came. Greedy for knowledge, daring lovers of truth, heirs of Savl, his principles and declarations, we were proud of each other."[72] In both Joyce and Sokolov, these names—TWC and HCE—represent a generalized presence rather than a particular character with individual traits. However, Sokolov inverts the Joycean original with his character's name, suggesting a terminal point of development in one sense, but also challenging any definitive solution to the problem of primacy. Thus, Those Who Came is/are the result of Here Comes Everybody, a take on character that universalizes and breaks apart identity. Devoid of any firm foundation in time, whether past or future, TWC simply live in the present: arrived, existing, wrapped up in the moment. This conception of a character without past or future emphasizes Sokolov's guiding interest in escaping from any kind of conflict with literary history. As the all-in-all and totally present, TWC need not find a precedent.

Sokolov stresses this point at the very conclusion of the novel in two ways. First, he has his hero speak of the immortality of nature. He describes how each plant, particularly the rhododendron, feels no sadness at the thought of death, for their seeds bear them into the future. He notes that "all nature, excepting man, is one undying, indestructible whole . . . it is only man, burdened by egotistical pity for himself, to whom dying feels offensive and bitter."[73] What Sokolov does throughout his novel, however, is present a single human capable of such a selfless unity with nature. Most importantly, the transformations that the Student, who is also Nymphaea Alba and TWC, undergoes bring him closer both to nature and to man in their symbolic connections, recalling again the universalizing aspects of both *Ulysses* and *Finnegans Wake*.

Second, Sokolov takes this maneuver even further by having his hero meet his author and become part of a crowd at the very end of the novel: "Happily chatting and counting again our pocket change, slapping each other on the shoulders and whistling silly songs, we walk out into the many-footed street and in some miraculous manner are transformed into passersby."[74] Through this open-ended leap into the unknown, TWC become part of the fabric of life, while the author (Sokolov's stand-in) elects to join his character in the texture of literature. Both hero and author are changed into part of this many-footed figure, Sokolov's recurring literary embodiment of life in all its complexities and movement. The imagined time of *A School for Fools* merges with the reader's real time, as the hero (language) becomes flesh in a kind of literary re-enactment of logos in its biblical incarnation. Rather than follow a past model, electing a forefather as Olesha, Nabokov, and Bitov did before him, Sokolov here welcomes the effervescence of the present moment, the "now." In breaking so radically with a traditional approach to character, Sokolov, following in Joyce's *Wake*, continues to unravel the cultural hierarchies set up around him. He sees Joyce's deconstruction of character in his final work as a fruitful alternative that allows the author to slip, almost unnoticed, into the text, championing style rather than content, one's accomplishments rather than the anxiety caused by predecessors.

Writing and Reading Fathers

Given the centrality of alternative approaches to character in Sokolov's work, it is worth taking a closer look at his depiction of father-son relationships in

A School for Fools.[75] In some of the book's most striking passages, the Student's father attempts to curb his disobedient tendencies by making him copy articles from newspapers. This act represents the father's imposition of a language and worldview on his son, something against which the Student rebels. This behavior, of course, takes us far from the paternal idolatry of Fyodor's projects in *The Gift*, wherein he uses the fathers' languages—Pushkin's prose and poetry, Konstantin Godunov-Cherdyntsev's scientific accounts—to escape his émigré plight. Bitov comes closer to Sokolov in this regard, suggesting that an overdependence on past culture restricts the movement of the present-day artist.[76]

Sokolov here also aligns himself with Joyce, who firmly recognized the power language holds over the creative individual. Compare, for example, Stephen's thoughts in *Portrait* during his conversation with the English Jesuit dean of studies: "The language in which we are speaking is his before it is mine. How different are the words *home, Christ, ale, master* on his lips and on mine! I cannot speak or write these words without unrest of spirit. His language, so familiar and so foreign, will always be for me an acquired speech. I have not made or accepted its words. My voice holds them at bay. My soul frets in the shadow of his language."[77] Stephen, an Irishman, recognizes that the English language for him is, as Marian Eide puts it, "a symptom of external controls" and that he must find a way to "write in the language of the master [Roman Catholicism and British imperial rule] without acceding to the colonial influence of the master's own aesthetic."[78] Sokolov uses the Student's tale in *A School for Fools* to dramatize much the same process. Making matters worse, the father's language—one of oppression and creative restrictions—represents a hostile takeover of the Russian language from within, as it were. The history of colonialism haunts Stephen's use of English, while the specter of Socialist Realism looms over Sokolov's Russian.

To rebel in Nymphaea's case means turning not just to any tongue but to a fearful cry beyond rational language.[79] Even while his father attempts to stifle his efforts to give voice to his concerns, as Vladimir Tumanov notes, Nymphaea makes himself heard: "I roared so loudly as I had never yelled before in my life, I wanted him to hear and understand what the cry of his son means: a-a-a-a-a-a-a-a! wolves on the walls even worse on the walls people people people's faces these are hospital walls that is time when you die quietly and terribly a-a-a-a-a."[80] The yell disrupts any sense of logic, order, or teleology that might be present in the Soviet speech that his father champions; it instead gives shape to the Student's and Sokolov's alternative approach to language, one that is totally individualized. As in Joyce's works, the Student must learn to use, or at least work around, the strictures of his paternal discourse to create something new.

Nymphaea describes an even more aggressive approach when he details a classmate's plan to "dissolve parents" in a "barrel of acid."[81] The use of the word "dissolve" (*rastvorit'*) is telling, for that is precisely what Sokolov's narrative attempts to do: dissolve away barriers in time, tradition, and style to find a new path. Through other key image clusters, Sokolov exhibits the desire to stretch the boundaries set up around the creative individual. First, as in *Ulysses*, as well as in *The Gift* and *Pushkin House*, the domestic space acts as a particularly potent symbol. Holding a conversation between his two identities, Nymphaea implores himself: "Run from *the house of your father* and don't look back, for, if you look back, you will behold the grief in your mother's eyes, and all will become bitter to you."[82] Analogous phrases appear elsewhere: "I emerge from *my father's house* and walk quietly"; "why are you [*vy*] shouting here, in *my house*"; "it wouldn't be very easy for him to live in *that* house"; "You can't imagine how I'm going to miss you after we've unstuck the label and you apply the cancellation [to a postage stamp] and I go back, to *the house of my father*."[83] These moments emphasize how the Student feels that he must flee from his father's house to find his true self.

As demonstrated in chapter 3, the familial (and familiar) home of the father is no less perilous for Stephen, who comments in "Proteus," "Houses of decay, mine, his and all."[84] Of course, Stephen's perspective inverts the Homeric model in which Telemachus hopes to rejoin his father in the domestic hearth, as well as the Nabokovian one by which Fyodor will fashion a new home for Russian culture with the metaphoric keys he has taken with him into emigration. For both the Student and Stephen, though, too many ills abide in these spaces. They require new environs, and they intend to carve them out using the primary tool available to them: language. Tellingly, though, Nymphaea uses his father's boat to transverse the river to reach Veta's dacha, "smear[ing] the oarlocks with thick dark water drawn from the river."[85] Symbolically, the water from the river represents his merger with nature, his departure from the father's materialistic, human-centric worldview. Yet, he must make use of the materials available to him. The Western and Russian timelines are truly not isomorphic with each other, at the very least in terms of cultural development. His failure to recognize this difference is partly what leads to Leva Odoevtsev's tragic end in *Pushkin House*, as he considers himself the innovator despite his deeply iterative nature. Sokolov's hero sees the relative values of those developments. For him, it does not matter who is first, only what one does with the tools.

Images related to his father's clothing further complicate Nymphaea's paternal relationship (and recall some of the imagery in *Ulysses*, *The Gift*, and *Pushkin House*). At different points, he explicitly mentions how he wears his "father's cap"; his "ordinary pants with cuffs, made out of hand-me-downs from [his] prosecutor father"; a "tie, watch, and briefcase. Like father's"; and "a dark duster with six buttons, made out of my prosecutor father's great-coat."[86] All these items denote the father's attempts to control the son by implicating him in a particular system of signification. They evoke Stephen's concerns regarding his borrowed shoes from Buck and Kavalerov's, Leva's, and Fyodor's respective fears about how little or how much they resemble their fathers. These articles of clothing serve as constant reminders of a connection to an order from which the characters wish to disengage.[87] It is a matter of how they dress themselves figuratively, which burdens they take on. In Nymphaea's case, as with the boat trip, he does not feel unable to thrive.

In depicting father-son relationships, Sokolov deploys similar themes and images as Joyce. Where they depart in method, however, is in Joyce's stress on the artist selecting a literary precedent to become a father (to) himself. In Sokolov's case, this step is revealed to be unnecessary. While Nymphaea may struggle against his father's influence, as embodied by his language, clothing, and house/dacha, he ultimately merges with his author, effectively choosing himself.

All the same, in a manner reminiscent of Bitov's explorations of the connections between Leva's generation and the modernist era, Sokolov also probes the Student's relationship with his grandparents. These absent figures form a bridge to the past in the Student's narrative. Still, their descriptions and his relationship with them are not devoid of ambiguity. Conversing with Norvegov, the Student explains that he can access the past, present, and future at will in a frenetic temporal simultaneity, thanks to a disease inherited from his grandmother: "Sometimes she lost her memory, it usually happened if she looked at something extraordinarily beautiful for a long time."[88] Indeed, such complete absorption into natural beauty plagues the Student, for example, when he transforms into the lily, Nymphaea Alba. Perhaps more than anything else—his cries into barrels, his reading habits, his flights of fancy—this approach to memory and time sets him apart from his parents, particularly his father, who wields a strictly teleological, materialistic view of time. It links the Student to the modernist age with its explorations of alternative views of time and memory (Henri Bergson, Proust, Nabokov). In this way, Sokolov subtly challenges the status quo and stakes a claim for a particular lineage.

For Nymphaea this process is not quite so straightforward. Recognizing his mother's suffering and self-denials, he says, "Grandmother, I try terribly, terribly hard, I'll definitely graduate from the school, please don't worry, and I'll become an engineer, like grandfather."[89] He mentions this profession several times. It is a vocation that emphasizes the creation of material things. And yet it represents the complete opposite of his other potential career, that of the

Akatovian biologist who studies nature, not machines. This distinction recalls Stephen and Bloom's conversation regarding the role of the poet in the latter's imagined utopian state, where "the brain and the brawn" will work together.[90] In both cases, the artist figures clearly prefer the idea of an art independent of societal needs. Moreover, the reference to a future as an engineer serves as a potential allusion to Stalin's "engineers of the human soul," that is, writers and artists. The image therefore gains multivalency as a both positive and negative symbol for past ways of life represented in turn by Nymphaea's two grandparents.

Nymphaea's predecessors become the Scylla and Charybdis of his symbolic world. On the one hand, he may follow the materialist path of the engineer. If so, he will renounce his special relationship with the natural world, perpetuate his father's philosophy, and join the ranks of Soviet world-builders. On the other hand, he may link himself to a different tradition, though at the cost of great pain for his mother and complete isolation from his surroundings. Sokolov highlights this division with a reference to "the key to *grandmother*" in a list of the contents found within Nymphaea's mother's purse during a trip to her grave.[91] In *Envy*, Babichev kicks Kavalerov out of his apartment. In *The Gift*, Fyodor takes the keys of Russian culture with him into exile, opening up unexplored vistas in the process. In *Pushkin House*, Leva traps himself in the past with the keys to the eponymous research institute. And in *Ulysses*, both Stephen and Bloom become keyless. For Stephen, this event serves as a push toward self-fulfillment and self-creation. In *A School for Fools*, the Student's "key to grandmother" represents the connection to the past that he feels thanks to his selective memory. The implication, however, is that this is no disease at all, but rather a gift. Able to commune with the past, with the deceased, he wields an achronological perspective that permits him to transcend any limitations brought on by an overdependence on past models. Sokolov, in essence, levels the cultural playing field. Unlike Stephen, who must transform the past in his own image to overcome his anxieties, Nymphaea believes he exists in the past, present, and future all at once, allowing him to come to a better understanding of his artistic essence, as both a descendent and a predecessor.

Reversing the Flow of Time

Attridge summarizes the elements of fiction that Joyce's prose destabilizes in the following way: "Plot, character, moral argument, teleological structure, chronological continuity, symbolism, emotional coherence, depiction of place, observance of lexical rules, authorial presence, linearity, identifiable voices, monolingualism, all these and more are rendered relative, seen as options with certain effects and certain drawbacks."[92] A more fitting description of Sokolov's own art would be difficult to find. To take one more case study, time undoubtedly ranks among both Joyce's and Sokolov's favorite topics. How they play with time, giving it shape in their texts and complicating it through multilayered, nonlinear plots, speaks to similarities in their artistic worldviews. In *A School for Fools*, the Student suggests that his two halves "don't understand time properly."[93] Sokolov grammaticalizes the Student's wandering mind by having him speak/write in all three tenses:

> Dear Leonardo, not long ago (just now, in a short time) I was floating (am floating, will float) along a big river in a rowboat. Before this (after this) I was often (will be) there and am well acquainted with the surroundings. It was (is, will be) very good weather, and the river—quiet and broad, and on the shore, on one of the shores, a cuckoo was cuckooing (is cuckooing, will be cuckooing), and when I put down (will put down) the oar to rest, it sang (will sing) to me of how many years of life I have left. But this was (is, will be) stupid on its part because I was quite sure (am sure, will be sure) that I will soon die, if I have not died already.[94]

This process, moreover, allows him to die, live, and repeatedly return to life, as he can experience all moments of his life in a simultaneity. Joyce uses the very same formulation in *Finnegans Wake*: "Teems of times and happy returns. The seim anew. Ordovico or viricordo. Anna was, Livia is, Plurabelle's to be."[95] Here, as with plot and character, the two writers take an innovative approach to time. Their characters, Nymphaea and Anna Livia Plurabelle, live multiple lives as they are born and reborn in the narrative fabric in various forms. Through this construction, they imply a universality and immortality of (human) nature. Time, simply put, loses meaning.

The fragment from *Finnegans Wake* quoted above ("Ordovico or viricordo") raises the question of Viconian cyclical time that, in fact, runs throughout both authors' oeuvres.[96] Scholars have noted that in his literary career, Joyce grew closer and closer to Giambattista Vico's (1668–1744) theory of historical recurrence described in his *New Science*.[97] Joyce constructs *Finnegans Wake*— and potentially *Ulysses*, as Margaret Church maintains in "The Language of Time"—along Vico's cyclical patterns of the divine age (Joyce's age of the parents), the heroic age (the age of the sons), the human age (the age of the people), and the *ricorso* (the recurrence of events).[98] On the one hand, Viconian narrative time provides an alternative to historicist accounts; on the other hand, it also acts as a force that counters life's volatility. In the chaos of time's passing, the recognition, conscious or unconscious, that one is a particular instance of an archetype may provide a sense of stability amid the flux.

Nymphaea's musings on time evince a similar understanding of history as a combination of chaos (flux) and recurrence (stability). He believes that "the days come whenever it comes into one's head, and sometimes several come immediately. And sometimes a day doesn't come for a long time."[99] Nymphaea's imagined interlocutor Leonardo puts this perspective in related terms: "In time nothing is in the past and future and it has nothing from the present."[100] Sokolov does not deny the past's influence. However, Leonardo here emphasizes that the past, as well as the future, means nothing beyond how it is construed in the present. In an interview, Sokolov essentially expresses this same thought: "History simply does not interest me; I don't believe that you can extract the future from it."[101] This foregrounding of the present is central to Joyce's thought as well. Discussing his final novel with Jacques Mercanton, Joyce once said, "There is no past, no future; everything flows in an eternal present."[102] We see the same in his fiction. In Ulysses, a novel dealing with a single day's events, Molly's soliloquy reflects her immediate thoughts (her menstrual cycle, her singing career), and yet they constantly reevaluate the past, suggesting Molly's inability to overcome her love for the flawed Bloom. In Finnegans Wake, Vico's theory of circular history structures the narrative as events—HCE's alleged crime of exposing himself foremost among them— retold in different guises. History, understood broadly, seems to be taking place, as it were, alongside the present.[103] Finally, in A School for Fools, Sokolov uses a combination of these approaches. The Student's narrative is obsessed with the present moment as it jumps from one idea to the next in real time, and yet the circularity of the novel is difficult to miss. Jasmina Vojvodić examines Sokolov's play with grammar, punctuation, and language to explain his use of simultaneity, a device she considers eminently modernist.[104] But there is more to the story.

As in Joyce's texts, the flux of a time out of joint in the modern world is stabilized by Nymphaea's ricorso. His chaotic story, which ebbs and flows, is grounded, among other things, by recurring motifs (transformations, natural images), situations (his bathroom conversation with Norvegov), and the structure itself (the second chapter's alternative perspectives on events from the primary narrative). These various kinds of recurrences allow the Student to continue living in his world devoid of linear time, while simultaneously creating an artistic framework within it.[105] Again, he—with Sokolov behind him— feels at home in this atemporal chronotope, where the past (along with the future) is no longer a burden, but rather a welcome sight.

Nymphaea finds affirmation for this view in an article that his father immediately denounces: "The philosopher wrote there that in his opinion time has a reverse aspect, that is, it moves not in the direction we suppose it should move, but in reverse."[106] This image of time flowing backward reappears several times in connection to the local river, the Lethe: "The Lethe, whose waters, always turned backward, bear out your boat" and "We fell silent, one could hear the Lethe flowing backward."[107] This conflation of time, memory, and river brings to mind Joyce's treatment of the same topics in *Ulysses* and *Finnegans Wake*. In the former, Stephen makes a claim for the power of his art and memory to overcome time: "You have spoken of the past and its phantoms. . . . If I call them into life across the waters of Lethe will not the poor ghosts troop to my call?"[108] This particular river, too, makes several appearances in the *Wake*, as in the following passage: "lethelulled between explosion and reexplosion (Donnaurwatteur! Hunderthunder!) from grosskopp to megapod, embalmed, of grand age, rich in death anticipated."[109] In all three cases the inability to recall the past brings on death, "anticipated" in Joyce, untimely in Sokolov. If Stephen fails to remember his classmates, or chooses to do so, they will remain in a mnemonic death. Likewise, "lethelulled" suggests the stillness of Lethean forgetting, and numerous funereal images appear in the same paragraph (coffins, urns, decrepitude). Finally, the Lethe in *A School for Fools* is also a river of death, as Nymphaea sees his teacher, Norvegov, stand across it following his death. To consider time a river that can flow in multiple directions means to overcome death. Of course, the idea of time flowing backward, away from death's grip, finds its greatest treatment at the conclusion/beginning of *Finnegans Wake*: "A way a lone a last a loved a long the / riverrun, past Eve and Adam's, from swerve of shore to bend of bay, brings us by a commodius vicus of recirculation back to Howth Castle and Environs."[110] As the river ALP flows into the wider ocean, she returns back to the beginning of the novel, taking the narrative along with her in the process.

Nymphaea describes this process with another metaphor when he mentions the trains that travel near his home in an "infinite curve": "One goes clockwise, the other counterclockwise. As a result, it is as if they mutually destroy each other, and together they destroy movement and time."[111] Having abolished character and plot, Sokolov also set his sights on time. In *Ulysses*, Stephen speaks out against the restrictions that come with a traditional understanding of time, and yet, for now, he remains trapped within the nightmare of history, particularly in its twin forms of British and Catholic rule and the image of his deceased mother. Nymphaea, by contrast, lives unburdened by the past, as his extreme simultaneity goes far beyond what Stephen considers possible. Again, this narrative move evinces a wish to break away from the need to live with a constant glance backward—the same glance that dooms Leva in *Pushkin House*.

Writing New Directions

If all these tactics and devices illustrate Sokolov's belief in a time without boundaries, best expressed thematically through Student So-and-So's selective memory, then Sokolov's approach to the theme of writing demonstrates his desire to merge traditions and thus symbolically to break the literary boundaries set up around him. Along the same lines, in an interview, he denies "historicism," in favor of viewing all writers, from Gogol to Ivan Bunin, as contemporaries.[112] Allusions to Joyce's fiction, as well as to Western fiction in general, establish the terms of Sokolov's polemics in his struggle against father figures and the Soviet system. Writing itself becomes a guard against historical metanarratives foisted on a culture or a writer.

A crucial image related to this theme is that of the literary forge. In the fourth chapter of Sokolov's novel, Nymphaea tells Norvegov about his composition, "My Morning." In response, Norvegov bemoans the fact that he did not discover Nymphaea's talents earlier, when he was still in charge of his classroom: "But, Student So-and-So, I'm afraid you will not escape those lessons, and with torturous pain you will have to memorize by heart excerpts and scraps of works that we call literature. You will read with disgust the filthy and petty freaks of the pen, and now and then it will be unbearable for you, but then, having passed through the *crucible* of this unhappiness, you will mature, you will rise over your own ashes like the Phoenix, you will understand— you will understand everything."[113] His mentor suggests that Nymphaea could have avoided many miseries had this talent only become apparent earlier. This exchange may be read metafictionally: Sokolov has come late and must work through the difficult lessons of literature, both the belated, positive ones from Modernism and the negative from Socialist Realism.[114] Through this process, he can come to a better understanding of his own art.

A similar construction can be found in Joyce's *Portrait*. Near the end of the novel, Stephen reflects on the events in his life and announces to himself: "Welcome, O life! I go to encounter for the millionth time the reality of experience and to *forge* in the smithy of my soul the uncreated conscience of my race."[115] Stephen intends to travel to Paris, where he can gain perspective and become a writer. By directly confronting the reality of the Irish, Stephen believes he will give voice to his nation and create a new art.

While some scholars emphasize the potential for irony inherent in Stephen's formulation, particularly in light of Joyce's later punning on the very same word ("forge") in *Finnegans Wake*, Norvegov's sermon highlights similar prospects.[116] He says that the Student will need to work through his Soviet existence in order to become hardened by the world and then to produce his own individual art. Like Stephen, Norvegov acknowledges that this process can be a demeaning, painful one, full of setbacks, particularly given the state of the Soviet world. An outspoken critic, Norvegov dunks his head in the Lethe to avoid hearing more about an unspecified hack writer: "I washed [my ears] in the waters of the reservoir you see before you, in order to purify them of the defilement of the aforementioned name and to meet the coming nonbeing in the whiteness of soul, body, thoughts, tongue, and ears."[117] These, then, are the two possible responses to the Soviet forge of writing as Norvegov describes it: willful ignorance or agonizing ordeal.

Nymphaea, Sokolov's version of the artist as a young man, however, offers an alternative. Having heard his master's words, he responds, "But dear teacher, we object, didn't the composition . . . convince you that we long ago understood and that we don't have to pass through any kind of literary crucibles?"[118] Norvegov unexpectedly agrees that from Nymphaea's "first words" he saw this test was a "false necessity" for his student.[119] Student So-and-So in this way echoes the resurrected Leva's sentiments from *Pushkin House* as he announces that the literary crucible that is so crucial to Stephen, his literary antecedent, and Norvegov, his forebear, does not hold nearly as much weight for him. Norvegov, despite his close ties to Nymphaea and his role as esteemed teacher, nonetheless belongs to the generation of the fathers by age, and for this reason he sees the only path to literary success as a struggle. The circumstances have changed, and Nymphaea—with Sokolov as author before him—has recognized the literary forge as a false lead. He will undoubtedly face challenges along the way, but with the general relativity of cultural values enveloping his generation, he might pursue his own art without concern for what surrounds or precedes him.

One key difference between Nymphaea and Stephen, among many, is their conception of the literary forge or crucible that they must endure—or not. Nymphaea, despite appearances to the contrary, is quite cognizant of the hold his father wields over him. Sokolov makes this point apparent in his use of recurring motifs, as well as the symbolic meanings attached to images, particularly ones related to violence and control. Despite these stultifying conditions, Nymphaea opts to take the path of the artist, focusing on language itself rather than the struggle of the writer. Stephen uses the challenge of overcoming forebears, their languages, and the Irish experience as his forge of the literary spirit. For Nymphaea, a creation from a much different epoch, it is enough to explore language, to elevate it on its own merits. The pull of the fathers to adopt their language / writing is equally strong in *Ulysses* and *Finnegans Wake*. Whether it be HCE, Simon Dedalus, Leopold Bloom, or Nymphaea's unnamed prosecutor father, the paternal figures all try to entrap their sons using language as a (literal, figurative, rhetorical) tool. In *A School for Fools*, though, Sokolov finds a way out through a ludic attitude to language that gestures toward that of the iconoclastic *Finnegans Wake*. Sokolov here suggests the relativity of *all* language. There may exist forms that assail his personal tastes—Socialist Realism and newspaper reports, for instance—but, in the end, language, too, permits Sokolov to transcend any self- or externally imposed limitations. As Norvegov asks, "Do words really prove anything?," Sokolov interrogates the possibility of pinning down any one meaning to a word.[120] In this way, he dissolves the struggle with the father-predecessors in favor of sheer play within language, a risky move that might lead to accusations of solipsistic posturing. If everyone is equal within language, then there can be no real fathers, so to speak.

Already Was Joyce

If the references to and echoes of Joyce in *A School for Fools* and even *Dog* remain largely implicit or coded, then in *Palisandriia* Sokolov treats Joyce quite directly.[121] In one scene, Sokolov's hero, Palisandr Dalberg, details a book titled *The History of Water Closets*: "In it, written in magnificent free verse, is carefully but accessibly traced all sewage systems from ancient, cave, and—through the Roman aqueducts—to present-day waste recycling of recent eras."[122] To make this already obvious parody of Bloom's bathroom habits and the catechism of "Ithaca" even less ambiguous, he adds that "Dublin's weekly *Finnegan's Week* called it 'the next *Iliad*.'"[123] Elsewhere, Palisandr acknowledges his debt to Joyce in his *Reminiscences of Old Age*, where instead of describing a single day, he devotes hundreds of pages to mere minutes.[124] Palisandr also undergoes a transformation that recalls the grotesqueries of "Circe" when he is revealed to be a hermaphrodite, and, finally, when he considers different options for his image of the motherland, he refers to the "milkmaid, the type in which she appeared to Joyce's student [*studiozusu*] in his tower upon the coast of the stormy-foamy [*burnopennogo*] sea of Guinness."[125] If not always in style, then certainly in spirit, *Palisandriia* itself recalls both *Ulysses* and *Finnegans Wake*. Modeled after the émigré memoir genre, the primary target of Sokolov's acerbic satire, Sokolov's novel envelops Russian history, as Palisandr lives multiple time periods at once through what he calls *uzhebylo*, his personal brand of déjà vu, or "already-was."[126] Time frames blur as they do in Sokolov's previous two novels, and characters likewise shift identities in Palisandr's episodic narrative. These allusions, some more direct than others, confirm Sokolov's familiarity and understanding of Joyce's texts.

In this way, in each of his three primary works Sokolov's literary dialogue with Joyce has shifted according to his aims and to his changing attitude toward history, art, and time. In his first novel, *A School for Fools*, the ties are largely thematic and stylistic. He reconfigures elements of Joyce's texts, including *Dubliners* and *A Portrait of the Artist*, to construct his own portrait of the artist as a young man, as well as his novel of generational conflicts. In *Between Dog and Wolf*, Sokolov turned to a *Wake*an language to overcome his alleged debt to Nabokov. This move, in turn, led to innovations in his treatment of character and time that can also be traced to Joyce's experiments. Finally, in *Palisandriia*, Joyce takes his place among many objects of parody in a narrative that disrupts historical determinism, complicates the reader's understanding of character with its protean hero, and takes no prisoners in its satirical depictions of everyone from Russian émigrés and Soviet bureaucrats to Western cultural luminaries and historical figures.

In a telling passage, Borden notes that the novelty of *A School for Fools* has led scholars to seek influences outside of the Russian canon.[127] He suggests that this move is not necessary; domestic sources, such as Valentin Kataev, can illuminate our understanding of Sokolov's methods just as well. Johnson, too, has written that Sokolov's "novels are intensely and almost entirely Russian in the range of their cultural allusions."[128] And yet for all these warnings, the West, especially Joyce, plays a great role in the Russian writer's work.

Joyce offered the novice artist alternatives in approaches to language, time, and writing itself in his early career. *A School for Fools* is replete with stylistic markers reminiscent of Joyce's methods. Where they differ, however, is in the critical theme of fathers and sons. Sokolov chooses to liberate himself of the dialectic that Stephen and Joyce so memorably engage in and that continues to play out in *Finnegans Wake*'s Viconian recurrences. Even if by his own admission Sokolov tried to overcome the fatherly influence of Nabokov on his language, his art reflects a desire to break away from these terms of engagement. It has been argued that Sokolov's novels demonstrate a move toward pessimism, toward a belief in the inescapability of time's hold on man. Should that be the case, *A School for Fools*, as the earliest of Sokolov's major works, then retains its optimism. The author is able to merge with his character, Student So-and-So, as they depart into the street, much like Stephen does at the end of *Ulysses*. This moment, full of freedom and hope, represents Sokolov's giving himself up to language. He does not fear his belated status, as Bitov initially does, because he can see the relativity of cultural and historical time. By plunging into the fabric of the language itself, where, as Samuel Beckett put it so succinctly with reference to Joyce, "form *is* content; content *is* form," Sokolov avoids the need to choose a particular literary antecedent.[129] Instead, the Russian language as a whole becomes the basis of his art and he—He Who Came—the equal of those who come before him.

CHAPTER 5

Mikhail Shishkin

Border Crossings

> But tell me, you must have had the sensation at least
> once that you were your father, right?
>
> —Mikhail Shishkin, *Maidenhair*

Then the curtain fell and changed everything.
The opportunity to publish once-censored works meant that authors would
now compete for readers' attention (and money) with writers from the 1920s
and 1930s, as if they were contemporaneous with one another. Additionally,
access to these "new" works meant that artists would continue to experience
past innovations in literature in ways far different from how their peers in the
West had received them.

When it comes to Joyce's legacy, the situation is no less complex today. On
the one hand, post-Soviet writers do not lack access to the Irish author's works,
either in translation or in the original, and many in fact can read his peculiar
forms of English. On the other hand, when his works were again published
in the late 1980s—most significantly, Sergei Khoruzhy's long-awaited translation of *Ulysses*—many of his techniques had by this point become old hat, familiar from other sources who had crept past the censors. The experience of
reading Joyce at this time thus brought on for some a kind of déjà vu. Finally,
authors who came of age during perestroika still faced the dilemma of reconciling the Joycean myth with the reality of his works. His was a name that had
become legendary. Would his texts hold up to scrutiny under the stark light
of glasnost?

Unsurprisingly, the same debates regarding Joyce's art that started in the
1920s stretched on as people developed new lines of dialogue with him. In writ-

ing about Joyce, whether in their literary works or in articles, they sought to determine where he fit into the canon in Russia. Reactions were mixed. Before addressing Mikhail Shishkin and his novel *Maidenhair* (*Venerin volos*, 2005), it would be worth considering one counterexample from a book written at approximately the same time.

In the early 1990s, Viktor Pelevin (1962–) developed a well-earned reputation as one of Russia's most promising and controversial writers. Equal parts Buddhist mystic and postmodern trickster, Pelevin in his prose joyfully blurs the line between the comic and the serious. In that sense, he and Shishkin are similar, but otherwise they could not be more different as writers. Pelevin's indiscriminating eye means that he is just as likely to set his sights on Batman as he is on Tolstoy. Over time, he has begun to repeat himself, taking up topical motifs such as vampires, drugs, and alternative worlds, while remaining just as popular among readers.

A case in point: Pelevin's 2004 novel *The Sacred Book of the Werewolf* (*Sviashchennaia kniga oborotnia*) purports to be the found manuscript of a centuries-old shape-shifter, A Hu-Li, who feeds on the sexual energies of men. Featuring Pelevin's characteristic offbeat mixture of pulp fiction, biting satire, and Eastern mysticism, *The Sacred Book* chronicles A Hu-Li's gradual self-enlightenment. Along the way, she—a were-fox—encounters a Federal Security Service captain, Alexander Sery, who turns out to be a werewolf himself. The individuals who write the foreword to A Hu-Li's book note its highly intertextual qualities, observing a "thick network of borrowings, imitations, rehashings, and allusions," which nonetheless is "not worthy of a serious literary or critical analysis."[1] In his typical ironic mode, Pelevin plays with the issue of literariness and intertextuality throughout this allegedly amateur book that quotes, recycles, and travesties classic plots.

Unsurprisingly, more than once in their courtship, A Hu-Li and Alexander discuss literature. When Joyce is mentioned, the latter flares up:

> "Joyce?" he asked, drawing closer. "The one who wrote *Ulysses*? I tried to read it. Boring stuff. Frankly, I simply don't understand why such books are necessary."
> "What do you mean?"
> "Look, no one reads it, *Ulysses*. Three people read it and then they live off of it their whole lives: they write articles, go to conferences. But no one else made it through."[2]

Without necessarily equating his character's words with his own, Pelevin here suggests what many, extending all the way back to Olesha in the 1930s, have purported to be the case regarding Joyce's popularity and readership. More of a figurehead for Modernism than a truly widely read and appreciated author, Joyce, according to Alexander, symbolizes a dead-end. A select handful manage to wend their way through his novels, publish some pieces about them, and thus "live off of" him, but the rest cannot even finish *Ulysses*, let alone comprehend its many layers. His import has simply been exaggerated.

Pelevin's take on Joyce situates the Irish writer in a role often attributed to him—that of an unreadable high modernist. As the product of the late Soviet era, as well as being a writer who achieved his fame at the beginning of the post-Soviet 1990s, Pelevin weaves all sorts of intertexts from both high and popular culture without necessarily prioritizing any one over the other. Joyce for him would readily embody a literature that champions hierarchies. Pelevin instead demolishes boundaries between the sacred and the profane, all the while ignoring those same tendencies in Joyce's work.

But naturally, one may read Joyce differently in the years since the Soviet Union's end. Shishkin's relationship with his Irish predecessor is much more positive and productive. He, too, recognizes the importance of Joyce's books to literary history, but, unlike Pelevin, Shishkin views it as a beneficial influence. In a 2005 interview, for example, he contrasts the Western tradition's "love of the word," which for him is exemplified by Joyce's texts, with the Russian tradition's "love of man," embodied by Nikolai Gogol's short story "The Overcoat."[3] He says that he wishes, like Sokolov, to direct Russian literature toward the combination of the two trends, with the result being an art that is at once technically proficient and thoroughly humanist. In a later interview, in 2010, he comments on how Russians "skipped Joyce and an entire generation of Western writers, their breakthroughs, their achievements."[4] He was nevertheless surprised to learn that he had read Joyce through other writers who came after him. While there clearly exist important exceptions to Shishkin's claim about Russians skipping Joyce, his comments recall some of Bitov's on influence and the indirect ways Soviet writers accessed Western writers. All the same, the lessons of Joyce's works made it to Shishkin, and by the time of *Maidenhair*'s composition, he revealed himself to be a true Joycean writer.

Though the ideological content informing their opinions is obviously much different, Shishkin and Pelevin may very well be compared here to Vsevolod Vishnevsky and Boris Poplavsky, on the one hand, and Karl Radek, on the other, last seen in the introduction arguing over *Ulysses*. Shishkin, Vishnevsky, and Poplavsky all understand the value of Western literature to Russian letters and the potential for Russian writers to create something noteworthy and new out of a combination of sources; the other two see in Joyce a form of literature totally foreign, unnecessary, and frequently misrepresented, if actually read at all. As such tensions demonstrate, Joyce's complex place in Russian literature carries on from the debates of the 1920s and 1930s into the twenty-first century.

In this final chapter, Shishkin's third novel, *Maidenhair*, which blends characters, plotlines, and time frames almost indiscriminately, is read in the context of Joyce's innovations in both *Ulysses* and *Finnegans Wake*. If Sokolov reconceptualized Joyce's project even further than his precursors and elevated language—the one single concern that unquestionably unites all these authors—to the highest position possible in *A School for Fools*, then Shishkin's *Maidenhair* takes yet another path in its response to Stephen's "Scylla and Charybdis" theory. To be sure, he remains just as fascinated and engaged with the literary word as a world-building tool. But in his response to Joyce, a new element, namely, an effort to merge traditions and to reintegrate Russian literature into world culture after the Soviet experiment, emerges. Joyce acts as a prism through which he sees this effort—both a means and a model.

Shishkin's engagement with Joyce operates on two interrelated levels. First, the by now familiar thematic links appear: parents and children, missing ancestors, the artist's inscription of life into art (and vice versa), echoing stories, the interaction between myth and a present-day, seemingly mundane existence. All of these elements, so central to Joyce's final two novels, play their roles in Shishkin's book. Second, as with Sokolov, a stylistic influence is much more readily apparent than in the works of Olesha, Nabokov, or Bitov. Among other reasons, this may be explained by Shishkin's ability to read Joyce in the original and his exposure to other Joycean-inflected writers. Most notably, Shishkin has made a name for himself as a "scissors and paste man," to borrow Joyce's tongue-in-cheek term.[5] For their method of collecting and incorporating bits and pieces of texts written by others into their own works, these authors have been accused, both in jest and in seriousness, of plagiarism, a charge that ultimately wilts away when the artists' poetics are studied closely. Additionally, Shishkin deploys a brand of stream of consciousness that might very well be called the stream of *collective* consciousness, for by the end of *Maidenhair* the reader hears not just the voice of a single character (à la Molly Bloom in her soliloquy) but a cacophony of sources and discrete personalities. These techniques provide valuable entry points into how Shishkin's and Joyce's novels resonate with each other. More importantly, they likewise speak to Shishkin's efforts to chart a new course for Russian literature, one that takes Joyce's works as a springboard because of their ability to bring together disparate voices and traditions.

So what has happened to Stephen's project in Russia? Stephen and Joyce selected a literary forefather, overthrew their biological fathers, created lasting art, and, in the process, became fathers to themselves. Olesha feared the impasse that prevented his pursuit of the same mission. Nabokov subverted it to retain the biological-cultural heritage that he had lost in emigration. Bitov tried it but ultimately recognized how Soviet policies had distorted his view of history and literary evolution, requiring something new. Sokolov ejected himself from the nightmare of history through the radical nature of his prose, preferring an existence divorced from these polemics. Are any of these options possible, relevant, or appealing to the post-Soviet artist? What precisely is left for Shishkin to do in this new environment?

If for Stephen the ultimate goal of his Shakespeare theory is to redefine his lineage and to become father to himself and his nation through revolutionary, timeless art, then Shishkin, responding to his time and place, modifies the scope of the equation. (After all, Buck Mulligan refers to Stephen's theory as "algebra.")[6] He comes out the other side of the end of history to put the pieces together and to reintegrate Russian literature into world culture. His protagonist is decidedly not the young artist seen repeatedly in the previous novels, the son in search of a substitute father. Instead, Shishkin's semiautobiographical hero, a Russian interpreter working in Switzerland and writing letters to his son that are never actually sent, begins as a weary father, cast adrift in a cruel world. This choice in hero in fact reflects a major difference from how previous writers would perceive Joyce's project.

Unlike Joyce, but perhaps like Sokolov, Shishkin does not elect a single forefather. Taking instead an anti-historicist view, he sees how everything repeats, how he is only one in a chain of fathers and sons. Yet, following in Joyce's footsteps, Shishkin takes up the voices of the past, working them through his creative filter and reformulating them according to his needs (parodic, sincere, or somewhere in between). As a result, all eras become equal, as Shishkin underscores the iterative nature of storytelling, a lesson that can be imbibed directly from Joyce's narrative experiments. By contrast, Sokolov's novel remains much more focused on a local level, that of the late Soviet Russian chronotope, even if the author and his stand-ins attempt to distance themselves from that political reality. Whereas Sokolov merges language, hero, and author together in an arguably solipsistic move, Shishkin emphasizes the recurrent nature of the stories we tell, and, in doing so, he highlights yet another aspect of Joyce's artistry than those who wrote before him, one that came to full fruition in *Finnegans Wake*: the universality of human experience. Fathers, sons, and holy ghosts can, indeed, all be one.

Shishkin's resurrection of the past and the fathers, in opposition to Nabokov's efforts in *The Gift* or to those of his nationalistic contemporaries in Russia today, is global in nature and achieved through his borrowings and reworkings of past bits of others' writing. The major difference, though, is that what occurs is no longer the struggle with forefathers witnessed in previous authors' texts, but simply a recuperation of a tradition's place in literary history. Through Shishkin's engagement with Joyce, his efforts to craft a cosmopolitan conception of Russian literature grow clearer. Reading Joyce in Russia after 1991 could conceivably mean becoming lost in the ahistorical jumble caused by the Soviet experiment's disruptions and repressions, taking the old for the new; instead, Shishkin uses these peculiar circumstances to his advantage.

Points of Contact

Reviewers of Shishkin's fiction, especially *Maidenhair* and *Pis'movnik* (2010; translated as *The Light and the Dark* by Andrew Bromfield), have not missed their Joycean echoes.[7] These comparisons typically focus on structural similarities such as Joyce's catechism in "Ithaca" and the sections of *Maidenhair* structured in a question-and-answer format, a parallel noted by Anna Arkhipova.[8] Like his Irish predecessor, Shishkin draws from "the clean and the dirty alike," argues S. Divakov, believing it all to be worthy of literature.[9] Muireann Maguire goes so far as to suggest that while Shishkin cannot be denied his place as a great modern writer, many of his novelties actually stem from the modernist Joyce.[10] However, these developments do not derive directly from Joyce so much as they pay homage to him and embody Shishkin's efforts to bring Russian literature into direct contact with the West that Joyce represents. Along the same lines, Vlad Tolstov compares Shishkin's prose to a fantastic dinner party, referencing some of Shishkin's favorite writers: "This is a blend of European and Russian prosaic traditions unique to us. This is James Joyce visiting Bunin, while Nabokov sets the table."[11] Tolstov's brilliant metaphor suggests that Joyce's presence in Shishkin's book is layered upon a Russian foundation, and, overall, these examples demonstrate how Shishkin's art has been framed as belonging to a particular heritage. Nonetheless, they predominantly operate on a superficial level.

Evgeniya Rogova, by contrast, has produced the fullest, if not the most nuanced, examination so far of the connections between the two writers. In her article "The Tradition of J. Joyce in M. Shishkin's Novel *Pis'movnik* (A Comparative Analysis of Motifs)," she explores thematic parallels, including the power of the word, the consubstantiality of all people, and the senselessness of history.[12] These motifs speak to Joyce's and Shishkin's shared concerns, to be sure, and yet they only go so far. Shishkin's response began earlier than his 2010 novel, and it goes beyond what the characters and narrators say, having an impact on the very structure and style of his books, as well as his broader poetics. To a greater degree than other writers of his generation, Shishkin's writings exemplify how Joyce symbolizes, in his words, "more than Joyce": a lost forefather, an alternate course, a luminary who can resurrect fossilized, long-dead language.

For his part, Shishkin has never been reticent to discuss Joyce's role as one of his main forebears. He readily admits to his literary apprenticeship under Joyce. According to Shishkin, his initial encounter with Joyce came when he started studying English at Moscow State Pedagogical Institute. There, he visited the Foreign Literature Library and picked up a copy of *Ulysses*, the only place where he could do so. He calls this experience his "battle with the Soviet mind-set [*sovka*], an attempt to save himself in that toxic atmosphere" and claims that he went there "to draw breath from the text."[13] Joyce had become a matter of life and death to Shishkin: "Joyce helped that youth survive."[14]

Ultimately, though, he did not finish *Ulysses* in its entirety until after he relocated to Zurich in 1995, following the publication of his debut works in Russia. Rather than encountering all the many surprises that he awaited in the book, he realized that much of it already looked familiar, that he had taken in Joyce's devices from others who had worked through and digested them much earlier. In a sense, for Shishkin, communing with Joyce through his own writing allows for a reintegration of his generation with world culture—a bridging of that unexpected gap. He demonstrates how his art is already part of a wider movement. He cultivates these connections that hid beneath the surface, yet nonetheless brought him into contact with this most eminent of literary forefathers.

Shishkin's enthusiasm for Joyce has not waned since those first encounters. In the essay "More than Joyce" (2018), which is part of Shishkin's efforts to write creative biographies of major cultural figures and was originally published in German, he positions the Irish author within Russian culture;[15] the essay in turn serves as a Rosetta stone, which, while ostensibly about Joyce's life and art, also sheds light on Shishkin's poetics by underscoring certain aspects of his own work that he shares with the Irish writer. It acts as a working through of Shishkin's own approach to writing, an exploration of the metaphysics of art through the lens of what he sees in his foreign predecessor, and, finally, a tool to merge Russian literature with a tradition once lost to writers and readers in Russia. In adopting Joyce's devices for his own purposes, in echoing the craftsmanship of his narratives, Shishkin demonstrates the value he places on Joyce's art. This is Shishkin's ultimate goal in writing about Joyce: to position himself and his brand of Russian literature within the Joycean lineage, recalibrating Russian letters from the cultural periphery to the center, just as Joyce managed to do with Irish literature during a very uncertain time in Ireland's cultural history.

The context—in both cases—is crucial. Although *Ulysses* takes place in 1904, Joyce composed his masterpiece between 1914 and 1921. During Easter Week of 1916, the Irish Volunteers and Irish Citizen Army took control of Dublin in an attempt to establish an independent republic in opposition to the Irish Home Rule movement, which supported Ireland's self-government within the United Kingdom. Although Home Rule gained traction, it was suspended at the beginning of World War I. Partly as a result, the Easter Rising factions began their rebellion. Within a few days, British forces quelled the insurrection, instituted martial law, arrested over a thousand participants and nonparticipants, and executed most of the movement's leaders. Two years later, after Irish republicans gained but refused a number of seats in the British Parliament, Irish independence was declared by the Sinn Féin party. A war then dragged on until 1921, when England partitioned Ireland into its two present parts.

Looking back to 1904, the situation may be less dramatic and bloody, but it was no less contentious. Episodes such as "Telemachus," "Scylla and Charybdis," and "Cyclops" are rampant with the politics of the era, when Irish writers debated how to establish a national tradition. Figures such as William Butler Yeats, Lady Gregory, and Edward Martyn developed the Irish National Theater. Oliver St. John Gogarty, the model for Buck Mulligan, published in John Eglinton's journal *Dana*. Artists engaged in the Irish Literary Revival (also known as the Celtic Revival or Celtic Twilight) drew on folklore and tradition. As Matthew Campbell puts it, these figures "sought subject matter in the longest past of Celtic myth and a bardic feudal order or in the imagined pre-Union golden age of the eighteenth century. Above all, they sought it in the authenticity that direct contact with the Irish language and Irish peasant culture might bring."[16] Joyce, of course, critiqued the Irish Revival's tendency to dwell on the past, cultural conservatism, and quaint use of folklore and myth. It is all part of the broader nightmare of history that Stephen mentions and that leads to the sense of paralysis that Joyce diagnosed in his homeland. As such, he opted to remain apart from Yeats's theatrical ventures and George "AE" Russell's projects, pursuing instead his singular path.[17]

In general, though, these two periods—1904 and 1916–21—are very clearly intertwined as moments in Irish history when the nation attempted to define itself vis-à-vis either the past or the future. *Ulysses* bears traces of its in-text historical context, as well as of the turbulent time of its composition. Would Ireland opt for the backward glance toward its heritage to fashion new works in a Romantic key, or would it accept modernity wholeheartedly and seek out new forms of thought, art, and politics? At the risk of oversimplification, this question is here painted as a binary opposition, which it often was not, in order to give a sense of why else a book like *Ulysses* might appeal to a Russian writer of the late 1990s and the early years of the twenty-first century.

Even more significantly, Joyce's novels bespeak the disputes regarding nationalism and literature's role in crafting a national identity that lie at the heart of Shishkin's *Maidenhair*, too. And for good reason. In much the same way as turn-of-the-century Ireland underwent an identity crisis, post-Soviet Russia faced the challenge of coming to terms with an uncertain future, a bloody past, and substantial unknowns in a quickly shifting present. *Maidenhair* is by no means a political novel in the strict sense, nor is it the blunt political instrument Ada Bernatskaya makes it out to be in what can only be called a quasi-scholarly hit piece, where she explains how Shishkin's book serves as a weapon in the so-called info-psychological war being waged against contemporary Russia.[18] But it *is* part of a broader context of changing value systems.

During the 1990s and into the early 2000s, many cultural figures wrestled with a number of accursed questions. Perhaps most importantly, they attempted to make sense of Russia's so-called historical mission. From journals to TV shows and from poetry to pulp, authors sought firm ground. Some landed on nationalist shores. As Boris Noordenbos writes, "In tandem with the decline of postmodernism and a groundswell of nostalgic and patriotic popular sentiment, prominent Russian writers claimed increasingly authoritative and politically committed positions in debates about Russian identity."[19] Noordenbos convincingly argues that in the late Soviet era and throughout the 1990s, the postmodern writer had opted for a more relativist perspective, rather than the traditional role of nation builder and spiritual guide for Russia.[20] To make matters more complex, the question of national identity remained deeply entwined with issues such as Russia's relationship with the West and its own imperial ambitions. As a part of a former empire, Russia now had to contend with the question of how to define itself politically, culturally, economically, and linguistically, among other things. For some, the turn to the West for models, just as it had been for centuries, was a welcome option. For others, it "created unsettling hybrid forms and unleashed uncertainties about Russia's relation to the cultures from which these ('progressive,' 'advanced,' 'universal') models were derived."[21] Writers as different as Alexander Solzhenitsyn (1918–2008), who returned to Russia in 1994, and Alexander Prokhanov (1938–), the author of ultranationalist texts, began to regurgitate ideas about Russia's and the Russian Orthodox Church's mission to save the world from the West's decadent expansion. The result in some camps has been an idealization of the nation's traditional roots, which has been parodied by writers such as Vladimir Sorokin (1955–) in his *Day of the Oprichnik* (*Den' oprichnika*, 2006).[22] Writers and readers alike endeavored to find somehow inherently Russian values that would bring stability to their precarious situation.

It is against this backdrop of rising nationalism, which echoes that experienced by Joyce in its religious and historical undertones, that Shishkin's engagement with the Irish writer should be read. He has remained separate, opting to not fall into any camps, whether political or literary, but still advocating his personal vision and beliefs. If in these works one can detect traces of his views, in his publicistic essays, particularly those written in the past ten years and during the expansion of Putinism, the question of Russia's identity is a primary topic. Shishkin's politics became a subject of intense scrutiny after the publication of his open letter declining participation in BookExpo America 2013 as part of the Russian delegation. Among other things, he claimed that he no longer wished to serve a state that created an "absolutely unacceptable and demeaning" situation within its borders: "I want to and will represent another Russia, my Russia, a country free of imposters, a country with a state structure that defends the right of the individual, not the right to corruption, a country with a free media, free elections, and free people."[23] Shishkin has become part of the debate regarding Russia's role in the world and the writer's position in crafting that same role. Shishkin's reformulation of Joyce's modernist experiment cannot engender a text identical to *Ulysses* or *Finnegans Wake*; different forces shaped *Maidenhair*. How he reads Joyce and furthermore how he frames that reading, however, speak to this same desire to give Russia a more cosmopolitan, democratic future and to provide contemporary Russian literature a meaningful place alongside the great works of the past.

Tales as Old as Time

If during the Soviet era writers associated themselves with Joyce as a means to symbolically extricate their art from the mire of Socialist Realism, then what Shishkin does with his Irish forefather is naturally different. For him, Joyce is ever-present, if belatedly discovered. In many respects, when Shishkin writes about Joyce in "More than Joyce," he actually writes about himself: "In some sense, of course, I wrote about my Joyce, projected him onto myself, myself onto him. I looked for what unites all true writers."[24] Joyce serves as a mirror with which Shishkin may interrogate his own art—or what he ultimately wants his art to become—and with which to reflect himself outward to readers.

At first glance, *Maidenhair* seems quite different than *Ulysses* or *Finnegans Wake*. Although its plot is relatively simple, the book's multifaceted structure can be difficult to summarize in a few words. Composed of three primary interlocking stories, it eventually unfolds into a narrative that grows increasingly concerned with mixing times and spaces, in first-, second-, and third-person accounts. *Maidenhair* opens with an unnamed Russian émigré whose experiences working as an interpreter in Switzerland draw heavily from Shishkin's biography. The letters he writes to his son, as well as excerpts from his reading and accounts of his travels in Italy, also appear here. Interspersed throughout the book are transcriptions of interviews with Russian speakers fleeing war-torn areas such as Chechnya. Nearly a hundred pages in, Shishkin introduces yet another plot thread: the diaries of Izabella (Bella) Yureva, a real and wildly popular singer who was born in 1899 and died in 2000. The reader learns about her childhood, her blossoming career, the terrors she witnesses during World War I, and the changes she observes during the early Soviet period.

Everything quickly shifts, though. The Interpreter's reading of Greek history, his knowledge of various myths, and his own biography begin to intertwine with the questions and answers, while two stream-of-consciousness sections near the end of the book rupture any sense of cohesion. In this new chronotope, Greek warriors interact with Chechen refugees, and the Interpreter imagines an encounter in Rome with one of his Soviet schoolteachers, Galpetra, whose image and life story also begin to overlap with that of Bella.

Envy, *The Gift*, *Pushkin House*, and even *A School for Fools* all present their own portraits of artists as young men. Some of their heroes are more talented than others; some gravitate toward alternative father figures, while others do everything in their power to remain independent. They each face difficulties emblematic of their own environments, from the NEP era or emigration in Germany to post-Stalinist Russia. Even with only the above short précis at hand, it should be clear that *Maidenhair* is not a Dedalian portrait in the usual sense. The singer Bella, if anyone, serves as the novel's representative young artist, while the Interpreter plays a more mature and more cynical role, at least initially. But on a structural level, within the texts' architecture, the parallels between Shishkin's and Joyce's books run quite deep.

First and foremost, the two authors exhibit a strong mutual interest in the iterative nature of stories (as already seen in *Maidenhair*'s convoluted and overlapping plot). If everything has already been told, their books imply, then the author's mission consists of (re)framing the fragments of the past in new compositions, in effect causing a simultaneity of experience. "More than Joyce" highlights this aspect of *Finnegans Wake*: "In [Joyce's] book everything happens concurrently, as in life."[25] Shishkin was not the first to notice this peculiar feature of Joyce's work, of course, which can be explained in a number of ways.

"Uniqueness of character is subordinated to narrative process," writes Vivian Heller, as the heroes "are reduced to names and those names are played against each other in a way that evokes the heroticisms, catastrophes and eccentricities transmitted by the ancient legacy of the past."[26] Through play with symbols and initials, Humphrey Chimpden Earwicker (HCE) becomes Haroun Childeric Eggeberth, Haveth Childers Everywhere, and Here Comes Everybody, while Anna Livia Plurabelle (ALP) becomes associated with an entire list of rivers and other female figures. This technique is seen most vividly in Joyce's use of sigla for his characters, something he detailed in a 1924 letter to Harriet Shaw Weaver.[27] These modulations allowed Joyce to transpose his characters from situation to situation, as he does on a reduced scale in *Ulysses* with Homer's *Odyssey*. They are thus rendered as mere vessels for ideas, types, and archetypes: Shem the Penman, HCE's son, embodies artistic trickery; Shaun the Postman, his brother, the jealous, cautious man of society; and ALP a feminine life force. In the published version of the book, the sigla's effects can be felt, as the reader must track how different personalities inhabit different names and bodies.

Naturally, the book's indeterminacy when it comes to such basic elements of fiction as character and setting has led to a plethora of readings that attempt to synthesize its assorted parts. Thus, Harry Burrell proposes that the *Wake* is, in fact, a retelling of the Bible—but with a twist: "Rather, taking the simple Fall story, and repeating it again and again with embellishments and interweaving fables, bits of history, jokes, and personal biography, he rewrites it in the sense of creating a new Bible with its own theology and rules of ethics."[28] We can read HCE and ALP as Adam and Eve, as the first line suggests, and their experience throughout the book as a continual fall from grace of various kinds.[29] But on another level, HCE is simply a "turnpiker" (a turnpike keeper), a "pikebailer" (a fisherman), and an "earwigger" (the subject of gossip).[30] His fall, in this reading, is the double crime of watching two young girls pee in Dublin's Phoenix Park and of exposing himself to them. Still, here he is called "good Dook Umphrey," a reference to Humphrey, Duke of Gloucester (1390–1447), a name that only further links him to Humpty Dumpty and *his* famous fall. HCE's experience (if he can be reduced to a stable identity) is replayed again and again in these various forms, in a way suggesting that there are certain *kinds* of people and certain *kinds* of stories. Beyond that, differences are negligible. One need only take a glance at Adaline Glasheen's massive *Third Census of "Finnegans Wake"* to understand how densely packed Joyce's book truly is with characters who blend into each other.[31] According to Glasheen, for instance, Shem plays the roles of no less a wide-ranging and multinational collection of figures than St. Laurence O'Toole, James Macpherson, the right

bank of the Liffey River, James (Joyce), Jacob, Homer, the Devil and the An-
gel, Stan and St. Michael, Cain and Abel, Sham, Ishmael, the Holy Ghost,
St. Paul, and many, many others. Each iteration fulfills his role depending on
the circumstances (and language) at hand.

Shishkin's characters, too, might be considered little more than similar vessels. In *Maidenhair*, the author even ironically jokes about this tendency in his
writing: "And one other little thing: what kind of heroes can there be without
a description of their external appearance?"[32] He effects part of this technique
by sharing scant detail regarding their appearances. In interviews, he has provided different explanations for this phenomenon, for example, this one, which
suggests the lofty goal of his art is no less than to bring people together: "My
main characters never have descriptions of their external appearance. Because
our looks are what divide us, disrupt intimacy, mutual understanding, other us
and make us foreign to one another. But if you take away external appearance,
then it suddenly becomes clear that inside people are unbelievably similar. . . .
My novels are about mutual understanding and human rapprochement."[33]
Who the characters fundamentally are matters very little since they are all essentially the same, and, thus, their various stories begin to recall each other.
This is, in fact, one of Shishkin's main points in *Maidenhair*: "All stories have already been told a hundred times. But you—this is your story. . . . The story is
the hand. You are the mitt. Stories change you, like mitts."[34] Individuals may
feel that their experiences are unique. They may feel that they are the first to
undergo some bliss or trauma. Shishkin suggests otherwise. The refugees who
come to Switzerland eventually transform in the question-and-answer sections
into entirely different figures. Whereas the first few entries are relatively
straightforward accounts of the horrific violence that these people witnessed in
their homes ("Then my mother threw herself at them with a knife. . . . One of
them shoved her against the wall, put his AK to her head, and fired"), later entries become far more complex.[35] One section begins as follows with generali-
ties and clichés: "So, you claim that you're searching for a haven for your weary,
wounded soul, exhausted from the humiliations and trials, from boors and
poverty, from scoundrels and fools, and that everywhere you go the impending danger of becoming evil's toy and victim threatens you, as if an inescap-
able curse lays on your line, and on everyone else, too, and how your
grandmothers and grandfathers suffered, so, too, the current generation suffers, and how the unborn are going to suffer."[36] It then turns out that the
protagonist of this question and answer section—largely a parody of the detective genre—is a rogue policeman seeking to root out corruption, and his story
becomes about the ensuing campaign waged against him. As a result of his
actions, his mother and sister are killed, and their corpses are found in a most

gruesome state. Then there are the Chechens fleeing their villages who are linked to Xenophon's Greek warriors seeking an end to their war. As *Maidenhair*'s narrator says, each of these stories has been told before; the stories are hands on which we—the gloves—are placed by fate, by chance, by choice. The fact that anyone can fit onto these hand-stories suggests that there are many common threads to the human experience.

Joyce's novels and *Maidenhair* are to a significant degree composed of such echoing stories. Shishkin emphasizes this technique in his essay on his predecessor: "The song about the drunken Finnegan . . . becomes a book-palimpsest. . . . Here, everything is as in life. Father becomes son, mother—daughter, a river—the ocean. People blend, overflow, splash, like words."[37] *Finnegans Wake*, but *Ulysses*, too, with its Homeric links and inversions and intersecting forking characters, served as a productive model for Shishkin to explore this particular artistic project. His characters, who exist in the mid-1990s and the Soviet era, in ancient Greece and civil war–era Russia, come to embody new forms of familiar tales, from Longus's *Daphnis and Chloe* (second century AD) and Xenophon's *Anabasis* (370 BC) to the detective stories of Edgar Allan Poe (1809–1849) and G. K. Chesterton (1874–1936).

This view shared by the Russian writer and his Irish precursor proposes a conception of literature that is much more expansive, and far less concerned with the local or national level. Instead, it suggests some inherent links between traditions, which bolsters Shishkin's attempts to reintegrate the Russian literary tradition with the West. Similar to how he seeks less to describe the individual features of his heroes, what makes them unique, he likewise repeatedly underscores the universality of his narratives and, therefore, the role of his fiction to speak not just for the Russian context but for a more collective, humanistic one.

Something Borrowed, Something New

In "Ithaca," Joyce's narrator pictures Leopold Bloom smiling to himself as he thinks about how "each one who enters imagines himself to be the first to enter whereas he is always the last term of a preceding series even if the first term of a succeeding one, each imagining himself to be first, last, only and alone whereas he is neither first nor last nor only nor alone in a series originating in and repeated to infinity."[38] Although Bloom—inspired by his Molly's recent infidelity—here considers sexual experiences, this thought nonetheless touches on influence and intertextuality. Finding the primary source of a development in literature will prove difficult, for the medium is an endless and constantly expanding interchange between writers. Joyce's works, particularly his final two novels, testify to this phenomenon by incorporating a vast number of allusions and direct citations. The sheer density of quotations from both popular and high culture led some to criticize Joyce's method, even as he refined his own understanding of what he was doing. As Scarlett Baron puts it in her study of Joyce's relationship with Gustave Flaubert (1821–1880), "Joyce's own understanding of literary relations shifts from an early concern with his own place within the literary tradition . . . towards an increasingly complex, proto-intertextual conceptualization of textual relations, in which the inevitability of repetition and relationality is acknowledged and embraced."[39] Shishkin seems to have picked up on this lesson much earlier and with greater ease, adopting it as his modus operandi from his first works on.

Joyce, in fact, wrote to the U.S. avant-garde composer George Antheil (1900–1959) in 1931, while composing "Work in Progress" (his name for *Finnegans Wake* before its publication), that he was "quite content to go down to posterity as a scissors and paste man," a term he felt was "harsh but not unjust."[40] He fully recognized how he had used and would continue to use other people's words. Joyce would parody this "scissors and paste man" epithet in *Finnegans Wake*, where he has Shaun mock his brother Shem the Penman's writing: "Every dimmed letter in it is a copy and not a few of the silbils and wholly words I can show you in my Kingdom of Heaven. . . . The last word in stolentelling."[41] Shaun accuses Shem of having plagiarized every "damned letter" in his works, which are also "dim" because they are copies, and suggests that some of the "syllables and whole/holy/hole-y words" can be found in the Bible, among other sources. Shem's texts, his angry brother proclaims, are "stolen tales" he "retells" as his own. Rather than simply copying materials (even if he sometimes *did* do just that), however, Joyce often reformulated them. Baron lists "the elision of quotation marks . . . , distortion, and decontextualization" as his three primary tools, at least in *Finnegans Wake*.[42] Trimming with scissors naturally leaves its trace; in changing his quotations, Joyce crafts something new out of borrowed materials.

A couple characteristic examples from Joyce and, afterward, a few more from Shishkin will suffice to illustrate the parallels in their approach. The first comes from "Oxen of the Sun," where Joyce parodies and manipulates a passage from Thomas Malory's (c. 1415–1471) own reworking of the Arthurian legend (see table 5.1).

The entire "Oxen" episode is replete with such lifted material that straddles the line between parody, transformation, and homage. Joyce was known to jot down such passages and bits from other works that he would later in-

Table 5.1

Malory, *Le Morte d'Arthur*, XXI.13: And thou were the courteoust knight that ever bare shield; and thou were truest friend to thy lover that ever bestrad hors. And thou were the kindest man that ever struck with sword; and thou were the goodliest person that ever cam among press of knights. And thou were the meekest man and the gentlest that ever ate in hall among ladies. And thou were the sternest knight to thy mortal foe that ever put spear in the rest.	Malory Parody in "Oxen": And sir Leopold that was the goodliest guest that ever sat in scholars' hall and that was the meekest man and the kindest that ever laid husbandly hand under hen and that was the very truest knight of the world one that ever did minion service to lady gentle pledged him courtly in the cup.

Source: Thomas Malory and James Joyce, quoted in Paul K. Saint-Amour, *The Copywrights: Intellectual Property and the Literary Imagination* (Ithaca, NY: Cornell University Press, 2003), 175.

Table 5.2

Flaubert, *La Tentation de saint Antoine*: Day at last dawns. . . . There in the middle, inside the very disc of the sun, radiates the face of Jesus Christ.	"Circe" (335–36, 340–41): *A cake of new clean lemon soap arises, diffusing light and perfume. . . . The freckled face of Sweny, the druggist, appears in the disc of the soapsun.*

Source: Gustave Flaubert and Joyce, quoted in Baron, "Strandentwining Cable," 171.

sert into his own texts, leading Jean-Michel Rabaté to call Joyce a "bricoleur" who "salvage[s] trivia" for his art.[43]

Another similar allusion is derived from Flaubert's *The Temptation of Saint Anthony* (1874) (see table 5.2). Joyce and Shishkin naturally are not unique in incorporating fragments from and alluding to other works. Nabokov, too, did the same with travelogues in Fyodor's biography of his father. The key difference is they take this approach to a different level than many others, radicalizing the intertextual nature of their works in frequency and extent. One effect of this technique, in these passages from Joyce's novel, is that his sources remain easily identifiable, but at the same time he dramatically transforms them through recontextualization. Soap becomes equated with Jesus Christ, Leopold Bloom with a chivalrous knight of yore. The result is less that Joyce has simply taken "wholly words" or that he playfully travesties his sources for the sake of a joke than that he equates his new figures (Bloom, Sweny, and so on) and their unremarkable actions with the heroes and heroics of the past. Furthermore, while Ireland was never far from Joyce's mind, particularly when writing *Ulysses*, the range of his sources, especially in *Finnegans Wake*, speaks to how languages and cultures intertwine as never before and likely never after. In this way, Irish, Russian, ancient Greek, and Italian referents— the list goes on—can all speak to one another in the *Wake*'s strange language.[44]

For readers acquainted with Shishkin's career and compositional techniques, this should all ring familiar.

When the poet Alexander Tankov (1953–) made his way through *Maidenhair*, he was shocked to learn that he had, in fact, already read it. More precisely, he discovered that one section of the novel—the diaries of Bella Yureva—bore more than a passing resemblance to Soviet writer Vera Panova's memoirs. In an article published in *Literary Gazette*, Tankov reproduced the offending passages alongside the original text, Panova's *On My Life, Books, and Readers* (1989), and laid out his charge against Shishkin, calling it not simply plagiarism but "an act of marauding [*maroderstvo*]."[45]

This short piece, in turn, led to a scandal that spread from online forums to literary journals. While some debated the merit of Shishkin's work in the comments sections of LiveJournal pages, Aleksei Karakovsky would go on to call Shishkin's novel a "parasitic text" in *Literary Questions (Voprosy literatury)*.[46] Irina Kaspe, however, classified it as an exemplar of the tendency toward "documentariness [*dokumentnost'*]" in Russian literature of the early 2000s.[47] The author himself only fanned the flames of controversy when he agreed to have an open letter published on a friend's blog. In it, Shishkin claimed that he strives "to write an ideal text, a text of texts that will consist of excerpts from everything ever written. From these fragments, a new mosaic should be composed. And from the old words comes out a fundamentally new book . . . because it's my choice, my painting of my world that never was and later will never be."[48] Shishkin thus engages in the same kind of intertextual practices as Joyce when he borrows and modifies elements of other people's works for his own purposes, as he attempts both to create something new out of borrowed material and to elevate that same material through recontextualization, giving it new life in the process.

This scandal fits within a much wider history of literary plagiarisms. Marilyn Randall, in her expansive study *Pragmatic Plagiarism: Authorship, Profit, and Power*, traces attitudes toward plagiarism from antiquity through the present day, summarizing that "the history of plagiarism can be divided roughly into discourses of apology and of condemnation."[49] In antiquity, she finds that a line was drawn between mere copying and transformation, a difference that implied inspiration was the meeting point between respectfully copying one's predecessors and individual innovation. Throughout the eighteenth century, particularly with the rise of the Romantic poet, emphasis shifted from imitation to originality. The next stage, emblematic of the modern era, involved maintaining the aura of the original writer, while finding ways to justify plagiarism. Randall suggests that critics now face the challenge of reconciling the idealized original, authoritative author with the challenging notion that "genius may in fact be a flair for creative imitation."[50] This crucial change has resulted in what she calls the euphemization of plagiarism: the so-called good author does not plagiarize but "uncover[s] gold from a dunghill" (as Virgil put it) or recovers "buried treasures that would otherwise be lost."[51] However, if authors are judged more severely, their plagiarism may be called a "conquest of foreign lands," which recalls Tankov's "act of marauding."[52] These tendencies are readily apparent in discussions of Joyce's and Shishkin's plagiarisms.[53]

Like *Finnegans Wake* before it, *Maidenhair* asks its reader to collaborate by (re)considering some conventions of literary art and to craft the text alongside the author by making sense of its foreign elements, not unlike what the novel's protagonist-interpreter does at his place of work or what the *Wake* requires of anyone who wishes to untangle its many-layered design. Whether artistic plagiarism proceeds from the author's intent or the reader's interpretation, to give an adequate reading of *Maidenhair*, we must also focus on its stylistic and thematic effects, which involves a perspective of history according to which subjects from disparate eras can come into contact with one other. This same background is at work in *Finnegans Wake* and even in *Ulysses*, where Joyce establishes his Homeric parallels and inversions and various other citations in order to position his heroes' experiences against a heroic past. It would be overly simplistic to suggest that these parallels make up the entirety of *Ulysses*'s meaning, just as it would be to say that Joyce's borrowings are only stolen words. Rather, his method of recontextualizing the words of both predecessors and contemporaries fashions something novel by creating explosive, unexpected connections.

Shishkin performs a similar tightrope act in citing so explicitly, as Joyce does with Flaubert or Malory. It is certainly not coincidental that *Maidenhair*'s first line is a quotation taken verbatim from Xenophon's *Anabasis*. The most extensive of Shishkin's borrowings come from the ancient Greek historian-soldier's account of Cyrus the Younger's failed attempt to seize the Persian throne from his brother Artaxerxes II. (Incidentally, Xenophon's epic plays no less an important role in *Ulysses*'s opening chapter, where Buck Mulligan calls out *"Thalatta! Thalatta!"*[54]—a reference to the soldiers' finally encountering the Black Sea after their failed war.) This initial reference-cum-citation in *Maidenhair*, thus, establishes the terms of Shishkin's poetics in the novel, something that continues to its final pages:

Sнisнкin: У Дария и Парисатиды было два сына, старший Артаксеркс и младший Кир.

Xenophon: У Дария и Парисатиды было два сына: старший Артаксеркс и младший Кир.

Translation: Darius and Parysatis had two sons born to them, of whom the elder was Artaxerxes and the younger Cyrus.[55]

After this opening where Shishkin only slightly changes the punctuation, follows a brief description of the Interpreter's office and the first question-and-answer section. However, Shishkin repeatedly modifies Xenophon's words in other passages. At one point, the Interpreter describes how he wishes to read before going to sleep and then begins quoting chapter 5 of the *Anabasis*. However, in this passage he takes more liberties with the original source (see table 5.3).

The quotation continues for several more lines, but this selection provides a sense of Shishkin's methods. Modifications of tense (*pakhli* [smelled] → *pakhnut* [smell]), as well as of deictic markers (*tam* [there], the removal of the reference to Arabia), are typical of Shishkin's insertions from other texts. Those passages that appear to be transcribed by the Interpreter from his reading of the *Anabasis* are logically transferred from the past tense into the present tense as he scans the lines, and they thus make clear that he retells the events from Xenophon's chronicle as opposed to only copying them word for word. At the same time, Shishkin makes adjustments that appear to be purely stylistic, such as reorganizing the order of a participial clause found a few sentences below the passage quoted below.

Beyond rearranging words and altering grammar, Shishkin omits details and combines his sources in other sections much as Joyce does.[56] In the two paragraphs that follow, a portion from chapter 8 of the *Anabasis* is wedded to material from chapter 7, and Shishkin cuts a few details largely related to troop movements and strategies undertaken by Cyrus and his forces.[57] The result is that Xenophon's original text loses some of its specificity. There could be no mistaking the source of Shishkin's words, but they lose their original flavor in place of a more generalized depiction of events. Shishkin is concerned here less with the minutiae of battle than with the emotional undercurrents, as well

Table 5.3

Shishkin Original: Хочется еще, прежде чем выключить свет и положить подушку на ухо, унестись на другой конец империи и пройти вместе с Киром по пустыне, имея Евфрат по правую руку, в пять переходов 35 парасангов. . . . Встречные растения—кустарники и тростники—все прекрасно пахнут, словно благовония.	**Xenophon in Russian Translation**: Отсюда Кир проходит по пустыне Аравии, имея Евфрат по правую руку, в пять переходов 35 парасангов. . . . Встречавшиеся там те или иные растения—кустарники или тростники—все прекрасно пахли, словно благовония.
English Translation of Shishkin: One still wants, before turning off the light and putting pillow to ear, to fly off to the other end of the empire and with Cyrus, keeping the Euphrates on the right, cross five stages through desert country, thirty-five parasangs. . . . Whatever else is met on the plain by way of shrub or reed, is always fragrant, like spices.	**English Translation of Xenophon**: Thence he marched through Arabia, keeping the Euphrates on the right, five stages through desert country, thirty-five parasangs. . . . Whatever else there was on the plain by way of shrub or reed, was always fragrant, like spices.

Sources: Shishkin, *Venerin volos*, 28; Ksenofont, *Anabasis*, 22–23; and Xenophon, *Anabasis*, 47.

as the ways these stories resonate through time, linking different lives. Both Shishkin and Joyce pursue this universalizing effect in their works.

Another major borrowing that likewise upends the original source's spatial-temporal foundations comes from Edgar Allan Poe's "Murders in the Rue Morgue" and appears in the question-and-answer section that details the policeman's battle against local corruption (see table 5.4).

As before, while largely transplanting much of Poe's passage to *Maidenhair*, Shishkin omits certain details, such as the ruined bed and teaspoons. Curiously, some French coins with Napoleon's visage remain in the scene as a trace from the original. He then adds another characteristically Russian image: the three-liter jar of mushroom kombucha. Finally, the murder victim, Madame L'Espanaye, becomes the policeman's sister and mother. Poe's Paris-set scene thus shifts. Nonetheless, the core narrative—a mysterious violent crime—remains intact. The murders and traumas exist in both times and countries.

Elsewhere in this section, Shishkin also refers to G. K. Chesterton's "The Miracle of Moon Crescent" and Agatha Christie's *And Then There Were None*, two

Table 5.4

Shishkin Original: В квартире все было вверх дном, повсюду раскидана поломанная мебель. На стуле лежала бритва с окровавленным лезвием. Две-три густые пряди длинных седых волос, вырванных, видимо, с корнем и слипшихся от крови, пристали к каминной решетке. На полу найдены были четыре наполеондора, одна серьга с топазом и два мешочка со старыми юбилейными рублями, которые здесь все автоматы принимают за пятифранковую монету с Вильгельмом Теллем. У окна разбитая трехлитровая банка с грибом—подсох, скукожился.

Poe in Russian Translation: Здесь все было вверх дном, повсюду раскидана поломанная мебель. В комнате стояла одна только кровать, но без постели, подушки и одеяло валялись на полу. На стуле лежала бритва с окровавленным лезвием. Две-три густые пряди длинных седых волос, вырванных, видимо, с корнем и слипшихся от крови, пристали к каминной решетке. На полу, под ногами, найдены четыре наполеондора, одна серьга с топазом, три столовые серебряные и три чайные мельхиоровые ложки и два мешочка с золотыми монетами—общим счетом без малого четыре тысячи франков.

Shishkin in English Translation: The apartment was in the wildest disorder—the furniture broken and thrown about in all directions. On the chair lay a razor, besmeared with blood. On the hearth were two or three long and thick tresses of gray human hair, also dabbled with blood, and seeming to have been pulled out by the roots. Upon the floor were found four Napoleons, an ear-ring of topaz, and two bags with old jubilee rubles, which all slot machines here take for five-franc coins with William Tell. Near the window was a broken three-liter jar with homemade kombucha inside—dried and shriveled now.

Poe Original: The apartment was in the wildest disorder—the furniture broken and thrown about in all directions. There was only one bedstead; and from this the bed had been removed, and thrown into the middle of the floor. On the chair lay a razor, besmeared with blood. On the hearth were two or three long and thick tresses of gray human hair, also dabbled with blood, and seeming to have been pulled out by the roots. Upon the floor were found four Napoleons, an ear-ring of topaz, three large silver spoons, three smaller of *metal d'Alger*, and two bags, containing nearly four thousand francs in gold.

Sources: Shishkin, *Venerin volos*, 47–48; Edgar Po, "Ubiistvo na ulitse Morg," in *Izbrannoe*, trans. V. Stanevits (Moskva: Gosudarstvennoe izdatel'stvo khudozhestvennoi literatury, 1958), 148; Edgar Allan Poe, "The Murders in the Rue Morgue," in *Selected Poetry, Tales, and Essays* (Boston: St. Martin's Press, 2015), 136. Shishkin's borrowing actually extends further.

other works of detective fiction.[58] The author paraphrases the former's plot, uses the character name Wynd, and focuses on the locked door at the heart of the mystery.[59] Shishkin also echoes Christie by incorporating her "plaster of red mud on the forehead" and "[gray] wool."[60] In this way, Shishkin brings together disparate items to craft a transnational point of view by which identities shatter and tales can be told and retold. For him, contemporary stories hold the same kinds of tragedy as those from the distant past in faraway locales.[61] At the same time, his Russian narrative becomes part of Poe's mystery.

In essence, Shishkin creates a metastyle out of his borrowings, as a number of key insertions both comment on his practice and realize the novel's thematics of identity and individuality, not unlike what we see in Joyce's works. The latter, too, quotes and reformulates alien materials to devise his polyphonic texts, multivalent characters, and global perspective in *Finnegans Wake*. Shishkin crafts a novelistic world where characters separated by thousands of miles and decades, if not centuries, are united by near identical experiences. The borrowings, in turn, serve to emphasize this view of the world in which history rhymes. Joyce, too, deploys such a style. The texture made up of borrowings and parodies of "Oxen of the Sun," for example, depends on the reader's recognizing the shifting styles, if not the particular sources of those voices, for part of its effect. The new context—a maternity hospital in Dublin, 1904—gives different meaning to these voices and styles, as they are used to describe much different scenarios than originally intended.

Instead of fearing or envying the words of his fathers, Shishkin, following in Joyce's footsteps, takes a ludic approach. For instance, early in the novel, Shishkin's Interpreter quotes without explanation a line from Anton Chekhov's (1860–1904) *The Seagull* in a letter to his son, adding only an interjection in the middle: "On the dam, you see, the neck of a broken bottle gleams and the shadow dims from the mill wheel."[62] This line comes from act 4 of Chekhov's play and is spoken by Konstantin Treplev, a would-be writer who struggles with his reputation. Here, he compares himself to the more successful Boris Trigorin, but the lines that follow in the original work are just as significant: "And all the same I come to the conclusion that it's not a matter of old or new forms, but rather that a person writes, not thinking about forms, writes because that's what freely pours out of his soul."[63] Understood within the context of Shishkin's palimpsestic borrowings, this passage offers a key to understanding the author's methods. He refers to a well-known example from Chekhov where a character, who wants desperately to be a writer of Romantic genius, struggles with questions of authenticity and originality. Joyce's efforts to destroy the traditional novelistic form in *Ulysses* and even more so in the *Wake* prefigure Shishkin's project. Shishkin, for his part, proclaims that the issue of new or old forms matters less than a commitment to the task at hand, to pouring out what is inside the writer's "soul"—a compendium of various other people's texts and voices. By doing so, Shishkin uses a citational technique that defines much of his work to question what literature might be when we understand the author not in broad Romantic terms as a genius, but rather as a translator/interpreter of the word and of literary history. Writing under the weight of this accumulated cultural baggage, Shishkin opts to engage directly with his predecessors. He minces no words about his practices, and a key line from one of the question-and-answer sections cannot be anything but an ironic commentary on his work: "If you're not caught, you're not a thief."[64] Although Tankov caught Shishkin, the latter maintains his innocence by advocating for a different relationship with the past and its cultural artifacts, one that embraces Joycean intertextuality. The fact that *Maidenhair* won both the National Bestseller and Big Book awards suggests that critics sided with Shishkin, too.

Furthermore, the way *Maidenhair* recalls and thereafter amends the words of the past imagines them as a literary landscape that the author can explore and rebuild. Joyce's project in *Ulysses* and *Finnegans Wake* offers a striking parallel, even a model, for Shishkin's work. "If Shishkin's novel focuses on modernity [Bella's 1920s and 1930s]," notes Sergey Oroby, "then it is only in order to depict it as transient, overturned [*oprokinutoi*] into the past."[65] This modernist past, in other words, is but one step in the development of literature, not its culmination, so it must not overwhelm new artists. All the same, its lessons and techniques may be adapted for new purposes.

For Shishkin, who writes after the fall of the Soviet Union and amid the chaos of a period when writers attempted to make sense of their new identities and Russia's role on the global stage, adopting this Joycean method is yet another means of inscribing himself, his art, and his Russian literature into world culture. By citing and reworking foreign elements alongside domestic ones in this neutral way—both sincere and parodic—Shishkin forges a link between contemporary Russian fiction and its Western predecessors. In light of the literary and political polemics of the 1990s and early 2000s, his act is even more meaningful. The Interpreter (and the author behind his hero) seeks not a father figure the way Nabokov's Fyodor does in order to establish a lineage; instead, he scrambles and reconstitutes many voices from many times and places to generate this sense of time in which all peoples may be equal. While he sees the general relativity of historical time like Sokolov, whose novels refuse to accept the laws of time, he draws on an even wider range of sources. In so doing, he merges the two traditions to rewrite these lines and disrupt the notion that Russia's ties to the West had been, or even should now be, irrevocably severed.

Answering Tragedy in the Affirmative

These links work on both the macro and micro levels. Describing *The Taking of Izmail* (written 1996–1998, published 1999 and 2000), his second, as yet untranslated novel, Shishkin wrote in his response to Tankov and other critics: "'The 'typical' reader, it goes without saying, is not obligated to guess without fail where each and every phrase comes from. To me it's important that the ideal reader knows everything. The simple reader immediately guesses that the 'Yes' that ends this section [of *Izmail*] is Joyce's 'yes' that ends his novel. But it's more important to me that the ideal reader knows that this 'yes' was Velimir Khlebnikov's answer to the question posed by the peasant girl in whose house he passed away: 'Well, is it hard to die?'"[66] Shishkin speaks of his perfect reader who should be able to identify the author's many sources, even ones nearly impossible to recognize hidden in single words, but there is even greater significance to his claim. First, in this example, but not only there, Shishkin unites Russian literature—embodied by Khlebnikov (1885–1922)—with Joyce. The word "yes" can thus represent how Shishkin's art transverses national borders. Given his comments regarding Russian literature's "love of man" and the West's "love of the word," it is curious, of course, that he brings together Khlebnikov, a Futurist Russian poet who helped develop *zaum'* (trans-sense) verse, with Joyce, who in a way developed his own trans-sense prose. But the context of Khlebnikov's exchange before his death links him to the humanity that Shishkin mentions elsewhere. His "yes" speaks of death and pain, while Molly's "yes" is a rejoinder against all that. It stands at the book's end as a firm affirmation of the will to live and to love.

This is not Shishkin's only Joycean "yes," however. Bella, in one of her later diary entries, writes about her unborn child and her love for her husband, Iosif Epstein: "And now I'm thinking about myself and how I would have answered her. Do I love him? Am I happy? Yes. Yes."[67] This moment directly parallels "Penelope," as Bella continues to see the good in her marriage despite rough times. Even closer to the end of *Maidenhair*, the book's many narratives collapse, blending into one another to form more than a dozen pages of prose divided into only two paragraphs and resembling stream of consciousness.[68] Not insignificantly, the first paragraph begins with the key word "Yes," just as Molly's soliloquy does.[69] This word and the section's initial portions are spoken by Galpetra, the Interpreter's former teacher, but soon after the text breaks down and begins to combine fragments of the many narrative threads the reader has encountered along the way, as well as a multitude of quotations derived from the Interpreter's (that is, Shishkin's) wide-ranging reading and stray bits of his writing.

The voices of multiple narrators can be heard throughout the ensuing pages, but one of the principal figures consists of a combination of Galpetra and Bella. These female figures, like Molly Bloom, evoke a sense of a life that refuses to be diminished by any personal tragedies, not least of which are the deaths of Molly's and Bella's young children. At one point in her soliloquy, Molly thinks about her son, Rudy, who died at eleven days: "I knew well Id never have another our 1st death too it was we were never the same since O Im not going to think myself into the glooms about that any more."[70] The same sorts of thoughts plague Galpetra: "How difficult it is to spend one's last years in solitude. And how I wanted a child! The child who was then, at the Ostankino Museum, inside me, never born, became a fish and swam away. How I prayed: Green, green grass, give me another little baby!"[71] The attentive reader knows that this is Galpetra's voice, since very early in the novel, during a field trip to Ostankino, the Interpreter recalls being surprised as a child that Galpetra could become pregnant. On the following page, too, the character imagines herself pregnant miraculously again and refers to the child as "sweetpea," Bella's nickname for her son before his birth.[72] What she explains as the birth of this new child turns out to be her death, previously described by the person living in her former apartment as a horrific mess, as she fell while adjusting a lamp and died covered in her own feces.[73] Thus, the two figures merge into one through the shared experience of losing children, the narration blurring the lines between their two lives. Despite being surrounded by great tragedy and death, *Maidenhair*'s characters nonetheless seek out life, hope, and resurrection through these kinds of connections to newer generations and rebirth, themes that resonate with Molly and "Penelope" in *Ulysses*. Language is what brings them all together. The shared "Yes" that begins both Molly's and Galpetra's soliloquies embodies such an outlook on life.

Both in "More than Joyce" and in *Maidenhair*, Shishkin associates this power of the word, which can preserve and even resurrect life in posterity, with a divine source. In the former, he writes that an author's innovations will seem like "hocus-pocus" to the uninitiated reader but will be entirely "comprehensible to God."[74] Such is the nature of *Finnegans Wake*, which effectively crafts a pre-Babelian, experimental linguistic space. Languages, dialects, and neologisms bleed into one another, and in this process Shishkin sees Joyce's desire to mix all cultures and to achieve a communion with a common point of origin. One of his most potent symbols in this effort is a tree—not just a single tree, but many that are all simultaneously one: the Tree of Life, the Tree of Knowledge, the mythical Norse tree Yggdrasil, and others. Close to the book's conclusion, HCE and Anna Livia are once more transformed into Adam and Eve figures and, afterward, into a tree representative of the prototypical family:

"Creatures of the wold approaching him, hollow mid ivy, for to claw and rub, hermits of the desert barking their infernal shins over her triliteral roots and his acorns and pinecorns shooting wide all sides out of him, plantitude out-sends of plenty to thousands . . . and her leaves, my darling dearest, sinsin-sinning since the night of time and each and all of their branches meeting and shaking twisty hands all over again in their new world through the ger-mination of its gemination from Ond's outset till Odd's end."[75] Joyce layers myths upon one another, amplifying his idea that stories are all iterations of tales already once told. The tree imagery, following Shishkin's logic, fur-thermore unites everyone in a kind of pantheistic fervor, while language—understood as a kind of natural force—not only represents life but sustains it by constantly creating these branches between peoples and stories.

Something similar takes place near the end of *Maidenhair* when the text erupts into the stream-of-consciousness section. One of its key motifs is the titular maidenhair, a grass that grows in different guises with greater frequency throughout the book's pages. The green grass, of course, calls to mind Howth Head, the site of Bloom's proposal to Molly when they lay by the seaside and of Molly's closing thoughts in *Ulysses*'s final episode. She remembers how they rested in the grass on that day and felt alive, and, in turn, the Interpreter's stream of consciousness recalls a day when Isolde, his wife, was hanging laundry, and he watched her. "You grab her heel," he writes, "kiss her ankle, and Isolde laughs, hops on one foot, uses the tube to smack you on your shoul-ders, on your head, loses her balance, falls, grabs onto your neck, and the mat-tress bucks and rears and dumps you on the grass [*travku*]."[76] Both novels thus feature this movement toward the green grass, a symbol for life and the sus-tainability of hope.

Indeed, *Maidenhair* concludes with a tour guide's call in the streets of Rome: "Where are you? Follow me! I'll show you the green, green grass [*travka-muravka*]!"[77] As the stream of consciousness shakes loose divisions between voices in the novel, Shishkin's own Babelian project is enacted; all his heroes, whether technically living or dead, come to coexist, as it were, on the pages and within the word itself. The fern, then, denotes this tectonic shift. As the anthropo-morphized maidenhair proclaims at one point in the book's furious conclusion, "Adiantum capillus veneris. The green, green grass from the genus adiantum. Maidenhair. The god of life. . . . I grew here before your Eternal City and I will grow after."[78] The novel closes with this symbol of life-affirming energy and un-stoppable growth, as the various narrative threads return to their source: the fern-cum-language that transcends all, even death. In proposing that nature will remain after the end of the so-called Eternal City (Rome), Shishkin also im-plies that literature (represented by the maidenhair) will preserve their lives.

By tapping into the threads of the green grass and using it as a motif throughout his novel, Shishkin aims for a kind of immortality in the written word.

Along the same lines, *"Finnegans Wake,"* writes Shishkin, is "an incantation for the resurrection of the dead, a magic spell of flesh risen from the grave."[79] He goes so far as to call the *Wake* a "book of immortal life."[80] *Maidenhair* repeats many such proclamations, as when one of Bella's lovers, who has been reading Xenophon's *Anabasis*, tells her, "[Xenophon's soldiers are] no better or worse than today's soldiers, who are shooting at someone right now. . . . Imagine, how many people have slipped by . . . and these Greek soldiers held on because he wrote them down. . . . Because he brought them to a very special sea. Thalassa is the sea of immortality."[81] Shishkin here conflates the preservation of the memory of others in writing with immortality. He sees in Joyce the profoundest expression of how words can reclaim that which has been lost. He is therefore not (simply) a symbol of the Western canon; rather, Joyce becomes a model for how a writer can manipulate words to fashion history itself. Shishkin's essay manifests this idea, as he aims to reintegrate Russian literature into Joyce's legacy through his narrative. He mentions in "More than Joyce" the stories of how Akhmatova read Joyce with Lidia Chukovskaya, how Sergei Eisenstein (1898–1948) dreamt of adapting *Ulysses* to film. Shishkin's engagement with Joyce operates on this metatextual level as well. As a re-interpreter of the past, he aims to demonstrate how Russian culture retained its vital links to Joyce even when thought impossible, and, in doing so today, he drafts this positivist tradition into which his work may fit.

Time's Arrow

Such creative rewritings of the past lie at the core of Shishkin's work and manifest themselves in multifarious ways. In "More than Joyce," Shishkin takes up the Ouroboros—the ancient Egyptian symbol depicting a snake eating its own tail—when discussing *Finnegans Wake*'s simultaneous beginning/end. He, like many others, initially uses this image to describe the *Wake*'s shape, as the final line segues into the opening line: "A way a lone a last a loved a long the / riverrun, past Eve and Adam's, from swerve of shore to bend of bay, brings us by a commodius vicus of recirculation back to Howth Castle and Environs."[82] But not long afterward in the essay, Shishkin changes his mind: "No, not so. The Ouroboros, of course, doesn't bite itself by the tail, but disgorges itself. It gives birth to itself through the mouth, like the word. Thus it changes the direction of the universe. And all human culture retreats into itself differently: *Finnegans Wake* births the Torah."[83] Shishkin, in this way, suggests that the artist can rewrite the past, making it seem as if the modern generates the ancient by somehow encompassing all that came before it.

In fact, this sense that the present or the future can engender the past runs deep within *Maidenhair*, where all plotlines can intersect no matter the time or space involved. In other words, all roads *do* lead to Rome in Shishkin's universe. His creative process, along with the texts that it produces, is the Ouroboros taking in the past and reformulating it in the process of spitting it out again. Looking backward produces no anxiety, only opportunity.

In the first stream of consciousness section, a stylistic representation of this idea takes shape when the narrative suddenly presents the reader with a series of untranslatable palindromes: "Ищи в себе свищи. . . . Тут как тут. . . . Там холмы, дым лохмат, невидим и дивен. А к ночи ж умер, о горе, мужичонка. . . . И нет тени. И ледены недели. И волнами луну, лиман, лови. . . . Косо сидел у леди сосок. И с репу перси. Узор плел прозу."[84] This section of *Maidenhair*, identified in the English translation, but not in the original, as a "notebook lost in the metro" by the Interpreter, blends together many different quotations from other sources and themes and motifs from the novel.[85] In other words, it recycles what has come before, as if the book is recovering these past materials. The palindromes, which task the reader with moving both forward and backward, play out this very collapse of time, where the present can retreat into the past and, in so doing, transform it.

Joyce's last two novels also exhibit this type of wordplay. Consider, for instance, *Ulysses*'s "Madam, I'm Adam" and "Able was I ere I saw Elba."[86] They become even more prominent in *Finnegans Wake*. Here are two examples: "And shall not Babel be with Lebab" and "Madas. Sadam."[87] Joyce's biblical "Madam, I'm Adam" and "Babel . . . Lebab" both direct readers toward the origins of language: the former represents what could have ostensibly been the first human exchange (Adam introducing himself to Eve were they English speakers) and the latter to the Tower of Babel and its fall. His own works, particularly *Finnegans Wake*, enact a total revolution of language itself, one that explores what it means both to communicate meaning through words and to scavenge the past for material.

Shishkin has similar ideas in mind when he departs from the more traditional parts of his narrative into the stream of *collective* consciousness, bringing together numerous voices through citations of numerous works. In the first of these two sections, the reader becomes acquainted with the contents of the Interpreter's notebook. In the second, the Interpreter ostensibly meets Galpetra on the streets of Rome, and they begin a conversation. It quickly becomes apparent, however, that everything is occurring within the narrator's mind and that he is pulling together stray bits of conversations he has held, jottings he has made in his notebooks, and quotations from his reading of various texts. The result is a procession of distinct voices that the Interpreter has imbibed through various means in his life. While it does not become the same kind of cacophony and multilingual chaos that *Finnegans Wake* does, this part of the book, more so than others, exhibits Shishkin's interest in blending traditions, shuttling between time frames through language and the echoes of past works. From this perspective, indeed, *Finnegans Wake* can give birth to the Torah, just as *Maidenhair* births its predecessors by recontextualizing them. The palindromes then function as an especially striking, emblematic symbol of this unexpected move between the present and the past.

The way Shishkin engages with history, particularly the modernist era, suggests that his work falls under the rubric of what David James and Urmila Seshagiri call Metamodernism. According to them, novels such as *Maidenhair*, which takes up Bella's narrative from roughly 1904 to Stalin's reign, "extend, reanimate, and repudiate twentieth-century modernist literature."[88] This frequently involves setting their contemporary works in the modernist period itself and using its archetypal devices, including stream of consciousness. In depicting the past in his work, Shishkin attempts to make sense of it and its effects on the present. *Maidenhair*, at least in part, might therefore be read as a working through of the continuities between prerevolutionary Russia, early Soviet Russia, and post-Soviet Russia. It goes much further than that, however, as Shishkin brings in Xenophon and ancient myth, but the centrality of Bella's narrative to *Maidenhair*'s plot and its thematic resonance grants it additional weight. At the same time, by incorporating the past into his works, Shishkin not only makes links between eras but actually rewrites it. Shishkin's text becomes the Joycean Ouroboros that spits out its own origins, and, on a higher level, the author can therefore become one with his forerunners while retaining his autonomy. In crossing these borders—metaphoric, literary, temporal—he develops his role as an interpreter of history.

Waking from the Nightmare of Paternity

Like the rest of the works previously analyzed, *Maidenhair* is also a book about parents and children. In this novel, at least, Shishkin articulates an obsession with father-son relations not unlike the ones that drive much of *Ulysses*. Significantly, it begins with a proclamation concerning parentage: "Darius and Parysatis had two sons born to them, of whom the elder was Artaxerxes and the younger Cyrus."[89] From its opening, then, *Maidenhair* is a book concerned with origins. Bella, in her story, also devotes a great deal of attention to her father and mother. She later relates the experience of becoming pregnant with her husband,

Iosif, as well as the birth and death of their young son, Volodya. Then there is the Interpreter, who writes unsent missives to his son, whom we see only in the protagonist's recollections of his time with his ex-wife, Isolde.

These various plot points together underscore just how taken Shishkin is with the question of paternity. He has in fact expressed the belief that there is a direct link between the experience of having a child and one's ability to create art, as when he explained his first novel's conception:

> I'm suffering on the second floor [of our dacha], and my wife is lying, reading something on the first floor. With terror I recognize that nothing will come of it, lay down on the couch, and pick up a copy of *Ogonek* [*Little Fire*]. . . . I open a posthumous interview with Andrei Tarkovsky and suddenly see the phrase: "And how can you make films, how can you write novels if you haven't held your child in your own hands?" Right then I understood: I don't have any children, so my novel doesn't come out. I went down to the first floor, and nine months later our son was born and my novel written. But when our son was born, I understood that compared to the birth of one's son a novel is utter nonsense.[90]

Reading various statements on parents and children throughout *Maidenhair* in this way sheds light on his notion of the creative drive. Whereas some of the previous authors (Olesha, Nabokov, Bitov) looked backward, toward their own father figures, in the process of inspiration, Shishkin inverts the formula, seeing inspiration in the creation of future generations—intimately linked to the past though they may be.

In the final question-and-answer section of the novel, the Interpreter imagines a conversation between himself and a girlfriend nicknamed the Princess Frog, who died by suicide. The two discuss how they feel themselves turning into their parents. The woman says, "Sometimes I caught myself thinking with horror that I understood and felt everything she [her mother] understood and felt at some time. Here you and I loved each other, but in my head I thought that maybe my mama loved my father exactly the same way when I was already somewhere near this world. . . . At that moment, she and I suddenly united, merged. And you have exactly the same kind of mole below your shoulder blade as my father did."[91] What she says calls to mind Stephen's proclamations in "Scylla and Charybdis": "And as the mole on my right breast is where it was when I was born, though all my body has been woven of new stuff time after time, so through the ghost of the unquiet father the image of the unliving son looks forth."[92] "So in the future," he continues, "the sister of the past, I may see myself as I sit here now but by reflection from that which then I shall be."[93] Stephen's speech is entirely wrapped up in his considerations of what paternity means, metaphysically and poetically speaking. Here, he suggests that as the human body constantly reinvents itself, so too may the creative artist fashion a new identity and, in so doing, may establish new bonds between the past and the future, the present and the future. For him, the mole is a symbol of the trace that remains, despite the body's constant renewal. For the Interpreter's (imagined, deceased, former) girlfriend, it results in certain anxieties similar to Stephen's—the fear of turning into one's parents, of inheriting their imperfections. All the same, in this mole, the child can be seen in the father, as if the former gives meaning to the latter.

When the Interpreter doubts her story, she asks whether he ever felt the same thing, and he responds, suddenly recalling an experience on a bumpy train car: "Never. Or rather, once, yes. . . . And for an instant the rattling car seemed to me a submarine and I was him, my father. He and I became a single whole. Time and everything else suddenly turned to nothing, to dust. I was my father."[94] Here, yet again, is the theme of echoing stories uniting generations. It is a passing moment—both in the Interpreter's recollection and in his conversation with his girlfriend—for they quickly move on, but it is a significant one. Whereas Olesha's hero, Kavalerov, freezes up at the thought that he has become his father when he recognizes him while gazing in a mirror, the Interpreter gains insight into the nature of time as he eventually views it when he remembers this sensation on the train. The structure of *Maidenhair* reflects this same epiphany, as characters blend in and out of one another, resulting in a simultaneity of different temporal planes. The son can feel at one with the father thanks to the transformative power of memory and art.

Considered from a different angle, if everything happens simultaneously, then there is no real space between *Maidenhair* and *Ulysses* or *Finnegans Wake*; they may yet occupy the same cultural territory. In giving birth to one's predecessors, through the creative reworking of past materials, one can become father to oneself and even reconfigure the sources (Western and Russian) of one's lineage in the process. One can leave behind those identifying marks— the moles—from which Stephen's "unliving sons" peer forth into the future. *Maidenhair* in this manner flips the Joycean script by focusing not on the young artist/son, but rather on the father (the Interpreter) who learns to read history more compassionately.

After the End of History

According to Shishkin's essay "Salvaged Language," he made it his top priority on reaching Zurich to visit Joyce's grave in the Fluntern Graveyard. As he approached the site, he became confused; a huge crowd was headed in the same direction and gathering nearby. Then it all became clear: they were burying Elias Canetti (1905–1994), the Bulgarian Nobel Prize–winning novelist, who had requested that he be buried near Joyce.[95]

Shishkin would deny that writing in Russian outside his homeland's borders is significant. And why should it be? His connection and familiarity with the contemporary language spoken by those within Russia may fall behind, but Russian remains his primary tool in crafting his view of the world. Where he lives plays little role in that. And yet the question of place clearly means a great deal to him, as it did to Joyce. Like Canetti, Shishkin has found both literal and metaphoric proximity to the great Irish writer. Joyce devoted over six hundred pages to Dublin alone, and in *Finnegans Wake* he threw in many additional locations and sights, building on its Irish foundation. *Maidenhair* focuses a great deal on Rome, at least a tourist's version of the city, along with Bella's tsarist Russian provinces and Soviet cities. Beyond that, we are shuttled between Xenophon's ancient world and the Chechen refugees' homes. Shishkin develops his transnational novel by traversing these multifarious boundaries.

A more minor point still worth mentioning is Shishkin's placement of "Zürich–Rome, 2002–2004" after the last lines in *Maidenhair*, which recalls Joyce's postscript to *Ulysses*: "Trieste–Zurich–Paris / 1914–1921."[96] There was little intentional in how Shishkin came to occupy the same city as Joyce: "I wrote in Joyce's cities not thinking at all about that, for he shared these cities with dozens of writers who are important to me. And in general, these were already my cities, not theirs."[97] Nonetheless, both writers' postscripts contextualize their works within a broader framework than their ostensible national origins; they evoke the cosmopolitanism that Russian nationalist critics decry in this post-Soviet era, as well as simultaneously positioning their authors as international figures. Additionally, much of *Maidenhair* focuses on people fleeing their homes in search of sanctuary, and Shishkin's project should be read in a similar light. His narrative positions humanity in general—and the author as an emblematic case—as refugees seeking meaning and companionship in an often dark and violent world. This concept informs Joyce's and Shishkin's fiction in significant ways, as they constantly look for a literary home, father, and compatriots. Neither one went into "exile" by force; they both willingly and consciously opted to depart for Europe, but remain(ed) free to return, more or less. For Joyce, escaping the bounds of Ireland, held "paralyzed" by backward-looking mind-sets and traditions, felt necessary for developing his art. Like Shishkin, he needed to gain that critical distance from his subject. In Shishkin's case, coming out of the Soviet era, there is yet another factor in the equation: whether or not Russia should align itself with the West. These links with Joyce serve as a potential means of bringing together the Russian tradition (the "love of man") with the Western tradition (the "love of the word"). And his response to Joyce becomes a political move. Russia remains central to his thought, and yet it is only one component among many.

There are, of course, very few simple, reliable keys for resolving questions of literary influence (or even dialogue). This may be acutely true when it comes to a writer with such immense reach and symbolic capital as James Joyce. What comes after him? Everything? Nothing? In the Russian context, where Soviet authorities excised him from the record for many decades, what might he represent to writers today? Among the most protean of artists, Joyce serves in some respects as a litmus test for a Russian writer's position vis-à-vis the West. He can be not only a great writer but an alternative path. But Joyce's future in Russia remains unclear, for his example can lead to many ends.

While, as Rogova suggests, the thematic links between Joyce's and Shishkin's works are numerous, "More than Joyce" clarifies how these same ideas populate *Maidenhair* and affect its very structure. The interpenetration of voices and cultures functions on the level of plot, to be sure, as Shishkin turns his focus from character to character and location to location, but it also renders the novel a "palimpsest-book," to borrow his term for *Finnegans Wake* in his essay.[98] Stories stack atop one another, as the author borrows and rewrites others. Although it is nowhere near as radical as the *Wake*, *Maidenhair* exhibits a stylistic influence that positions Shishkin within a particular strand of the Russian Joycean tradition. He takes just as much from the fabric of Joyce's writing as he does from his creative philosophy of literature and history.

What reading "More than Joyce" alongside *Maidenhair* allows the reader to see most clearly of all, however, is the conflation of art and life that Shishkin emphasizes throughout the essay. At a couple key—and surprising—moments, he enigmatically mentions that something in Joyce's books is "as in life," as when everything happens simultaneously or when older generations turn into younger ones. For him, the nature of Joyce's worldview manifested itself not only in some texts that relatively few people read but also in the way its narrative framework reflects, perhaps even somehow shapes, human experience itself. This, then, is Joyce's greatest parallel to Shishkin's art: an understanding of the writer's near-mythical task. What is at stake is how words can make sense of a world that seems so disjointed and chaotic—and in *Maidenhair* always by means of innovative techniques.[99] He aims through both his fiction and his nonfiction to bridge his work with the giants of the past. For Shishkin, to fail to cross this border between art and life, to fail to achieve this mission, means to be less than a true author.

Conclusion

How Joyce Is Read in Russia

> It seems history is to blame.
>
> —James Joyce, *Ulysses*

Act I: The Territory of Slow Reading

The Moscow-based Joyce reading group Territory of Slow Reading meets every Sunday, give or take the occasional holiday break, and promptly at 10 a.m. In their hour-long conversations, they pull apart and discuss the significance of Joyce's *Ulysses* episode by episode. Their membership is flexible, including the dozens on their Facebook page, but, more often than not, a handful gathers each time in a dedicated Zoom video call. Their target goal each Sunday: a section of the mammoth book. Founded in 2016 by Zinaida and Aleksei Odollamsky, the group has taken detours to cover *A Portrait of the Artist as a Young Man* and *The Odyssey*, as well as other Joyce-related texts, contexts, and scholarly works. On June 16, they also join thousands around the world by organizing a Bloomsday walk and reading—a celebration of Leopold Bloom's peripatetic escapades in *Ulysses*. They themselves stroll around Moscow and read fragments at such sites as the Arbat and Patriarch's Ponds, treating Muscovites to a peculiar sight. Some dressed in quasi-Victorian attire, they round off the day with drinks at a pub.

In early June 2019, I gladly agreed to join the group for one of their Sunday gatherings. The circumstances were perfect: Working in the RGALI archives at the time, I was not limited by the eight-hour time difference that would have otherwise required my waking up (or staying up) at two in the morning to discuss Joyce. On this particular date, right in the middle of a merciless heatwave, they were forging ahead with their discussion of episode 10, "Wandering Rocks," and its nineteen constituent vignettes. It was a serious, yet playful conversation about Joyce's work: "God created the world in six days, and Joyce in one day. He gifted us the seventh day."

When I asked the group why they read Joyce in the first place, one particularly excitable member, Wilhelm Shenrok (identified as Nikolai on Zoom), a German-born painter of highly erotic and parodic art, shifted to the topic of the patriarchy. Joyce is, for him, the embodiment of an art that liberates the human sexual drive, rebalances the divide between men and women, and shows the possibilities of interpersonal connections. It was to some extent difficult to tell just how genuinely Shenrok intended this explanation, but his remarks and the episode's other focus on money led to comments concerning the inability of today's so-called Russian intelligentsia to tackle such weighty— and everyday—topics head-on. "We get lost [*putaemsia*] when we talk about money, sex, and so on." Joyce, then, offers an alternative: "His language allows one to talk about new topics. God is the father. He gives everything." The seventh day was a good day.

This is, after all, everything that the selected case studies of this book have suggested. Joyce accorded them, and Russian culture more broadly, the opportunity to probe taboos, to break previously unyielding boundaries, to disrupt hierarchies. On the one hand, it is what compelled both Yury Olesha and Andrei Bitov to use Joyce's ideas to test what electing a different, nonbiological father figure would mean for their heroes, what it would do to one's psyche in disparate periods of Soviet history. On the other hand, it made Vladimir Nabokov resolute in his defense of the patriarchal, hierarchical order of literary relations—more reactionary, in a manner of speaking, toward narratives in Modernism that challenged biological and cultural Fathers.

In my conversation with the Moscow Joyce group, then, I noted similar themes and ideas, a familiar pull toward the flexible Joyce, the one who could represent so much to multifarious Russian intellectuals. Over the course of the past one hundred years, Joyce's image evolved with the times. That goes without saying. But in the Russian context, he became an emblem deeply tied to the politics and social order, as well as the literary tradition, of the changing regimes. In his plasticity, he nevertheless retained a nearly universal attraction, whether positively or negatively charged. At the beginning of the tumultuous twentieth century, countless debates about lineages raged, and writers were no less immune than others to such issues. If, as the Russian Futurists proclaimed, the classics should be thrown overboard from the steamship of modernity, or if Ezra Pound's dictum to "make it new" entrenched itself into the cultural psyche, then Joyce's art was prepared to become a major part of that novel steamship. Authors would come to view him as a name to be associated with, someone whose star could illuminate their own in the literary pantheon. His name was likewise a talisman of sorts in the gloom of the Soviet era when experimentation was severely limited in the public realm. He was, indeed, generous in his symbolic value, too.

Act II: Changing Responses

One way to tell the Joyce-in-Russia story examined so far is to consider how Russian writers' use of Joyce has answered the evolving preoccupations and intellectual needs of their ages. As demonstrated in chapter 1, for example, many of Olesha's texts concern themselves with the desire to eradicate the seed of an unwanted father figure not only from history but even from one's very being. In Envy, as well as in the trilogy of short stories "I Look into the Past," "Liompa," and "Human Material" composed in 1928, Olesha's narrators probe this very issue.[1] This struggle between generations would remain a common and critical anxiety for Olesha, as he had to decide whether he would side with the Soviet zeitgeist or resist it. Ultimately, ambivalence won out. The Joycean subtext of Olesha's Envy makes clear the meaning of Nikolai Kavalerov's decision when he does not head out into the dark night like Stephen Dedalus, but rather stays in Anechka's room with Ivan Babichev. Olesha's short novel in this way exemplifies a particular point in time—in both its composition and later developments in intertextual theory—when such paternal relations were viewed as intrinsically vertical and antagonistic. More specifically, Envy enacts what Harold Bloom calls a "kenosis" of Joyce: "a revisionary act in which an 'emptying' or 'ebbing' takes place *in relation to the precursor*. . . . 'Undoing' the precursor's strength *in oneself* serves also to 'isolate' the latecomer-poet."[2] Olesha's self-humbling extends itself to Joyce to show the limitations of his predecessor's project, its unsuitability to the new Soviet Russia and, therefore, to the world at large. This so-called emptying manifests itself on a narrative level, too, when Envy unexpectedly shifts from the first- to the third-person halfway through the novel. Although some argue that the second part continues to be narrated in Kavalerov's voice, it appears that he yields control, as the story turns its focus toward Ivan Babichev. This half is then all about Kavalerov's fall to paternal substitutes, as Olesha's intertextual exchange with Joyce reflects precisely this problematic relationship with predecessors that intertextual analyses, such as Bloom's, address.

Nabokov, too, evinces a similar attitude toward literary relations with his (in)famously strong opinions on writers both contemporaneous and dead. Most significantly, in *The Gift* and *Bend Sinister*, he endeavors to honor and correct Joyce's steps in *Ulysses*. He failed to translate Joyce's novel in a literal sense, despite his offer to do so in the early 1930s, but through *The Gift* he fashioned a creative rewriting of the modernist pillar of fatherly relationships that, all things considered, proved more closely aligned with his vision than any literal translation. Nabokov's art, at this point at least, exemplifies Bloomian clinamen, or "misprision proper": "A poet swerves away from his precursor, by so reading his precursor's poem as to execute a *clinamen* in relation to it. This [corrective move] implies that the precursor poem went accurately up to a certain point, but then should have swerved."[3] Nabokov clearly appreciates how Stephen-Joyce merge themselves with Shakespeare and Homer, their elected forefathers, but, even as he operates within the Joycean framework, he resents that this process does so at the expense of the biological relations between real father and son.[4] This attitude infects the novel itself. The search for a father manifests in the gradual development of the book's styles as a movement through the history of Russian letters since Pushkin's time across each of its five chapters.[5] *The Gift*, like *Envy* before it, represents this earlier step in intertextual theory with a kind of antagonism and competition at the heart of relationships between authors.

For the Oleshas and Nabokovs of the world, Joyce's contemporaries, the author of *Ulysses* enjoyed such an immense mythology that he became a father figure with whom one had to wage literary war. In a time of modernist hierarchies, grand societal experiments, and artistic genius, it was only natural that the response to him, especially the early Soviet Russian response, would exhibit shades of a battle of titans that emphasized the struggle to overcome one's history. There was a considerable paradigm shift in the post-Stalin age, however. With the breakdown of stable hierarchies and challenges both internal and external to the great metanarratives of the twentieth century (Stalinism, Modernism, Xism, Yism, Zism), our understanding of intertextual relations was likewise altered irrevocably.

This development is quite palpable in Andrei Bitov's *Pushkin House*, a novel that exhibits the growing pains of the transition from a combative, Bloomian paradigm of intertext to a decidedly more playful one. Bitov's Leva Odoevtsev, like Kavalerov and Fyodor Godunov-Cherdyntsev before him, tries to alter his pedigree, which results in a narrative structure that keeps looping in on itself. Each new iteration of Leva's paternity, in a sense, requires a new (hi)story. Between the assorted versions of Leva's life and Bitov's ludic use of many subtexts and quotations, a new attitude emerges. Rather than fearing the past or, worse, actively competing with it, Bitov's novel seeks to turn it into revelatory fun and adopts fragments of previous works to adorn itself. Less weighed down by his predecessors' accomplishments, Bitov saw in Joyce the possibility of escaping history's grip by enacting a "Hooligans Wake," a fitting alternative title Bitov considered for *Pushkin House* according to his own commentary.[6] Like Finnegan brought back to life by whiskey in the titular Irish song, the Russian tradition that was stamped out by the Soviet regime is resurrected and put to clever use by Bitov. His *Pushkin House* pulls back from what Patricia Yaeger calls the "agon" of Bloomian intertext toward "a queer poetics where style . . . becomes the dress of thought."[7] On the one hand, Bitov seems to challenge some of the basic ideas of T. S. Eliot's famous essay "Tradition and the Individual Talent." In this classic modernist statement, Eliot wrote that "you cannot value [a writer] alone; you must set him, for contrast and comparison, among the dead."[8] Bitov's *Pushkin House* rebels against this view. On the other hand, Bitov's use of past texts aligns with Eliot's (at the time) provocative belief that "what happens when a new work of art is created is something that happens simultaneously to all the works of art which preceded it."[9] The present, in other words, defines the past just as much as the past defines the present. And this is the lesson, adapted from Joyce's Shakespeare project, that Leva has learned by the novel's end, even if he must die and be resurrected for it to sink in. *Pushkin House*, in this way, fully encapsulates Eliot's "historical sense" through which an author "write[s] not merely with his own generation in his bones, but with a feeling that the whole of the literature of Europe . . . and within it the whole of the literature of his own country has a simultaneous existence."[10]

When it comes to radicalizing literature and intertext, however, Sasha Sokolov takes things even further. His *School for Fools* engages Joyce in a totally different manner, namely, through style. Style becomes an intertextual referent itself, where the stream of consciousness recalls and challenges Joyce's model in its deliberate multivoicedness and disruption of narrative time. Everything is deeply folded or entangled. Various classes of referents merge, becoming inseparable from Sokolov's (and the narrator's) own words and eradicating any sort of modernist hierarchies between his present and the past. Everything occurs simultaneously. If in the final lines the narrator and protagonist meld with the style itself, joining the many-footed creature that stalks the book's pages, then Sokolov adapts the Joycean model to transcend paternal-filial strife. The structure of the book, driven by its persistently conversing twin voices, flows unreservedly, referring to a number of authors, works, and cultural touchstones and reflecting this deeply entangled view of intertextuality where no one figure holds greater weight or pride of place over another. It would be a mistake to deem the protagonist or his narrative schizophrenic, but it is not coincidental that Fredric Jameson applied this exact term in his critique of capitalism. "The schizophrenic," Jameson writes, "is reduced to an experience of pure material signifiers, or, in other words, a series of pure and unrelated realities."[11] The present is entirely divorced from a sense of historicity. The difference between this analysis and Sokolov's novel is that the latter finds release from the strictures of Soviet reality in the author's literary representation of an existence with multiple presents. The break from linear time, which is inspired by Joyce's innovative novels, becomes liberating in these circumstances.

And what of the post-Soviet era—the confused age of Boris Yeltsin and Vladimir Putin when everyone suddenly became a contemporary of Joyce, if only for a brief moment starting in the early 1990s? Mikhail Shishkin's *Maidenhair*, as an emblematic case study of one brand of contemporary prose deeply concerned with the history of Russian letters, demands a *Wake*an understanding of literary relations. It conceives of all texts as up for grabs, a shared body of work that gifted writers might dip into at will. On a micro scale, Shishkin's adherence to this view aligns him with the late Joyce, who sought to craft a universal, almost pre-Babelian language in the *Wake*; the two authors cultivate a common transhuman grammar and historical-literary outlook where everything repeats in an eternal recurrence recalling Giambattista Vico's theory of history. To be sure, *Maidenhair* looks quite different than *Ulysses* or *Finnegans Wake*, particularly in plot, but the similarities in their deep structure and philosophical underpinnings are profound. On a macro scale, too, *Maidenhair* presents such a turn to the poetics of borrowing and plagiarism common to postmodern intertextuality. Here, the writer and the reader work together to excavate the treasures of the past. Such an approach naturally has its precedents (ancient, Romantic, modernist), but the density increases in this time period. Again, Joycean style and the intertextual tendencies of its era have an impact on *Maidenhair*'s construction, as the various competing/conversing narratives alternate and echo one another. At its core, Shishkin uses Joyce's model to initiate a radical intervention in Russian letters, bringing the tradition back into the realm of world literature.

For all these reasons, evaluating the Russian response to Joyce as a history of the past many decades of intertextual theory and practice helps shed light on several key features of twentieth-century Russian prose. First, it emphasizes, as do the individual case studies, the fickle, contextually based nature of how we link stories together. What was sheer theft in one era turns out to be a perfectly acceptable brand of honoring a precursor in another. For these five authors in particular, Joyce also offered different paths toward (re)claiming their literary genealogies. What they drew from Joyce's novels speaks to how they each conceptualized their respective generation's place in history. Joyce comes to personify the trajectory of world literature as it has become more tightly bound, inclusive, and interconnected. Reading the various Russian responses to him as stops along the tracks of intertextuality's development underscores how we have come both to read Joyce, in particular, and to read, in general, much differently. These writers have all grappled with what it means to live and create in a post-Joycean world, to operate belatedly. For the earlier set of authors, this position meant combating predecessors to make room for oneself; for the later group, it means accepting belatedness as a position of potential benefit, as well as welcoming filiation as a means to inherit something valuable.

Act III: Alternative Histories

This version of the Joyce-in-Russia story might also be counterbalanced with an explicit awareness of the heterogeneous fertility of borrowings and of Joycean intertextuality in particular. A book on intertextuality is necessarily a book of literary history, one prerequisite for which is a working assumption that history can be recounted and interpreted in a coherent manner. This position is not to be surrendered; much can be learned regarding the con/texts of the Russian writers spotlighted from this perspective.

However, the first thing for a literary historian to consider is the possibility that there is something intrinsically oppositional in the situation of a writer vis-à-vis history. Comparing the modern artist to the historian, Hayden White suggests that for the former, "history is not only a substantive burden imposed upon the present by the past in the form of outmoded institutions, ideas, and values, but also *the way of looking at the world* which gives to these outmoded forms their specious authority."[12] The twentieth- and twenty-first-century Russian authors featured throughout this book, for instance, sought to curb White's "substantive burden" to varying degrees of success. They each found an entry point into Joyce's writings, but this theme, along with other related ones, served as a catalyst for how they interpreted the Irish writer. Their readings of Joyce thus speak not only to their understanding of his work but also to their efforts to situate themselves within shifting historical factors and legacies, as well as an evolving comprehension of intertextual relations. The writer's struggle with history, according to this line of reasoning, is an attempted liberation from a worldview that stifles one's current reality with concerns about the past. This concept is vital to Joyce's fiction, particularly as concerns his own artist figures, Stephen and Shem. When Stephen calls history a "nightmare from which [he is] trying to awake," he has in mind the hold of the past embodied by his father, England, and Catholicism.[13] He also means the weight of literary history that looms over him as a budding writer. Its alleged inescapability terrifies Stephen. *Ulysses*, then, represents a working through of these ideas, as Stephen attempts to shake free from the stranglehold of this multitude of fathers, both literal and figurative, by means of his Shakespeare theory.

But the writer's and historian's craft is *also* essentially dependent on their worldviews. As White suggests in his *Metahistory*, all historians, including those of literature, turn stories into history by shaping them through a mode of emplotment (romance, comedy, tragedy, satire); a mode of argument (formist, mechanistic, organicist, contextualist); a mode of ideological implication (anarchist, radical, conservative, liberal); and a trope that provides a deep structure (metaphor, metonymy, synecdoche, irony). Historians, in other words, must inevitably "*pre*figure the [historical] field": the agents, figures, events, and ideas that make up the story.[14] How they piece everything together is defined by the modes in which they operate, which are, in turn, determined by their general worldview and outlook on the nature of their subjects. The writing of history for White is therefore a poetic act—not a purely academic, objective one. Finally, and most radically, White maintains that, in effect like a writer of fiction, "the historian both creates his object of analysis and predetermines the modality of the conceptual strategies he will use to explain it."[15] White's model is particularly attractive for the present discussion, since his overlapping grid structure of historical modes is so similar to *Ulysses*'s own architecture.

To conclude this study, then, we might try at least to imagine what a polyphonic approach to a history that is not yet concluded can yield, especially if applied to more recent materials in the Russian Joyce story. The modes in which most of the present book has been operating are metonymy / tragedy / contextualist / liberal. This particular combination places the individual writers against a shared, if gradually shifting, background (liberal, contextualist), understands these figures to represent a broader experience (metonymy), and recognizes their individual losses (tragedy). We do not have the space to attempt all of White's modes, of course, but we can do two things: (1) enlist the heterogeneous voices of contemporary Russian writers and (2) do so in a way roughly corresponding to another of White's modes, that of metaphor / romance / representational / anarchist. In this reading, we see likenesses across differences, Joyce as a once or continuing heroic figure, the uniqueness of individual writers, and a simultaneous community among them. This exercise invites further questions: How has Joyce come to be read in the past thirty or so years? What does he represent to the latest generations of writers, critics, and readers? How do they conceive of his influence—that knotty word!—now that he has been successfully reincorporated into the canon on Russian soil? How is this history being shaped *today* by living writers? To answer such questions, I have conducted interviews and corresponded with a wide range of authors, critics, and readers of Joyce in Russia, who themselves reflect assorted backgrounds, experiences, and ideologies. My goal here is to further refine the Joyce-in-Russia question to emphasize its continued, developing relevance.

Act IV: Joycean Echoes
Cast of Characters

Babikov, Andrei: b. 1974. Moscow. Author of short stories, poetry, and the novel *The Greenhouse* (2010). Scholar, translator, and editor of several Russian edition works by Nabokov.

Buksha, Ksenia: b. 1983. Leningrad. Poet, artist, and author of numerous books including *The Freedom Factory* (2013), a novel that has drawn comparisons to *Ulysses* for its use of multiple styles in its description of a factory over several decades.

Bykov, Dmitry: b. 1967. Moscow. Writer, poet, journalist, literary critic, radio and TV host, activist, and author of dozens of books, including biographies of Boris Pasternak and Maxim Gorky. Has lectured on Joyce.

Glazova, Anna: b. 1973. Dubna. Resides in Hamburg. Poet, translator from English and German, and independent scholar. Published five books of poetry. Received a PhD in German and comparative literature from Northwestern University.

Ilianen, Alexander: b. 1958. Leningrad. Queer poet and prose writer. Author of the books *And Finn* (1997), *The Road to Y* (2000), *The Vanity Boutique* (2007), and *Pension* (2015). Serializes works in progress on VKontakte (Russia's Facebook).[16] Recipient of the Andrey Bely Award.

Ilichevsky, Alexander: b. 1970. Sumgait. Resides in Israel. Author of several novels, including *Matisse* (2006), *The Persian* (2009), and *Newton's Sketch* (2019). Studied theoretical physics.

Kukulin, Ilya: b. 1969. Moscow. Author, poet, literary critic, and professor. Research interests include the history of education in Eastern Europe, Russia's internal colonization, contemporary Russian literature, and political discourses in Russian social media.

Ragozin, Dmitry: b. 1962. Moscow. Prose writer and translator from Japanese. Works include "The Battlefield" (2000) and *The Fiancée* (2013).

Rubinstein, Lev: b. 1947. Poet, essayist, and activist. Worked as a bibliographer. One of the founders of Moscow Conceptualism.

Salnikov, Aleksei: b. 1978. Tartu. Writer and poet. Winner of the National Bestseller Prize for *The Petrovs in and around the Flu* (2017).

Skidan, Alexander: b. 1965. Leningrad. Poet, critic, and translator. Widely translated. Poetry collections include *Delirium* (1993), *In the Re-reading* (1998), and *Red Shifting* (2005).

Sluzhitel, Grigory: b. 1983. Moscow. Author and actor. Completed studies at the Russian Institute of Theatre Arts. Author of *Savely's Days* (2018), a novel written from the perspective of a highly philosophical cat who spends his life wandering around Moscow.

Sokolov, Ivan: b. 1991. Leningrad. Poet. PhD student at the University of California, Berkeley. Organized several poetry readings and events in Russia, including a polyphonic, multilingual performance involving Joyce's work.

Solovev, Sergei: b. 1959. Kiev. Resides in Munich. Poet, writer, and painter. Leads tour groups in India. Translated Joyce's erotic love letters to his wife, Nora.

Stepnova, Marina: b. 1971. Efremov. Resides in Moscow. Author of many short stories and four novels. Works as a screenwriter.

Zinik, Zinovy: b. 1945. Moscow. Resides in London. Emigrated in 1975. Regular contributor to BBC Radio and the *Times Literary Supplement*. Prose often focuses on exiles of various stripes and includes *The Mushroom Picker* (1986) and *The Orgone Box* (2017).

First Contact

Alexander Ilianen: As usual, it began with rumors. That there's some significant writer . . .

Marina Stepnova: In 1989, I read *A Portrait of the Artist as a Young Man*. I was eighteen years old, and it affected me profoundly, so much so that I remember even today how I shook all night following the description of hell, and, in the morning, I literally ran to church to confess, even though

I've never been particularly religious, especially at eighteen. That's the magic power of art in action for you.

Anna Glazova: For me, Joyce was very important at a certain age. I read *Ulysses* in Khinkis and Khoruzhy's translation at fourteen or fifteen, when the entire novel was published in chapters by *Foreign Literature* [*Inostrannaia literatura*]. I don't remember how I got my hands on it, or how I found out about Joyce to begin with. I do remember that I was in the hospital with pneumonia and without interruptions, going over pieces over and over, reading the initial chapters, which are relatively "simple" to understand. It was like being drunk or like an infection, superimposed on a disease, with a fever. After that, I began to write some prose under the influence of this reading.

Ilya Kukulin: I first read Joyce in the early 1990s.

Ivan Sokolov: I always had a copy of *Ulysses* around. It was probably my parents', from the early 1990s. The yellow edition. They saw it as a supreme achievement, of course, but said, "Maybe don't read it." Then I joined the English Department at St. Petersburg State University. Before starting my third year and becoming one of Andrei Astvatsaturov's students, I heard some recordings of his lectures. He did something really great. He said, "*Ulysses* is a great book. A powerful book. But only one hundred people have actually read it."[17] That made me want to read it.

Sergei Solovev: I read *Ulysses* in translation in *Foreign Literature* in 1989 in very interesting circumstances. At that time, I was working as a restoration artist, and I repainted provincial churches with two friends, near Kiev, in Ukraine, in Gogolesque conditions. After every two or three hours, we had a break, and we would go to a small lake. I had that journal, and I read it over the course of the two or three months that we worked there. I'm no exception. It made an immense impression on me.

Dmitry Bykov: In 1988, when I was in the army, sometimes it was possible to get an issue of *Foreign Literature* with a piece of the novel and the detailed commentary from the library of our military unit.

Aleksei Salnikov: I started reading him quite late. I was closer to thirty then. He was often mentioned just after perestroika! He fell into this stream of publications, having become fashionable by means of the publication itself. Volumes of Joyce stood in many intelligentsia's homes, sometimes with uncut pages. My friend and teacher Evgeny Turenko promised to bow at the feet of anyone who read *Ulysses*, but, at the same time, he didn't let anyone read the book. I don't even know whether he had read *Ulysses* himself.

Ksenia Buksha: In 1997 or 1998, I was fourteen to fifteen years old, and I was reading everything. Then in 1999, in our lyceum's foreign literature classes, there was a teacher, Galina Viktorovna Yakovleva, a university instructor, who talked about a real variety of texts, including modernists. Then I read Virginia Woolf in the original and, after that, Joyce. There's a general sense of recognition and freedom associated with these texts: "Aha, this is my spiritual homeland." I experienced the exact same feeling from [Alexander] Vvedensky's poems, [Kazimir] Malevich's paintings, from Sasha Sokolov and Venichka Erofeev. A lack of emphasis on the plot, the subject. I was never interested in the story, neither as a child nor later. I didn't read books from beginning to end. Why all this hierarchy? Why should something "interesting" only come from simulating the movement of time? It's stupid.

Alexander Ilichevsky: The freedom of action in writing that I adopt for myself wouldn't be possible without Joyce. His multifaceted vision and method of composition really resonated with me.

A Joyce for All

Ilianen: The fact is, he's a writer for writers, no? But, at the moment, many people write.

Andrei Babikov: He was a hooligan; he wasn't a professional writer in the sense that he didn't write for profit or with a particular audience in mind.

Salnikov: Joyce is a lesson. Any book for a writer is a lesson in skill, even a work forgotten by others, something insignificant—anything can still teach you in terms of writing.

Buksha: I'd say he's one of those writers who managed to express their own thing in their own way. Successful attempts of this kind give me hope. All of a sudden, one day I'll also be able to say what I want to say, as clearly as possible.

Zinovy Zinik: You probably can't appreciate the full meaning that's hidden behind the lines, but you enjoy the imagery. You enjoy the words.

Dmitry Ragozin: The Russian language isn't capable of such word games as Joyce's.

Babikov: It's impossible to write that way. Joyce destroyed the novel.

Buksha: To say that he "changed" something is impossible. There's no technical progress in literature.

Ragozin: I see Joyce as a kind of stylistic realism, a realism that is filtered through all sorts of styles and stylistic lenses. There's the stream of consciousness, of course, but, in general, it's a matter of how the words and phrases add up to more than the plot.

Salnikov: In some way, Joyce affirmed the right of the Russian classics (I have in mind, of course, Dostoevsky and Tolstoy) to write verbosely, long-windedly, with a strong focus on details, leaving the plot somewhere to the side of the whole enormous narrative. He showed that the plot is sometimes not as important as the text itself.

Buksha: There's too much plot, characters, emotions, and primitive psycho-therapy these days. We don't have many novels. Not only in Russia, I think. This is probably a phase. *Ulysses* in general is a peculiar thing, where the technique cannot be scraped off from the essence.

Salnikov: It's an example of how to turn fleeting reality into literature.

Zinik: You can play with *Ulysses* yourself. It's a kind of interactive novel. It's one of the first interactive novels.

Stepnova: After reading Joyce for the first time, I began to think about how it is possible—and necessary—to write in such a way that the text physically affects the reader.

Glazova: I think that he means a lot to a novice author, because he's absolutely not ashamed to show all the machinery of his techniques. He's very generous in this sense.

Bykov: For me, Joyce is the founder of total realism, which touches on all aspects of being, from the religious to the physiological. He is Tolstoy's main successor, and he pulled off Tolstoy's dream of producing a detailed description of a single day in a fictional character's life. *Ulysses* brought European prose of the twentieth century to a close, and no one has gone further yet. Mark Z. Danielewski's methods are more or less promising, although this is just a development of Joyce's narrative techniques.[18] To surpass *Ulysses*, a new conception of man is necessary. This isn't yet apparent, unfortunately. This new conception of man that we see in Joyce could not appear in the USSR, and post-Soviet Russia hasn't yet matured. Russia should offer a new narrative form, and I am looking for it.

The Russian Joyce

Stepnova: The early nineties brought on a real barrage of a very different kind of literature. From the age of sixteen to twenty, I read as many books as a normal person reads in a lifetime. On the one hand, it was a wonderful adventure. On the other hand, under such an avalanche, it was difficult to understand the true position of this or that novel or writer. And yes, all these writers, read at once, became almost contemporaries, which is wrong. But it's no longer possible to alter this feeling, alas.

Salnikov: It's not worth putting the question of reading that way. If we talk about the peculiar connection between times, about the beginning of the twentieth century and the twenty-first century, then we should definitely turn to Joyce, who represented the Irish of that time. As far as I recall, the Irish were a kind of bogeyman for the rest of Europe, like Muslims in our time. A hundred years will pass, and, since human nature is unchangeable, someone will again be frightened on the basis of nationality, faith, or they'll think up something else to fear. Just to understand that, you should probably read Joyce. To demonstrate that, with the exception of everyday details, people have not particularly changed much. Their minds are also full of jealousy, envy, and sadness. In this regard, his maximally accurate focus, with which we see the movement of the thoughts of each of his characters, is especially valuable.

Solovev: We read Homer at the same time, even though he wrote long ago. It's all the same.

Glazova: I think Joyce has had and continues to have a strong influence on Russian literature. In the nineties, everyone who thought it was important to catch up with the development of European literature, which was largely neglected because of the Iron Curtain, read him in one gulp. The interest at that time resembled the excitement in Europe around *Ulysses* at the time of its original publication, though for other reasons. Several of my friends, such as Sasha Skidan and Andrei Senkov, remembered this moment well, and for them the Russian translation of *Ulysses* remained a significant literary event in their memory.

Salnikov: Our generation apparently fell right into this stream of "returned" literature during its adolescence. Plus, it's not just literature that flooded in. Music and movies, too. They complemented each other. For adults, it was probably like a fountain! Such sudden freedom. And we thought it should be that way. We weren't particularly hooked by the USSR, only slightly.

Solovev: If we're talking about the Soviet response, it seems to me *Ulysses* was linked to the myth in which we lived. The Soviet Union was essentially a ship that also set off in search of the Golden Fleece—communism—and all those experiences that Odysseus underwent are the same terrible myth. He leaves his homeland, the same as Russia leaving the nineteenth century, and he sets off on some terrible adventure, like the terrible Soviet Union. That enormous ship, all the episodes of his experience . . . he keeps moving, although more hallucinations come to him, and it's unclear which shore he will find. That was 1989, even if perestroika was allegedly already there. Reading *Ulysses*, and that one day where we see human life without time, that was the experience of every thinking person in the Soviet Union. That was normal. Every thinking person lived that way. No single day had limits, because time had a mythological quality.

Salnikov: I'd venture to propose that the huge volumes of Socialist Realism were also written not without Joyce's influence. They were not stupid people, after all. They probably wanted something more than to just describe the adventures of kolkhoz farmers, workers, and party members. Something probably burst through.

Bykov: *Ulysses* is absolutely universal and close to Russians no more, no less than to Greeks or Latin Americans.

Ilianen: There was a time when they kept Dostoevsky out of the curriculum, too. It's connected, I think. In Joyce, there's a rich world, polyphony, like in Dostoevsky, and maybe people found shelter in Joyce, saved themselves in Joyce, through Joyce.

Ilichevsky: I've absorbed as much as he wrote as possible. His influence is obvious as far as language lessons can influence a literate person. He showed that the inner world of a person can be polyphonic. He revealed the infinity of the world of perception.

Zinik: Sociologically, it's interesting why he came to be of focus to people of my generation. Of course, we knew about the first translation of Joyce in the 1920s. Joyce's reputation of the 1920s was of a kind of avant-garde, anticapitalist, revolutionary writer. He was taken up as an example of the progressive writers of Western Europe.

Everything was under the aura of the myth about James Joyce. So the question is, What's the real James Joyce got to do with this? The core of it is the sense of being an internal exile while in Soviet Moscow or the Soviet Union in general. It's the notion of the internal exile living in a world with two languages, practically, because the language of private conversations differed drastically from the language of the outside world. Not necessarily propaganda but public language. Everyone read *The Portrait of the Artist*, so everyone knew this quotation about exile, silence, and cunning, and that's very relevant for a person who feels divided from the public life of the country. I mean, for God's sake, Bloom's a Jew, and he's not a Jew. He's a person in between. The in-betweenness. An internal dilemma for everyone who found himself between two cultures. I wouldn't call it "underground" culture. To call it underground is a bit unfair, because for that you have to have a kind of surface, but there was no reality from which one would go into the underground, because we didn't regard the outside world as real. It was a kind of process of creating something while sitting on an island in the middle of nowhere, basically.[19]

So the mythology of Joyce is the mythology of becoming bilingual in a way, in different forms, or the character of this notion of being bilingual. Exile, no exile. It's just a brilliant book. It's very provocative, because it touches the basic elemental dilemma of the modern world, and that's probably why it's still so readable now. It's all about identity.

For Joyce, it was the question of living in your own country, not to be forced to participate, not to love your home, or your land, or your church, not to deal with what is forced on me. That was the illusion of those who left, like my generation. The paradox is that, by removing yourself, you probably contributed more to the horrors of your motherland than if you had stayed. The sense of complicity never leaves you. It's a kind of Catholic thing, is it not?

Grigory Sluzhitel: The planet has split apart into thousands of contiguous circles. *Ulysses*'s main theme—loss, restlessness, and the search for your corner in a divided world—can't help but be appealing today.

Salnikov: As for the change in the reception of his texts over the past thirty years, it seems that Joyce has been perceived better, simply because people have been trained to operate with a hypertext with a lot of references and memes. Likewise, Postmodernism also made the reader more tolerant and attentive.

Bykov: In general, Modernism is characterized by a desire for total self-control, while Postmodernism, that is, anti-Modernism, is characterized by a thirst for oblivion and seduction. So this isn't at all a Joycean time. He's interesting only to those seekers of new forms, metamodernists, of whom there aren't many.

Babikov: After 2005, there appeared a new generation for whom Joyce is passé. He hasn't been an influence.

Buksha: I'm completely different than Joyce. My texts are never so divided. The speed is much greater. I guess Joyce is the origin point of what people like me are doing now, but the origin is already very far away.

I. Sokolov: Bohemian society, the circle from which I come, isn't interested in big novels. I was interested in perpetuating Modernism.

Salnikov: Well, what can I say about the comparisons critics make between Joyce and my *Petrovs*? I'm flattered, of course. This is better than finding similarities with, I don't know, authors of ironic detective stories, humorous fantasy novels, better than comparing my books to *Fifty Shades of Grey*, *The Hunger Games*, *Twilight*.[20] I'm just trying to get rid of the story in my head, all these characters who won't disappear until you put a stop to the end of the novel.

Ilianen: A Russian Joyce isn't necessary. There's the Russian [Eugene] Vodolazkin, Shishkin, [Maria] Stepanova, and so on. Plus, Joyce has his peculiarities. It's not easy being Joyce, and it's not necessary. It's like the Northern Venice. You know that that's what they sometimes call our city. Petersburg isn't at all like Venice. Or Moscow being the Third Rome. It's stupid, but understandable where it begins, and I'm not opposed to such conventions, but they're still silly and amusing. Someone called Proust the French Oblomov. Okay.

Glazova: I don't think any Russian writers can be called Joyce's heir, but, in some sense, you can trace some overlapping ideas: for instance, the attempt to record the city's life and streets through a consciousness. At that time, a public language in different social strata arose, in different geographical locations and with different central themes and moods. Proust, [Robert] Musil, [Alfred] Döblin—they had a sensitivity to the spirit of the time similar to Joyce's. Bely's *Petersburg* naturally comes to mind, albeit with its special nervous—and poetic—note. You can, of course, say that this novel is the "Russian Joyce," but it will be the same half-true, half-crooked definition as "Petersburg is the Northern Venice."

I. Sokolov: Perhaps this is more a concern for the older generations.[21]

Sluzhitel: Of course, I wanted to create my own Moscow [in *Savely's Days*], like Joyce created his Dublin of June 16, 1904. My Moscow, regardless of the many actual and recognizable signs, is not real. Besides, in general, is there truly realism in literature? I think not. Every writer, and Joyce is a great example of this, thinks up his own reality that over time replaces its real-life prototype. No matter what Dublin was actually like at the beginning of the previous century, today we see it through Joyce's eyes.

Bykov: And why do we need a Russian Joyce when we already have an Irish one?

Stepnova: I don't think there's a Russian Joyce today. He hasn't been published, at least.

Buksha: There's no Russian Joyce, and there cannot be one, but if you want, you can think of someone like Venichka Erofeev, for example.

Glazova: There *is* one case I'm familiar with: not long ago, Sergei Solovev translated Joyce's love letters to his young wife, in which obscenities are intertwined with a tender sense of intimacy, and all this is invested with the same epic, large-scale style as in *Ulysses* and *Finnegan*. Solovev exhibits a tendency to distill everything eroticized into an even more sublime, pure extract of sensuality than Joyce himself. And again, as in the translation of *Ulysses*, it sounds sophisticated and virtuosic; that is, it appears that Joyce's very style makes authors think, comprehend his text in this way.

No Limits

Solovev: My version of Joyce's letters to Nora isn't exactly a translation. I tried to stay close to the text, but I played my own music and provided my own figurative structure. It's a jazz improvisation on this theme . . .

I. Sokolov: Sexual liberation isn't incorporated into the Russian canon. It's a matter of tearing apart mores on an elevated level. That's really a question of the intelligentsia.

Solovev: I was surprised to learn that they call me one of the founders of erotic Russian verse . . . Everything came together with fate and biography. I lived with a woman similar to her, Nora . . . I lived in that place, Trieste . . .

Kukulin: I was shocked by Joyce's presentation of sexual nature, the profanity of the stream of consciousness.

Solovev: No borders in this case existed for me. Or almost didn't. In any case, I always tried to go beyond what's acceptable in terms of forthrightness . . .

Bykov: Well, *Ulysses* is also one of those books, according to V. I. Novikov's definition, alone with which you can admit everything—even what you do not admit to yourself.

Solovev: It's a paradoxical situation. Despite our very rich language, which is very plastic, very attuned to feeling, it gives us endless possibilities to describe things in this territory . . . After two hundred years, we still don't have anything along these lines, only limits . . .

Salnikov: What struck me most about *Ulysses* was its honesty. Honesty in the most intimate details. Not the savoring of naturalism we see in, for example, [Émile] Zola, but this movement of the characters' thoughts that's shown without embellishment, their way of life.

Solovev: Joyce was an open man, full of life. Brave. Really brave. He didn't fear showing his weaknesses. So when I ran across Joyce's letters, it was a meeting between two people who completely understand each other, in the full sense of the word. A joyful meeting in which we spoke in one language . . .

Two Dissenters

Lev Rubinstein: The fact is that Joyce didn't play any particular or noticeable role in my literary biography.

It goes without saying that in my youth I read all the translations of *Ulysses* that I could find. And, of course, I was interested in Joyce's work and biography. That was important for an author of my generation and of my circle. And, of course, for a long time I took him as one of the symbols of literary innovation.

But it all turned out to be not for very long. My artistic interests shifted in a new direction—toward the latest in fine arts and music. Because of these various things, there arose in my mind those ideas that soon became the main factors in my poetry and prose.

Yet Joyce remained in my consciousness a deeply respected and honored influence, but one that is practically unread and, most importantly, entirely distant from what I considered and now consider relevant for myself.

Unfortunately, I can't say more than that.

Alexander Skidan: To be honest, your question took me by surprise. I really don't know Joyce well, and I've never studied him. Moreover, I tried to read *Ulysses* and only managed two or three chapters. Back then, I liked his *Giacomo Joyce* with his "love me—love my umbrella."

It was a long time ago, around 1990, it's hard to remember. That was when I read a few chapters with Khoruzhy's commentary for the first time and gave up. Then, a couple of years later, a separate edition came out, and I also tried to read it, and again I could not get any further than the second or third chapter. It became boring, I wasn't taken by the situation; there was a feeling that it was a demonstration of "naked technique," perhaps a deceptive one. It's also possible that I was unnecessarily immersed in the commentary. It overwhelmed me with cultural references, especially to antiquity and ancient mythology. At the time, all this seemed dead to me. Perhaps it was also the myth of Joyce himself as a great genius that interfered and overwhelmed me.

That's all I can say.

Foreign Influence

Stepnova: Joyce for me is a figure analogous to [Miguel de] Cervantes. At some point, *The Ingenious Gentleman Don Quixote of La Mancha* was a living, important book for living readers. This novel changed lives, altered worldviews. So, what happened? Today no one, other than specialists, reads *Don Quixote*. It's simply impossible. But everyone knows who Don Quixote is, what Quixotism means; they remember windmills and Dulcinea. The novel became part of not only world culture but humanity's everyday culture. Thus, as a novel, it's dead. More or less the same thing happened to *Ulysses*, at least for me. The novel exerted an enormous influence not only on literature but on world culture. Everyone's heard about it; everyone knows about it. But only a handful have read it, and only a hundredth of those understood it. Joyce proved to be the author of a novel of genius, whose genius is transmitted through the air, like flu. I contend that Joyce himself would be pleased. He wanted literary immortality, he constructed it completely consciously, and he achieved it.

Ilianen: It's possible to live there, in his books. I love Joyce precisely for that reason. Almost physically. I was just walking home along the Neva. There was a miraculous breeze along the river. It was easy to breathe. I have asthma, like Proust; therefore, when it's easy to breathe, it's very healthy. A book's "air," in which you can find yourself, means the place where you can breathe. To understand is one thing. The intellectual component. It's very important. But there's also beauty. It's simply nice, pleasant, beautiful there; you want to be there. You want to run away from somewhere, and you want to be somewhere else, to stay there. In *Ulysses*, it's nice, comfortable. I opted to stop at *Ulysses*.

Zinik: Why Russians are mad about Ireland, I don't know. Being under the influence of Pavel Ulitin, for a while, naively probably, I would compare my situation. I would use a lot of biographical episodes and relations between Beckett and Joyce, that of the mentor or guru and his pupil, follower, disciple. For me, the accent moved from this myth about Ireland and exile to that of Joyce's concrete relations with other characters in his life. And then the rebellion. I imitated Ulitin's style for years in Moscow, then broke away from it drastically, like Beckett from Joyce.[22] I started writing proper fiction. It was a kind of fighting against Joyce stylistically, for me personally. It's a change in point of view. While in Moscow, you looked up at Joyce as a monumental figure of this mythology of exile, but while you're in exile, you look back at Moscow from London's point of view, like Joyce would have on Dublin.

Bykov: To be completely honest, Joyce is for me the most readable, fascinating, fun, and genial author of the notorious triad of major modernists (Proust, Joyce, [Franz] Kafka). I love Kafka, I'm completely cold toward Proust and sincerely do not understand the reasons for his fame, but only Joyce am I able to reread for pleasure.

Stepnova: I didn't read Joyce in the original, and therefore I can't fully take pleasure in or rage against him. For precisely this reason, I completely understand and recognize Joyce's place on the literary Olympus, but, as a reader, I don't love *Ulysses*. It irritates me that I don't catch all its layers. It even pains me. And it once stunned with its audacity. At eighteen, I couldn't believe at all that you could write like that.

Sluzhitel: In some sense, knowing Joyce is a cultural initiation.

Glazova: I had had deep dives into literary texts before, but when Joyce
happened, he stuck with me for a long time. It had something to do with
growing up, with puberty. For me, reading Joyce was an initiation. And I
returned to him many times, later, when I learned enough English; I read
Ulysses in English several times and read *A Portrait of the Artist as a Young
Man* and *Dubliners*. I even took a course on *Ulysses* when I was studying
for my master's degree. But in my school days, Joyce was for me a portal
to literature in general. My family read books, but not systematically.
Joyce, whom I discovered then for myself, contained entire worlds, with
his explicit task of creating a linguistic archive for the reality where the
author lived. But over time, Joyce ceased to fascinate me so much. Immer-
sion in the stream of consciousness no longer seems absolute, and his
linguistic sophistication, along with all the richness of references to other
authors and contexts that requires detailed commentary, no longer seems
particularly difficult. Now I prefer *Dubliners* to *Ulysses*, and, above all, I
love the story "The Dead." It's accurate in feeling and very memorable in
how the hero's self-perception shifts.

I began to write poetry very late by average standards, at twenty-six
to twenty-seven. So, even though I was thirty when my first book was
published, these are early poems, and you see this in a deep dependence on my reading. My own voice sounds only latently, under a layer
of "that which I read." Hence the numerous references to various
literary texts and contexts, to Joyce, Kafka, Greek myths, and religious
figures. I especially remembered Bloom's lemon soap, which I refer to
in some poems, because it forms a sort of comic double of Bloom-
Ulysses.[23] It serves him in the style of Sancho Panza under Don Quixote: Bloom travels around Dublin, and the soap travels from his pocket
to his other pocket and from one thought to another. It's a mixture of
sublimity with comicality. This is also Bloom's odyssey with the
soap—an epic, but the hero sometimes sneaks a ridiculous sniff under
his armpit. And as the sublime—[it's] the universal rising of soap over
the horizon of Ireland.

Stepnova: Joyce is a mountain on the horizon. Big, immense, strange. But the
view from my own writerly window faces entirely different mountains.

Sluzhitel: For a person whose native language isn't English, reading *Ulysses*,
and even more so *Finnegans Wake*, is essentially pointless (despite the
monumental and amazing work of Khoruzhy). I don't count Joyce
among my favorite writers, but to write in the twenty-first century as if

Joyce never existed is already impossible. Joyce is a mountain whose outline is visible in any weather. Literature, like culture in general, is a chain reaction. For a person for whom reading is a way of life, avoiding Joyce is impossible.

Salnikov: You see, any writer somehow, sometimes even unconsciously, plunders a lot from many contemporaries, and, it goes without saying, from the classics, and from people on the streets, and from daily happenings. This is called "influence"—the influence of time, the influence of literature. No one is fixated on one author, for the simple reason that this influence will be too obvious. The reader immediately dismisses such inept "thieves." Why read an obvious imitator, if we have the original? Here he is, this style is *his* style, and, therefore, by default it's better, covered with the patina of time. It's the same with painting.

Each author, at first unconsciously, chooses his teachers and imitates them, then expands his circle of reading and becomes a little more biased. The author no longer recklessly drags any old trash from his father's nest but chooses trinkets that seem valuable to him.

Ilianen: One wishes to rewrite things. You see, all literature is parody in an etymological sense. Joyce parodied Homer. Everyone parodies everyone else. They rewrite. Dostoevsky rewrote Balzac. Tolstoy—Flaubert. You read Proust, and you want to rewrite him. It's important to assimilate what you read.

To read them is a great effort. You need a lot of time. In my opinion, Joyce . . . and here I return to my thought about writers for writers, to read him is labor. And pleasure, of course. The same as with Proust, Kafka. For me, it's pleasure. Sadomasochistic.

He inspired me.

Salnikov: His work is a readerly adventure that you can plunge into for several years. Many Russian readers sometimes perceive *Ulysses* as a kind of test or trial. Reading this novel is something like climbing a large mountain. It requires the same concentration as a serious excursion. You see, the edition that I have, half of it consists of very long footnotes, so when you read, you involuntarily refer to these footnotes, and while you read the footnote, you forget what, in fact, was discussed in the main text.[24] As on sticks for Nordic walking, you rely on two bookmarks to avoid stumbling.

Joyce, like Nabokov, infected me with his contemplativeness. They showed me that everyday details can be interesting regardless of the plot, of some basic idea of the text, that you can fill the narrative with these little things almost for your own pleasure, for the pleasure of the text itself. Since the text wants to move in this direction anyway, why not let go of the reins sometimes?

Act V: Days of a Joycean Future Past

If we ourselves "let go of the reins" a bit, it becomes clear that the history of Joyce in Russia remains a process still in motion, despite Joyce's official canonization within the Russian sphere. Whether it is due to the legacy of his heavily politicized reception, his own extensive self-mythologization, or some other, harder-to-define factor, Joyce, it should be clear by now, remains a controversial figure among living Russian writers. He is innovative, yet old-fashioned. He is alien to individual writers, yet immensely relevant to all. He deserves close attention, but no one, apparently, reads him. Behind all these contradictory frictions, though, lies the near-universal recognition of Joyce's significance, particularly with regard to the liberating nature of his art. As Buksha suggests, he is at once an origin source whose innovations feel simultaneously quite distant and tangible today.

The five case studies of this book, in tandem with the voices featured in its conclusion, stress how Joyce became and continues to be emblematic of exactly this desire for freedom. This freedom has naturally taken a variety of forms, but undergirding many of them is the hope to combat a historical narrative that aims to restrict the artist's identity. A man out of time, Olesha saw in Joyce's work a solution to his precarious state as an individualist writer in the newly formed Soviet Union, as he turned to the West. Meanwhile, Nabokov, as an émigré writer, sought to recover the past taken from him by the 1917 revolution by "translating" Joyce's text and even adopting an inverted Joycean model. Then Bitov opted to disengage from the war with the past, seeing the futility of doing so, while Sasha Sokolov reconceptualized time—and thus intertextual connections—as untethered from a linear, hierarchal scheme. Shishkin rewrote history, as it were, by bringing the present into dialogue with the past through extensive direct quotations of his predecessors and recycled narratives. Yet they, like Joyce, aim to liberate themselves from a constricting sense of belatedness.

In the statements collected from Bykov, Buksha, Glazova, and other contemporary writers, we see this very process before our eyes; responding to my questions, they conceptualize their position in relation to Joyce and everything he represents. Being a latecomer, as Bitov's novel argues, presents certain possibilities, even if they are sometimes difficult to discern in the moment. Joyce's novels, then, manifest a belief in the power of previous words to activate these new potentialities if younger authors can manage to render them through their own language, style, or modes.

Despite their various differences, these writers make up a community that recognizes not only Joyce's impact but also a much vaster unity among story-tellers. Writing about the Irish "race," Joyce had the following to say in the 1907 essay "Ireland: Island of Saints and Sages":

> Our civilization is an immense woven fabric in which very different ele-ments are mixed, in which Nordic rapacity is reconciled to Roman law, and new Bourgeois conventions to the remains of Siriac religion. In such a fabric, it is pointless searching for a thread that has remained pure, vir-gin and uninfluenced by other threads nearby. What race or language (if we except those few which a humorous will seems to have preserved in ice, such as the people of Iceland) can nowadays claim to be pure?[25]

For Joyce, it was senseless to think of a society as untouched by foreign influ-ences—a purity left only to the imagination of tyrants. Rather, much like his own fiction with its literally countless references, everything is interwoven. What has been said before will be said again in new formulations. As Salnikov puts it, since Joyce's time, "people have not particularly changed much. Their minds are also full of jealousy, envy, and sadness." Joyce's texts give voice to the same stories that the Russian writers attempted to share throughout the tempestuous twentieth century and into this new one. Going even further back, Ilianen saw in Joyce a return to Dostoevsky's polyphony, something that had been repressed in the Soviet era and was brought back to life through a foreign emissary.

This literary zone of contact fuels the novels of the Russian Joyceans, and in their engagement with the Irish writer's theories, they found much to shape their own visions and responses to the worlds around them. In Joyce, they could breathe the liberating "air" that Ilianen speaks of, that was necessary to escape themselves and a tradition in desperate need of estrangement. But this transformation cuts both ways. "Strong writers," as Harold Bloom writes in his controversial *Western Canon*, "have the wit to transform [their] forerunners into composite and therefore partly imaginary beings."[26] Indeed, Joyce became a remarkably plastic symbol for Olesha, Nabokov, Bitov, Sokolov, and Shish-kin, who all viewed him as a crucial element in their escape from oppressive histories. Fluctuating political, cultural, and personal realities would dictate how exactly they could read Joyce, literally and figuratively, yet they found in his writings the means to beget their own lineage through the literary word.

NOTES

Introduction

1. Vs. V. Vishnevskii, "V Evrope: Iz putevogo dnevnika" in *"Russkaia odisseia" Dzheimsa Dzhoisa*, ed. Ekaterina Genieva (Moskva: Rudomino, 2005), 38.

2. Zhitomirsky's translation was preceded by excerpts in French and Spanish (1924) and published the same year as selections in German.

3. Karl Radek, "Iz doklada 'Sovremennaia mirovaia literatura i zadachi proletarsk-ogo iskusstva,'" in Genieva, *"Russkaia odisseia" Dzheimsa Dzhoisa*, 95.

4. Boris Poplavskii, "Po povodu . . . 'Atlantidy–Evropy' . . . 'Noveishei russkoi literatury' . . . Dzhoisa," *Chisla* 4 (1930–31): 173–74.

5. Such views, of course, were not unique to Soviet readers. *Ulysses* was essentially banned in the United States from 1921 to 1933 on charges of obscenity, which were eventually struck down by Judge John M. Woolsey. For the novel's publication history, see Kevin Birmingham, *The Most Dangerous Book: The Battle for James Joyce's "Ulysses"* (New York: Penguin Books, 2014).

6. On the history of the Khinkis-Khoruzhy translation, see Emily Tall, "Behind the Scenes: How *Ulysses* Was Finally Published in the Soviet Union," *Slavic Review* 49, no. 2 (1990): 183–99.

7. For documentation of Joyce's own reading in Russian literature, see Neil Cornwell, *James Joyce and the Russians* (London: Macmillan Press, 1992), 26.

8. Sokolov also emigrated, but he completed his first novel in Soviet Russia.

9. Heinrich F. Plett, "Intertextualities," in *Intertextuality*, ed. Heinrich F. Plett (New York: Walter de Gruyter, 1991), 25.

10. Ibid.

11. Ibid., 26–27.

12. Julia Kristeva, *The Portable Kristeva*, ed. Kelly Oliver (New York: Columbia University Press, 2002), 446.

13. Ibid.

14. Ibid.

15. Julia Kristeva, "Word, Dialogue and Novel," trans. Alice Jardine, Thomas Gora, and Léon S. Roudiez, in *The Kristeva Reader*, ed. Toril Moi (New York: Columbia University Press, 1986), 36.

16. Julia Kristeva, "The Bounded Text," in *Desire in Language: A Semiotic Approach to Literature and Art*, ed. Leon S. Roudiez, trans. Thomas Gora, Alice Jardine, and Leon S. Roudiez (New York: Columbia University Press, 1980), 36.

17. Harold Bloom, *The Anxiety of Influence: A Theory of Poetry*, 2nd ed. (New York: Oxford University Press, 1997), 5.

18. Ibid., 7.

19. Ibid., xxiii.

20. Ibid., 14.

21. Harold Bloom, *The Anatomy of Influence: Literature as a Way of Life* (New Haven, CT: Yale University Press, 2011), 6.

22. Gregory Machacek, "Allusion," *PMLA* 122, no. 2 (2007): 524–25.

23. Gérard Genette, *Palimpsests: Literature in the Second Degree*, trans. Channa Newman and Claude Doubinsky (Lincoln: University of Nebraska Press, 1997), 5.

24. Ibid., 397–98.

25. Patricia Yaeger, "Editor's Column: The Polyphony Issue," *PMLA* 122, no. 2 (2007): 436.

26. Ibid.

27. Ibid., 438.

28. Ibid.

29. Ibid.

30. Ibid., 440.

31. Ibid., 440, 442.

32. James Joyce, *Letters of James Joyce*, vol. 1, ed. Stuart Gilbert (New York: Viking Press, 1966), 297.

33. Yaeger, "Editor's Column," 440.

34. Ibid., 443.

35. Mary Orr, *Intertextuality: Debates and Contexts* (Cambridge, UK: Polity Press, 2003), 84.

36. Joseph Brodsky, *Less than One: Selected Essays* (New York: Farrar, Straus and Giroux, 1986), 271.

37. *The Gift* was not published in full until 1952. Political disagreements prevented its fourth chapter—a subversive biography of the nineteenth-century author-critic Nikolai Chernyshevsky—from being included in the émigré journal *Contemporary Notes* (*Sovremennye zapiski*).

38. Mikhail Shishkin, "Mat i molitva—eto priblizitel'no odno i to zhe," *Gazeta* 105 (June 9, 2005): 26.

39. Edward W. Said, *The World, the Text, and the Critic* (Cambridge, MA: Harvard University Press, 1983), 16.

40. Hayden White, "The Burden of History," *History and Theory* 5, no. 2 (1966): 123.

41. Ibid.

42. Eleazar M. Meletinsky, *The Poetics of Myth*, trans. Guy Lanoue and Alexandre Sadetsky (New York: Garland Publishing, 1998), xix.

1. Yury Olesha

1. Iurii Olesha, "Velikoe narodnoe iskusstvo," *Literaturnaia gazeta* 17 (March 20, 1936): 3. Olesha quotes Leopold Bloom's thought from episode 6 ("Hades") in *Ulysses*: "A corpse is meat gone bad. Well and what's cheese? Corpse of milk." James Joyce, *Ulysses* (New York: Random House, 1986), 94.

2. Iurii Olesha, *Povesti i rasskazy* (Moskva: Khudozhestvennaia literatura, 1965), 427–30.

3. Benedikt Sarnov, *Stalin i pisateli* (Moskva: Eksmo, 2009), 1:146. Arkady Belinkov essentially made the same politically minded argument in his seminal study of Olesha. See Arkadii Belinkov, *Sdacha i gibel' sovetskogo intelligenta. Iurii Olesha* (Moskva: RIK "Kul'tura," 1997).

4. Joyce, *Ulysses*, 644.

5. Olesha, "Velikoe narodnoe iskusstvo," 3.

6. E.Z. [Evgenii Zamiatin], "Angliia i Amerika," *Sovremennyi Zapad* 2 (1923): 229.

7. Cornwell, *James Joyce and the Russians*, 89. Nils Åke Nilsson and Elizabeth Klosty Beaujour have also explicated Zamiatin's influence as artist and thinker on Olesha. See Nils Åke Nilsson, "Through the Wrong End of Binoculars: An Introduction to Jurij Oleša," in *Major Soviet Writers: Essays in Criticism*, ed. Edward J. Brown (New York: Oxford University Press, 1973), 268; and Elizabeth Klosty Beaujour, *The Invisible Land: A Study of the Artistic Imagination of Iurii Olesha* (New York: Columbia University Press, 1970), 141.

8. Cornwell, *James Joyce and the Russians*, 14. Fitch has written extensively on the expatriate community that gathered in Paris. Litvinov, who had some personal contact with Joyce, was an English writer and the wife of Soviet diplomat Maxim Litvinov. Beach owned the famed Shakespeare and Company bookshop in Paris and published the first book edition of *Ulysses* in 1922.

9. The history of the novel's translation constitutes a protracted and elaborate tale, one that has been traced at length in Emily Tall's articles "Behind the Scenes"; "Correspondence between Three Slavic Translators of *Ulysses*: Maciej Słomczyński, Aloys Skoumal, and Viktor Khinkis," *Slavic Review* 49, no. 4 (1990): 625–33; "Interview with Victor Khinkis, Russian Translator of *Ulysses*," *James Joyce Quarterly* 17, no. 4 (1980): 349–53; "James Joyce Returns to the Soviet Union," *James Joyce Quarterly* 17, no. 4 (1980): 341–47; and "The Joyce Centenary in the Soviet Union: Making Way for *Ulysses*," *James Joyce Quarterly* 21, no. 2 (1984): 107–22; and in Ludmilla S. Voitkovska's "James Joyce and the Soviet Reader: Problems of Contact," *Canadian Journal of Irish Studies* 16, no. 2 (1990): 21–26; as well as Cornwell's *James Joyce and the Russians*; and Neil Cornwell, "More on Joyce and Russia: Or *Ulysses* on the Moscow River," *Joyce Studies Annual* (1994): 176–86.

10. Dzhems Dzhois, "Uliss," in *Novinki zapada. Al'manakh No. 1*, trans. V. Zhitomirskii (Moskva-Leningrad: Zemlia i Fabrika, 1925), 65–94. For a complete Russian translation history of Joyce, see Ekaterina Genieva, *"Russkaia odisseia" Dzheimsa Dzhoisa* (Moskva: Rudomino, 2005).

11. E. L. Lann, foreword to "Uliss," by Dzhems Dzhois, in *Novinki Zapada. Al'manakh No. 1*, trans. V. Zhitomirskii (Moskva-Leningrad: Zemlia i Fabrika, 1925), 61–64.

12. In fact, Olesha's manuscripts show that he alternated between first- and third-person narration throughout the book's composition. For example, the version contained in individual file 5 features a first-person account. The one in file 8 begins with a first-person account of the narrator's living space, then eventually switches to third person and proceeds to flip back and forth as Olesha experiments with the perspective. It was only in the final version that everything settled into place with the first half of the book in first person and the second in third person. The writer's manuscripts can be found at the Russian State Archive of Literature and Art (RGALI). A problem worth noting is that Olesha frequently rewrote passages many times over,

leaving multiple pages numbered the same way even within a single archival file. Furthermore, in some cases, they are twice numbered: once by Olesha and, seemingly, again by those who prepared the manuscripts for preservation. Thus, one page can be labeled 1 by Olesha but 13 by the archivist. Another difficulty of Olesha's *Zavist'* (*Envy*) manuscripts is that with only three exceptions (files 4, 6, and 17) they are all dated "[1924–27]," that is, the general range during which Olesha worked on the novel. Materials housed at RGALI are organized in the following manner: fond (*fond*), inventory (*opis'*), individual file (*edinnoe khranenie*), and page (*list*).

13. Vsevolod Vishnevskii, "Znat' Zapad!," *Literaturnyi kritik* 7 (1933): 79–95. While in emigration, Mirsky himself published highly complimentary remarks about *Ulysses* in the 1928 Parisian annual *Versty*. See D. S. Mirskii, "Dzhois ('Ulysses,' 1922)," *Versty* 3 (1928): 147–49. Having converted to Marxism, however, he requested a pardon from Soviet authorities and attempted to make up for his past transgressions through a series of articles. They failed to make a difference: he perished in a labor camp in 1939. See D. S. Mirskii, "Dzheims Dzhois," *God shestnadtsatyi* 1 (1933): 428–50; D. S. Mirskii, "Dos-Passos, sovetskaia literatura i Zapad," *Literaturnyi kritik* 1 (1933): 111–26; and D. S. Mirskii, "O formalizme," *God shestnadtsatyi* 2 (1933): 490–517.

14. Vishnevskii, "Znat' Zapad!," 94. A close friend of Olesha, Valentin Stenich, editor at the Mysl' publishing house, oversaw E. N. Fetodova's 1927 translation of *Dubliners* and himself translated three episodes from *Ulysses* before the tide turned completely against Joyce. For some commentary on these debates, see E. D. Gal'tsova, "Zapadnye pisateli-modernisty v zhurnale 'Literaturnyi kritik': Prust, Dzhois, Dos Passos," in *Postizhenie Zapada: Inostrannaia kul'tura v sovetskoi literature, iskusstve i teorii 1917–1941 gg.* (Moskva: IMLI RAN, 2015), 669–86; and Hans Günther, "Soviet Literary Criticism and the Formulation of the Aesthetics of Socialist Realism, 1932–1940," in *A History of Russian Literary Theory and Criticism: The Soviet Age and Beyond*, ed. Evgeny Dobrenko and Galin Tihanov (Pittsburgh: University of Pittsburgh Press, 2011), 97–100.

15. Genieva, "Russkaia odisseia," 6.

16. Iurii Olesha, quoted in V. Pertsov, "My zhivem vpervye": O tvorchestve Iuriia Oleshi (Moskva: Sovetskii pisatel', 1976), 95.

17. Lev Nikulin, untitled memoir, in *Vospominaniia o Iurii Oleshe*, ed. E. Pel'son and O. Suok-Olesha (Moskva: Sovetskii pisatel', 1975), 68.

18. Ibid., 69.

19. Olesha, *Povesti*, 422.

20. Iurii Olesha, "Beseda s chitateliami," *Literaturnyi kritik* 12 (1935): 165.

21. Ibid.

22. Ibid.

23. Iurii Olesha, *Kniga proshchaniia* (Moskva: Vagrius, 1999), 154.

24. Evgeny Dobrenko, "Socialist Realism," in *The Cambridge Companion to Twentieth-Century Russian Literature*, ed. Evgeny Dobrenko and Marina Balina (Cambridge: Cambridge University Press, 2011), 97–98.

25. Ibid., 100. For more on the cultural politics of the Soviet 1920s, see Evgeny Dobrenko, "Literary Criticism and the Transformations of the Literary Field during the Cultural Revolution, 1928–1932," in *A History of Russian Literary Theory and Criticism: The Soviet Age and Beyond*, ed. Evgeny Dobrenko and Galin Tihanov (Pittsburgh: University of Pittsburgh Press, 2011), 43–63; Dobrenko, "Socialist Realism"; Sheila

Fitzpatrick, "The 'Soft' Line on Culture and Its Enemies: Soviet Cultural Policy, 1922–1927," *Slavic Review* 33, no. 2 (1974): 267–87; Sheila Fitzpatrick, Alexander Rabinowitch, and Richard Stites, eds., *Russia in the Era of NEP: Explorations in Soviet Society and Culture* (Bloomington: Indiana University Press, 1991); Natalia Kornienko, "Literary Criticism and Cultural Policy during the New Economic Policy, 1921–1927," in *A History of Russian Literary Theory and Criticism: The Soviet Age and Beyond*, ed. Evgeny Dobrenko and Galin Tihanov (Pittsburgh: University of Pittsburgh Press, 2011), 17–42; Robert Maguire, *Red Virgin Soil: Soviet Literature in the 1920's* (Evanston, IL: Northwestern University Press, 2000); and Stepan Sheshukov, *Neistovye revniteli: Iz istorii literaturnoi bor'by 20-kh godov* (Moskva: Moskovskii rabochii, 1970).

26. For passing comparisons, see Nilsson, "Through the Wrong End of Binoculars," 273, on *ostranenie* (defamiliarization) and epiphany; Kazimiera Ingdahl, *The Artist and the Creative Act* (Stockholm: Almqvist and Wiksell International, 1984), 99, on epiphany and "solar visions" in *Envy*; and Boris Volodin, "Dzheims Dzhois," in *Pamiatnye knizhnye daty* (Moskva: Kniga, 1982), 165, on Joycean "echoes" in *Envy*.

27. Olesha, *Povesti*, 19. On a page labeled 33 of individual file 6 of the *Zavist'* manuscripts, Olesha introduces these "juices" in Babichev's body. This file is dated "[1924]–31/V/1926," that is, after the publication of the *Ulysses* fragments in the USSR. It also stands to note how Olesha generally begins to shift the focus from Ivan to Andrei in this manuscript.

28. Joyce, *Ulysses*, 3.

29. Ibid., 56.

30. For alternative comparisons to Sinclair Lewis's *Babbitt* (1922) and Mikhail Bulgakov's *Heart of a Dog* (completed 1925), see Rimgaila Salys, "Understanding *Envy*," in *Olesha's "Envy": A Critical Companion*, ed. Rimgaila Salys (Evanston, IL: Northwestern University Press, 1999), 3–43; and Alexander Zholkovsky, *Text Counter Text: Rereadings in Russian Literary History* (Stanford, CA: Stanford University Press, 1994), 191.

31. Olesha, *Povesti*, 21.

32. Joyce, *Ulysses*, 7.

33. Ibid., 6.

34. This tension between characters has likewise been a point of contention in Joyce scholarship, where readers must decide just how generously to read Buck's personality and Stephen's assessments. See, for instance, Adaline Glasheen, "Queries about Mulligan as Heretic Mocker and Rhetorician," *A Wake Newslitter* 14, no. 5 (1977): 71. For more on Buck and his real-life model, Oliver St. John Gogarty, and Joyce's complicated relationship with both, consider James F. Carens, "Joyce and Gogarty," in *New Light on Joyce: From the Dublin Symposium*, ed. Fritz Senn (Bloomington: Indiana University Press, 1972), 28–45; Elisabetta Cecconi, "Buck Mulligan: Characterisation Process," in *"Who Chose This Face for Me?": Joyce's Creation of Secondary Characters in "Ulysses"* (Bern: Peter Lang, 2007), 41–86; Cheryl Temple Herr, *Joyce and the Art of Shaving* (Dublin: National Library of Ireland, 2004); J. B. Lyons, "A Roland for Your Oliver," in *Oliver St. John Gogarty: The Man of Many Talents* (Dublin: Blackwater Press, 1960), 211–23; and Ulick O'Connor, "James Joyce and Oliver St. John Gogarty: A Famous Friendship," *Texas Quarterly* 3, no. 2 (1960): 189–210.

35. Olesha, *Povesti*, 19, 20.

36. Joyce, *Ulysses*, 6.

37. Ibid.

38. In his memoir, *No Day without a Line* (*Ni dnia bez strochki*), Olesha, too, recounts a similar experience of gazing into mirrors to determine whom he more closely resembles: his father or his mother. Iurii Olesha, *Zavist'. Ni dnia bez strochki* (Riga: Liesma, 1987), 117. In one of the manuscripts to *Zavist'*, Olesha has his narrator see himself in a mirror before Andrei Babichev walks into the room (individual file 8, page 69).

39. Joyce, *Ulysses*, 12.

40. Olesha, *Povesti*, 21.

41. Ibid., 20.

42. Joyce, *Ulysses*, 12.

43. Ibid., 13.

44. Eliot Borenstein, *Men without Women: Masculinity and Revolution in Russian Fiction, 1917–1929* (Durham, NC: Duke University Press, 2001), 167.

45. Olesha, *Povesti*, 63.

46. Ibid., 23.

47. On the significance of milk and food imagery in the novels, see Liesl Olson, *Modernism and the Ordinary* (New York: Oxford University Press, 2009), 46; and William E. Harkins, "The Theme of Sterility in Olesha's *Envy*," in *Olesha's "Envy": A Critical Companion*, ed. Rimgaila Salys (Evanston, IL: Northwestern University Press, 1999), 66. Even how these items are detailed through lists speaks to the marked contrasts between the earthly father figures and the poetic sons. Consider Olesha, *Povesti*, 21, 22, 23, 23–24, 24, 38, 46, 63, 98; and Joyce, *Ulysses*, 45, 544.

48. William M. Schutte, *Joyce and Shakespeare: A Study in the Meaning of "Ulysses"* (New Haven, CT: Yale University Press, 1957), 73.

49. Olesha, *Povesti*, 58.

50. Joyce, *Ulysses*, 18.

51. Olesha, *Povesti*, 82.

52. L. H. Platt, "*Ulysses* 15 and the Irish Literary Theatre," in *Reading Joyce's "Circe*," ed. Andrew Gibson (Amsterdam: Rodopi, 1994), 55.

53. Olesha, *Povesti*, 76.

54. Joyce, *Ulysses*, 58.

55. Ibid., 235.

56. Olesha, *Povesti*, 86.

57. Ibid., 105.

58. Joyce, *Ulysses*, 299.

59. Olesha, *Povesti*, 80.

60. Ibid., 87.

61. Joyce, *Ulysses*, 526.

62. Ibid., 527.

63. Ibid., 393.

64. Olesha, *Povesti*, 99.

65. Borenstein, *Men without Women*, 304.

66. Joyce, *Ulysses*, 549.

67. Ibid., 10.

68. Olesha, *Povesti*, 116.

69. Ibid., 120.

70. Ibid., 119.

71. Olesha, *Zavist'*, 119.

72. Joyce, *Ulysses*, 160.

73. Said, *The World, the Text, and the Critic*, 17.

74. Compare Molly's musings about taking Stephen as a lover, not to mention Bloom's apparent support for such a possibility. Joyce, *Ulysses*, 638.

75. Of relevance here is the controversial 1926 Soviet Family Code. This new code gave legal recognition to "de facto marriage" based on cohabitation, abolished collective paternity of orphans, and altered alimony standards. Babichev's concerns—adopting Makarov and the establishment of a communal kitchen—and Kavalerov and Ivan's sharing of Anechka are very much a part of the debate surrounding the Family Code. For further details, see Wendy Z. Goldman, *Women, the State and Revolution: Soviet Family Policy and Social Life, 1917–1936* (New York: Cambridge University Press, 1995).

76. Olesha, *Povesti*, 282.

77. Ibid.

78. Olesha, *Zavist'*, 116. Coincidentally, Olesha's stepson, Igor, committed self-defenestration in front of his mother and stepfather in 1939.

79. Olesha, *Povesti*, 89.

80. Borenstein, *Men without Women*, 126, 161.

81. Katerina Clark, *The Soviet Novel: History as Ritual* (Chicago: University of Chicago Press, 1985), 168–70.

82. Olesha, *Povesti*, 34 (italics mine).

83. Joyce, *Ulysses*, 32.

84. Ibid., 159.

85. M. O. Chudakova, *Masterstvo Iuriia Oleshi* (Moskva: Nauka, 1972), 19.

86. See "I Look into the Past" for another fictionalized representation of this desire regarding France. Olesha, *Povesti*, 282. Consider also the various references to European literature throughout *No Day without a Line*, for example, the German Expressionists. Olesha, *Zavist'*, 293. On the contrary, in "Human Material" (1928), Olesha's autobiographical narrator claims, presaging the Futurist poet Vladimir Mayakovsky's (1893–1930) proclamations in "At the Top of My Voice" (1930), that he wants to grip by the throat that version of himself "who thinks that the distance between us [Russia] and Europe is only a geographical distance." Olesha, *Povesti*, 245.

87. Joyce, *Ulysses*, 171.

88. Ibid., 28.

89. Elizabeth Klosty Beaujour, "On Choosing One's Ancestors: Some Afterthoughts on *Envy*," *Ulbandus Review* 2, no. 1 (1979): 32.

90. Olesha, quoted in Pertsov, "My zhivem vpervye," 282–83.

91. Olesha uses literary and mythical archetypes, thereby partaking in what T. S. Eliot famously called the mythic method to enrich his characterization and associative poetics, but nowhere does this device achieve Joycean depth or breadth. On the subject of myth in *Envy*, consider Janet G. Tucker, *Revolution Betrayed: Jurij Oleša's "Envy"* (Columbus, OH: Slavica Publishers, 1996).

92. Joyce, *Ulysses*, 8, 50.

93. Olesha, *Povesti*, 60.

94. This cloud image appears on the second page explicitly numbered 3 in individual file 4, which Olesha produced in September 1924.

2. Vladimir Nabokov

1. Terrence Killeen's article "Nabokov . . . Léon . . . Joyce" in the *Irish Times* describes the letter in question, which is part of the James Joyce–Paul Léon papers housed in Dublin's National Library. Vladimir Nabokov, quoted in Terrence Killeen, "Nabokov . . . Léon . . . Joyce," *Irish Times*, June 13, 1992.

2. Vladimir Nabokov, *Strong Opinions* (New York: Vintage Books, 1990), 102.

3. Ibid., 102–3.

4. Compare Nabokov's comments on Gogol, Dostoevsky, and Proust: ibid., 103, 148, 197.

5. Ibid., 102.

6. Vladimir Nabokov, *Lectures on "Ulysses": Facsimile of the Manuscript* (Bloomfield Hills, MI: Bruccoli Clark, 1980), 320.

7. Consider, for instance, Gennadii Barabtarlo, *Sochinenie Nabokova* (Sankt-Peterburg: Izdatel'stvo Ivana Limbakha, 2011), 296.

8. For previous comparisons between Nabokov and Joyce, see Julian Moynahan, "Nabokov and Joyce," in *The Garland Companion to Vladimir Nabokov*, ed. Vladimir E. Alexandrov (New York: Garland Publishing, 1995), 434; and Michael H. Begnal, *"Bend Sinister*: Joyce, Shakespeare, Nabokov," *Modern Language Studies* 15, no. 4 (1985): 22–27.

9. For differing accounts of these meetings, see Nabokov, *Strong Opinions*, 86; Richard Ellmann, *James Joyce* (Oxford: Oxford University Press, 1983), 616; Michael H. Begnal, "Joyce, Nabokov, and the Hungarian National Soccer Team," *James Joyce Quarterly* 31, no. 4 (1994): 522–23; and Lucie Léon Noel, "Playback," *TriQuarterly* 17 (1970): 219.

10. Margaret McBride, *"Ulysses" and the Metamorphosis of Stephen Dedalus* (Lewisburg, PA: Bucknell University Press, 2001), 182.

11. Alexander Dolinin, *"The Gift,"* in *The Garland Companion to Vladimir Nabokov*, ed. Vladimir E. Alexandrov (New York: Garland Publishing, 1995), 139.

12. Pekka Tammi, *Problems of Nabokov's Poetics: A Narratological Analysis* (Helsinki: Suomalainen Tiedeakatemia, 1985), 86.

13. Sergei Davydov, *"Teksty-matreški" Vladimira Nabokova* (Munich: Verlag Otto Sagner, 1982).

14. Consider, for instance, Nora Buhks, "Roman-oboroten': O *Dare* V. Nabokova," *Cahiers du Monde russe et soviétique* 31, no. 4 (1990): 587–624; Edward J. Brown, "Nabokov, Chernyshevsky, Olesha and the Gift of Sight," *Stanford Slavic Studies* 4, no. 2 (1992): 280–94; Anat Ben-Amos, "The Role of Literature in *The Gift*," *Nabokov Studies* 4 (1997): 117–49; Stephen H. Blackwell, *Zina's Paradox: The Figured Reader in Nabokov's "Gift"* (New York: Peter Lang, 2000); Paul D. Morris, "Nabokov's Poetic Gift: The Poetry in and of *Dar*," *Russian Literature* 48, no. 4 (2000): 457–69; and Victoria Ivleva, "A Vest Reinvested in *The Gift*," *Russian Review* 68, no. 2 (2009): 283–301.

15. Justin Weir, *The Author as Hero: Self and Tradition in Bulgakov, Pasternak, and Nabokov* (Evanston, IL: Northwestern University Press, 2002), xxi.

16. Vladimir Nabokov, *The Gift*, trans. Michael Scammell (New York: Vintage Books, 1991), 340. Vladimir Nabokov, *Sobranie sochinenii russkogo perioda* (Sankt-

Peterburg: Simpozium, 2000), 4:515. Citations from *The Gift* refer to Michael Scammell's English translation (E), which the author edited, and to the original Russian version (R) included in the fourth volume of the Simpozium edition of Nabokov's collected works.

17. Nabokov also took issue with Joyce's Homeric parallels and the so-called stream of consciousness technique. See Vladimir Nabokov, *Lectures on Literature*, ed. Fredson Bowers (New York: Harcourt, Brace, Jovanovich, 1980), 288, 363.

18. Monika Greenleaf, "Fathers, Sons and Impostors: Pushkin's Trace in *The Gift*," *Slavic Review* 53, no. 1 (1994): 144. Vladimir E. Alexandrov, too, counters Greenleaf by suggesting that "Russian literature was neither specially privileged, nor of course an end in itself for him." Vladimir E. Alexandrov, *Nabokov's Otherworld* (Princeton, NJ: Princeton University Press, 1991), 136. To consider *The Gift* a singularly Russocentric work, in other words, is too limited a view.

19. Poplavskii, "Po povodu," 171.

20. Vladislav Khodasevich, quoted in David M. Bethea, *Khodasevich: His Life and Art* (Princeton, NJ: Princeton University Press, 1983), 327.

21. Adamovich saw the same in Nabokov: "Meanwhile, wittingly or not, it's as if [Nabokov] plows the soil for some future Pushkin who will again proceed to put our poetry in order. Maybe this new Pushkin will not appear." Georgii Adamovich, *Odinochestvo i svoboda* (Sankt-Peterburg: Aleteiia, 2002), 222.

22. Numerous scholars have called *The Gift* a "portrait of the artist as a young man" in the Joycean tradition, though nearly always as a generic shorthand. See, for example, Ben-Amos, "The Role of Literature in *The Gift*," 142; L. L. Lee, *Vladimir Nabokov* (Boston: Twayne, 1976), 81; Brian Boyd, *Vladimir Nabokov: The Russian Years* (Princeton, NJ: Princeton University Press, 1990), 447; Tammi, *Problems of Nabokov's Poetics*, 86; and Roger B. Salomon, "*The Gift*: Nabokov's Portrait of the Artist," in *Critical Essays on Vladimir Nabokov*, ed. Phyllis A. Roth (Boston: G. K. Hall, 1984), 185.

23. Ellmann, *James Joyce*, 22, 610.

24. James Joyce, *Finnegans Wake* (London: Wordsworth Editions, 2012), 620, lines 32–33. All further references to *Finnegans Wake* are to this edition, with both page number and line cited; most editions of *Finnegans Wake* are paginated identically.

25. Joyce, *Ulysses*, 170.

26. Nabokov, *The Gift*, E98/R280–81.

27. Cf. Boyd, *Vladimir Nabokov*, 466.

28. Sergei Davydov, "Weighing Nabokov's *Gift* on Pushkin's Scales," in *Cultural Mythologies of Russian Modernism: From the Golden Age to the Silver Age*, ed. Boris Gasparov, Robert P. Hughes, and Irina Paperno (Berkeley: University of California Press, 1992), 421.

29. Bloom, *The Anxiety of Influence*, 30.

30. S. Ia. Senderovich, "Pushkin v 'Dare' Nabokova," in *Figura sokrytiia: Izbrannye raboty* (Moskva: Iazyki slavianskikh kul'tur, 2012), 2:493.

31. Hugh Kenner, *Ulysses* (Baltimore: Johns Hopkins University Press, 1987), 114. On the correspondences between Stephen's version of Shakespeare and Bloom, see McBride, *"Ulysses" and the Metamorphosis of Stephen Dedalus*, 82–84, 89. Consider also Schutte's pioneering *Joyce and Shakespeare*.

32. Nabokov, *The Gift*, E137/R319.

33. A. S. Pushkin, *Sobranie sochinenii v desiati tomakh*, vol. 2, *Stikhotvoreniia 1823–1836* (Moskva: Gosudarstvennoe izdatel'stvo khudozhestvennoi literatury, 1959), 305–6.

34. Nabokov, *The Gift*, E138/R320.

35. Nabokov, *The Gift*, E310/R484.

36. Senderovich, "Pushkin v 'Dare' Nabokova," 517.

37. See Schutte, *Joyce and Shakespeare*, 153–77, for an extensive line-by-line comparison.

38. See Dieter E. Zimmer and Sabine Hartmann, "'The Amazing Music of Truth': Nabokov's Sources for Godunov's Central Asian Travels in *The Gift*," *Nabokov Studies* 7 (2002–3): 33–74, for a nearly exhaustive account of these sources; and Irina Paperno's earlier "How Nabokov's *Gift* Is Made," *Stanford Slavic Studies* 4, no. 2 (1992): 295–322, for further discussion of the transformation of authentic sources within *The Gift*. In *Vladimir Nabokov: A Critical Study of the Novels* (New York: Cambridge University Press, 1984), David Rampton offers a less sympathetic take on how this process is repeated for parodic effect in Fyodor's Chernyshevsky book.

39. Schutte, *Joyce and Shakespeare*, 54.

40. Nabokov, *The Gift*, E205/R385.

41. In *Strong Opinions*, Nabokov interrogates an interviewer's use of the word "life" as a general concept. See Nabokov, *Strong Opinions*, 118.

42. Joyce, *Ulysses*, 170.

43. David M. Bethea, *The Superstitious Muse: Thinking Russian Literature Mythopoetically* (Brighton, MA: Academic Studies Press, 2009), 140–41.

44. Nabokov, *The Gift*, E342/R517.

45. Joyce, *Ulysses*, 153. According to Don Gifford's annotations to *Ulysses*, Joyce here reworks a line from St. Augustine's *De immortalitate animae*: "But the intention to act is of the present, through which the future flows into the past." Don Gifford, *"Ulysses" Annotated: Notes for James Joyce's "Ulysses,"* 2nd ed. (Berkeley: University of California Press, 1989), 199. Christoph Henry-Thommes does not raise this potential allusion in his comparative study of Nabokov's and Augustine's autobiographical texts. His analysis of quotations from the *Confessions* in *Lolita* and *Ada* shows that Nabokov undoubtedly did read Augustine at some point, as when *Ada*'s Van Veen "ferociously attacks [the] Augustinian idea of time as a flow or sequence of events." Christoph Henry-Thommes, *Recollection, Memory, and Imagination: Selected Autobiographical Novels of Vladimir Nabokov* (Heidelberg: Winter, 2006), 159. Nabokov is not equivalent to either Fyodor or Van, but this change marks a curious inversion of what Fyodor writes.

46. Vladimir Nabokov, *Novels and Memoirs 1941–1951: The Real Life of Sebastian Knight; Bend Sinister; Speak, Memory: An Autobiography Revisited*, ed. Brian Boyd, Library of America (New York: Literary Classics of the United States, 1996), 178. All citations from *Bend Sinister* refer to the Library of America edition, *Novels and Memoirs 1941–1951*.

47. Joyce, *Ulysses*, 28.

48. Nabokov, *Lectures on "Ulysses,"* 355.

49. Robert Spoo, *James Joyce and the Language of History: Dedalus's Nightmare* (New York: Oxford University Press, 1994), 13.

50. Nabokov, *Lectures on Literature*, 378.

51. Ibid., 373.

52. Spoo, *James Joyce and the Language of History*, 90.

53. Nabokov, *Novels and Memoirs*, 370.

54. Nabokov, *Strong Opinions*, 141.

55. Nabokov, *The Gift*, E156/R337.

56. Weir, *The Author as Hero*, 90; Blackwell, *Zina's Paradox*, 154.

57. Nabokov, *The Gift*, E139/R321.

58. Nabokov, *The Gift*, E98/R80–81.

59. Nabokov, *The Gift*, E331/R506 (italics mine).

60. Nabokov, *Lectures on "Ulysses,"* 297.

61. Joyce, *Ulysses*, 37.

62. Ibid., 39.

63. Ibid. (italics mine).

64. Ibid., 5.

65. Ibid., 18, 38.

66. Julian W. Connolly, *Nabokov's Early Fiction: Patterns of Self and Other* (Cambridge: Cambridge University Press, 1992), 210–11.

67. Nabokov, *Novels and Memoirs*, 358.

68. Nabokov, *The Gift*, E64/R249.

69. Nabokov, *The Gift*, E64/R250.

70. Weir suggests that this scene is a parodic response to Pushkin's podiatric fixation. Weir, *The Author as Hero*, 83. See also Davydov, *"Teksty-matreški,"* 422–23. *The Gift*'s narrator also provides self-aware commentary on the exploitation of female legs in literature. Nabokov, *The Gift*, E163/R343–44. For a similar moment in *Ulysses*, see Joyce, *Ulysses*, 301.

71. Joyce, *Ulysses*, 187.

72. Ibid., 41.

73. Ibid., 31.

74. Ibid., 173.

75. Ibid., 42.

76. Nabokov, *The Gift*, E18.

77. Nabokov, *The Gift*, R205.

78. Nabokov, *The Gift*, E18.

79. Joyce, *Ulysses*, 31.

80. My thanks to S.A. Karpukhin for bringing this parallel to my attention.

81. Herbert Grabes, "Nabokov and Shakespeare: The English Works," in *The Garland Companion to Vladimir Nabokov*, ed. Vladimir E. Alexandrov (New York: Garland Publishing, 1995), 499; Samuel Schuman, *Nabokov's Shakespeare* (New York: Bloomsbury, 2014).

82. Nabokov, *Lectures on Literature*, 326. Coincidentally, in a 1928 letter mixed with praise and critique, H. G. Wells wrote to Joyce, "You have turned your back on common men, on their elementary needs and their restricted time and intelligence and you have elaborated. What is the result? Vast riddles. Your last two works have been more amusing and exciting to write than they will ever be to read." Joyce, *Letters of James Joyce*, 1:275.

83. John Burt Foster Jr., for example, treats this section at length in terms of his thesis regarding Nabokov's connections to European Modernism and his "art of

memory." John Burt Foster Jr., *Nabokov's Art of Memory and European Modernism* (Princeton, NJ: Princeton University Press, 1993), 170.

84. Consider Begnal, *"Bend Sinister,"* 23–24; and Michael Seidel, "Nabokov on Joyce, Shakespeare, Telemachus, and Hamlet," *James Joyce Quarterly* 20, no. 3 (1983): 359.

85. On the multilayered quality of Nabokov's allusions, see Pekka Tammi, "Seventeen Remarks on *Poligenetičnost'* in Nabokov's Prose," *Studia slavica finlandensia* 7 (1990): 192; and Yuri Leving, *Keys to "The Gift": A Guide to Vladimir Nabokov's Novel* (Brighton, MA: Academic Studies Press, 2011), 277.

86. Nabokov, *Novels and Memoirs*, 252. Nabokov here also encodes an additional reference to Pushkin, who was famously called Proteus by Nikolai Gnedich (1784–1833), further uniting the father of Russian poetry with the father of English literature: "Pushkin, Proteus / With your flexible tongue and the magic of your hymns." Nikolai Ivanovich Gnedich, *Stikhotvorenii* (Leningrad: Sovetskii pisatel', 1956), 148. Gnedich, incidentally, translated Homer's *Iliad* into Russian.

87. Boyd, in Nabokov, *Novels and Memoirs*, 684.

88. Nabokov, *Novels and Memoirs*, 252.

89. Eric Naiman, *Nabokov, Perversely* (Ithaca, NY: Cornell University Press, 2010), 50.

90. Joyce, *Ulysses*, 175.

91. Naiman, *Nabokov, Perversely*, 64.

92. Nabokov, *Novels and Memoirs*, 258.

93. Ibid., 259 (italics mine).

94. Nabokov, *The Gift*, E139/R321.

95. Nabokov, *The Gift*, E364/R359.

96. Nabokov, *Strong Opinions*, 218.

97. Ibid., 219.

98. Ibid., 95.

99. Joyce, *Ulysses*, 339.

100. Nabokov, *The Gift*, E204/R384.

101. For some brief remarks on this occasion, see Nabokov, *Strong Opinions*, 86; Boyd, *Vladimir Nabokov*, 434; and Begnal, "Joyce, Nabokov," 520–21.

102. Vladimir Nabokov, "Pushkin, or the Real and the Plausible," *New York Review of Books* 35 (March 31, 1988): 39.

103. Vladimir Nabokov, foreword to *Glory*, by Vladimir Nabokov (New York: Vintage Books, 1991), xii.

104. Nabokov, "Pushkin," 39 (italics mine).

105. Ibid., 40.

106. Nabokov, *The Gift*, E139/R321.

107. Nabokov, *Novels and Memoirs*, 305.

108. Ibid., 178.

109. Foster, *Nabokov's Art*, 176.

110. Nabokov, *Novels and Memoirs*, 345.

111. Ibid.

112. See Alexandrov, *Nabokov's Otherworld*, 3. Major texts that have been analyzed as "ghost stories" include *Pale Fire, Transparent Things,* "Signs and Symbols," and "The Vane Sisters."

113. Polina Barskova, "Filial Feelings and Paternal Patterns: Transformations of *Hamlet* in *The Gift*," *Nabokov Studies* 9, no. 1 (2005): 204.

114. Ibid. 205. See Brian Boyd, "'The Expected Stress Did Not Come': A Note on 'Father's Butterflies,'" *Nabokovian* 45 (2000): 28, for another iteration of this claim that explicitly mentions *Ulysses*'s conclusion.

115. Joyce, *Ulysses*, 474.

116. Nabokov, *The Gift*, E354/R530. The execution theme was crucial in Nabokov's thinking at this time. He paused his work on *The Gift* to complete *Invitation to a Beheading (Priglashenie na kazn')* "in one fortnight of wonderful excitement and sustained inspiration." Nabokov, *Strong Opinions*, 68.

117. Nabokov, *The Gift*, E355/R530.

118. Nabokov, *The Gift*, E98/R280–81.

119. Nabokov, *Novels and Memoirs*, 351–52; Nabokov, *The Gift*, E355/R530.

120. Nabokov, *The Gift*, E362–63/R538.

121. Borenstein, *Men without Women*, 125.

3. Andrei Bitov

1. Cornwell, *James Joyce and the Russians*, 111–12. See R. Miller-Budnitskaia, "Filosofiia kul'tury Dzhemza Dzhoisa," *Internatsional'naia literatura* 2 (1937): 188–209; and A. Startsev, "Dzhois pered 'Ulissom,'" *Internatsional'naia literatura* 1 (1937): 196–202.

2. Andrei Platonov, "Iz stat'i 'O likvidatsii' chelovechestva (Po povodu romana K. Chapeka 'Voina s salamandrami,'" in *"Russkaia odisseia" Dzheimsa Dzhoisa*, ed. Ekaterina Genieva (Moskva: Rudomino, 2005), 100–101.

3. A.S. [A. Startsev], "Dzhems Dzhois," *Internatsional'naia literatura* 2 (1941): 241.

4. A brief, unsigned entry on Joyce appeared in the second edition of the *Great Soviet Encyclopedia* in 1952. Anonymous, "Dzhois," in *Bol'shaia sovetskaia entsiklopediia*, 2nd ed. (Moskva: Gosudarstvennoe nauchnoe izdatel'stvo "Bol'shaia sovetskaia entsiklopediia," 1952), 14:231.

5. Anna Akhmatova, "Listki iz dnevnika," in Genieva, *"Russkaia odisseia" Dzheimsa Dzhoisa*, 112.

6. Lidiia Chukovskaia, *Zapiski ob Anne Akhmatovoi*, vol. 1 (Paris: YMCA-Press, 1984), 18.

7. Anna Akhmatova, *Sobranie sochinenii v shesti tomakh*, vol. 3, *Poemy. Pro domo mea. Teatr* (Moskva: Ellis Lak, 1998), 21. Compare "He could not leave his mother an orphan," from Joyce, *Ulysses*, 339. Akhmatova later used this same line as the epigraph to *Shards (Cherepki*, 1930s, 1958). See Anna Akhmatova, *Cherepki*, in *Pamiati A. A. Akhmatovoi. Stikhi, pis'ma, vospominaniia* (Paris: YMCA-Press, 1974), 15.

8. See Cornwell's *James Joyce and the Russians*, especially 113–17, for a more detailed account of Joyce's critical reception in the 1950s and 1960s. Consider also Emily Tall, "The Reception of James Joyce in Russia," in *The Reception of James Joyce in Europe*, ed. Geert Lernout and Wim Van Mierlo, vol. 1, *Germany, Northern and East Central Europe* (New York: Thoemmes Continuum, 2004), 244–57.

9. A reprint of the 1937 edition of *Dublintsy (Dubliners)* appeared in 1966, and *A Portrait of the Artist as a Young Man* was finally published in a Russian translation by Maria Bogoslovskaia-Bobrova in *Inostrannaia literatura* in 1976. See Dzheims Dzhois, *Portret khudozhnika v iunosti*, trans. M. P. Bogoslovskaia-Bobrova, *Inostrannaia literatura* 10 (1976): 171–98; 11 (1976): 119–74; 12 (1976): 139–82. Galina S. Griffiths mentions that, in an interview with Bitov, he described his English education to her. Galina

S. Griffiths, "The Monuments of Russian Culture: *Pushkin House* as the Museum of the Soviet School Curriculum" (PhD diss., University of Kansas, 2005), 18.

10. Viktor Erofeev, "Pamiatnik proshedshemu vremeni: Andrei Bitov. Pushkinskii dom," *Oktiabr'* 6 (1988): 203.

11. Andrei Bitov, *Pushkinskii dom*, in *Imperiia v chetyrekh izmereniiakh*, vol. 2, *Pushkinskii dom* (Khar'kov: Folio, 1996), 369–70. All further references to *Pushkin House* (*Pushkinskii dom*) are to the version included in this edition, which features all additions to the novel including Bitov's commentary and the supplement to the commentary, *Scraps* (*Obrezki*).

12. Ann Komaromi, "The Window to the West in Andrei Bitov's *Pushkin House*," in *"Pushkin House" by Andrei Bitov: A Casebook*, ed. Ekaterina Sukhanova (Normal, IL: Dalkey Archive Press, 2005), 96.

13. For glancing references to Joyce in studies about Bitov, see Susan Brownsberger, afterword to *Pushkin House*, by Andrei Bitov (Ann Arbor, MI: Ardis, 1990), 360; Iurii Karabchievskii, "Tochka boli. O romane Andreia Bitova 'Pushkinskii dom,'" *Grani* 106 (1977): 200; I. Skoropanova, "Klassika v postmodernistskoi sisteme koordinat: 'Pushkinskii dom' Andreia Bitova," in *Russkaia postmodernistskaia literatura: Uchebnoe posobie* (Moskva: Izd-vo "Flinta" and Izd-vo "Nauka," 2000), 127; and Solomon Volkov, *St. Petersburg: A Cultural History*, trans. Antonina W. Bouis (New York: Free Press, 1995), 524.

14. Bitov, *Pushkinskii dom*, 11, 130, 355, 370. Other studies that analyze non-Russian intertextual links in Bitov's work include Harold D. Baker, "Bitov Reading Proust through the Windows of *Pushkin House*," *Slavic and East European Journal* 41, no. 4 (1997): 604–26; Peter I. Barta, "Bitov's Perilous Passage: 'Penelopa,' Odysseus and Plato on the Nevskii," *Slavonic and East European Review* 76, no. 4 (1998): 633–42; Susan Brownsberger, "'Man in a Landscape': Toward an Understanding of Bitov's Design," *Russian Literature* 61, no. 4 (2007): 393–416, on Dante; Ellen Chances, *Andrei Bitov: The Ecology of Inspiration* (New York: Cambridge University Press, 1993), 226, on Charles Dickens and Proust; V. Ermilov, "Budem tochnymi . . . ," *Literaturnaia gazeta*, April 16, 1964, 3, on Laurence Sterne; Komaromi, "The Window to the West"; Ronald Meyer, "Andrej Bitov's *Puškinskij dom*" (PhD diss., Indiana University, 1986), on Dickens and Dumas; and Kurt Shaw, "French Connections: The *Three Musketeers* Motif in Andrei Bitov's *Pushkinskii dom*," *Canadian Slavonic Papers* 37, no. 1–2 (1995): 187–99.

15. Bitov, *Pushkinskii dom*, 369.

16. Ibid., 387.

17. Ibid.

18. Ibid., 386.

19. Andrei Bitov, quoted in Vitalii Amurskii, *Zapechatlennye golosa: Parizhskie besedy s russkimi pisateliami i poetami* (Moskva: Izdatel'stvo "MIK," 1998), 38.

20. Bitov, *Pushkinskii dom*, 386.

21. Ibid. (italics mine).

22. Bitov, quoted in Amurskii, *Zapechatlennye golosa*, 39.

23. I. P. Smirnov, quoted in Stanislav Savitskii, "Kak postroili 'Pushkinskii dom' (Dos'e)," in *Pushkinskii dom*, by Andrei Bitov (Sankt-Peterburg: Izdatel'stvo Ivana Limbakha, 1999), 469.

24. Although Bitov does not explain what he means by "hypernovel," he likely has in mind texts that reject a linear plot in favor of multiple, often overlapping, story

lines and that are extremely metatextual. Other examples include Nabokov's *Pale Fire* (1962), Julio Cortázar's *Hopscotch* (1963), and Italo Calvino's *If on a Winter's Night a Traveler* . . . (1979). The "one day (in the life) of . . ." trope heralded in large part by *Ulysses* found a welcome home in Russian literature. Consider, for example, Valentin Kataev's *Time, Forward* (*Vremia, vpered!*, 1933); Alexander Solzhenitsyn's *One Day in the Life of Ivan Denisovich* (*Odin den' Ivana Denisovicha*, 1962); Venedikt Erofeev's *Moskva–Petushki* (written 1969–70); Chingiz Aitmatov's *One Day Lasts More than a Hundred Years* (*I dol'she veka dlitsia den'*, 1980); and Vladimir Sorokin's *Day of the Oprichnik* (*Den' oprichnika*, 2006). Savitskii, "Kak postroili 'Pushkinskii dom' (Dos'e)," 476.

25. Andrei Bitov, *Novyi Gulliver* (Tenafly, NJ: Hermitage Publishers, 1997), 39.

26. Cf. Komaromi, "The Window to the West," 98.

27. See Chances, *Andrei Bitov*, 8–9, for a concise explanation of Ginzburg's intellectual impact on Bitov. See also Lidiia Ginzburg's "Pole napriazheniia," *Literaturnaia gazeta*, January 5, 1986, 7, for her remarks on Bitov.

28. Bitov, *Pushkinskii dom*, 374.

29. Ginzburg's comments on Joyce, particularly his narration, can be found in both her critical works and her journals: Lidiia Ginzburg, *Chelovek za pis'mennym stolom: Esse. Iz vozpominanii. Chetyre povestvovaniia* (Leningrad: Sovetskii pisatel', Leningradskoe otdelenie, 1989), 172; *O psikhologicheskoi proze* (Moskva: Intrada, 1999), 308; and *O literaturnom geroe* (Leningrad: Sovetskii pisatel', Leningradskoe otdelenie, 1979), 12, 332, 137.

30. Andrei Bitov, *My prosnulis' v neznakomoi strane* (Leningrad: Sovetskii pisatel', 1991), 5.

31. Ibid.

32. Bitov, *Pushkinskii dom*, 386.

33. Chances, *Andrei Bitov*, 237.

34. For a similar development of this theme, consider Bitov's novella "Pushkin's Photograph (1799–2099)," which features Leva's descendant time traveling to photograph and record Russia's national poet. See Andrei Bitov, "Fotografiia Pushkina (1799–2099)," in *Imperiia v chetyrekh izmereniiakh*, vol. 2, *Pushkinskii dom* (Khar'kov: Folio, 1996), 399–437.

35. Mark Lipovetsky, *Russian Postmodernist Fiction: Dialogue with Chaos* (Armonk, NY: M. E. Sharpe, 1999), 8.

36. Denis Kozlov and Eleonory Gilburd, "The Thaw as an Event in Russian History," in *The Thaw: Soviet Society and Culture during the 1950s and 1960s*, ed. Denis Kozlov and Eleonory Gilburd (Toronto: University of Toronto Press, 2013), 38.

37. Stephen V. Bittner, *The Many Lives of Khrushchev's Thaw: Experience and Memory in Moscow's Arbat* (Ithaca, NY: Cornell University Press, 2008), 76.

38. For more on the Thaw and literary trends during this period, see Liudmila Alekseeva and Paul Goldberg, *The Thaw Generation: Coming of Age in the Post-Stalin Era* (Pittsburgh: University of Pittsburgh Press, 1993); Vera Apukhtina, *Molodoi geroi v sovetskoi proze: 60-e gody* (Moskva: Znanie, 1971); Sergei Chuprinin, "Non–Past Time: On the Traits of the 'Thaw' Period in the History of the Contemporary Literary Process," *Russian Studies in Literature* 28, no. 4 (1992): 4–21; and T. A. Sivokhina and M. R. Zezina, *Apogei rezhima lichnoi vlasti. "Ottepel'." Povorot k neostalinizmu: Obshchestvenno-politicheskaia zhizn' v SSSR v seredine 40-kh–60-e gody* (Moskva: Izdatel'stvo Moskovskogo universiteta, 1993).

39. John Barth, *The Friday Book: Essays and Other Nonfiction* (New York: G. P. Putnam's Sons, 1984), 203.

40. Consider V. N. Toporov, *Peterburgskii tekst russkoi literatury: Izbrannye trudy* (Sankt-Petersburg: Iskusstvo-SPB, 2003); and Iu. M. Lotman, "Simvolika Peterburga i problemy semiotiki goroda," in *Izbrannye stat'i v trekh tomakh* (Tallinn: Aleksandra, 1992), 2:9–21. See also Pekka Pesonen, "Bitov's Text as Text: The Petersburg Text as a Context in Andrey Bitov's Prose," in *Literary Tradition and Practice in Russian Culture: Papers from an International Conference on the Occasion of the Seventieth Birthday of Yury Mikhailovich Lotman*, ed. Valentina Polukhina, Joe Andrew, and Robert Reid (Amsterdam: Rodopi, 1993), 325–41; and Henrietta Mondry, "*Literaturnost'* as a Key to Andrey Bitov's *Pushkin House*," in *The Waking Sphinx: South African Essays on Russian Culture*, ed. Henrietta Mondry (Johannesburg: University of Witwatersrand, 1989), 3–19.

41. Joyce, *Ulysses*, 527.

42. Compare Stephen's proclamation about past acquaintances: "If I call them into life across the waters of Lethe will not the poor ghosts troop to my call?" Ibid., 339.

43. Andrei Bitov, "Andrei Bitov," interview by Elisabeth Rich, trans. Adam Perri, *South Central Review* 12, no. 3–4 (1995): 28.

44. Bitov, *Pushkinskii dom*, 342.

45. Ibid., 52.

46. Peter I. Barta, *Bely, Joyce, and Döblin: Peripatetics in the City Novel* (Gainesville: University Press of Florida, 1996), xv.

47. Joyce, *Ulysses*, 35.

48. Ibid., 19.

49. Ibid., 537, 632.

50. Ibid., 495 (italics mine).

51. Ibid., 174.

52. Recall Stephen's three defenses for the artist from *A Portrait of the Artist as a Young Man*: "silence, exile and cunning." James Joyce, *A Portrait of the Artist as a Young Man* (New York: Penguin Books, 1993), 269.

53. Bitov, *Pushkinskii dom*, 39.

54. Ibid.

55. Ellen Chances, "The Energy of Honesty, or Brussels Lace, Mandelstam, 'Stolen Air,' and Inner Freedom: A Visit to the Creative Workshop of Andrei Bitov's *Pushkin House*," in *"Pushkin House" by Andrei Bitov: A Casebook*, ed. Ekaterina Sukhanova (Normal, IL: Dalkey Archive Press, 2005), 47.

56. Bitov, *Pushkinskii dom*, 334.

57. Komaromi, "The Window to the West," 98.

58. Bitov, *Pushkinskii dom*, 17.

59. Joyce, *Ulysses*, 170.

60. Bitov, *Pushkinskii dom*, 18–19.

61. Morris Beja, introduction to "The Mystical Estate or the Legal Fiction: Paternity in *Ulysses*," in *James Joyce: The Augmented Ninth; Proceedings from the Ninth International James Joyce Symposium, Frankfurt, 1984*, ed. Bernard Benstock (Syracuse, NY: Syracuse University Press, 1988), 217.

62. Joyce, *Ulysses*, 32.

63. Olesha, *Povesti*, 34.

64. Bitov, *Pushkinskii dom*, 21.

65. Ibid.

66. Ibid., 31.

67. Joyce, *Ulysses*, 463.

68. Harold Bloom reads this scene as a sign of anxiety of influence on Joyce's part. Harold Bloom, introduction to *Modern Critical Views: James Joyce*, ed. Harold Bloom (New York: Chelsea House Publishers, 1986), 5. Though the reindeer's horns certainly emphasize the characters' sense of having been usurped and cuckolded, he takes matters too far here.

69. Bitov, *Pushkinskii dom*, 43.

70. Ibid., 47.

71. Italics mine.

72. Bitov, *Pushkinskii dom*, 53.

73. Joyce, *Ulysses*, 173.

74. Bitov, *Pushkinskii dom*, 19.

75. Ibid.

76. Ibid., 46.

77. Ibid., 47.

78. Joyce, *Ulysses*, 171.

79. Bitov, *Pushkinskii dom*, 85. Later in the novel, Leva and Mitishatev part ways after a gathering. The former feels "relief and joy" as he begins to doubt his suspicions about Mitishatev becoming romantically involved with his girlfriend, Faina (ibid., 164). Leva suggests that "at the core" of his being stands "the kernel, the seed" (*iadryshko, zernyshko*) amid a bright light (ibid.). The irony of the situation, evident only to the reader, is that Mitishatev probably returns to Faina's for an assignation. The two words for seed used in these separate passages may be different, and yet the results are dire for Leva. Even the language of Bitov's novel implicates Leva in the system of belatedness and treachery, embodied by his tormentor and rival.

80. Ibid., 22. Russian: "otets—eto ego otets, chto emu, Leve,—tozhe nuzhen otets, kak okazalsia odnazhdi nuzhen i ottsy—ego otets, Levin ded, otets ottsa."

81. Ibid., 49.

82. For a Freudian reading of Leva's experience with absent fathers and grandfathers, see Slobodanka M. Vladiv-Glover, "The 1960s and the Rediscovery of the Other in Russian Culture: Andrei Bitov," in *Russian Postmodernism: New Perspectives on Post-Soviet Culture*, ed. Mikhail N. Epstein, Alexander A. Genis, and Slobodanka M. Vladiv-Glover, trans. Slobodanka M. Vladiv-Glover (New York: Berghahn Books, 1999), 31–86.

83. Bitov, *Pushkinskii dom*, 50.

84. Ibid., 51–52.

85. Ibid., 73.

86. Ibid.

87. Ibid.

88. In the commentary written in 1971, years after Modest Platonovich's speech, Bitov doubts his character. According to him, people say all sorts of things, for example, that Russia will soon see *A Portrait of the Artist* translated and that the Olympics will be held in Moscow in 1980. Bitov, *Pushkinskii dom*, 366. A translation did, in fact, appear in *Inostrannaia literatura* in 1976.

89. On the topic of *Envy*, Bitov may well have had Olesha, along with Mikhail Bakhtin, in mind when writing Modest Platonovich's speech. See Priscilla Meyer, introduction to *Life in Windy Weather: Short Stories*, by Andrei Bitov, ed. Priscilla Meyer (Ann Arbor: Ardis, 1986), 10; and Vol'f Shmid, "Andrei Bitov—master 'ostrovidedeniia,'" in *Proza kak poeziia: Stat'i o povestvovanii v russkoi literature* (Sankt-Peterburg: Gumanitarnoe agenstvo "Akademicheskii prospect," 1994), 212, for some comparisons of Bitov with Olesha.

90. Fredric Jameson, "*Ulysses* in History," in *Modern Critical Views: James Joyce*, ed. Harold Bloom (New York: Chelsea House Publishers, 1986), 174.

91. Joyce, *Ulysses*, 548.

92. Bitov, *Pushkinskii dom*, 71.

93. Ibid., 249.

94. Ibid., 88.

95. Ibid., 103–4.

96. Ibid., 48.

97. Joyce, *Ulysses*, 15.

98. Karen Lawrence, "Paternity as Legal Fiction in *Ulysses*," in *James Joyce: The Augmented Ninth; Proceedings from the Ninth International James Joyce Symposium, Frankfurt, 1984*, ed. Bernard Benstock (Syracuse, NY: Syracuse University Press, 1988), 233.

99. Joyce, *Ulysses*, 171.

100. Bitov, *Pushkinskii dom*, 227.

101. Ibid., 228. Bitov also began *Pushkin House* at this age.

102. Ibid., 237.

103. Ibid.

104. Vladiv-Glover, "Rediscovery of the Other," 56.

105. Bitov, *Pushkinskii dom*, 17.

106. Ibid., 239.

107. Ibid., 234.

108. Ibid., 241–42.

109. Joyce, *Ulysses*, 159–60.

110. Andrei Bitov, preface to *Life in Windy Weather: Short Stories*, by Andrei Bitov, ed. Priscilla Meyer (Ann Arbor: Ardis, 1986), 15.

111. Consider Osip Mandelstam's claim in his essay "The Word and Culture" that "yesterday has not yet been born. . . . I want Pushkin, and Catullus all over again, and the historical Ovid, Pushkin, and Catullus don't satisfy me. . . . Thus, there has not been a single poet. We are free from the burden of recollections." Osip Mandel'shtam, "Slovo i kul'tura," in *Sochineniia* (Moskva: Khudozhestvennaia literatura, 1990), 169–70. Clare Cavanagh writes that Mandelstam, Pound, and Eliot, like Joyce, all championed the idea that dead poets "will remain dead to the present age unless their potential is tapped by a self-proclaimed 'spiritual heir' and translated into a new idiom for another generation, another tradition or nation." Clare Cavanagh, *Osip Mandelstam and the Modernist Creation of Tradition* (Princeton, NJ: Princeton University Press, 1994), 26. Bitov and the other subjects of this study do, indeed, translate Joyce's ideas into their respective contexts, leading to unexpected combinations. On the subject of Mandelstam in Bitov's writings, see Chances, "The Energy of Honesty."

112. Bitov, *Pushkinskii dom*, 137.

113. Joyce, *Ulysses*, 3.

114. Bitov, *Pushkinskii dom*, 195–96, 254–58, 300, 304, 307–9.

115. On Bitov and the Odoevskys, see Chances, *Andrei Bitov*, 224–25, 254.

116. Bitov, *Pushkinskii dom*, 257.

117. Joyce, *Ulysses*, 273.

118. Bitov, *Pushkinskii dom*, 262.

119. Ibid.

120. Ibid., 197.

121. Joyce, *Ulysses*, 280.

122. Incidentally, Dmitry Anuchin published an ethnographic study, *A. S. Pushkin (An Anthropological Sketch)* (1899), on Pushkin's racial origins, with particular emphasis on his great-grandfather, Abram Gannibal (1696–1781), and his potential Semitic roots. See D. N. Anuchin, *A. S. Pushkin (Antropologicheskii eskiz)* (Moskva: Tipografiia Russkikh vedomostei, 1899). My thanks to Irina Shevelenko for bringing this connection to my attention.

123. Bitov, *Pushkinskii dom*, 275.

124. Joyce, *Ulysses*, 157. Note the Bitovian number: twenty-seven, give or take a year.

125. Bitov, *Pushkinskii dom*, 270.

126. Ibid., 269. He likely has in mind Akhmatova and Tsvetaeva. See Ronald Meyer, "Jealous Poetess or Pushkinist? Anna Achmatova in the Works of Andrej Bitov," *Russian Literature* 61, no. 4 (2007): 453–64, on Bitov and Akhmatova.

127. In the commentary to *Pushkin House*, Bitov writes about the dramatic effect that reading *The Gift* had on him when he had already composed most of his own novel. Bitov, *Pushkinskii dom*, 388–89. See Marina von Hirsch, "The Presence of Nabokov in Bitov's Fiction and Nonfiction: Bitov and Nabokov, Bitov on Nabokov, Nabokov in Bitov," *Nabokov Studies* 6 (2000–2001): 57–74, for an analysis of Nabokov's impact on Bitov's writing.

128. Nabokov, *The Gift*, E350/R526.

129. Bitov, *Pushkinskii dom*, 286.

130. Generally speaking, Russian commentators have perceived Bitov's glorification of Pushkin, while Western scholars note his subversive tendencies. Consider Natal'ia Ivanova, *Tochka zreniia: O proze poslednykh let* (Moskva: Sovetskii pisatel', 1988), 194; V. V. Karpova, *Avtor v sovremennoi russkoi postmodernistskoi literature (na materiale romana A. Bitova "Pushkinskii dom")* (Borisoglebsk: GOU VPO "Borisoglebskii gosudarstvennyi pedagogicheskii institut," 2005), 82; Komaromi, "The Window to the West," 89–92, 94–96; Ronald Meyer, "Andrei Bitov's Memoir of Pushkin," *Studies in Comparative Communism* 21, no. 3–4 (1988): 381–87; Meyer, "Jealous Poetess or Pushkinist?"; Stephanie Sandler, *Commemorating Pushkin: Russia's Myth of a National Poet* (Stanford, CA: Stanford University Press, 2004), chap. 7, especially 279; and Ekaterina Sukhanova, "With Pushkin in the Background: An Invitation to Andrei Bitov's *Pushkin House*," in *"Pushkin House" by Andrei Bitov: A Casebook*, ed. Ekaterina Sukhanova (Normal, IL: Dalkey Archive Press, 2005), 13–16.

131. Bitov, *Pushkinskii dom*, 349.

132. Ibid., 315.

133. Marina von Hirsch's series of essays on Bitov's metafiction and metacommentary provide insights into several devices central to the writer's oeuvre. See Marina von Hirsch, "In the Context of Metafiction: Commentary as a Principal Narrative

Structure in Bitov's *Pushkin House*," in *"Pushkin House" by Andrei Bitov: A Casebook*, ed. Ekaterina Sukhanova (Normal, IL: Dalkey Archive Press, 2005), 103–31; "Commentary *Ad Infinitum* in Andrej Bitov's Unified Narrative," *Russian Literature* 61, no. 4 (2007): 465–89; and "The Illusion of Infinity: Andrei Bitov's Innovative Poetics of Commentary," *Russian Studies in Literature* 44, no. 2 (2008): 77–89.

134. Bitov, *Pushkinskii dom*, 324.

135. Ibid., 335. Modest Platonovich's face also appears to Leva when he writes about Pushkin at the literary institute before Mitishatev's arrival. Ibid., 252.

136. Ibid., 335. The narrator of Bitov's semiautobiographical travelogue *A Georgian Album* (*Gruzinskii al'bom*, 1970–73, 1980–83) relates how witnesses to Pushkin's duel changed the location of the event in their descriptions after the fact. See Andrei Bitov, *Gruzinskii al'bom*, in *Imperiia v chetyrekh izmereniiakh*, vol. 3, *Kavkazskii plennik* (Khar'kov: Folio, 1996), 312.

137. Sven Spieker, *Figures of Memory and Forgetting in Andrej Bitov's Prose: Postmodernism and the Quest for History* (Frankfurt am Main: Peter Lang, 1996), 138–39.

138. Bitov, *Pushkinskii dom*, 342.

139. Andrei Bitov, *Prepodavatel' simmetrii: Roman-ekho* (Moskva: Fortuna El, 2008), 365.

140. Garry Leonard, "The History of Now: Commodity Culture and Everyday Life in Joyce," in *Joyce and the Subject of History*, ed. Mark A. Wollaeger, Victor Luftig, and Robert Spoo (Ann Arbor: University of Michigan Press, 1996), 20.

141. Bitov, *Pushkinskii dom*, 351.

4. Sasha Sokolov

1. D. Barton Johnson, "Saša Sokolov and Vladimir Nabokov," *Russian Language Journal* 41 (1987): 155.

2. For more on Sokolov's response to Nabokov in terms of style and authorial persona, see Lisa Ryoko Wakamiya, "Transformation, Forgetting and Fate: Self-Representation in the Essays of Sasha Sokolov," *Canadian-American Slavic Studies* 40, no. 2–4 (2006): 326.

3. Columbia University Press published Alexander Boguslawski's translation only in late 2017. See Sasha Sokolov, *Between Dog and Wolf*, trans. Alexander Boguslawski (New York: Columbia University Press, 2017).

4. Consider, for instance, Johnson, "Saša Sokolov and Vladimir Nabokov," 155; Richard C. Borden, *The Art of Writing Badly: Valentin Kataev's Mauvism and the Rebirth of Russian Modernism* (Evanston, IL: Northwestern University Press, 1999), 389; and Elena Kravchenko, *The Prose of Sasha Sokolov: Reflections on/of the Real* (London: Modern Humanities Research Association, 2013), 8.

5. Nabokov, *Strong Opinions*, 151, 102.

6. See D. G. Zhantieva, *Dzheimz Dzhois* (Moskva: Vyssh. shkola, 1967); and Ekaterina Genieva, "Khudozhestvennaia proza Dzheimsa Dzhoisa" (PhD diss., Moskovskii universitet, 1972).

7. Sokolov alternatively recalls the date as February 19. See Sasha Sokolov, "'Ia vsiu zhizn' vybiraiu luchshee. Chashche vsego bessoznatel'no . . .': Beseda Iriny Vrubel'-Golubkinoi s Sashei Sokolovym," *Zerkalo* 37 (2011), https://magazines.gorky.media/zerkalo/2011/37/ya-vsyu-zhizn-vybirayu-luchshee-chashhe-vsego-bessoznatelno-8230.html.

8. Ibid.

9. Ibid.

10. Ibid.

11. Sasha Sokolov, quoted in John Glad, "Sasha Sokolov (1986)," in *Conversations in Exile: Russian Writers Abroad*, ed. John Glad, trans. Richard and Joanna Robin (Durham, NC: Duke University Press, 1993), 183.

12. Sasha Sokolov, quoted in Viktor Erofeev, "Vremia dlia chastnykh besed . . . ," *Oktiabr'* 8 (1989): 199. Just a few years earlier, in a taped interview with Johnson, Sokolov had suggested a comparison between a scene in *Dog* in which a character becomes the rain and the snowy conclusion of Joyce's "The Dead." Sasha Sokolov, interview by D. Barton Johnson, audiocassette A13599/CS, December 4, 1985, 13:51–14:31, Sasha Sokolov Collection, Special Research Collections, University of California, Santa Barbara.

13. Sasha Sokolov, *Trevozhnaia kukolka* (Sankt-Peterburg: Izdatel'skii dom "Azbuka-klassika," 2007), 154–55.

14. Ibid., 73.

15. For these kinds of passing references, consider Igor Burikhin, review of *Mezhdu sobakoi i volkom*, by S. Sokolov, *Grani* 118 (1980): 273; Aleksandr Genis, "'Lessons of *Shkola dlia durakov*' (Over the Barrier: A Special Broadcast in Honor of Sasha Sokolov's 60th Birthday)," *Canadian-American Slavic Studies* 40, no. 2–4 (2006): 345; D. Barton Johnson, "Sasha Sokolov's *Between Dog and Wolf* and the Modernist Tradition," in *The Third Wave: Russian Literature in Emigration*, ed. Olga Matich and Michael Henry Heim (Ann Arbor, MI: Ardis, 1984), 216; Borden, *The Art of Writing Badly*, 389; Arnold McMillin, "Aberration of the Future: The Avant-Garde Novels of Sasha Sokolov," in *From Pushkin to "Palisandriia": Essays on the Russian Novel in Honour of Richard Freeborn*, ed. Arnold McMillin (London: Macmillan, 1990), 234–35; Fred Moody, "Madness and the Pattern of Freedom in Sasha Sokolov's *A School for Fools*," *Russian Literature Triquarterly* 16 (1979): 15; Alexandra Heidi Karriker, "Double Vision: Sasha Sokolov's *School for Fools*," *World Literature Today* 53, no. 4 (1979): 613; and Sergei Orobii, "Istoriia odnogo uchenichestva (Vladimir Nabokov–Sasha Sokolov–Mikhail Shishkin)," *Novoe literaturnoe obozrenie* 6 (2012): 293–308. More broadly, Sokolov's style and use of language have drawn wide critical attention: D. Barton Johnson, "A Structural Analysis of Sasha Sokolov's *School for Fools*: A Paradigmatic Novel," in *Fiction and Drama in Eastern and Southeastern Europe: Evolution and Experiment in the Postwar Period*, ed. Henrik Birnbaum and Thomas Eekman (Columbus, OH: Slavica Publishers, 1980), 207–37; Alexander Boguslawski, "Sokolov's *A School for Fools*: An Escape from Socialist Realism," *Slavic and East European Journal* 27, no. 1 (1983): 91–97; Cynthia Simmons, "Cohesion and Coherence in Pathological Discourse and Its Literary Representation in Sasha Sokolov's *Škola dlja durakov*," *International Journal of Slavic Linguistics and Poetics* 33 (1986): 71–96; Cynthia Simmons, *Their Father's Voice: Vassily Aksyonov, Venedikt Erofeev, Eduard Limonov, and Sasha Sokolov* (New York: Peter Lang, 1993), 125–58; T. D. Brainina, "Iazykovaia igra v proizvedeniiakh Sashi Sokolova," in *Iazyk kak tvorchestvo*, ed. Viktor Petrovich Grigor'ev, Iu. Petrova, and N. A. Fateeva (Moskva: Institut russkogo iazyka RAN, 1996), 276–83; Mikhail Iur'evich Egorov, "O postmodernistskikh aspektakh poetiki romana Sashi Sokolova *Shkola dlia durakov*," *Iaroslavskii pedagogicheskii vestnik* 2 (2002): 38–42; Mikhail Iur'evich Egorov, "Spontannost' pis'ma kak printsip produtsirovaniia teksta v romane Sashi Sokolova *Shkola dlia durakov*," in *Literatura, iazyk,*

kul'tura: Materialy konferentsii "Chteniia Ushinskogo" fakul'teta russkoi filologii i kul'tury (Iaroslavl': Izdatel'stvo Iaroslavskogo gosudartsvennogo pedagogicheskogo instituta imeni K. D. Ushinskogo, 2002), 64–66; Mikhail Iur'evich Egorov, "Ustanovka na inde-terminirovannoe produtsirovanie teksta v romane Sashi Sokolova 'Shkola dlia dura-kov,'" *Canadian-American Slavic Studies* 40, no. 2–4 (2006): 179–99; and José Vergara, "The Embodied Language of Sasha Sokolov's *A School for Fools*," *Slavonic and East European Review* 97, no. 3 (2019): 426–50.

16. Bitov, *Pushkinskii dom*, 386.

17. Both names for the hero will be used interchangeably. Any patterns that exist in their usage throughout the novel to distinguish the protagonist's identities are ulti-mately destabilized by exceptions and discrepancies.

18. Sasha Sokolov, *Shkola dlia durakov. Mezhdu sobakoi i volkom* (Moskva: Ogonek-Variant, 1990), 16.

19. Sasha Sokolov, "Beseda s Sashei Sokolovym: 'Nuzhno zabyt' vse staroe i vspom-nit' vse novoe,'" by Ol'ga Matich, *Russkaia mysl'* 3571 (1985): 12. Nabokov, among many others, made the same claim. See Vladimir Nabokov, *Ada, or Ardor* (New York: Vintage Books, 1990), 283.

20. Sokolov, "'Ia vsiu zhizn' vybiraiu luchshee.'"

21. Joyce, *Ulysses*, 616.

22. Joyce, *Finnegans Wake*, 620.33–621.2.

23. Nabokov, *Lectures on "Ulysses,"* 362.

24. Derek Attridge, *Joyce Effects: On Language, Theory, and History* (Cambridge: Cam-bridge University Press, 2000), 104.

25. Boguslawski, "Sokolov's *A School for Fools*," 91; Simmons, *Their Father's Voice*, 134.

26. Vladimir Bondarenko, *Zhivi opasno* (Moskva: PoRog, 2006), 511; Moody, "Madness and the Pattern of Freedom," 9. For other applications of the term "stream of consciousness" to *School*, see Borden, *The Art of Writing Badly*, 313; Vári Erzsébet, "'Literatura [. . .]—iskusstvo obrashcheniia so slovom': Zametki o povesti 'Shkola dlia durakov' Sashi Sokolova," *Studia Slavica Academiae Scientiarum Hungaricae* 47 (2002): 428; Johnson, "Structural Analysis," 221; Lipovetsky, *Russian Postmodernist Fic-tion*, 88, 90; and Vladimir Tumanov, "A Tale Told by Two Idiots: Krik idiota v 'Shkole dlia durakov' S. Sokolova i v 'Shume i iarosti' U. Folknera," *Russian Language Journal* 48, no. 159–61 (1994): 138. Some of Sokolov's earliest readers, too, found this phrase to be the most apt in describing his book. None other than the distinguished scholar of Russian culture Simon Karlinsky writes in an unpublished letter responding to Ar-dis publisher Carl Proffer's request for an advertising blurb: "While it *is* a new experi-ence to read that kind of Joycean stream-of-consciousness prose in Russian, I happen to have a built-in aversion to literary works dealing with split personalities." Simon Karlinsky, letter to Carl Proffer, January 5, 1976, box 4, folder 6, Sasha Sokolov Collec-tion, Special Research Collections, University of California, Santa Barbara.

27. Anonymous, review of "*Škola dlja durakov*," by Saša Sokolov, *Russian Language Journal* 31, no. 108 (1977): 189.

28. See Vergara, "Embodied Language," 429–40, for more on this reconsideration of stream of consciousness beyond Joyce.

29. Erzsébet, "'Literatura,'" 428.

30. Consider, for example, Gerald Smith, "The Verse in Sasha Sokolov's *Between Dog and Wolf*," *Canadian-American Slavic Studies* 21, no. 3–4 (1987): 319–39.

31. See Alexander Zholkovsky, "The Stylistic Roots of *Palisandriia*," *Canadian-American Slavic Studies* 21, no. 3–4 (1987): 369–400.

32. Viktor Shklovskii, "Parodiinyi roman ('Tristram Shendi' Sterna)," in *O teorii romana* (Moskva: Federatsiia, 1929), 204.

33. Johnson, "Structural Analysis," 230.

34. Borden, *The Art of Writing Badly*, 314. Sokolov himself refers to Homer when Student So-and-So says, "We cannot enumerate a single ship." Sokolov, *Shkola dlia durakov*, 17.

35. Sokolov, *Shkola dlia durakov*, 11–12.

36. Ibid., 156.

37. Joyce, *Ulysses*, 592–93.

38. Ibid., 268.

39. Sasha Sokolov, quoted in David Remnick, "Wellspring of the Russian Writer: Thirsting for His Native Language, Sasha Sokolov Returns," *Washington Post*, September 28, 1989.

40. On Sokolov's so-called word worship and linguistic pantheism, see Petr Vail' and Aleksandr Genis, "Uroki *Shkoly dlia durakov*," *Literaturnoe obozrenie* 1, no. 2 (1993): 13.

41. Joseph Brodsky, "Nobel Lecture," trans. Barry Rubin, The Nobel Prize, 2011, https://www.nobelprize.org/prizes/literature/1987/brodsky/25498-joseph-brodsky-nobel-lecture-1987.

42. Joyce, *Ulysses*, 578–79. See Karen Lawrence, *The Odyssey of Style in "Ulysses"* (Princeton, NJ: Princeton University Press, 1981), 181.

43. Sokolov, *Shkola dlia durakov*, 11.

44. Ibid., 124.

45. Ibid., 12.

46. D. Barton Johnson, "Background Notes on Sokolov's *School for Fools* and *Between Dog and Wolf*: Conversations with the Author," *Canadian-American Slavic Studies* 40, no. 2–4 (2006): 334.

47. David Hayman, *"Ulysses": The Mechanics of Meaning* (Madison: University of Wisconsin Press, 1982), 84.

48. Johnson's conversations with Sokolov concerning the novel's second chapter are available as part of the Sasha Sokolov Collection at the University of California, Santa Barbara. See audiocassettes A13591/CS, Sokolov interviewed by Johnson, June 20, 1983 (12:39–14:05), and A13599/CS, Sokolov interviewed by Johnson, December 4, 1985 (33:20–35:50).

49. Joseph Frank, "Spatial Form in Modern Literature," in *The Widening Gyre: Crisis and Mastery in Modern Literature* (New Brunswick, NJ: Rutgers University Press, 1963), 16.

50. Joyce, *Ulysses*, 185.

51. Of all of Joyce's works, *Dubliners* had been translated into Russian the most frequently and fully by Sokolov's time. A version of "Sisters" appeared in 1926 in Paris; an edition (without "The Sisters," "Grace," "An Encounter," and "A Mother") in 1927 in Leningrad; "Eveline" in 1927; "A Mother" and "A Painful Case" in 1936; a complete edition in 1937; "Araby" in 1946; a reprint of the full 1937 translation in 1966; and "The Dead" in 1975. See Genieva, *"Russkaia odisseia,"* 139–41, for bibliographic information on these publications.

52. Alexandra Heidi Karriker, "Narrative Shifts and Cyclic Patterns in *A School for Fools*," *Canadian-American Slavic Studies* 21, no. 3–4 (1987): 292.

53. James Joyce, *Selected Letters of James Joyce*, ed. Richard Ellmann (New York: Viking Press, 1976), 83.

54. James Joyce, *Dubliners*, ed. Margot Norris, Hans Walter Gabler, and Walter Hettche (New York: W. W. Norton, 2006), 3.

55. Ibid., 194.

56. Ibid. Compare the similarly wistful ending of Anton Chekhov's "Lady with a Lapdog." Anton Chekhov, "Dama s sobachkoi," in *Izbrannye proizvedeniia* (Moskva: Izdatel'stvo Khudozhestvennaia literatura, 1964), 3:189. On the theme of Joyce and Chekhov, see Sidney Monas, "Joyce and Russia," *Joyce Studies Annual* 4 (1993): 205–6.

57. Sokolov, *Shkola dlia durakov*, 60.

58. Ibid., 77.

59. Joyce, *Dubliners*, 194.

60. Sokolov, *Trevozhnaia kukolka*, 52.

61. Leona Toker, "Gamesman's Sketches (Found in a Bottle): A Reading of Sasha Sokolov's *Between Dog and Wolf*," *Canadian-American Slavic Studies* 21, no. 3–4 (1987): 354.

62. See, for instance, Harry Burrell, *Narrative Design in "Finnegans Wake": The "Wake" Lock Picked* (Gainesville: University Press of Florida, 1996), 89–90.

63. Colin MacCabe, "An Introduction to *Finnegans Wake*," in *James Joyce's "Finnegans Wake": A Casebook*, ed. John Harty III (New York: Garland Publishing, 1999), 28; Northrop Frye, "Cycle and Apocalypse in *Finnegans Wake*," in *Vico and Joyce*, ed. Donald Phillip Verene (Albany: State University of New York Press, 1987), 16.

64. Joyce, *Finnegans Wake*, 306.5–6.

65. Sokolov, *Shkola dlia durakov*, 170, 35.

66. Joyce, *Ulysses*, 175.

67. Sokolov, *Shkola dlia durakov*, 51.

68. Joyce, *Ulysses*, 31.

69. Sokolov, *Shkola dlia durakov*, 32.

70. Joyce, *Finnegans Wake*, 32.19–21.

71. For other interpretations of TWC's origins based on linguistics and religion, see Johnson, "Structural Analysis," 214; and Cynthia Simmons, "Incarnations of the Hero Archetype in Sokolov's *School for Fools*," in *The Supernatural in Slavic and Baltic Literature: Essays in Honour of Victor Terras*, ed. Amy Mandelker and Roberta Reeder (Columbus, OH: Slavica Publishers, 1988), 281. In Sokolov's polyvalent world, the options are not mutually exclusive. However, a literary reference aligns well with Sokolov's poetics.

72. Sokolov, *Shkola dlia durakov*, 181.

73. Ibid., 183.

74. Ibid. Compare the end of Nabokov's *Invitation to a Beheading* when its hero departs into an unknown world full of "beings akin to him." Nabokov, *Sobranie sochinenii russkogo perioda*, 187.

75. Past treatments of this theme in Sokolov's work include D. Barton Johnson, "Sasha Sokolov's Twilight Cosmos: Themes and Motifs," *Slavic Review* 45 (1986): 644; Olga Matich, "Sasha Sokolov and His Literary Context," *Canadian-American Slavic Studies* 21, no. 3–4 (1987): 305; and Lisa Ryoko Wakamiya, "Overcoming Death and Denotation in Saša Sokolov's *School for Fools*," *Die Welt der Slaven* 50 (2005): 64. For some comments by Sokolov on his own father's presence in his life, see Remnick, "Wellspring of the Russian Writer."

76. On Bitov's views on Sokolov's art, see Andrei Bitov, "Grust' vsego cheloveka," *Oktiabr'* 3 (1989): 157–58.

77. Joyce, *A Portrait of the Artist as a Young Man*, 205.

78. Marian Eide, "The Woman of the Ballyhoura Hills: James Joyce and the Politics of Creativity," in *James Joyce's "A Portrait of the Artist as a Young Man": A Casebook*, ed. Mark A. Wollaeger (New York: Oxford University Press, 2003), 301.

79. For an extended consideration of Nymphaea's cries and their similarities to Benjy's tormented screams in Faulkner's *The Sound and the Fury*, see Tumanov, "A Tale Told by Two Idiots."

80. Sokolov, *Shkola dlia durakov*, 98.

81. Ibid., 152.

82. Ibid., 86 (italics mine).

83. Ibid., 57, 97, 119, 133 (italics mine).

84. Joyce, *Ulysses*, 43.

85. Sokolov, *Shkola dlia durakov*, 57.

86. Ibid., 107, 120, 150, 157.

87. For more on clothing imagery in Sokolov's novel, see Richard C. Borden, "Time, Backward! Sasha Sokolov and Valentin Kataev," *Canadian-American Slavic Studies* 21, no. 3–4 (1987): 247–63; and D. Barton Johnson, "The Galoshes Manifesto: A Motif in the Novels of Sasha Sokolov," *Oxford Slavonic Papers* 22 (1989): 155–79.

88. Sokolov, *Shkola dlia durakov*, 29.

89. Ibid., 100.

90. Joyce, *Ulysses*, 527.

91. Sokolov, *Shkola dlia durakov*, 156.

92. Derek Attridge, *Peculiar Language: Literature as Difference from the Renaissance to James Joyce* (New York: Routledge, 2004), 233.

93. Sokolov, *Shkola dlia durakov*, 19.

94. Ibid., 28.

95. Joyce, *Finnegans Wake*, 215.24.

96. On Vico and Sokolov, consider Alexander Boguslawski, "Vremia Palisandra Dal'berga," *Russian Language Journal* 142–43 (1989): 225.

97. See, for example, Margaret Church, "The Language of Time—Thomas Mann and James Joyce," *Study of Time* 3 (1978): 500–511; Margaret Church, *Time and Reality: Studies in Contemporary Fiction* (Chapel Hill: University of North Carolina Press, 1963); and MacCabe, "An Introduction to *Finnegans Wake*."

98. Church, "The Language of Time," 509.

99. Sokolov, *Shkola dlia durakov*, 27.

100. Ibid., 26.

101. A. Voronel' and N. Voronel', "Ia khochu podniat' russkuiu prozu do urovnia poezii . . . ," *22* 35 (1984): 184.

102. James Joyce, quoted in Gordon Bowker, *James Joyce: A New Biography* (New York: Farrar, Straus and Giroux, 2012), 301.

103. Compare to Gary Saul Morson's similar notion of "sideshadowing" and its effects on narrative, in Gary Saul Morson, "Sideshadowing and Tempics," *New Literary History* 29, no. 4 (1998): 599–624.

104. Jasmina Vojvodić, "Otkliki simul'tanizma v postmodernistskoi proze (*Shkola dlia durakov* S. Sokolova)," *Russian Literature* 51, no. 3 (2002): 363–64.

105. Sokolov presents a more negative view of this circularity of time in *Palisandriia*, where the protagonist, Palisandr Dalberg, remains caught in an endless cycle of déjà vu. On Sokolov's novels, time, memory, and aesthetics, see Alexander Boguslawski, "Death in the Works of Sasha Sokolov," *Canadian-American Slavic Studies* 21, no. 3–4 (1987): 241–42; Anna Brodsky, "The Death of Genius in the Works of Sasha Sokolov and Liudmila Petrushevskaia," *Canadian-American Slavic Studies* 40, no. 2–4 (2006): 287, 295; Larissa Rudova, "Reading *Palisandriia*: Of Menippean Satire and Sots-Art," in *Endquote: Sots-Art Literature and Soviet Grand Style*, ed. Marina Balina, Nancy Condee, and Evgeny Dobrenko (Evanston, IL: Northwestern University Press, 2000), 217–218; Larissa Rudova, "The Dystopian Vision in Sasha Sokolov's *Palisandriia*," *Canadian-American Slavic Studies* 40, no. 2–4 (2006): 167–70; Hanna Kolb, "The Dissolution of Reality in Sasha Sokolov's *Mezhdu sobakoi i volkom*," in *Reconstructing the Canon: Russian Writing in the 1980s*, ed. Arnold McMillin (London: Harwood Academic Publishers, 2000), 199; Johnson, "Sasha Sokolov's Twilight Cosmos," 641–42; and Borden, "Time, Backward!"

106. Sokolov, *Shkola dlia durakov*, 104.

107. Ibid., 141, 165.

108. Joyce, *Ulysses*, 339.

109. Joyce, *Finnegans Wake*, 78.4–6.

110. Ibid., 628.15–16/3.1–3.

111. Sokolov, *Shkola dlia durakov*, 135.

112. Voronel' and Voronel', "Ia khochu podniat' russkuiu prozu," 184.

113. Sokolov, *Shkola dlia durakov*, 136 (italics mine).

114. While *School* may be read as ultimately apolitical, see Boguslawski, "Sokolov's *A School for Fools*," for an analysis of *A School for Fools* as a text written in response to Socialist Realism. Consider also Ludmilla L. Litus, "Saša Sokolov's *Škola dlja durakov*: Aesopian Language and Intertextual Play," *Slavic and East European Journal* 41, no. 1 (1997): 114–34.

115. Joyce, *A Portrait of the Artist as a Young Man*, 275–76 (italics mine).

116. Cf. Charles Peake, *James Joyce, the Citizen and the Artist* (Stanford, CA: Stanford University Press, 1977), 83; and William York Tindall, *A Reader's Guide to James Joyce* (Syracuse, NY: Syracuse University Press, 1995), 67.

117. Sokolov, *Shkola dlia durakov*, 48.

118. Ibid., 136.

119. Ibid., 137.

120. Ibid., 125.

121. The English translation was published under a much different name. See Sasha Sokolov, *Astrophobia*, trans. Michael Henry Heim (New York: Grove Weidenfeld, 1989).

122. Ibid., 164.

123. Ibid., 165.

124. Ibid., 234.

125. Ibid., 285.

126. Ibid., 220.

127. Borden, "Time, Backward!," 247.

128. Johnson, "Sokolov's *Between Dog and Wolf*," 215.

129. Samuel Beckett, "Dante . . . Bruno. Vico . . Joyce," in *Our Exagmination Round his Factification for Incamination of Work in Progress* (New York: New Directions, 1972), 14.

5. Mikhail Shishkin

1. Viktor Pelevin, *Sviashchennaia kniga oborotnia* (Moskva: Eksmo, 2004), 5.

2. Ibid., 157–58.

3. Shishkin, "Mat i molitva," 26.

4. Mikhail Shishkin, "Pisatel' dolzhen oshchutit' vsesilie," interview by Sergei Ivanov, *Kontrakty UA*, August 4, 2010, http://kontrakty.ua/article/37875.

5. Joyce, *Letters of James Joyce*, 1:297.

6. Joyce, *Ulysses*, 15.

7. Mikhail Shishkin, *Pis'movnik* (Moskva: Astrel', 2010); Mikhail Shishkin, *The Light and the Dark*, trans. Andrew Bromfield (London: Quercus, 2013).

8. Anna Arkhipova, "Venerin volos Shishkina," *Starland.ru*, June 21, 2011.

9. S. Divakov, "Direct Speech in a State of Flux," *Russian Studies in Literature* 51, no. 1 (2014–15): 10.

10. Muireann Maguire, review of *Maidenhair*, by Mikhail Shishkin, *Slavic and East European Journal* 59, no. 1 (2015): 140.

11. Vlad Tolstov, review of *Pis'movnik*, by Mikhail Shishkin, *NewsLab.ru*, December 13, 2011, https://newslab.ru/article/389029. For further references to Joyce and Shishkin in reviews and interviews, see Boris Fishman, "Dear Sasha, Dear Volodya," review of *The Light and the Dark*, by Mikhail Shishkin, *New York Times*, January 10, 2014, https://www.nytimes.com/2014/01/12/books/review/the-light-and-the-dark-by-mikhail-shishkin.html; Elena Makeenko, "Iazyk, vremia, smert': Kak ustroeny romany Mikhaila Shishkina," *Afisha Daily*, May 5, 2017, https://daily.afisha.ru/brain/5350-yazyk-vremya-smert-kak-ustroeny-romany-mihaila-shishkina; Maryam Omidi, "The Light and Dark of It: How Russia's Greatest Living Writer Became a Refusenik," *Calvert Journal*, April 16, 2013, https://www.calvertjournal.com/articles/show/771/mikhail-shishkin-light-dark-russian-writer-author-corrupt-criminal-regime; and Christopher Tauchen, review of *Maidenhair*, by Mikhail Shishkin, *Words without Borders*, November 2012, https://www.wordswithoutborders.org/book-review/mikhail-shishkins-maidenhair.

12. E. N. Rogova, "Traditsii D. Dzhoisa v romane M. Shishkina 'Pismov'nik' (Sopostavitel'nyi analiz motivov)," *Siuzhetologiia i siuzhetografiia* 2 (2014): 141–50. For a narrower comparative study of the two authors' works, see also E. N. Rogova, "Motiv kalligrafii v tvorchestve Dzh. Dzhoisa i M. Shishkina," in *Dergachevskie chteniia—2014. Russkaia literatura: Tipy khudozhestvennogo soznaniia i dialog kul'turno-natsional'nykh traditsii; Materialy XI Vserossiiskoi nauchnoi konferentsii s mezhdunarodnym uchastiem, Ekaterinburg, 6–7 oktiabria 2014 g.* (Ekaterinburg: Izdatel'stvo Ural'skogo universiteta, 2014), 338–42.

13. Mikhail Shishkin, e-mail message to the author, October 8, 2018.

14. Ibid.

15. See Michail Schischkin, "Die letzten Tage von James Joyce: Eine historische Reportage," *Das Magazin*, July 13, 2018, https://www.dasmagazin.ch/2018/07/13/die-letzten-tage-von-james-joyce.

16. Michael Campbell, "Nineteenth-Century Lyric Nationalism," in *James Joyce in Context*, ed. John McCourt (New York: Cambridge University Press, 2009), 184.

17. For more on Joyce's place in the Irish Revival, see also Claire Hutton, "The Irish Revival," in *James Joyce in Context*, ed. John McCourt (New York: Cambridge University Press, 2009), 195–204.

18. A. A. Bernatskaia, "Simptomy informatsionno-psikhologicheskoi voiny, ili chem pakhnet pokinutaia rodina (na materiale romana M. P. Shishkina 'Venerin volos')," *Ekologiia iazyka i kommunikativnaia praktika* 1 (2016): 239–58. Ingunn Lunde, on the contrary, considers Shishkin's political engagement in various genres that inform his poetics. See Ingunn Lunde, "'A Revolution for Russia's Words': Rhetoric and Style in Mixail Šiškin's Political Essays," *Zeitschrift für Slawistik* 61, no. 2 (2016): 249–61.

19. Boris Noordenbos, *Post-Soviet Literature and the Search for a Russian Identity* (New York: Palgrave Macmillan, 2016), 1.

20. Ibid., 6.

21. Ibid., 20.

22. Vladimir Sorokin, *Den' oprichnika* (Moskva: Zakharov, 2006).

23. Mikhail Shishkin, "Open letter to the Federal Agency for the Press and Mass Communications and the International Office of the Boris Yeltsin Presidential Center," *Faust*, February 27, 2013, https://faustkultur.de/1085-0-Brief-Schischkin_Russ Deutsch.html.

24. Mikhail Shishkin, e-mail message to author, October 8, 2018.

25. Mikhail Shishkin, "Bol'she chem Dzhois," *Colta*, January 13, 2019, https://www.colta.ru/articles/literature/20202-bolshe-chem-dzhoys.

26. Vivian Heller, *Joyce, Decadence, and Emancipation* (Urbana: University of Illinois Press, 199), 162–63.

27. Joyce, *Letters of James Joyce*, 1:213.

28. Burrell, *Narrative Design in "Finnegans Wake,"* 9.

29. Joyce, *Finnegans Wake*, 3.1.

30. Ibid., 31.26–28.

31. Adaline Glasheen, *Third Census of "Finnegans Wake": An Index of the Characters and Their Roles* (Berkeley: University of California Press, 1977).

32. Mikhail Shishkin, *Venerin volos* (Moskva: AST, 2014), 154.

33. Mikhail Shishkin, "Mikhail Shishkin: Vse pisateli dolzhny poluchit' po Nobelevskoi premii," interview by Elizaveta Fomina, *Postimees*, June 6, 2016, https://rus.postimees .ee/3719763/mihail-shishkin-vse-pisateli-dolzhny-poluchit-po-nobelevskoy-premii. For an alternative, more egocentric explanation, where Shishkin suggests that all his male characters are manifestations of himself and his female character projections of an imagined woman, see Anna Griboedova, "Mikhail Shishkin: 'The Idea behind Letter-Book Came to Me Overnight,'" Russkiy Mir Foundation, November 30, 2011, https://russkiymir.ru/en/publications/140274/.

34. Shishkin, *Venerin volos*, 56, 131.

35. Ibid., 11.

36. Ibid., 34.

37. Shishkin, "Bol'she chem Dzhois."

38. Joyce, *Ulysses*, 601.

39. Scarlett Baron, *"Strandentwining Cable": Joyce, Flaubert, and Intertextuality* (New York: Oxford University Press, 2012), 11.

40. Joyce, *Letters of James Joyce*, 1:297.

41. Joyce, *Finnegans Wake*, 424.33–35.

42. Baron, *"Strandentwining Cable,"* 268.

43. Jean-Michel Rabaté, "The Fourfold Root of Yawn's Unreason: Chapter III.3," in *How Joyce Wrote "Finnegans Wake": A Chapter-by-Chapter Genetic Guide*, ed. Luca Crispi and Sam Slote (Madison: University of Wisconsin Press, 2007), 403–4.

44. Even a quick glance at Weldon Thornton's *Allusions in "Ulysses": An Annotated List* (Chapel Hill: University of North Carolina Press, 1968) or James S. Atherton's *The Books at the Wake: A Study of Literary Allusions in James Joyce's "Finnegans Wake"* (Mamaroneck, NY: Paul P. Appel, 1974) reveals just how many sources Joyce drew from.

45. Aleksandr Tankov, "Shestvie perepershchikov," *Literaturnaia gazeta*, 2006, http://old.lgz.ru/archives/html_arch/lg112006/Polosy/8_2.htm.

46. Aleksei Karakovskii, "Parazitnyi tekst i massovoe knigozdanie," *Voprosy literatury* 3 (2011), https://voplit.ru/article/parazitnyj-tekst-i-massovoe-knigoizdanie/. For nonacademic online discussions, see, for example, Oleg Lur'e, "Igry marodera: Nekotorye podrobnosti o 'pisatele' Shishkine," LiveJournal, March 9, 2013, http://oleglurie-new.livejournal.com/85580.html; "Russkii buker Mikhail Shishkin ulichen v plagiate," 988, LiveJournal, March 8, 2013, http://988.livejournal.com/361509.html; Aptsvet, "Vorovat' durno," LiveJournal, March 24, 2006, http://aptsvet.livejournal.com/62716.html; or Liv Pirogov, "Prigovor sebe, Rossii i zhizni," *Nezavisimaia gazeta*, April 4, 2006, http://www.ng.ru/ng_exlibris/2006-04-06/1_prigovor.html?id_user=Y.

47. I. M. Kaspe, *Kogda govoriat veshchi: Dokument i dokumentnost' v russkoi literature 2000-kh* (Moskva: Gosudarstvennyi universitet Vysshaia shkola ekonomiki, 2010), 25.

48. Mezh_du, ". . . nanosit otvetnyi udar," LiveJournal, March 30, 2006, http://mezh-du.livejournal.com/9359.html.

49. Marilyn Randall, *Pragmatic Plagiarism: Authorship, Profit, and Power* (Toronto: University of Toronto Press, 2001), 3.

50. Ibid., 55.

51. Ibid., 101, 103, 106.

52. Ibid., 106.

53. There are many other fascinating studies of originality, imitation, translation, and plagiarism, though, perhaps not surprisingly, not in the Russian language. Consider Gerald L. Bruns, "The Originality of Texts in a Manuscript Culture," *Comparative Literature* 32, no. 2 (1980): 113–29; Morris Freedman, "The Persistence of Plagiarism, the Riddle of Originality," *Virginia Quarterly Review* 70, no. 3 (1994): 504–17; Rebecca Moore Howard, *Standing in the Shadow of Giants: Plagiarists, Authors, Collaborators* (Stamford, CT: Ablex Publishing, 1999); and Siva Vaidhyanathan, *Copyrights and Copywrongs: The Rise of Intellectual Property and How It Threatens Creativity* (New York: New York University Press, 2001).

54. Joyce, *Ulysses*, 5.

55. Shishkin, *Venerin volos*, 7; Ksenofont, *Anabasis*, trans. M. I. Masimova (Moskva: Izdatel'stvo Akademii nauk SSSR, 1951), 7; Xenophon, *Anabasis*, trans. Carleton L. Brownson (Cambridge, MA: Harvard University Press, 1992), 3. Where possible, I cite (1) Shishkin in the original Russian, (2) his source in Russian translation, and (3) my translation of Shishkin based on (4) a translation of his source.

56. Consider also Shishkin, *Venerin volos*, 103; Ksenofont, *Anabasis*, 28–29; and Xenophon, *Anabasis*, 63, 65.

57. Ksenofont, *Anabasis*, 31–32; Xenophon, *Anabasis*, 73.

58. G. K. Chesterton, "The Miracle of Moon Crescent," in *The Incredulity of Father Brown* (New York: Cassell, 1926), 97–132; Agatha Christie, *And Then There Were None* (New York: St. Martin's Press, 2001).

59. Shishkin, *Venerin volos*, 42–44.

60. Ibid., 81; Christie, *And Then There Were None*, 270.

61. For a more detailed typological analysis of Shishkin's borrowings, see José Vergara, "'Return That Which Does Not Belong to You': Mikhail Shishkin's Borrowings in *Maidenhair*," *Russian Review* 78, no. 2 (2019): 300–321.

62. Shishkin, *Venerin volos*, 24.

63. Anton Chekhov, *Chaika*, in *Izbrannye proizvedeniia* (Moskva: Izdatel'stvo Khudozhestvennaia literatura, 1964), 3:451.

64. Shishkin, *Venerin volos*, 50.

65. Sergei Orobii, *"Babilonskaia bashnia" Mikhaila Shishkina: Opyt modernizatsii russkoi prozy* (Blagoveshchensk: Izdatel'stvo BGPU, 2011),142.

66. Mezh_du, "... nanosit otvetnyi udar." It is telling, too, that Tankov did not refer to *Izmail* in his article. *Izmail*, with its own sets of borrowings, serves as a manifesto for Shishkin's poetics.

67. Shishkin, *Venerin volos*, 468.

68. This passage is preceded by a similar one shortly before. Ibid., 469–85.

69. Ibid., 519.

70. Joyce, *Ulysses*, 640.

71. Shishkin, *Venerin volos*, 538.

72. Ibid., 539.

73. Ibid.

74. Shishkin, "Bol'she chem Dzhois."

75. Joyce, *Finnegans Wake*, 505.2–13.

76. Shishkin, *Venerin volos*, 522.

77. Ibid., 541.

78. Ibid., 534.

79. Shishkin, "Bol'she chem Dzhois."

80. Ibid.

81. Shishkin, *Venerin volos*, 316.

82. Joyce, *Finnegans Wake*, 628.15–16/3.1–3.

83. Shishkin, "Bol'she chem Dzhois."

84. Shishkin, *Venerin volos*, 484. Note the curious, though purely coincidental, palindrome in the page number. Marian Schwartz ably makes do with some English alternatives in her English rendition: "Never odd or even. . . . Name now one man. . . . Drawn, I sit; serene rest is inward. . . . He did die, did he? . . . No devil lived on. Won't lovers revolt now? O stone, be not so. . . . Drab as a fool, aloof as a bard. Lid off a daffodil. O stone, be not so." Mikhail Shishkin, *Maidenhair*, trans. Marian Schwartz (Rochester, NY: Open Letter Books, 2012), 453.

85. Shishkin, *Maidenhair*, 453.

86. Joyce, *Ulysses*, 113.

87. Joyce, *Finnegans Wake*, 258.10–11; 496.21.

88. David James and Urmila Seshagiri, "Metamodernism: Narratives of Continuity and Revolution," *PMLA* 129, no. 1 (2014): 89.

89. Shishkin, *Venerin volos*, 7. This line is directly drawn from Xenophon.

90. Shishkin, "Mikhail Shishkin."

91. Shishkin, *Venerin volos*, 436–37.

92. Joyce, *Ulysses*, 159–60.

93. Ibid., 160.

94. Shishkin, *Venerin volos*, 437–38. The Interpreter also refers to his father's time as a submariner on pages 97 and 218, which helps the careful reader determine the speaker in this question and answer.

95. Mikhail Shishkin, "Spasennyi iazik," in *Pal'to s khliastikom* (Moskva: AST, 2017), 200.

96. Shishkin, *Venerin volos*, 541; Joyce, *Ulysses*, 644.

97. Mikhail Shishkin, e-mail message to the author, August 20, 2019.

98. Shishkin, "Bol'she chem Dzhois."

99. Curiously, Shishkin sees a progression toward stylistic simplicity in his art as he comes to a better understanding of death, his primary theme: "If in *Maidenhair* there are still whole pages constructed exclusively upon the 'sounds' of phrases, . . . then in *Pis'movnik*, there's nothing like that. . . . But for me these novels are an attempt to deal with death. And the closer I get to an understanding of something important, the less necessary 'devices' are." Mikhail Shishkin, e-mail message to the author, August 20, 2019.

Conclusion

1. See, for instance, the exchange between dying grandfather and grandson in "Liompa." Iurii Olesha, "Liompa," in *Povesti i rasskazy* (Moskva: Khudozhestvennaia literatura, 1965), 265–66.

2. Bloom, *The Anxiety of Influence*, 87–88.

3. Ibid., 14.

4. For a sense of Nabokov's views on the Bard and how the roots of his dialogue with Joyce may go back many years, perhaps even to the early 1920s, see his 1924 poem "Shakespeare." Vladimir Nabokov, "Shakespeare," trans. Dmitri Nabokov, *Nabokovian* 20 (1988): 15–16. The poem also concerns the artist's ability to escape death through art. For both Nabokov and Joyce, Shakespeare became an intermediary and, therefore, a medium for descendants' rights.

5. Consider Sergei Davydov, "*The Gift*: Nabokov's Aesthetic Exorcism of Chernyshevskii," *Canadian-American Slavic Studies* 19, no. 3 (1985): 359–60.

6. Bitov, *Pushkinskii dom*, 342.

7. Yaeger, "Editor's Column," 438.

8. T. S. Eliot, "Tradition and the Individual Talent," in *Selected Essays: New Edition* (New York: Harcourt, Brace, 1950), 3.

9. Ibid., 5.

10. Ibid., 4.

11. Fredric Jameson, *Postmodernism, or, The Cultural Logic of Late Capitalism* (Durham, NC: Duke University Press, 1991), 27.

12. White, "The Burden of History," 123.

13. Joyce, *Ulysses*, 28.

14. Hayden White, *Metahistory: The Historical Imagination in Nineteenth-Century Europe* (Baltimore: Johns Hopkins University Press, 1973), 30.

15. Ibid., 31.

16. Directly before I contacted Ilianen, he had coincidentally written several posts referencing *Ulysses*, particularly the scene on the beach with Bloom and Gerty. In the lead-up to and following my interview, Ilianen mentioned me several times on his public page, allowing me to become part of his project. See the posts made on VKontakte on August 24 and 26, September 4, 8, 10, 11, 14, and 25, and November 5, 2019, https://vk.com/id311972610.

17. A number of my interlocutors expressed this sentiment, though its validity is entirely another matter. A popular Russian literary blogger, Knigagid (Evgenia Vlasenko), conducted what she calls a "synchronous reading" with her followers. She started reading *Ulysses* at the beginning of 2020 and aimed to finish it before Bloomsday. In a livestream on Instagram, however, she expressed great frustration with the project, especially in comparison with her previous experience reading David Foster Wallace's gargantuan *Infinite Jest*. Vlasenko's videos and interviews are available on YouTube, https://www.youtube.com/knigagid, and Instagram, https://www.instagram.com/knigagid.

18. The novels of the U.S. writer Danielewski, including *House of Leaves* (2000) and *Only Revolutions* (2006), are also "interactive novels"—literally. They require the reader to physically turn the book in their hands to read text that has been placed upside-down, backward, and in other arrangements.

19. Note the multivalency of emigration. Zinik's conception of the exilic Joyce contrasts strongly with that of Nabokov, who saw this facet of Joyce's biography as a negative for personal reasons.

20. The real danger of making such comparisons is that Salnikov will hear them.

21. Those generations disagree. To be sure, attempts to find a Russian Joyce have been made, but the way his ideas have infected and influenced Russian authors and what he represented to them resonates much more strongly.

22. *Glazova*: My departure from Joyce coincided with my reading of Beckett, who, after all, later became estranged from Joyce as a teacher. He records a consciousness that is devoid of everything and that strips away the subject. Consciousness without a subject! This is really complicated; this is a completely new milestone in human thinking.

23. See the poems "prometheus" and "flowers" from Glazova's collection *Let Water* (*Pust' i voda*). Anna Glazova, *Pust' i voda* (Moskva: OGI, 2003). The entire volume is available at Vavilon, http://www.vavilon.ru/texts/glazova1.html.

24. *Bykov*: Reading Joyce requires less effort (his complexity is exaggerated by those readers who have read the novel to the end and want to be proud of themselves) than it does interest.

Buksha: For some reason, everyone is struck by *Ulysses*'s length. But for such a novel, there's no difference. It's like the sea. You swim in it, and it's all the same whether there are twenty, two hundred, or two thousand meters under your stomach. If a person complains that a novel is long, it's obvious that they're trying to read it linearly, which, in the case of Joyce, isn't quite adequate.

25. James Joyce, "Ireland: Island of Saints and Sages," in *Occasional, Critical, and Political Writing*, ed. Kevin Barry (Oxford: Oxford University Press, 2000), 118.

26. Harold Bloom, *The Western Canon: The Books and School of the Ages* (New York: Harcourt Brace, 1994), 11.

BIBLIOGRAPHY

Adamovich, Georgii. *Odinochestvo i svoboda*. Sankt-Peterburg: Aleteiia, 2002.

Akhmatova, Anna. *Cherepki*. In *Pamiati A. A. Akhmatovoi. Stikhi, pis'ma, vospomina-niia*, 15–16. Paris: YMCA-Press, 1974.

——. "Listki iz dnevnika." In *"Russkaia odisseia" Dzheimsa Dzhoisa*, edited by Ekaterina Genieva, 112. Moskva: Rudomino, 2005.

——. *Sobranie sochinenii v shesti tomakh*. Vol. 3, *Poemy. Pro domo mea. Teatr*. Moskva: Ellis Lak, 1998.

Alekseeva, Liudmila, and Paul Goldberg. *The Thaw Generation: Coming of Age in the Post-Stalin Era*. Pittsburgh: University of Pittsburgh Press, 1993.

Alexandrov, Vladimir E. *Nabokov's Otherworld*. Princeton, NJ: Princeton University Press, 1991.

Amurskii, Vitalii. *Zapechatlennye golosa: Parizhskie besedy s russkimi pisateliami i poetami*. Moskva: Izdatel'stvo "MIK," 1998.

Anonymous. "Dzhois." In *Bol'shaia sovetskaia entsiklopediia*, 14:231. 2nd ed. Moskva: Gosudarstvennoe nauchnoe izdatel'stvo "Bol'shaia sovetskaia entsiklopediia," 1952.

Anonymous. Review of *Škola dlja durakov*, by Saša Sokolov. *Russian Language Journal* 31, no. 108 (1977): 188–93.

Anuchin, D. N. *A. S. Pushkin (Antropologicheskii eskiz)*. Moskva: Tipografiia Russkikh vedomostei, 1899.

Aptsvet. "Vorovat' durno." LiveJournal, March 24, 2006. http://aptsvet.livejournal .com/62716.html.

Apukhtina, Vera. *Molodoi geroi v sovetskoi proze: 60-e gody*. Moskva: Znanie, 1971.

Arkhipova, Anna. "Venerin volos Shishkina." *Starland.ru*, June 21, 2011. http:// starland.ru/venerin-volos-shishkina.

A.S. [A. Startsev]. "Dzhems Dzhois." *Internatsional'naia literatura* 2 (1941): 241.

Atherton, James S. *The Books at the Wake: A Study of Literary Allusions in James Joyce's "Finnegans Wake."* Mamaroneck, NY: Paul P. Appel, 1974.

Attridge, Derek. *Joyce Effects: On Language, Theory, and History*. Cambridge: Cambridge University Press, 2000.

——. *Peculiar Language: Literature as Difference from the Renaissance to James Joyce*. New York: Routledge, 2004.

Baker, Harold D. "Bitov Reading Proust through the Windows of *Pushkin House*." *Slavic and East European Journal* 41, no. 4 (1997): 604–26.

Barabtarlo, Gennadii. *Sochinenie Nabokova*. Sankt-Peterburg: Izdatel'stvo Ivana Limbakha, 2011.

Baron, Scarlett. *"Strandentwining Cable": Joyce, Flaubert, and Intertextuality*. New York: Oxford University Press, 2012.

Barskova, Polina. "Filial Feelings and Paternal Patterns: Transformations of *Hamlet* in *The Gift*." *Nabokov Studies* 9, no. 1 (2005): 191–208.

Barta, Peter I. *Bely, Joyce, and Döblin: Peripatetics in the City Novel*. Gainesville: University Press of Florida, 1996.

——. "Bitov's Perilous Passage: 'Penelopa,' Odysseus and Plato on the Nevskii." *Slavonic and East European Review* 76, no. 4 (1998): 633–42.

Barth, John. *The Friday Book: Essays and Other Nonfiction*. New York: G. P. Putnam's Sons, 1984.

Beaujour, Elizabeth Klosty. *The Invisible Land: A Study of the Artistic Imagination of Iurii Olesha*. New York: Columbia University Press, 1970.

——. "On Choosing One's Ancestors: Some Afterthoughts on *Envy*." *Ulbandus Review* 2, no. 1 (1979): 24–36.

Beckett, Samuel. "Dante . . . Bruno. Vico . . Joyce." In *Our Exagmination Round His Factification for Incamination of Work in Progress*, 3–22. New York: New Directions, 1972.

Begnal, Michael H. "*Bend Sinister*: Joyce, Shakespeare, Nabokov." *Modern Language Studies* 15, no. 4 (1985): 22–27.

——. "Joyce, Nabokov, and the Hungarian National Soccer Team." *James Joyce Quarterly* 31, no. 4 (1994): 519–25.

Beja, Morris. Introduction to "The Mystical Estate or the Legal Fiction: Paternity in *Ulysses*." In *James Joyce: The Augmented Ninth; Proceedings from the Ninth International James Joyce Symposium, Frankfurt, 1984*, edited by Bernard Benstock, 215–18. Syracuse, NY: Syracuse University Press, 1988.

Belinkov, Arkadii. *Sdacha i gibel' sovetskogo intelligenta. Iurii Olesha*. Moskva: RIK "Kul'tura," 1997.

Ben-Amos, Anat. "The Role of Literature in *The Gift*." *Nabokov Studies* 4 (1997): 117–49.

Bernatskaia, A. A. "Simptomy informatsionno-psikhologicheskoi voiny, ili chem pakhnet pokinutaia rodina (na materiale romana M. P. Shishkina 'Venerin volos')." *Ekologiia iazyka i kommunikativnaia praktika* 1 (2016): 239–58.

Bethea, David M. *Khodasevich: His Life and Art*. Princeton, NJ: Princeton University Press, 1983.

——. *The Superstitious Muse: Thinking Russian Literature Mythopoetically*. Brighton, MA: Academic Studies Press, 2009.

Birmingham, Kevin. *The Most Dangerous Book: The Battle for James Joyce's "Ulysses."* New York: Penguin Books, 2014.

Bitov, Andrei. "Andrei Bitov." Interview by Elisabeth Rich. Translated by Adam Perri. *South Central Review* 12, no. 3–4 (1995): 28–35.

——. "Fotografiia Pushkina (1799–2099)." In *Imperiia v chetyrekh izmereniiakh*, vol. 2, *Pushkinskii dom*, 399–437. Khar'kov: Folio, 1996.

——. "Grust' vsego cheloveka." *Oktiabr'* 3 (1989): 157–58.

——. *Gruzinskii al'bom*. In *Imperiia v chetyrekh izmereniiakh*, vol. 3, *Kavkazskii plennik*, 187–326. Khar'kov: Folio, 1996.

——. *My prosnulis' v neznakomoi strane*. Leningrad: Sovetskii pisatel', 1991.

——. *Novyi Gulliver*. Tenafly, NJ: Hermitage Publishers, 1997.

——. Preface to *Life in Windy Weather: Short Stories*, by Andrei Bitov, 15. Edited by Priscilla Meyer. Ann Arbor: Ardis, 1986.

——. *Prepodavatel' simmetrii: Roman-ekho*. Moskva: Fortuna El, 2008.

——. *Pushkinskii dom*. In *Imperiia v chetyrekh izmereniiakh*, vol. 2, *Pushkinskii dom*, 5–396. Khar'kov: Folio, 1996.

Bittner, Stephen V. *The Many Lives of Khrushchev's Thaw: Experience and Memory in Moscow's Arbat*. Ithaca, NY: Cornell University Press, 2008.

Blackwell, Stephen H. *Zina's Paradox: The Figured Reader in Nabokov's "Gift."* New York: Peter Lang, 2000.

Bloom, Harold. *The Anatomy of Influence: Literature as a Way of Life*. New Haven, CT: Yale University Press, 2011.

——. *The Anxiety of Influence: A Theory of Poetry*. 2nd ed. New York: Oxford University Press, 1997.

——. Introduction to *Modern Critical Views: James Joyce*, edited by Harold Bloom, 1–6. New York: Chelsea House Publishers, 1986.

——. *The Western Canon: The Books and School of the Ages*. New York: Harcourt, Brace, 1994.

Boguslawski, Alexander. "Death in the Works of Sasha Sokolov." *Canadian-American Slavic Studies* 21, no. 3–4 (1987): 231–46.

——. "Sokolov's *A School for Fools*: An Escape from Socialist Realism." *Slavic and East European Journal* 27, no. 1 (1983): 91–97.

——. "Vremia Palisandra Dal'berga." *Russian Language Journal* 142–43 (1989): 221–29.

Bondarenko, Vladimir. *Zhivi opasno*. Moskva: PoRog, 2006.

Borden, Richard C. *The Art of Writing Badly: Valentin Kataev's Mauvism and the Rebirth of Russian Modernism*. Evanston, IL: Northwestern University Press, 1999.

——. "Time, Backward! Sasha Sokolov and Valentin Kataev." *Canadian-American Slavic Studies* 21, no. 3–4 (1987): 247–63.

Borenstein, Eliot. *Men without Women: Masculinity and Revolution in Russian Fiction, 1917–1929*. Durham, NC: Duke University Press, 2001.

Bowker, Gordon. *James Joyce: A New Biography*. New York: Farrar, Straus and Giroux, 2012.

Boyd, Brian. "'The Expected Stress Did Not Come': A Note on 'Father's Butterflies.'" *Nabokovian* 45 (2000): 22–29.

——. *Vladimir Nabokov: The Russian Years*. Princeton, NJ: Princeton University Press, 1990.

Brainina, T. D. "Iazykovaia igra v proizvedeniiakh Sashi Sokolova." In *Iazyk kak tvorchestvo*, edited by Viktor Petrovich Grigor'ev, Iu. Petrova, and N. A. Fateeva, 276–83. Moskva: Institut russkogo iazyka RAN, 1996.

Brodsky, Anna. "The Death of Genius in the Works of Sasha Sokolov and Liudmila Petrushevskaia." *Canadian-American Slavic Studies* 40, no. 2–4 (2006): 279–304.

Brodsky, Joseph. *Less than One: Selected Essays*. New York: Farrar, Straus and Giroux, 1986.

——. "Nobel Lecture." Translated by Barry Rubin. The Nobel Prize, 2011. https://www.nobelprize.org/prizes/literature/1987/brodsky/25498-joseph-brodsky-nobel-lecture-1987.

Brown, Edward J. "Nabokov, Chernyshevsky, Olesha and the Gift of Sight." *Stanford Slavic Studies* 4, no. 2 (1992): 280–94.

Brownsberger, Susan. Afterword to *Pushkin House*, by Andrei Bitov, 359–71. Ann Arbor, MI: Ardis, 1990.

——. "'Man in a Landscape': Toward an Understanding of Bitov's Design." *Russian Literature* 61, no. 4 (2007): 393–416.

Bruns, Gerald L. "The Originality of Texts in a Manuscript Culture." *Comparative Literature* 32, no. 2 (1980): 113–29.

Buhks, Nora. "Roman-oboroten': O *Dare* V. Nabokova." *Cahiers du Monde russe et soviétique* 31, no. 4 (1990): 587–624.

Burikhin, Igor. Review of *Mezhdu sobakoi i volkom*, by S. Sokolov. *Grani* 118 (1980): 273–74.

Burrell, Harry. *Narrative Design in "Finnegans Wake": The "Wake" Lock Picked*. Gainesville: University Press of Florida, 1996.

Campbell, Matthew. "Nineteenth-Century Lyric Nationalism." In *James Joyce in Context*, edited by John McCourt, 184–94. New York: Cambridge University Press, 2009.

Carens, James F. "Joyce and Gogarty." In *New Light on Joyce: From the Dublin Symposium*, edited by Fritz Senn, 28–45. Bloomington: Indiana University Press, 1972.

Cavanagh, Clare. *Osip Mandelstam and the Modernist Creation of Tradition*. Princeton, NJ: Princeton University Press, 1994.

Cecconi, Elisabetta. "Buck Mulligan: Characterisation Process." In *"Who Chose This Face for Me?": Joyce's Creation of Secondary Characters in "Ulysses,"* 41–86. Bern: Peter Lang, 2007.

Chances, Ellen. *Andrei Bitov: The Ecology of Inspiration*. New York: Cambridge University Press, 1993.

——. "The Energy of Honesty, or Brussels Lace, Mandelstam, 'Stolen Air,' and Inner Freedom: A Visit to the Creative Workshop of Andrei Bitov's *Pushkin House*." In *"Pushkin House" by Andrei Bitov: A Casebook*, edited by Ekaterina Sukhanova, 21–57. Normal, IL: Dalkey Archive Press, 2005.

Chekhov, Anton. *Chaika*. In *Izbrannye proizvedeniia*, 3:404–55. Moskva: Izdatel'stvo Khudozhestvennaia literatura, 1964.

——. "Dama s sobachkoi." In *Izbrannye proizvedeniia*, 3:173–89. Moskva: Izdatel'stvo Khudozhestvennaia literatura, 1964.

Chesterton, G. K. "The Miracle of Moon Crescent." In *The Incredulity of Father Brown*, 97–132. New York: Cassell, 1926.

Christie, Agatha. *And Then There Were None*. New York: St. Martin's Press, 2001.

Chudakova, M. O. *Masterstvo Iuriia Oleshi*. Moskva: Nauka, 1972.

Chukovskaia, Lidiia. *Zapiski ob Anne Akhmatovoi*. Vol. 1. Paris: YMCA-Press, 1984.

Chuprinin, Sergei. "Non–Past Time: On the Traits of the 'Thaw' Period in the History of the Contemporary Literary Process." *Russian Studies in Literature* 28, no. 4 (1992): 4–21.

Church, Margaret. "The Language of Time—Thomas Mann and James Joyce." *Study of Time* 3 (1978): 500–511.

——. *Time and Reality: Studies in Contemporary Fiction*. Chapel Hill: University of North Carolina Press, 1963.

Clark, Katerina. *The Soviet Novel: History as Ritual*. Chicago: University of Chicago Press, 1985.

Connolly, Julian W. *Nabokov's Early Fiction: Patterns of Self and Other*. Cambridge: Cambridge University Press, 1992.

Cornwell, Neil. *James Joyce and the Russians*. London: Macmillan Press, 1992.

——. "More on Joyce and Russia: Or *Ulysses* on the Moscow River." *Joyce Studies Annual* (1994): 176–86.

Davydov, Sergei. "*The Gift*: Nabokov's Aesthetic Exorcism of Chernyshevskii." *Canadian-American Slavic Studies* 19, no. 3 (1985): 357–74.

——. "*Teksty-matreški*" *Vladimira Nabokova*. Munich: Verlag Otto Sagner, 1982.

——. "Weighing Nabokov's *Gift* on Pushkin's Scales." In *Cultural Mythologies of Russian Modernism: From the Golden Age to the Silver Age*, edited by Boris Gasparov, Robert P. Hughes, and Irina Paperno, 415–28. Berkeley: University of California Press, 1992.

Divakov, S. "Direct Speech in a State of Flux." *Russian Studies in Literature* 51, no. 1 (2014–15): 7–17.

Dobrenko, Evgeny. "Literary Criticism and the Transformations of the Literary Field during the Cultural Revolution, 1928–1932." In *A History of Russian Literary Theory and Criticism: The Soviet Age and Beyond*, edited by Evgeny Dobrenko and Galin Tihanov, 43–63. Pittsburgh: University of Pittsburgh Press, 2011.

——. "Socialist Realism." In *The Cambridge Companion to Twentieth-Century Russian Literature*, edited by Evgeny Dobrenko and Marina Balina, 97–113. Cambridge: Cambridge University Press, 2011.

Dolinin, Alexander. "*The Gift*." In *The Garland Companion to Vladimir Nabokov*, edited by Vladimir E. Alexandrov, 135–69. New York: Garland Publishing, 1995.

Dzhois, Dzheims. *Portret khudozhnika v iunosti*. Translated by M. P. Bogoslovskaia-Bobrova. *Inostrannaia literatura* 10 (1976): 171–98; 11 (1976): 119–74; 12 (1976): 139–82.

Dzhois, Dzhems. *Dublintsy*. Translated by E. N. Fedotova. Leningrad: Mysl', 1927.

——. "Pokhorony Patrika Dignema." Translated by V. Stenich. *Zvezda* 11 (1934): 116–42.

——. "Uliss." In *Novinki zapada. Al'manakh No. 1*, translated by V. Zhitomirskii, 65–94. Moskva-Leningrad: Zemlia i Fabrika, 1925.

Egorov, Mikhail Iur'evich. "O postmodernistskikh aspektakh poetiki romana Sashi Sokolova *Shkola dlia durakov*." *Iaroslavskii pedagogicheskii vestnik* 2 (2002): 38–42.

——. "Spontannost' pis'ma kak printsip produtsirovaniia teksta v romane Sashi Sokolova *Shkola dlia durakov*." In *Literatura, iazyk, kul'tura: Materialy konferentsii "Chteniia Ushinskogo" fakul'teta russkoi filologii i kul'tury*, 64–66. Iaroslavl': Izdatel'stvo Iaroslavskogo gosudartsvennogo pedagogicheskogo instituta imeni K. D. Ushinskogo, 2002.

——. "Ustanovka na indeterminirovannoe produtsirovanie teksta v romane Sashi Sokolova 'Shkola dlia durakov.'" *Canadian-American Slavic Studies* 40, no. 2–4 (2006): 179–99.

Eide, Marian. "The Woman of the Ballyhoura Hills: James Joyce and the Politics of Creativity." In *James Joyce's "A Portrait of the Artist as a Young Man": A Casebook*, edited by Mark A. Wollaeger, 297–317. New York: Oxford University Press, 2003.

Eliot, T. S. "Tradition and the Individual Talent." In *Selected Essays: New Edition*, 3–11. New York: Harcourt, Brace, 1950.

Ellmann, Richard. *James Joyce*. Oxford: Oxford University Press, 1983.

Ermilov, V. "Budem tochnymi . . ." *Literaturnaia gazeta*, April 16, 1964, 3.

Erofeev, Viktor. "Pamiatnik proshedshemu vremeni: Andrei Bitov. Pushkinskii dom." *Oktiabr'* 6 (1988): 203–4.

——. "Vremia dlia chastnykh besed . . ." *Oktiabr'* 8 (1989): 195–202.

Erzsébet, Vári. "'Literatura [. . .]—iskusstvo obrashcheniia so slovom': Zametki o povesti 'Shkola dlia durakov' Sashi Sokolova." *Studia Slavica Academiae Scientiarum Hungaricae* 47 (2002): 427–50.

E.Z. [Evgenii Zamiatin]. "Angliia i Amerika." *Sovremennyi Zapad* 2 (1923): 229.

Fishman, Boris. "Dear Sasha, Dear Volodya." Review of *The Light and the Dark*, by Mikhail Shishkin. *New York Times*, January 10, 2014. https://www.nytimes .com/2014/01/12/books/review/the-light-and-the-dark-by-mikhail-shishkin .html.

Fitzpatrick, Sheila. "The 'Soft' Line on Culture and Its Enemies: Soviet Cultural Policy, 1922–1927." *Slavic Review* 33, no. 2 (1974): 267–87.

Fitzpatrick, Sheila, Alexander Rabinowitch, and Richard Stites, eds. *Russia in the Era of NEP: Explorations in Soviet Society and Culture*. Bloomington: Indiana University Press, 1991.

Foster, John Burt, Jr. *Nabokov's Art of Memory and European Modernism*. Princeton, NJ: Princeton University Press, 1993.

Frank, Joseph. "Spatial Form in Modern Literature." In *The Widening Gyre: Crisis and Mastery in Modern Literature*, 3–62. New Brunswick, NJ: Rutgers University Press, 1963.

Freedman, Morris. "The Persistence of Plagiarism, the Riddle of Originality." *Virginia Quarterly Review* 70, no. 3 (1994): 504–17.

Frye, Northrop. "Cycle and Apocalypse in *Finnegans Wake*." In *Vico and Joyce*, edited by Donald Phillip Verene, 3–19. Albany: State University of New York Press, 1987.

Gal'tsova, E. D. "Zapadnye pisateli-modernisty v zhurnale 'Literaturnyi kritik': Prust, Dzhois, Dos Passos." In *Postizhenie Zapada: Inostrannaia kul'tura v sovetskoi literature, iskusstve i teorii 1917–1941 gg.*, 669–86. Moskva: IMLI RAN, 2015.

Genette, Gérard. *Palimpsests: Literature in the Second Degree*. Translated by Channa Newman and Claude Doubinsky. Lincoln: University of Nebraska Press, 1997.

Genieva, Ekaterina. "Khudozhestvennaia proza Dzheimsa Dzhoisa." PhD diss., Moskovskii universitet, 1972.

——. *"Russkaia odisseia" Dzheimsa Dzhoisa*. Moskva: Rudomino, 2005.

Genis, Aleksandr. "'Lessons of *Shkola dlia durakov*' (Over the Barrier: A Special Broadcast in Honor of Sasha Sokolov's 60th Birthday)." *Canadian-American Slavic Studies* 40, no. 2–4 (2006): 341–49.

Gifford, Don. *"Ulysses" Annotated: Notes for James Joyce's "Ulysses."* 2nd ed. Berkeley: University of California Press, 1989.

Ginzburg, Lidiia. *Chelovek za pis'mennym stolom: Esse. Iz vozpominanii. Chetyre povestvovaniia*. Leningrad: Sovetskii pisatel', Leningradskoe otdelenie, 1989.

——. *O literaturnom geroe*. Leningrad: Sovetskii pisatel', Leningradskoe otdelenie, 1979.

——. *O psikhologicheskoi proze*. Moskva: Intrada, 1999.

——. "Pole napriazheniia." *Literaturnaia gazeta*, January 5, 1986, 7.

Glad, John. "Sasha Sokolov (1986)." In *Conversations in Exile: Russian Writers Abroad*, edited by John Glad, translated by Richard and Joanna Robin, 174–85. Durham, NC: Duke University Press, 1993.

Glasheen, Adaline. "Queries about Mulligan as Heretic Mocker and Rhetorician." *A Wake Newslitter* 14, no. 5 (1977): 71–76.

——. *Third Census of "Finnegans Wake": An Index of the Characters and Their Roles*. Berkeley: University of California Press, 1977.

Glazova, Anna. *Pust' i voda*. Moskva: OGI, 2003.

Gnedich, Nikolai Ivanovich. *Stikhotvoreniia*. Leningrad: Sovetskii pisatel', 1956.

Goldman, Wendy Z. *Women, the State and Revolution: Soviet Family Policy and Social Life, 1917–1936*. New York: Cambridge University Press, 1995.

Grabes, Herbert. "Nabokov and Shakespeare: The English Works." In *The Garland Companion to Vladimir Nabokov*, edited by Vladimir E. Alexandrov, 496–512. New York: Garland Publishing, 1995.

Greenleaf, Monika. "Fathers, Sons and Impostors: Pushkin's Trace in *The Gift*." *Slavic Review* 53, no. 1 (1994): 140–58.

Griboedova, Anna. "Mikhail Shishkin: 'The Idea behind Letter-Book Came to Me Overnight.'" Russkiy Mir Foundation, November 30, 2011. https://russkiymir .ru/en/publications/140274.

Griffiths, Galina S. "The Monuments of Russian Culture: *Pushkin House* as the Museum of the Soviet School Curriculum." PhD diss., University of Kansas, 2005.

Günther, Hans. "Soviet Literary Criticism and the Formulation of the Aesthetics of Socialist Realism, 1932–1940." In *A History of Russian Literary Theory and Criticism: The Soviet Age and Beyond*, edited by Evgeny Dobrenko and Galin Tihanov, 90–108. Pittsburgh: University of Pittsburgh Press, 2011.

Harkins, William E. "The Theme of Sterility in Olesha's *Envy*." In *Olesha's "Envy": A Critical Companion*, edited by Rimgaila Salys, 61–81. Evanston, IL: Northwestern University Press, 1999.

Hayman, David. *"Ulysses": The Mechanics of Meaning*. Madison: University of Wisconsin Press, 1982.

Heller, Vivian. *Joyce, Decadence, and Emancipation*. Urbana: University of Illinois Press, 1995.

Henry-Thommes, Christoph. *Recollection, Memory, and Imagination: Selected Autobiographical Novels of Vladimir Nabokov*. Heidelberg: Winter, 2006.

Herr, Cheryl Temple. *Joyce and the Art of Shaving*. Dublin: National Library of Ireland, 2004.

Howard, Rebecca Moore. *Standing in the Shadow of Giants: Plagiarists, Authors, Collaborators*. Stamford, CT: Ablex Publishing, 1999.

Hutton, Clare. "The Irish Revival." In *James Joyce in Context*, edited by John McCourt, 195–204. New York: Cambridge University Press, 2009.

Ingdahl, Kazimiera. *The Artist and the Creative Act*. Stockholm: Almqvist and Wiksell International, 1984.

Ivanova, Natal'ia. *Tochka zreniia: O proze poslednykh let*. Moskva: Sovetskii pisatel', 1988.

Ivleva, Victoria. "A Vest Reinvested in *The Gift*." *Russian Review* 68, no. 2 (2009): 283–301.

James, David, and Urmila Seshagiri. "Metamodernism: Narratives of Continuity and Revolution." *PMLA* 129, no. 1 (2014): 87–100.

Jameson, Fredric. *Postmodernism, or, The Cultural Logic of Late Capitalism*. Durham, NC: Duke University Press, 1991.

——. "*Ulysses* in History." In *Modern Critical Views: James Joyce*, edited by Harold Bloom, 173–88. New York: Chelsea House Publishers, 1986.

Johnson, D. Barton. "Background Notes on Sokolov's *School for Fools* and *Between Dog and Wolf*: Conversations with the Author." *Canadian-American Slavic Studies* 40, no. 2–4 (2006): 331–39.

——. "The Galoshes Manifesto: A Motif in the Novels of Sasha Sokolov." *Oxford Slavonic Papers* 22 (1989): 155–79.

——. "Saša Sokolov and Vladimir Nabokov." *Russian Language Journal* 41 (1987): 153–62.

——. "Sasha Sokolov's *Between Dog and Wolf* and the Modernist Tradition." In *The Third Wave: Russian Literature in Emigration*, edited by Olga Matich and Michael Henry Heim, 208–17. Ann Arbor, MI: Ardis, 1984.

——. "Sasha Sokolov's Twilight Cosmos: Themes and Motifs." *Slavic Review* 45 (1986): 639–49.

——. "A Structural Analysis of Sasha Sokolov's *School for Fools*: A Paradigmatic Novel." In *Fiction and Drama in Eastern and Southeastern Europe: Evolution and Experiment in the Postwar Period*, edited by Henrik Birnbaum and Thomas Eekman, 207–37. Columbus, OH: Slavica Publishers, 1980.

Joyce, James. *Dubliners*. Edited by Margot Norris, Hans Walter Gabler, and Walter Hettche. New York: W. W. Norton, 2006.

——. *Finnegans Wake*. London: Wordsworth Editions, 2012.

——. "Ireland: Island of Saints and Sages." In *Occasional, Critical, and Political Writing*, edited by Kevin Barry, 108–26. Oxford: Oxford University Press, 2000.

——. *Letters of James Joyce*. Vol. 1, edited by Stuart Gilbert. New York: Viking Press, 1966.

——. *A Portrait of the Artist as a Young Man*. New York: Penguin Books, 1993.

——. *Selected Letters of James Joyce*. Edited by Richard Ellmann. New York: Viking Press, 1976.

——. *Ulysses*. New York: Random House, 1986.

Karabchievskii, Iurii. "Tochka boli. O romane Andreia Bitova 'Pushkinskii dom.'" *Grani* 106 (1977): 141–203.

Karakovskii, Aleksei. "Parazitnyi tekst i massovoe knigozdanie." *Voprosy literatury* 3 (2011). https://voplit.ru/article/parazitnyj-tekst-i-massovoe-knigoizdanie.

Karlinsky, Simon. Letter to Carl Proffer. January 5, 1976. Box 4, folder 6. Sasha Sokolov Collection, Special Research Collections, University of California, Santa Barbara.

Karpova, V. V. *Avtor v sovremennoi russkoi postmodernistskoi literature (na materiale romana A. Bitova "Pushkinskii dom")*. Borisoglebsk: GOU VPO "Borisoglebskii gosudarstvennyi pedagogicheskii institut," 2005.

Karriker, Alexandra Heidi. "Double Vision: Sasha Sokolov's *School for Fools*." *World Literature Today* 53, no. 4 (1979): 610–14.

——. "Narrative Shifts and Cyclic Patterns in *A School for Fools*." *Canadian-American Slavic Studies* 21, no. 3–4 (1987): 287–99.

Kaspe, I. M. *Kogda govoriat veshchi: Dokument i dokumentnost' v russkoi literature 2000-kh*. Moskva: Gosudarstvennyi universitet Vysshaia shkola ekonomiki, 2010.

Kenner, Hugh. *Ulysses*. Baltimore: Johns Hopkins University Press, 1987.

Khoruzhii, Sergei. "*Uliss" v russkom zerkale*. Sankt-Peterburg: Azbuka, 2015.

Killeen, Terence. "Nabokov . . . Léon . . . Joyce." *Irish Times*, June 13, 1992.

Kolb, Hanna. "The Dissolution of Reality in Sasha Sokolov's *Mezhdu sobakoi i volkom*." In *Reconstructing the Canon: Russian Writing in the 1980s*, edited by Arnold McMillin, 193–223. London: Harwood Academic Publishers, 2000.

Komaromi, Ann. "The Window to the West in Andrei Bitov's *Pushkin House*." In *"Pushkin House" by Andrei Bitov: A Casebook*, edited by Ekaterina Sukhanova, 78–102. Normal, IL: Dalkey Archive Press, 2005.

Kornienko, Natalia. "Literary Criticism and Cultural Policy during the New Economic Policy, 1921–1927." In *A History of Russian Literary Theory and Criticism: The Soviet Age and Beyond*, edited by Evgeny Dobrenko and Galin Tihanov, 17–42. Pittsburgh: University of Pittsburgh Press, 2011.

Kozlov, Denis, and Eleonory Gilburd. "The Thaw as an Event in Russian History." In *The Thaw: Soviet Society and Culture during the 1950s and 1960s*, edited by Denis Kozlov and Eleonory Gilburd, 18–81. Toronto: University of Toronto Press, 2013.

Kravchenko, Elena. *The Prose of Sasha Sokolov: Reflections on/of the Real*. London: Modern Humanities Research Association, 2013.

Kristeva, Julia. "The Bounded Text." In *Desire in Language: A Semiotic Approach to Literature and Art*, edited by Leon S. Roudiez, translated by Thomas Gora, Alice Jardine, and Leon S. Roudiez, 36–63. New York: Columbia University Press, 1980.

——. *The Portable Kristeva*. Edited by Kelly Oliver. New York: Columbia University Press, 2002.

——. "Word, Dialogue and Novel." Translated by Alice Jardine, Thomas Gora, and Léon S. Roudiez. In *The Kristeva Reader*, edited by Toril Moi, 34–61. New York: Columbia University Press, 1986.

Ksenofont. *Anabasis*. Translated by M. I. Masimova. Moskva: Izdatel'stvo Akademii nauk SSSR, 1951.

Lann, E. L. Foreword to "Uliss," by Dzhems Dzhois. In *Novinki zapada. Al'manakh No. 1*, translated by V. Zhitomirskii, 61–64. Moskva-Leningrad: Zemlia i Fabrika, 1925.

Lawrence, Karen. *The Odyssey of Style in "Ulysses."* Princeton, NJ: Princeton University Press, 1981.

——. "Paternity as Legal Fiction in *Ulysses*." In *James Joyce: The Augmented Ninth; Proceedings from the Ninth International James Joyce Symposium, Frankfurt, 1984*, edited by Bernard Benstock, 233–43. Syracuse, NY: Syracuse University Press, 1988.

Lee, L. L. *Vladimir Nabokov*. Boston: Twayne, 1976.

Leonard, Garry. "The History of Now: Commodity Culture and Everyday Life in Joyce." In *Joyce and the Subject of History*, edited by Mark A. Wollaeger, Victor Luftig, and Robert Spoo, 13–26. Ann Arbor: University of Michigan Press, 1996.

Leving, Yuri. *Keys to "The Gift": A Guide to Vladimir Nabokov's Novel*. Brighton, MA: Academic Studies Press, 2011.

Lipovetsky, Mark. *Russian Postmodernist Fiction: Dialogue with Chaos*. Armonk, NY: M. E. Sharpe, 1999.

Litus, Ludmilla L. "Saša Sokolov's *Škola dlja durakov*: Aesopian Language and Intertextual Play." *Slavic and East European Journal* 41, no. 1 (1997): 114–34.

Lotman, Iu. M. "Simvolika Peterburga i problemy semiotiki goroda." In *Izbrannye stat'i v trekh tomakh*, 2:9–21. Tallinn: Aleksandra, 1992.

Lunde, Ingunn. "'A Revolution for Russia's Words': Rhetoric and Style in Mixail Šiškin's Political Essays." *Zeitschrift für Slawistik* 61, no. 2 (2016): 249–61.

Lur'e, Oleg. "Igry marodera: Nekotorye podrobnosti o 'pisatele' Shishkine." LiveJournal, March 9, 2013. http://oleglurie-new.livejournal.com/85580.html.

Lyons, J. B. "A Roland for Your Oliver." In *Oliver St. John Gogarty: The Man of Many Talents*, 211–23. Dublin: Blackwater Press, 1960.

MacCabe, Colin. "An Introduction to *Finnegans Wake*." In *James Joyce's "Finnegans Wake": A Casebook*, edited by John Harty III, 23–32. New York: Garland Publishing, 1999.

Machacek, Gregory. "Allusion." *PMLA* 122, no. 2 (2007): 522–36.

Maguire, Muireann. Review of *Maidenhair*, by Mikhail Shishkin. *Slavic and East European Journal* 59, no. 1 (2015): 139–40.

Maguire, Robert. *Red Virgin Soil: Soviet Literature in the 1920's*. Evanston, IL: Northwestern University Press, 2000.

Makeenko, Elena. "Iazyk, vremia, smert': Kak ustroeny romany Mikhaila Shishkina." *Afisha Daily*, May 5, 2017. https://daily.afisha.ru/brain/5350-yazyk-vremya-smert-kak-ustroeny-romany-mihaila-shishkina.

Mandel'shtam, Osip. "Slovo i kul'tura." In *Sochineniia*, 167–72. Moskva: Khudozhestvennaia literatura, 1990.

Matich, Olga. "Sasha Sokolov and His Literary Context." *Canadian-American Slavic Studies* 21, no. 3–4 (1987): 301–19.

McBride, Margaret. *"Ulysses" and the Metamorphosis of Stephen Dedalus*. Lewisburg, PA: Bucknell University Press, 2001.

McMillin, Arnold. "Aberration of the Future: The Avant-Garde Novels of Sasha Sokolov." In *From Pushkin to "Palisandriia": Essays on the Russian Novel in Honour of Richard Freeborn*, edited by Arnold McMillin, 229–43. London: Macmillan, 1990.

Meletinsky, Eleazar M. *The Poetics of Myth*. Translated by Guy Lanoue and Alexandre Sadetsky. New York: Garland Publishing, 1998.

Meyer, Priscilla. Introduction to *Life in Windy Weather: Short Stories*, by Andrei Bitov, 7–11. Edited by Priscilla Meyer. Ann Arbor: Ardis, 1986.

Meyer, Ronald. "Andrei Bitov's Memoir of Pushkin." *Studies in Comparative Communism* 21, no. 3–4 (1988): 379–87.

——. "Andrej Bitov's *Puškinskij dom*." PhD diss., Indiana University, 1986.

——. "Jealous Poetess or Pushkinist? Anna Achmatova in the Works of Andrej Bitov." *Russian Literature* 61, no. 4 (2007): 453–64.

Mezh_du. ". . . nanosit otvetnyi udar." LiveJournal, March 30, 2006. http://mezh-du.livejournal.com/9359.html.

Miller-Budnitskaia, R. "Filosofiia kul'tury Dzhemza Dzhoisa." *Internatsional'naia literatura* 2 (1937): 188–209.

Mirskii, D. S. "Dos-Passos, sovetskaia literatura i Zapad." *Literaturnyi kritik* 1 (1933): 111–26.

——. "Dzheims Dzhois." *God shestnadtsatyi* 1 (1933): 428–50.

——. "Dzhois ('Ulysses,' 1922)." *Versty* 3 (1928): 147–49.

——. "O formalizme." *God shestnadtsatyi* 2 (1933): 490–517.

Monas, Sidney. "Joyce and Russia." *Joyce Studies Annual* 4 (1993): 201–13.

Mondry, Henrietta. *"Literaturnost'* as a Key to Andrey Bitov's *Pushkin House."* In *The Waking Sphinx: South African Essays on Russian Culture,* edited by Henrietta Mondry, 3–19. Johannesburg: University of Witwatersrand, 1989.

Moody, Fred. "Madness and the Pattern of Freedom in Sasha Sokolov's *A School for Fools." Russian Literature Triquarterly* 16 (1979): 7–32.

Morris, Paul D. "Nabokov's Poetic Gift: The Poetry in and of *Dar." Russian Literature* 48, no. 4 (2000): 457–69.

Morson, Gary Saul. "Sideshadowing and Tempics." *New Literary History* 29, no. 4 (1998): 599–624.

Moynahan, Julian. "Nabokov and Joyce." In *The Garland Companion to Vladimir Nabokov,* edited by Vladimir E. Alexandrov, 433–44. New York: Garland Publishing, 1995.

Nabokov, Vladimir. *Ada, or Ardor.* New York: Vintage Books, 1990.

——. Foreword to *Glory,* by Vladimir Nabokov, ix–xiv. New York: Vintage Books, 1991.

——. *The Gift.* Translated by Michael Scammell. New York: Vintage Books, 1991.

——. *Lectures on Literature.* Edited by Fredson Bowers. New York: Harcourt, Brace, Jovanovich, 1980.

——. *Lectures on "Ulysses": Facsimile of the Manuscript.* Bloomfield Hills, MI: Bruccoli Clark, 1980.

——. *Novels and Memoirs 1941–1951: The Real Life of Sebastian Knight; Bend Sinister; Speak, Memory: An Autobiography Revisited,* edited by Brian Boyd. Library of America. New York: Literary Classics of the United States, 1996.

——. "Pushkin, or the Real and the Plausible." *New York Review of Books* 35 (March 31, 1988): 38–42.

——. "Shakespeare." Translated by Dmitri Nabokov. *Nabokovian* 20 (1988): 15–16.

——. *Sobranie sochinenii russkogo perioda.* Vol. 4. Sankt-Peterburg: Simpozium, 2000.

——. *Strong Opinions.* New York: Vintage Books, 1990.

Naiman, Eric. *Nabokov, Perversely.* Ithaca, NY: Cornell University Press, 2010.

Nikulin, Lev. Untitled memoir. In *Vospominaniia o Iurii Oleshe,* edited by E. Pel'son and O. Suok-Olesha, 66–80. Moskva: Sovetskii pisatel', 1975.

Nilsson, Nils Åke. "Through the Wrong End of Binoculars: An Introduction to Jurij Oleša." In *Major Soviet Writers: Essays in Criticism,* edited by Edward J. Brown, 254–79. New York: Oxford University Press, 1973.

Noel, Lucie Léon. "Playback." *TriQuarterly* 17 (1970): 209–19.

Noordenbos, Boris. *Post-Soviet Literature and the Search for a Russian Identity.* New York: Palgrave Macmillan, 2016.

O'Connor, Ulick. "James Joyce and Oliver St. John Gogarty: A Famous Friendship." *Texas Quarterly* 3, no. 2 (1960): 189–210.

Olesha, Iurii. "Beseda s chitateliami." *Literaturnyi kritik* 12 (1935): 152–65.

——. *Kniga proshchaniia.* Moskva: Vagrius, 1999.

——. "Liompa." In *Povesti i rasskazy,* 262–66. Moskva: Khudozhestvennaia literatura, 1965.

——. *Povesti i rasskazy.* Moskva: Khudozhestvennaia literatura, 1965.

——. "Velikoe narodnoe iskusstvo." *Literaturnaia gazeta* 17 (March 20, 1936): 3.

——. *Zavist'* manuscripts. Rossiiskii gosudarstvennyi arkhiv literatury i iskusstva (RGALI). Fond 358, opis' 2, edinnye khraneniia 4–18.

——. *Zavist'. Ni dnia bez strochki.* Riga: Liesma, 1987.

Olson, Liesl. *Modernism and the Ordinary.* New York: Oxford University Press, 2009.

Omidi, Maryam. "The Light and Dark of It: How Russia's Greatest Living Writer Became a Refusenik." *Calvert Journal,* April 16, 2013. https://www.calvertjournal .com/articles/show/771/mikhail-shishkin-light-dark-russian-writer-author -corrupt-criminal-regime.

Orobii, Sergei. *"Babilonskaia bashnia" Mikhaila Shishkina: Opyt modernizatsii russkoi prozy.* Blagoveshchensk: Izdatel'stvo BGPU, 2011.

——. "Istoriia odnogo uchenichestva (Vladimir Nabokov–Sasha Sokolov–Mikhail Shishkin)." *Novoe literaturnoe obozrenie* 6 (2012): 293–308.

Orr, Mary. *Intertextuality: Debates and Contexts.* Cambridge, UK: Polity Press, 2003.

Paperno, Irina. "How Nabokov's *Gift* Is Made." *Stanford Slavic Studies* 4, no. 2 (1992): 295–322.

——. "Pushkin v zhizni cheloveka Serebrianogo veka." In *Cultural Mythologies of Russian Modernism: From the Golden Age to the Silver Age,* edited by Boris Gasparov, Robert P. Hughes, and Irina Paperno, 19–51. Berkeley: University of California Press, 1992.

Peake, Charles. *James Joyce, the Citizen and the Artist.* Stanford, CA: Stanford University Press, 1977.

Pelevin, Viktor. *Sviashchennaia kniga oborotnia.* Moskva: Eksmo, 2004.

Pel'son, E., and O. Suok-Olesha, eds. *Vospominaniia o Iurii Oleshe.* Moskva: Sovetskii pisatel', 1975.

Pertsov, V. *"My zhivem vpervye": O tvorchestve Iuriia Oleshi.* Moskva: Sovetskii pisatel', 1976.

Pesonen, Pekka. "Bitov's Text as Text: The Petersburg Text as a Context in Andrey Bitov's Prose." In *Literary Tradition and Practice in Russian Culture: Papers from an International Conference on the Occasion of the Seventieth Birthday of Yury Mikhailovich Lotman,* edited by Valentina Polukhina, Joe Andrew, and Robert Reid, 325–41. Amsterdam: Rodopi, 1993.

Pirogov, Liv. "Prigovor sebe, Rossii i zhizni." *Nezavisimaia gazeta,* April 4, 2006. http://www.ng.ru/ng_exlibris/2006-04-06/1_prigovor.html?id_user=Y.

Platonov, Andrei. "Iz stat'i 'O likvidatsii' chelovechestva (Po povodu romana K. Chapeka 'Voina s salamandrami.'" In *"Russkaia odisseia" Dzheimsa Dzhoisa,* edited by Ekaterina Genieva, 100–101. Moskva: Rudomino, 2005.

Platt, L. H. "*Ulysses* 15 and the Irish Literary Theatre." In *Reading Joyce's "Circe,"* edited by Andrew Gibson, 33–62. Amsterdam: Rodopi, 1994.

Plett, Heinrich F. "Intertextualities." In *Intertextuality,* edited by Heinrich F. Plett, 3–29. New York: Walter de Gruyter, 1991.

Po, Edgar. "Ubiistvo na ulitse Morg." In *Izbrannoe,* translated by V. Stanevits, 141–68. Moskva: Gosudarstvennoe izdatel'stvo khudozhestvennoi literatury, 1958.

Poe, Edgar Allan. "The Murders in the Rue Morgue." In *Selected Poetry, Tales, and Essays,* 128–57. Boston: St. Martin's Press, 2015.

Poplavskii, Boris. "Po povodu . . . 'Atlantidy–Evropy' . . . 'Noveishei russkoi literatury' . . . Dzhoisa." *Chisla* 4 (1930–31): 161–75.

Pushkin, A. S. *Sobranie sochinenii v desiati tomakh.* Vol. 2, *Stikhotvoreniia 1823–1836.* Moskva: Gosudarstvennoe izdatel'stvo khudozhestvennoi literatury, 1959.

Rabaté, Jean-Michel. "The Fourfold Root of Yawn's Unreason: Chapter III.3." In *How Joyce Wrote "Finnegans Wake": A Chapter-by-Chapter Genetic Guide*, edited by Luca Crispi and Sam Slote, 384–409. Madison: University of Wisconsin Press, 2007.

Radek, Karl. "Iz doklada 'Sovremennaia mirovaia literatura i zadachi proletarskogo iskusstva.'" In *Russkaia odisseia*, edited by Ekaterina Genieva, 95. Moskva: Rudomino, 2005.

Rampton, David. *Vladimir Nabokov: A Critical Study of the Novels*. New York: Cambridge University Press, 1984.

Randall, Marilyn. *Pragmatic Plagiarism: Authorship, Profit, and Power*. Toronto: University of Toronto Press, 2001.

Remnick, David. "Wellspring of the Russian Writer: Thirsting for His Native Language, Sasha Sokolov Returns." *Washington Post*, September 28, 1989.

Rogova, E. N. "Motiv kalligrafii v tvorchestve Dzh. Dzhoisa i M. Shishkina." In *Dergachevskie chteniia—2014. Russkaia literatura: Tipy khudozhestvennogo soznaniia i dialog kul'turno-natsional'nykh traditsii; Materialy XI Vserossiiskoi nauchnoi konferentsii s mezhdunarodnym uchastiem, Ekaterinburg, 6–7 oktiabria 2014 g.*, 338–42. Ekaterinburg: Izdatel'stvo Ural'skogo universiteta, 2014.

——. "Traditsii D. Dzhoisa v romane M. Shishkina 'Pismov'nik' (Sopostavitel'nyi analiz motivov)." *Siuzhetologiia i siuzhetografiia* 2 (2014): 141–50.

Rudova, Larissa. "The Dystopian Vision in Sasha Sokolov's *Palisandriia*." *Canadian-American Slavic Studies* 40, no. 2–4 (2006): 163–77.

——. "Reading *Palisandriia*: Of Menippean Satire and Sots-Art." In *Endquote: Sots-Art Literature and Soviet Grand Style*, edited by Marina Balina, Nancy Condee, and Evgeny Dobrenko, 211–24. Evanston, IL: Northwestern University Press, 2000.

"Russkii buker Mikhail Shishkin ulichen v plagiate." 988, LiveJournal, March 8, 2013. http://988.livejournal.com/361509.html.

Said, Edward W. *The World, the Text, and the Critic*. Cambridge, MA: Harvard University Press, 1983.

Saint-Amour, Paul K. *The Copywrights: Intellectual Property and the Literary Imagination*. Ithaca, NY: Cornell University Press, 2003.

Salomon, Roger B. "*The Gift*: Nabokov's Portrait of the Artist." In *Critical Essays on Vladimir Nabokov*, edited by Phyllis A. Roth, 185–201. Boston: G. K. Hall, 1984.

Salys, Rimgaila. "Understanding *Envy*." In *Olesha's "Envy": A Critical Companion*, edited by Rimgaila Salys, 3–43. Evanston, IL: Northwestern University Press, 1999.

Sandler, Stephanie. *Commemorating Pushkin: Russia's Myth of a National Poet*. Stanford, CA: Stanford University Press, 2004.

Sarnov, Benedikt. *Stalin i pisateli*. Vol. 1. Moskva: Eksmo, 2009.

Savitskii, Stanislav. "Kak postroili 'Pushkinskii dom' (Dos'e)." In *Pushkinskii dom*, by Andrei Bitov, 423–76. Sankt-Peterburg: Izdatel'stvo Ivana Limbakha, 1999.

Schischkin, Michail. "Die letzten Tage von James Joyce: Eine historische Reportage." *Das Magazin*, July 13, 2018. https://www.dasmagazin.ch/2018/07/13/die-letzten-tage-von-james-joyce.

Schuman, Samuel. *Nabokov's Shakespeare*. New York: Bloomsbury, 2014.

Schutte, William M. *Joyce and Shakespeare: A Study in the Meaning of "Ulysses."* New Haven, CT: Yale University Press, 1957.

Seidel, Michael. "Nabokov on Joyce, Shakespeare, Telemachus, and Hamlet." *James Joyce Quarterly* 20, no. 3 (1983): 358–59.

Senderovich, S. Ia. "Pushkin v 'Dare' Nabokova." In *Figura sokrytiia: Izbrannye raboty*, 2:493–532. Moskva: Iazyki slavianskikh kul'tur, 2012.

Shaw, Kurt. "French Connections: The *Three Musketeers* Motif in Andrei Bitov's *Pushkinskii dom.*" *Canadian Slavonic Papers* 37, no. 1–2 (1995): 187–99.

Sheshukov, Stepan. *Neistovye revniteli: Iz istorii literaturnoi bor'by 20-kh godov*. Moskva: Moskovskii rabochii, 1970.

Shishkin, Mikhail. "Bol'she chem Dzhois." *Colta*, January 13, 2019. https://www .colta.ru/articles/literature/20202-bolshe-chem-dzhoys.

——. *The Light and the Dark*. Translated by Andrew Bromfield. London: Quercus, 2013.

——. *Maidenhair*. Translated by Marian Schwartz. Rochester, NY: Open Letter Books, 2012.

——. "Mat i molitva—eto priblizitel'no odno i to zhe." *Gazeta* 105 (June 9, 2005): 26.

——. "Mikhail Shishkin: Vse pisateli dolzhny poluchit' po Nobelevskoi premii." Interview by Elizaveta Fomina. *Postimees*, June 6, 2016. https://rus.postimees.ee /3719763/mihail-shishkin-vse-pisateli-dolzhny-poluchit-po-nobelevskoy-premii.

——. "Open letter to the Federal Agency for the Press and Mass Communications and the International Office of the Boris Yeltsin Presidential Center." *Faust*, February 27, 2013. https://faustkultur.de/1085-0-Brief-Schischkin _RussDeutsch.html.

——. "Pisatel' dolzhen oshchutit' vsesilie." Interview by Sergei Ivanov. *Kontrakty UA*, August 4, 2010. http://kontrakty.ua/article/37875.

——. *Pis'movnik*. Moskva: Astrel', 2010.

——. "Spasennyi iazik." In *Pal'to s khliastikom*, 197–218. Moskva: AST, 2017.

——. *Venerin volos*. Moskva: AST, 2014.

Shklovskii, Viktor. "Parodiinyi roman ('Tristram Shendi' Sterna)." In *O teorii romana*, 177–204. Moskva: Federatsiia, 1929.

Shmid, Vol'f. "Andrei Bitov—master 'ostrovidedeniia.'" In *Proza kak poeziia: Stat'i o povestvovanii v russkoi literature*. Sankt-Peterburg: Gumanitarnoe agenstvo "Akademicheskii prospect," 1994.

Simmons, Cynthia. "Cohesion and Coherence in Pathological Discourse and Its Literary Representation in Sasha Sokolov's *Škola dlja durakov.*" *International Journal of Slavic Linguistics and Poetics* 33 (1986): 71–96.

——. "Incarnations of the Hero Archetype in Sokolov's *School for Fools.*" In *The Supernatural in Slavic and Baltic Literature: Essays in Honour of Victor Terras*, edited by Amy Mandelker and Roberta Reeder, 275–89. Columbus, OH: Slavica Publishers, 1988.

——. *Their Father's Voice: Vassily Aksyonov, Venedikt Erofeev, Eduard Limonov, and Sasha Sokolov*. New York: Peter Lang, 1993.

Sivokhina, T. A., and M. R. Zezina. *Apogei rezhima lichnoi vlasti. "Ottepel'." Povorot k neostalinizmu: Obshchestvenno-politicheskaia zhizn' v SSSR v seredine 40-kh–60-e gody*. Moskva: Izdatel'stvo Moskovskogo universiteta, 1993.

Skoropanova, I. "Klassika v postmodernistskoi sisteme koordinat: 'Pushkinskii dom' Andreia Bitova." In *Russkaia postmodernistskaia literatura: Uchebnoe posobie*, 113–44. Moskva: Izd-vo "Flinta" and Izd-vo "Nauka," 2000.

Smith, Gerald. "The Verse in Sasha Sokolov's *Between Dog and Wolf*." *Canadian-American Slavic Studies* 21, no. 3–4 (1987): 319–39.

Sokolov, Sasha. *Astrophobia*. Translated by Michael Henry Heim. New York: Grove Weidenfeld, 1989.

——. "Beseda s Sashei Sokolovym: 'Nuzhno zabyt' vse staroe i vspomnit' vse novoe.'" Interview by Ol'ga Matich. *Russkaia mysl'* 3571 (1985): 12.

——. *Between Dog and Wolf*. Translated by Alexander Boguslawski. New York: Columbia University Press, 2017.

——. "Gazibo." In *Triptikh*, 59–165. Moskva: OGI, 2011.

——. "'Ia vsiu zhizn' vybiraiu luchshee. Chashche vsego bessoznatel'no . . .': Beseda Iriny Vrubel'-Golubkinoi s Sashei Sokolovym." Interview by Irina Vrubel'-Golubkina. *Zerkalo* 37 (2011). https://magazines.gorky.media/zerkalo/2011/37/ya-vsyu-zhizn-vybirayu-luchshee-chashhe-vsego-bessoznatelno-8230.html.

——. Interviews by D. Barton Johnson. Audiocassettes A13591/CS and A13599/CS. June 20, 1983, and December 4, 1985. Sasha Sokolov Collection, Special Research Collections, University of California, Santa Barbara.

——. *Palisandriia*. Ann Arbor, MI: Ardis, 1985.

——. *Shkola dlia durakov. Mezhdu sobakoi i volkom*. Moskva: Ogonek-Variant, 1990.

——. *Trevozhnaia kukolka*. Sankt-Peterburg: Izdatel'skii dom "Azbuka-klassika," 2007.

Sorokin, Vladimir. *Den' oprichnika*. Moskva: Zakharov, 2006.

Spieker, Sven. *Figures of Memory and Forgetting in Andrej Bitov's Prose: Postmodernism and the Quest for History*. Frankfurt am Main: Peter Lang, 1996.

Spoo, Robert. *James Joyce and the Language of History: Dedalus's Nightmare*. New York: Oxford University Press, 1994.

Startsev, A. "Dzhois pered 'Ulissom.'" *Internatsional'naia literatura* 1 (1937): 196–202.

Sukhanova, Ekaterina. "With Pushkin in the Background: An Invitation to Andrei Bitov's *Pushkin House*." In *"Pushkin House" by Andrei Bitov: A Casebook*, edited by Ekaterina Sukhanova, 1–20. Normal, IL: Dalkey Archive Press, 2005.

Tall, Emily. "Behind the Scenes: How *Ulysses* Was Finally Published in the Soviet Union." *Slavic Review* 49, no. 2 (1990): 183–99.

——. "Correspondence between Three Slavic Translators of *Ulysses*: Maciej Słomczyński, Aloys Skoumal, and Viktor Khinkis." *Slavic Review* 49, no. 4 (1990): 625–33.

——. "Interview with Victor Khinkis, Russian Translator of *Ulysses*." *James Joyce Quarterly* 17, no. 4 (1980): 349–53.

——. "James Joyce Returns to the Soviet Union." *James Joyce Quarterly* 17, no. 4 (1980): 341–47.

——. "The Joyce Centenary in the Soviet Union: Making Way for *Ulysses*." *James Joyce Quarterly* 21, no. 2 (1984): 107–22.

——. "The Reception of James Joyce in Russia." In *The Reception of James Joyce in Europe*, edited by Geert Lernout and Wim Van Mierlo, vol. 1, *Germany, Northern and East Central Europe*, 244–57. New York: Thoemmes Continuum, 2004.

Tammi, Pekka. *Problems of Nabokov's Poetics: A Narratological Analysis*. Helsinki: Suomalainen Tiedeakatemia, 1985.

——. "Seventeen Remarks on *Poligenetičnost'* in Nabokov's Prose." *Studia slavica finlandensia* 7 (1990): 189–232.

Tankov, Aleksandr. "Shestvie perepershchikov." *Literaturnaia gazeta*, 2006. http://old
.lgz.ru/archives/html_arch/lg112006/Polosy/8_2.htm.

Tauchen, Christopher. Review of *Maidenhair*, by Mikhail Shishkin. *Words without
Borders*, November 2012. https://www.wordswithoutborders.org/book
-review/mikhail-shishkins-maidenhair.

Thornton, Weldon. *Allusions in "Ulysses": An Annotated List*. Chapel Hill: University
of North Carolina Press, 1968.

Tindall, William York. *A Reader's Guide to James Joyce*. Syracuse, NY: Syracuse
University Press, 1995.

Toker, Leona. "Gamesman's Sketches (Found in a Bottle): A Reading of Sasha
Sokolov's *Between Dog and Wolf*." *Canadian-American Slavic Studies* 21, no. 3–4
(1987): 347–67.

Tolstov, Vlad. Review of *Pis'movnik*, by Mikhail Shishkin. *NewsLab.ru*, December 13,
2011. https://newslab.ru/article/389029.

Toporov, V. N. *Peterburgskii tekst russkoi literatury: Izbrannye trudy*. Sankt-Petersburg:
Iskusstvo-SPB, 2003.

Tucker, Janet G. *Revolution Betrayed: Jurij Oleša's "Envy."* Columbus, OH: Slavica
Publishers, 1996.

Tumanov, Vladimir. "A Tale Told by Two Idiots: Krik idiota v 'Shkole dlia durakov'
S. Sokolova i v 'Shume i iarosti' U. Folknera." *Russian Language Journal* 48,
no. 159–61 (1994): 137–54.

Vaidhyanathan, Siva. *Copyrights and Copywrongs: The Rise of Intellectual Property and
How It Threatens Creativity*. New York: New York University Press, 2001.

Vail', Petr, and Aleksandr Genis. "Uroki *Shkoly dlia durakov*." *Literaturnoe obozrenie* 1,
no. 2 (1993): 13–16.

Vergara, José. "The Embodied Language of Sasha Sokolov's *A School for Fools*."
Slavonic and East European Review 97, no. 3 (2019): 426–50.

——. "Kavalerov and Dedalus as Rebellious Sons and Artists: Yury Olesha's Dialogue
with *Ulysses* in *Envy*." *Slavic and East European Journal* 58, no. 4 (2014): 606–25.

——. "'Return That Which Does Not Belong to You': Mikhail Shishkin's Borrowings
in *Maidenhair*." *Russian Review* 78, no. 2 (2019): 300–321.

Vishnevskii, Vs. V. "V Evrope: Iz putevogo dnevnika." In *"Russkaia odisseia" Dzheimsa
Dzhoisa*, edited by Ekaterina Genieva, 37–38. Moskva: Rudomino, 2005

Vishnevskii, Vsevolod. "Znat' Zapad!" *Literaturnyi kritik* 7 (1933): 79–95.

Vladiv-Glover, Slobodanka M. "The 1960s and the Rediscovery of the Other in
Russian Culture: Andrei Bitov." In *Russian Postmodernism: New Perspectives on
Post-Soviet Culture*, edited by Mikhail N. Epstein, Alexander A. Genis, and
Slobodanka M. Vladiv-Glover, translated by Slobodanka M. Vladiv-Glover,
31–86. New York: Berghahn Books, 1999.

Voitkovska, Ludmilla S. "James Joyce and the Soviet Reader: Problems of Contact."
Canadian Journal of Irish Studies 16, no. 2 (1990): 21–26.

Vojvodić, Jasmina. "Otkliki simul'tanizma v postmodernistskoi proze (*Shkola dlia
durakov* S. Sokolova)." *Russian Literature* 51, no. 3 (2002): 355–70.

Volkov, Solomon. *St. Petersburg: A Cultural History*. Translated by Antonina W. Bouis.
New York: Free Press, 1995.

Volodin, Boris. "Dzheims Dzhois." In *Pamiatnye knizhnye daty*, 162–65. Moskva:
Kniga, 1982.

von Hirsch, Marina. "Commentary *Ad Infinitum* in Andrej Bitov's Unified Narrative." *Russian Literature* 61, no. 4 (2007): 465–89.

——. "The Illusion of Infinity: Andrei Bitov's Innovative Poetics of Commentary." *Russian Studies in Literature* 44, no. 2 (2008): 77–89.

——. "In the Context of Metafiction: Commentary as a Principal Narrative Structure in Bitov's *Pushkin House*." In *"Pushkin House" by Andrei Bitov: A Casebook*, edited by Ekaterina Sukhanova, 103–31. Normal, IL: Dalkey Archive Press, 2005.

——. "The Presence of Nabokov in Bitov's Fiction and Nonfiction: Bitov and Nabokov, Bitov on Nabokov, Nabokov in Bitov." *Nabokov Studies* 6 (2000–2001): 57–74.

Voronel', A., and N. Voronel'. "Ia khochu podniat' russkuiu prozu do urovnia poezii . . ." *22* 35 (1984): 179–86.

Wakamiya, Lisa Ryoko. "Overcoming Death and Denotation in Saša Sokolov's *School for Fools*." *Die Welt der Slaven* 50 (2005): 57–70.

——. "Transformation, Forgetting and Fate: Self-Representation in the Essays of Sasha Sokolov." *Canadian-American Slavic Studies* 40, no. 2–4 (2006): 317–29.

Weir, Justin. *The Author as Hero: Self and Tradition in Bulgakov, Pasternak, and Nabokov*. Evanston, IL: Northwestern University Press, 2002.

White, Hayden. "The Burden of History." *History and Theory* 5, no. 2 (1966): 111–34.

——. *Metahistory: The Historical Imagination in Nineteenth-Century Europe*. Baltimore: Johns Hopkins University Press, 1973.

Xenophon. *Anabasis*. Translated by Carleton L. Brownson. Cambridge, MA: Harvard University Press, 1992.

Yaeger, Patricia. "Editor's Column: The Polyphony Issue." *PMLA* 122, no. 2 (2007): 433–48.

Zhantieva, D. G. *Dzheimz Dzhois*. Moskva: Vyssh. shkola, 1967.

Zholkovsky, Alexander. "The Stylistic Roots of *Palisandriia*." *Canadian-American Slavic Studies* 21, no. 3–4 (1987): 369–400.

——. *Text Counter Text: Rereadings in Russian Literary History*. Stanford, CA: Stanford University Press, 1994.

Zimmer, Dieter E., and Sabine Hartmann. "'The Amazing Music of Truth': Nabokov's Sources for Godunov's Central Asian Travels in *The Gift*." *Nabokov Studies* 7 (2002–3): 33–74.

Author Interviews and Correspondence

Interview with Andrei Babikov, May 31, 2019, Moscow, Russia
Personal Correspondence with Ksenia Buksha, September 8 and 9, 2019
Personal Correspondence with Dmitry Bykov, August 20, 2019
Personal Correspondence with Anna Glazova, September 5, 2019
Skype Interview with Alexander Ilianen, September 9, 2019
Personal Correspondence with Alexander Ilichevsky, June 20, 2020
Interview with Ilya Kukulin, June 1, 2019, Moscow, Russia
Interview with Dmitry Ragozin, June 7, 2019, Moscow, Russia
Personal Correspondence with Lev Rubinstein, September 4, 2019
Personal Correspondence with Aleksei Salnikov, February 18 and March 10, 2020
Personal Correspondence with Mikhail Shishkin, August 10, 16, 18, and 20, 2019
Personal Correspondence with Alexander Skidan, November 11 and 14, 2019

Personal Correspondence with Grigory Sluzhitel, June 6, 2020
Interview with Ivan Sokolov, February 9, 2020, San Diego, California, USA
Skype Interview with Sergei Solovev, August 13, 2019
Personal Correspondence with Marina Stepnova, September 25 and October 15, 2019
Zoom Interview with Territory of Slow Reading, Joyce Reading Group, June 2, 2019
Skype Interview with Zinovy Zinik, August 23, 2019

Archives Consulted

Donald Barton Johnson Papers, Special Research Collections, University of Califor-
    nia, Santa Barbara, USA
Rossiiskii gosudarstvennyi arkhiv literatury i iskusstva (Russian State Archive of
    Literature and Art), Moscow, Russia
Sasha Sokolov Collection, Special Research Collections, University of California,
    Santa Barbara, USA
Zürich James Joyce Foundation, Zurich, Switzerland

INDEX

CPSIA information can be obtained
at www.ICGtesting.com
Printed in the USA
LVHW111530240921
698678LV00017B/450/J

9 781501 759901